Changing Perspectives in the Scientific Study of Religion

Contemporary Religious Movements:
A Wiley-Interscience Series

Edited by IRVING I. ZARETSKY

EDITED BY

Allan W. Eister

Changing Perspectives in the Scientific Study of Religion

A WILEY-INTERSCIENCE PUBLICATION

JOHN WILEY & SONS, New York • London • Sydney • Toronto

Library of Congress Cataloging in Publication Data:

Eister, Allan W.
  Changing perspectives in the scientific study of religion.

  (Contemporary religious movements)
  "A Wiley-Interscience publication."
  1. Religion—Study and teaching. 2. Religion and sociology. I. Title.

BL41.E37   200'.7   74-2092

ISBN 0-471-23476-1

Printed in the United States of America

10 9 8 7 6 5 4 3 2 1

Changing Perspectives in the Scientific Study of Religion

Edited by Allan W. Eister

Errata

p. 168   line missing between lines 22 and 23:

"ends in a form that the self can consciously accept and a definition of"

p. 174   line 19 should be *replaced* by:

"teens were transformed at once into young adults. They were ex-"

p. 180   line 36:

for "the relation of father to dependent child" read "the relation of chief to commoner was conceived as an idealization of the relation of father to dependent child"

Contributors

DAVID BAKAN is professor of psychology at York University, Toronto. Well-known for his work on *Sigmund Freud and the Jewish Mystical Tradition* (1958), he has also written *Disease, Pain and Suffering: Toward a Psychology of Human Suffering* (1968); *The Duality of Human Existence* (1966); *On Method: Toward the Reconstruction of Psychological Investigation* (1967); and *Slaughter of the Innocents* (1971) in addition to other publications.

RALPH W. BURHOE is research professor in theology and science at the Meadville/Lombard Theological School and editor of *Zygon: Journal of Religion and Science* which he has guided from its inception in 1966. Cofounder and honorary president of the Institute of Religion in an Age of Science, he is also a Fellow of the American Association for the Advancement of Science, a member of the Society for the Scientific Study of Religion (in which he has been an active officer), former Executive Officer of the American Academy of Arts and Sciences. He is editor and author of *Science and Human Values in the Twenty-First Century* (1971) and (with Hudson Hoagland) *Evolution and Man's Progress* (1962) and of more than fifty published articles on science and human values.

ALLAN W. EISTER is professor of sociology and chairman of the department of sociology and anthropology at Wellesley College. In addition to earlier work in history and on the relations of the United States with developing countries he has written on the sociology of new religious movements, including *Drawing-Room Conversion: A Sociological Account of the Oxford Group Movement* (1950), and has edited (with Constant Jacquet and Lauris Whitman) *Sociology and Religion: Proceedings of the Hazen International Conference on The Sociology of Religion* (1962). He also initiated the book reviews section of the *Journal for the Scientific Study of Religion*.

JOHANNES FABIAN is professor of anthropology at the National University of Zaire in Africa. In addition to *Jamaa: A Charismatic Renewal*

Movement in Katanga (1971), he has written articles on cognitive anthropology, philosophy of the social sciences, and anthropology of religion.

RICHARD K. FENN is associate professor of sociology at the University of Maine. He has published articles on secularization and on the problems of integration and of the legitimation of social behavior in pluralistic societies in the *Review of Religious Research* and in the *Journal for the Scientific Study of Religion.*

WARD H. GOODENOUGH is professor of anthropology at the University of Pennsylvania. Former president of the American Ethnological Society and of the Society for Applied Anthropology, he is the author of *Property, Kin and Community on Truk* (1951); *Cooperation in Change: an Anthropological Approach to Community Development* (1963); and *Description and Comparison in Cultural Anthropology* (1970). He has also edited *Explorations in Cultural Anthropology* (1964).

PHILLIP E. HAMMOND is professor of sociology at the University of Arizona. Presently secretary and council member of the Society for the Scientific Study of Religion, he is giving research attention now to law and retirement as these relate to religion. His books include *Sociologists at Work* (1964); *The Campus Clergyman* (1966); *Religion in Social Context: Tradition and Transition* (with N. J. Demerath III, 1968); *American Mosaic: Social Patterns of Religion in the United States* (with Benton Johnson, 1970); and *School Prayer Decisions: From Court Policy to Local Practice* (with K. M. Dolbeare, 1971).

DAVID O. MOBERG is professor of sociology and chairman of the department of sociology and anthropology at Marquette University. In addition to serving recently as editor of the *Review of Religious Research,* he is a member of the council of the Society for the Scientific Study of Religion and has written *The Church as a Social Institution* (1962); *The Church and the Older Person* (with Robert Gray, 1962); *The Great Reversal: Evangelism vs Social Concern* (1972); and numerous articles and monographs.

BENJAMIN NELSON is professor of sociology and history in the graduate faculty of the New School for Social Research. A former vice-president and member of the council of the Society for the Scientific Study of Religion, he has also·been a member of the American Society for the Study of Religion and is president of the United States Society for the Comparative Study of Civilizations. His publications include *The Idea of Usury: From Tribal Brotherhood to Universal Otherhood* (1949, 1969) and numerous chapters in books on themes related to religion, culture, social organization, and psychoanalysis. Since its inception in 1956 he has been principal advisory editor (in humanities and social sciences) for Harper Torchbooks.

TALCOTT PARSONS is professor of sociology, *emeritus,* at Harvard University, presently visiting professor at the University of Pennsylvania. In addition to having been president of the American and of the Eastern Sociological Societies, he has also been president of the American Academy of Arts and Sciences, a Fellow of the American Association for the Advancement of Science, and president of the Society for the Scientific Study of Religion. His books include, in addition to several recognized as classic works in sociological theory and the general theory of action, *The System of Modern Societies* (1971); *Societies: Evolutionary and Comparative Perspectives* (1966); *Sociological Theory and Modern Society* (1968); *Politics and Social Structure* (1969); and *The American University* (with Gerald M. Platt, 1973).

DONALD R. PLOCH is program director for sociology at the National Science Foundation. His research interests include both the sociology of religion and sociological research methods. Currently he is completing a study of theological education and a series of papers on measures of association for ordered sets. His publications include articles on "Theorizing and Statistics" and "On the Uses of Theology" and others and a monograph on *Higher Education: Faculty as Professionalization and Change Agents* (1972).

PAUL W. PRUYSER is Henry M. Pfeiffer Professor at the Menninger Foundation. With a Ph.D. in clinical psychology, he was director of the Foundation's professional training program. His main professional interests are personality theory, the teaching of clinical mental health knowledge and skills, and the psychology of religion. Recently elected president of the Society for the Scientific Study of Religion, he has been a member of the council and has been on the editorial board of its *Journal* as well as of the Bulletin of the Menninger Clinic. He is coauthor (with Karl Menninger and Martin Mayman) of *The Vital Balance* (1963), *A Manual for Psychiatric Case Study,* and *A Dynamic*

Psychology of Religion (1968). A new book, *Between Belief and Unbelief,* is forthcoming.

ROLAND ROBERTSON is professor of sociology at the University of Pittsburgh, having taught previously in England (at the universities of Leeds, Essex, and York, where he was department chairman). His books include *The Sociological Interpretation of Religion* (1970); *Sociology of Religion* (which he edited in 1969); and two which he coauthored—*International Systems and the Modernization of Societies* (1968) and *Deviance, Crime and Socio-Legal Control* (1973). In addition, two books are forthcoming—*Culture and Culture Change* and *Knowledge, Religion and Science.*

W. CLARK ROOF is assistant professor of sociology at the University of Massachusetts, Amherst. His research interests in the sociology of religion center in a local-cosmopolitan theory of religion in modern society, multivariate explanations, and the measurement of religiosity.

DAVID N. RUTH is associate professor of sociology and chairman of the department of sociology at Georgetown University. He has served as a research consultant in programs concerned with mental and general health, the developing societies in Southeast Asia, and a variety of federally sponsored projects. His current research interests are in social interaction and in religion and society.

CLARENCE H. SNELLING, JR., is professor of teaching ministries in the Iliff School of Theology. In addition to serving pastorates in Louisiana and in New Jersey, he was research director for Morris County (New Jersey) Community Chest and Council and has been interested in the religious needs and behavior of young persons.

VICTOR W. TURNER is professor of social thought and anthropology at the University of Chicago, having taught previously in England (Manchester University). Earlier he was research officer at the Rhodes-Livingstone Institute in Northern Rhodesia. In addition to membership in the Royal Anthropological Institute, he is also a member of the American Academy of Arts and Sciences, the American Anthropological Association, and the International African Institute and was a Fellow of the Center for Advanced Study in the Behavioral Sciences. His books include *Schism and Continuity in an African Society* (1957); *Chihamba The White Spirit* (1962); *The Forest of Symbols* (1967); *The Drums of Affliction* (1968); *The Ritual Process* (1969);

and *Dramas, Fields and Metaphors: Essays in Comparative Symbology* (1974).

OLIVER READ WHITLEY is professor of the sociology of religion at the Iliff School of Theology. During World War II he served as a chaplain in the United States Navy. His books include *Trumpet Call of Reformation* (1958); *Religious Behavior: Where Sociology and Religion Meet* (1964); *The Church: Mirror or Window?* (1969); and chapters and articles in other books and journals.

Foreword

In the study of contemporary religious movements we are concerned with specific case studies as well as with theoretical paradigms that account for ethnographic data collected about them over a period of time in both Western and non-Western societies. The subject of this book is the search for paradigms for use in data analysis, and the conceptualization of frameworks within which issues can be systematically and consistently observed in field research. The book discusses the various professional approaches of social scientists to religion and society. The chapters range from definitional questions of what we mean by religion, religiosity, and religious institutions to current interpretations of behavior along the dimensions of structure, metaphor systems, and symbolization processes. Collectively they point to new directions in the scientific study of religion.

To understand the worldwide religious revival of the last decade, as a result of both indigenous grass roots awakenings and diffusion through missionary activity and the communications media, we must focus on the religious group as a limited social unit and its relationship to the larger surrounding society. The analysis of a religious movement could usefully begin with an investigation of its institutionalization process. We need to distinguish between phenomena that are called movements by virtue of their diffusion—the widespread incidence of individuals who practice meditation or use drugs, for example—and those that are organized for shared and collective religious performance and are institutionally based.

Decentralized or diffuse religious movements, frequently described as social trends, are exemplified by the drug culture, the practice of meditative techniques, or such geographical loci as occult book shops, astrology kiosks and computers, and sidewalk churches. The unit of analysis in researching such movements has usually been the individual's quest for religious experience and the information he derives therefrom. Data have been gathered by professional health scientists from clinical observations of their patients and by social scientists from observations of current happenings in their social environment. The research thus takes place within the researcher's workaday world. These data have led to some general formulations in the domain of culture and personality—how the self is constituted in various social settings at various times—and to some conclusions on cultural history and the long-range evolution of religious and social patterns in a society. An example of this style of analysis is Nathan Adler's work on the Antinomian personality [1].

For cross-cultural research on religious groups, however, the centralized movement that is institutionalized into an *ecclesia* has been a more manageable unit for field observation and analysis [2]. Among such groups in contemporary America are Spiritualism, Mormonism, Jehovah Witnesses, Pentecostalism, Christian Science, the International Society for Krishna Consciousness, Subud Movement, Satanic churches, Scientology, Theosophy, Seventh Day Adventists, and New Thought Churches. Their study more closely approximates traditional research of religious institutions in non-Western societies where the unit of observations has been geographically localized, culturally acknowledged, socially tolerated, and institutionalized.

The study of centrally organized religious movements presents the scholar with a particular challenge—to describe and analyze the process of institution building, the creation of contexts and settings, of a new church from the viewpoint of the significant factors faced by its members and leadership. That is, how does a group accomplish its institutional goals and accommodate itself to the public order of the larger society so as to exist as a *bona fide* religious institution open to the public at large. The participants in such movements, especially in the United States, have themselves publicly acknowledged that their doctrines, their ritual, and their religious activities are greatly shaped through accommodations to secular pressures. Such adjustments are present in the relationship between church and state, between religious movements and mainstream orthodox churches, which are lobby groups in our political process, between a religious movement and a parallel, competing movement, and between a religious movement and the professions licensed by the state to care for the specific needs of the individual. To the degree that we can focus on the areas that significantly influence religious movements, we would gain a more pragmatic understanding of the phenomenon itself, as well as of the larger society in which the institutions are built and maintained. Three other books in this series deal in part with some of these issues: Felicitas Goodman, Jeannette H. Henney, and Esther J. Pressell, *Trance, Healing, and Hallucination* (1974), B. Z. Sobel, *Hebrew Christianity* (1974), and Edward A. Tiryakian, *On the Margin of the Visible* (1974).

In addition to the structure of a movement, we are also interested in the content of its activities. As the contributors to this book point out, some areas require greater scholarly attention. We need longitudinal studies of particular religious movements. Most of the material collected in the past has been in a single-time frame, and we have little information on how a movement changes through time. We lack sound quantitative data on the whole range of currently active movements. Membership, recruitment, frequency and intensity of church participation, and multiple affiliation with several organizations are issues that are relevant to the analysis of a movement, but about which we frequently lack data. Furthermore, we need evaluation studies of the success of the movements in terms of their own stated goals and in terms of the functional analysis we perform of their activities. This is a necessary area for further work if our arguments on the functional utility of movements in terms of the structure of society and the needs of the individual are to be more than mere hypotheses. We currently lack a firm data base on which to rest many of our claims and research on the role of religious movements as agencies for dealing with personal needs of their members.

This volume, in reexamining the current approaches to the study of religious institutions, serves the important function of periodically reassessing the direction of our research.

IRVING I. ZARETSKY

New Haven, Connecticut
December 1973

1. Nathan Adler, *The Underground Stream* [New York: Harper and Row (Harper Torchbooks, 1972].
2. Irving I. Zaretsky and Mark P. Leone, *Religious Movements in Contemporary America* (Princeton: Princeton University Press, 1974).

Preface

This book rests on the premise that important, yet subtle, changes—reinterpretations, new directions, new methods—are occurring in the scientific study of religion; and it is intended to document some of these developments. The general outline began to take shape in the fall of 1970, when the editor (at the invitation of the then president of the Society for the Scientific Study of Religion, Joseph H. Fichter, and the Society's Council) was asked to propose a theme for the annual meetings of the Society in 1971 at Chicago and to help organize the overall program. Several of the papers included here were invited specifically for the conference and have been rewritten for this book. Other, with one exception, were selected from papers contributed by their authors to the general sessions. (The exception is the chapter by Snelling and Whitley, which was presented to the annual meetings of the Society in Boston in 1972.)

For some time it has seemed clear not only that there is a resurgence of interest in the phenomena of "religion" but also that concepts and theories about religion have been undergoing reexamination. That the nature of science, including its relation to religion, is also being reexamined seemed equally evident.

The invitation to prospective participants at Chicago raised such questions as: "Are current social scientific conceptions of 'religion' and of 'faith' adequate in the collective opinion of social scientists for describing and analyzing the object of our studies?" "Do social scientists fully respect the canons of scientific inquiry in the study of religion?" "What, exactly, is the nature of 'unbelief'?" Other questions, both narrower and broader, invited critical reassessment of venerable theories regarding the nature and function of religion in societies, the character and varieties of religious organizations, the nature of—and appropriate dimensions for describing and analyzing—"religiosity," religious "commitment," and so on; and these led to many other questions reaching to the very center of current inquiry into the nature and use of symbols, the symbolization process, and much more.

This is only one of a growing number of organizations and conferences giving attention to the phenomena of religion. In 1971 and 1972 alone, for example, active, well-attended meetings were held by the Religious Research Association, the (American) Association for the Sociology of Religion, and the American Academy of Religion. An International Congress of Learned Societies in the Field of Religion took place (in Los Angeles), not to mention the various conferences of social scientists and others interested in the study of religion in Europe and elsewhere.

Marked though uneven growth of interest in the objective study of religious phenomena is demonstrated both by the rapid rise in the size and number of associations and by the increased numbers of meetings they held and of journals and publications generally devoted to the subject.

That this interest is *not* universal among social scientists, however, is equally evident from the marginal position in professional society meetings to which discussions of religion are often relegated or the still slender financial support available for basic research in the field, understandable though political and other obstacles to such research may be. The situation may be changing; and it is partly to document this possible trend, as well as to review some of the substantive developments in several of the disciplines themselves, that this particular set of papers has been brought together.

Much of the development focussed upon here no doubt reflects pressures of circumstances outside of the academy. Some, however, appears to stem from the thinking of social scientists themselves—from within the disciplines as they have been evolving. Some reflects the personal needs and concerns of individual students and others to whom the problems are experienced as existential rather than as "academic." But whatever the reason, new questions and new conceptions, new directions of investigation and new types of research methods do seem to be emerging in profusion.

It would be a mistake, of course, to assume that a totally coherent new approach to religion has emerged. For many years—at least since social scientists have given closer attention to the appearance of complex, pluralistic societies (not to mention the older traditions of radical skeptical inquiry which some have identified with "secularity")—religion has occupied an anomalous position in the university. Even to *define* religion has defied social scientific attempts to achieve some sort of working consensus for research purposes, for analysis and description. Both Emile Durkheim and Max Weber, in sociology, warned against premature attempts to specify what religion *is*. Edward Tylor, writing two or three decades earlier, was less hesitant than many anthropologists who came after him in his willingness to identify religion as "the belief in Spiritual Beings" (though some contemporary scholars seemed prepared, on the surface at least, to return to his early conception). In psychology and psychiatry, substantive and apodictic definitions of religion are even rarer.

"Religion," it seems clear, is not identical with "faith" and ought not to be confused with it, especially if the functions of religion are not the same as the functions of faith, if the vocabulary or the behavior consequences of each are not identical. Religion, as the cultural and institutional expression of faith, one might suppose, stands in relation to faith approximately as a building stands in relation to the intentions, aspirations, and designs of the architect and of those who commissioned its construction. Or, to change the metaphor, religious phenomena may best be perceived as sociocultural *artifacts,* as the precipitates or distillates of human experiences as captured, formulated, reflected upon, and shared in the form of symbols, rites, and other patterns. But they are patterns which seem to have compelling, and in a sense ultimate, worth and significance to those who "accept" them, "believe" in them, or, as Horace Kallen puts it, "bet their lives" on them, on their efficacy and on their "reliability." Religion may differ in this respect from many or all of the other orders of phenomena with which social scientists deal, although, undoubtedly there will be many who would dispute this claim or any of the implications arising from it.

Almost inevitably in the selection and ordering of papers in a volume of this sort the editor will have introduced his own biases, perhaps inadvertently intruding interpretations of the papers which the authors themselves had not intended (and may not agree with). But the hope is, nevertheless, to present the work of the several contributors with a minimum of gloss—as nearly as possible without editorial "distortion."

What we have here, then, is a range of searching thoughts, inquiries, investigations suggestive of the vigor with which the study of religion is currently being pursued. In the face of a veritable explosion of theoretical writing and research on many aspects of religion, religious institutions, and religious organization, much that must be recognized as "representative" of impressive current work in the field has had to be "left out." We have not been able to include here, for example, samplings of the recent theory and research being devoted to specific types of religious organizations, studies like Bryan Wilson's of "third world" sectarian movements, Douglas Walrath's and Donald A. Krueckeberg's of local congregations; or like John Biersdorf's or William Newman's of specific religious roles and role-preparation, or like Thomas Robbins', Richard Anthony's and others of "new" religious movements. New ideas for studying the dynamics and structures of religious movements generally (like those of John Snook and Barbara Hargrove), or church ritual (like those by Samuel Mueller, David R. Gibbs and James R. Wood), have not been touched. But the hope remains that the collection nevertheless fulfills the promise of bringing together evidence not only that "new bottles" are needed but that many exist.

There remains the pleasant opportunity of acknowledging, with many thanks, the cooperation afforded by the contributors themselves and the numerous expressions of goodwill offered by colleagues who have read portions of the manuscript. Copyright holders and editors who have kindly extended permission to quote or to reprint materials included in their publications include Miss A. Milford of the Clarendon Press, Oxford, and Professor John H. Goldthorpe, editor of *Sociology*, for inclusion of the paper by Roland Robertson, published with revisions under a different title in that journal; Professor Arien Mack, editor of *Social Research*, for portions of a paper "The 'Gift of Life' and Its Reciprocation" by Talcott Parsons, Renée Fox, and Victor Lidz and published in the autumn, 1972, issue of *Social Research* (Volume 39, No. 3); Robert N. Bellah, for selected passages from "Christianity and Symbolic Realism" in Volume 9 of the *Journal for the Scientific Study of Religion* (reprinted in *Beyond Belief*, 1970); The Barre Publishing Company (Barre, Massachusetts) for permission to quote C. K. Shipton from *Law and Authority in Colonial America*, edited by George A. Billias (© 1965); Basic Books, New York, for excerpts from "What is Religion?" Chapter 1, *The Psychology of Religious Experience* by Erwin R. Goodenough (© 1965); The Buddhist Society (London) for quotation from D. T. Suzuki's *On Indian Mahayana Buddhism* (© 1968); Cornell University Press for passages from *Law and Social Action* by Alexander Pekelis (1950); Doubleday and Company for use of Table 50, pp. 324–325 in *The Religious Factor* by Gerhard Lenski, revised edition, paperback, 1963); Faber and Faber (London) for quotation from Audrey Richards, *Chisungu* (© 1956); Fortress Press, Philadelphia, for passages from Harold S. Bender, *The Anabaptists and Religious Liberty in the 16th Century* (© 1953); The Free Press and the Macmillan Company for quotations from Max Weber, *Theory of Social and Economic Organization* (A. M. Henderson and T. Parsons, translators, 1947), and from C. J. H. Hayes, *Nationalism and Religion* (© 1960); Harper and Row for permission to quote from *Religion, Order and Law* by David Little (© 1969) and to use Figure 1 and Tables 50 and 51 (pp. 132 and 134) from *Christian Beliefs and Anti-Semitism* by Charles Y. Glock and Rodney Stark (© 1966 by Anti-Defamation League of B'nai B'rith); Harvard University Press for a brief passage from Lawrence Kohlberg in *Moral Education*, edited by James M. Gustafson (1970); Oxford University Press (London) for permission to quote from *Secularism and Moral Change* by Alisdair MacIntyre (© 1967); Random House for quotations from *Religion: An Anthropological View* by Anthony F. C. Wallace (© 1966) and from *Comparative Ethnic Relations* by Richard A. Schermerhorn (© 1970); the University of Chicago Press for quotations from *The American Supreme Court* by Robert McCloskey (© 1960) and from an article by Clyde Kluckhohn in Volume 1 of *Zygon* (1966); John Wiley and Sons for permission to quote from *Environment, Power and Society* by Howard T. Odum (© 1971).

Several manuscripts were read and evaluated by colleagues on the Program committee of the SSSR—Harold W. Melvin, Jr., William Newman, and Arnold Dashefsky—and by Robert Towler.

Irving Zaretsky, who wrote the Foreword, offered numerous helpful suggestions; he and Eric Valentine, editor of Wiley-Interscience, encouraged this book very nearly from its inception. For this the contributors and I am deeply appreciative.

For assistance in preparation of the manuscript for publication I wish to thank here Virginia DeLorey, Myrtle M. Holman and Sylvia Kanal as well as Wellesley College through its Committee on Faculty Awards.

Continuing thanks for our on-going—and to me always stimulating—discussions about religion and how religious phenomena are to be approached (and best understood) go to my good friend, Bryan Wilson, and to my wife, Dorothy Zulick Eister, who worked with me in preparing the index.

ALLAN W. EISTER

Wellesley, Massachusetts
March 1974

Contents

Changing Perspectives in the Scientific Study of Religion

Introduction

The current surge of interest in the phenomena of "religion"—especially if it signals *renewed* interest in these phenomena—calls special attention to changes in the ways in which "religion" and "faith" (and the various beliefs and practices taken to be related to them) are being approached. Whether this be in the conceptualizations used for capturing and describing religious phenomena, in theories purporting to identify their consequences for human social organization and behavior or in methods employed in their close study, there are significant changes occurring in current thinking about religion.

Well-worn orthodoxies in our ideas about religion (and to some extent about science as well)—and various hypotheses about religion which had seemed to serve us reasonably well—no longer satisfy many social scientists as adequate for describing the objects of their investigations, whether they are studying belief systems, new religious movements, ritual practices, organizational structures, or behavior thought to be associated in some way with these.

Different scholars, of course, perceive problems in different ways—and

1

at different levels of analysis. The once widely-accepted thesis, for example, that religion—or more precisely, what has been identified as *sacred* in every society—serves a necessary integrative function in human societies (and as such must exist as a universal phenomenon in all societies) has been challenged in the face of pluralistic patterns of social organization on one hand and of pervasive skepticism and doubts as to the possibility of attaining anything approaching moral consensus on the other. Whether religion is definable in terms of the functions which it performs (for example, *"religion* is whatever is sacred in the society") [1] or in terms that imply either stability in the institutions of religion or reliability in the responses of "believers" in diverse stuations, even within the same culture, suggests another current question. Conceivably *religion* may not be definable in *general* terms. Further, the validity of certain kinds of functional analysis, once hailed as a scientifically sanitary path for bypassing or escaping thorny theological or other faith-filled positions held by actors, has been called up for reexamination. So too our ideas as to the nature of belief, unbelief and disbelief, of "secularism"—especially the extent to which it in fact exists—and of symbols and the symbolization processes in religious communication.

Where some seek to define religion in terms of the object or objects "toward" which it is taken to be being directed or in terms of distinctive attitudes or postures toward those objects (sometimes with accompanying indicators or specific measures of religiosity), others have moved on to ask, not so insistently what religion *is*, but, rather, how language that is called religious is used. Is the "reality" spoken of by present-day scholars (like Peter Berger and Thomas Luckmann or Harold Garfinkel and Harvey Sacks among others) [2] best handled as indivisible rather than divisable into such familiar dichotomies as "natural" and "supernatural" —a distinction which Durkheim, we recall, thought may have been a "modern" conception, beyond the ken of primitive peoples—as "this-worldly" and "other-worldly," "sacred and secular," "mental" (or even "spiritual") and "material" [3]?

To the extent they have turned attention away from the "substance" or "content" explicit in religious belief systems (or implicit in rites or cultus and the like) and toward symbols having their own reality as cultural artifacts regardless of what they "express," "point to," or "stand for " (that is, symbolize), modern scholars, from Alfred North Whitehead, Kenneth Burke, or Mircea Eliade to Edmund Leach or Mary Douglas have as frequently added to, rather than reduced, the subtlety and complexity of the problems in studying religion. Like the functionalists before them they have, intentionally or otherwise, directed attention away from questions of the "truth value" once felt to be inherent in dogmas and other statements, and from questions for which there seem not to be any answers, or at least no "ultimate" answers.

Whether *what* is being symbolized is in some sense inherent to human experience, "structurally binary" (as many have assumed), or is something that is *not* so structured, not "given" but still evolving (and possibly through the very process of being symbolized thereby attaining the status of "reality" by being "creatively expressed"), is one of the questions currently before us [4].

Indeed, what is distinctive about the approach or approaches to religion taken by many students today may be a heightened awareness of the great subtlety and complexity of the phenomena of faith, and of the need to approach these phenomena with more sensitivity and imagination (and with greater intellectual discipline) than seems to have been exhibited by many who studied them in the past.

Against these issues, questions relative to the adequacy of such standard concepts as *church, sect,* or other types of religious organization, the utility of various role concepts and of different indices of religiosity, and so on might seem to pale; yet they too engage the lively interest of still other students in the social sciences.

Questions of the larger order being vigorously put forward at this time —and on a wide range of "fronts"—suggest that there may well be specific sociological and related changes in the needs and conditions of contemporary society, beyond those incidental to the growth of the social sciences themselves, that ought to be located. This we shall not attempt to do. We are here pointing only to what we take to be representative changes in theories, conceptions and methods in the scientific study of religion.

That "established" conceptions and hypotheses may once have served the intellectual purposes of those who held them is not in question. Ideas such as older structural and functional views of religious institutions, or the willingness to speak about "religion" as though it were a generic phenomenon, about "religions" as though they were readily identifiable, or about "religious responses" as though they were reliable and consistent in the behavioral systems of actors, have been defended by their adherents but are no longer satisfactory for many scholars.

While religion in mid-Victorian England, for example, was thought of as essentially a matter of *beliefs,* with a whole generation of scholars directing their efforts toward the discovery of how man came to believe in gods or a god, such a conception became too narrow to comprehend all the modes and levels of human orientation to human experience later seen to be an integral part of "religion."

Even the concept of religion itself in time was pointed out as derived from a Latin word (or words) limiting its reference to a range of phenomena linked in a rather special way to Western cultures (see Cohn, 1964). Some scholars now find the word "religion" quite unsatisfactory for coping with the variety of belief systems, ritual practices, and so forth encountered in different cultures—or even among different groups and individuals within a given culture.

Again, it is not our intention to demonstrate or describe the entire gamut of questions, fascinating as they are (and no doubt will continue to be). Rather, it is to direct attention to a series of papers which are rich with insights and suggestions for further research into the phenomena of "religion" as social scientists have at least minimally come to recognize it.

In the two opening papers of the present collection, by Burhoe and by Robertson respectively, the authors take opposing points of view. Burhoe, while entirely willing to entertain the idea that there is no demonstrable (or at least reliable) association between "religious" affirmations or even practices on one hand and any (or even some) predictably recurrent patterns of behavior on the other, nevertheless envisages a "science of religion" and calls for increasing cooperation among the sciences, biological as well as social, to create such a science.

Robertson, by contrast, seems to "view with alarm" a tendency—if only latent in some cases—for certain social scientists, to become "religious" about religion, that is, to become apologists or even protagonists, in however subtle a manner, for one or another faith instead of remaining neutral scholars. His paper diagrams a range of alternatives as he sees them.

What Professors Turner and Nelson do in the papers which follow is to suggest, I think, that social scientists cannot penetrate very far into the nature and workings of religion if they are tied to conceptions of religion as *fixed* or static in a given culture or at different points in time. Rather, belief systems, institutions, and the various sociocultural and behavioral expressions of religion might better be thought of as occasionally, perhaps periodically, in flux—in a state of "anti-structure" or, as Victor Turner puts it, of liminality. It is possible, Turner implies, that both in our conceptions of the nature of religion and in our ideas about its consequences —including latent as well as manifest functions which religion has been shown to be performing—we may have fastened upon thinking which has prematurely hardened and to which we tend to remain anchored. Theories and concepts alike may need to be recast in order to include the newer insights which the scientific study of religion itself, as Burhoe points out, has been producing.

Like Clifford Geertz and several others writing today, Turner rejects a conception of religion as describable, for social science purposes, in any fixed or universal terms. Religion, or the faith or faiths which it presumably expresses in cultural terms, is not properly studied in abstract forms but rather in terms of specific sets of symbols (and of the institutions related to them) which are "believed in"—accepted and acted upon by groups of human beings who share them.

Benjamin Nelson presents the arresting thesis that, in human society, a combination of essential ingredients is required for the formation of human consciousness and of human cultures. These include, but go beyond, elements conventionally recognized as part of the "moral basis" of societies or, more accurately, the basis for their maintenance through consensus on moral codes, however this may be accomplished. Without raising explicitly the question of the "functional necessity of religion" or of a sense of the sacred, Professor Nelson conveys an awareness, similar to that developed by Professor Turner drawing on different data, of fluidity—of liminality—at the foundation of social order.

Related to this perspective is another, to which we have already alluded but which may need to be emphasized, namely, that the symbols and institutions which deeply move "believers" may be (or may need to be seen as) *culturally specific*. Each "religion" as the symbolic (and cultural-institutional) vehicle for maintaining a faith is specific to the particular group—tribe, community, or society—which shares it. There is no religion "in general" because there is no faith in general. Faith, it is suggested, is operative—that is, religion is "functioning" in relation to behavior and/or social organization—only when it is vested in specific objects or "powers." It is operative only when presented in specific symbol systems, specific acts (including rituals), or specific structures shared in some way by given groups or, more accurately, by individuals in given groups. In other words, it is only in terms of specific symbols, specific rites or other expression of faith, that actors act in "religious" ways or *are* "religious"— that religion or, more precisely, faith does not and perhaps cannot exist in the generic terms used by some social scientists to describe religion or religious behavior. (This assumes, of course, that "faith" is an essential element in what is defined as religion.)

Here we might recall the point emphasized by Geertz and others that "faith," even for the most devout persons, is not consistently operative at all times and in all circumstances but is often irregularly "acted upon"— and may sometimes be specific to the situations in which the actors find themselves.

To suggest that religious phenomena are, at base, phenomena of faith and that they need to be studied as having culturally specific "contents" is not at all to plunge social scientists into questions which they, as scientists, cannot answer. Social scientists are not expected to answer questions concerning such issues as ontological "reality" (or the existential or other character or qualities) of the *objects* of symbolization, of worship, of faith. These are matters generally conceded to lie outside of the competence of scientists. All that is required of social scientists, we submit, is that the symbols, rites, religious obligations, belief systems of actors be taken seriously as data, as phenomena beyond which it is not necessary to probe— as data, in fact, which must not be "reduced" to some category of "reality" which may fit the biases of the observer more closely than it serves the purposes of scientific study. It is enough for most scientific purposes that symbols and other cultural data be accepted as "real." Whether the objects of reference of symbols are "empirical" or "nonempirical," "material" or "spiritual," "immanent" or "transcendant," "rational" or "irrational," or metaphysically existent, subsistent, or nonexistent may be for theologians but not for social scientists to say [5]. It is essential that scientists understand *what* is being said *about* the nature of God without, as scientists, adding anything to or subtracting anything from the statements [6]. Taking such steps in order to try to understand the actors' orientations, perceptions, or intents (which Max Scheler, Max Weber, and others urged as essential to the understanding of human social behavior) does not require that the observer accept the faith of the actors on the latters' terms. But he must take the elements of that faith seriously—understand and respect them as facts and not as "mistaken perceptions," "false consciousness," or fictions [7].

Social scientists, nevertheless, must be permitted—indeed must demand—freedom to gather data in their own terms, to formulate and test hypotheses which produce verifiable propositions about the behavior of "religious" persons, religious organizations and movements. How to accomplish this without becoming mired in controversy, committed willy-nilly to one theological position or another, is a problem which was partly resolved, as we have seen, by the invention of the functional analysis of religion. Inherent in funtionalism as many social scientists used it was a tendency to attempt to treat religion in general terms, that is, to assume that it had some generic or universal quality. Without careful analytic constraints, as we have observed, it ran some risk of either becoming excessively reductionist or tautological.

To say this, however, is not to disparage in any way the valuable— indeed, as we have argued, crucial—contributions which functional analysis, properly controlled, has made to the scientific study of religion. One of the enduring achievements (and, for social scientists, methodologically "necessary" advances) which functional analysis made possible was, as he noted, the study of religion asking only what demonstrable consequences religious beliefs, practices, rites, etc., had and removing from consideration all questions having to do with the "truth value" or with the validity or invalidity of particular beliefs, the "rightness" or efficacy of given sacraments, and the like.

Probably the most broadly conceived and, until recently at least, most widely and firmly held theories about religion found in the literature of the social sciences have been those concerned with the functions that religion, or what is identified as religion, might have with respect to human societies. Émile Durkheim in his classic formulation characterized religion as that which is sacred to a tribe or to a society and which, by virtue of the shared responses (feelings, practices, etc.) that it invokes and the needs that it fills for groups and for individuals, functions to integrate or unite that society into a moral community. Although both of the two papers following Nelson's, those by Phillip Hammond and by Richard Fenn, concern the functions which religion performs for societies, each challenge in its way theories which see religion as functional to the *whole* of the structural order of modern societies or which start from the premise that religion, however defined, supplies the sole or necessary basis for moral consensus in every human society or for the integration and maintenance of every society. Both raise basic questions, Hammond proposing a reinterpretation of what it means to speak of religion as being "integrative" in pluralistic societies and Fenn challenging the thesis directly. Their arguments, I believe, strike deep into the theoretical position formulated by Durkheim and still central to the understanding which many social scientists appear to have of religion itself. If, as Durkheim argued in *The Elementary Forms of the Religious Life,* religion (or the cultic or mythic expression of "that which is sacred," together with the social organization of "believers," which he called "the Church") is sociologically necessary in order for human beings to accept authority and constraint (and thus avoid anomie), then a religion, or what has to be regarded as a religion, is itself a necessity and will be found universally as a part of every functioning society or social system. Many present-day social scientists, however, recognize no such logical (or *socio*logical) necessity. They and others feel that so much evidence of a decline of "religion," even in the broad terms which Durkheim used, has been abduced that the original formulation must be called into question.

One way out of the difficulty, of course, is to redefine "religion" even more broadly to include not only "that which is sacred" but also that which is, in some sense, "ultimate" perhaps the "ground of being" in Paul Tillich's sense, or the foundation and source of "meaning" in a metaphysical or an ontological sense. Thus "historical materialism" and the Marxist view of History as a moving force become "religion" or, as some might prefer, "functional equivalents" of religion. This "solution," however, fails to satisfy for some the nagging sense that the posture of faith involves something more or other than this something not so readily cast in philosophical or intellectual terms. Intellectually sophisticated as are Marx's and Engels' view of History in this sense or G.W.F. Hegel's Idea of Freedom, and interesting as are other concepts in vogue at different times in the past few centuries (as, for example, the "Invisible Hand" or Bergson's "élan vital" and the like), none of these seems to capture satisfactorily the full range of behavior, attitudes, responses—the *phenomena*—which are the empirical manifests of human faith.

It is to the exploration of these and related problems that the group of papers following Hammond's and Fenn's direct attention. Ward Goodenough, like many anthropologists, takes the position that religion (faith) is not best approached as "beliefs" but rather as responses of human beings to the problems—or to what they perceive to be the problems—of their individual (or collective) common human condition.

Paul Pruyser in his discussion of "unbelief" follows a somewhat similar line of inquiry into what one might call the "faith components" implicated in the total perspective upon their life experiences on the part of human beings, including, of course, social scientists themselves. For Pruyser (as for an apparently growing number of others) the phenomena of "unbelief" are as problematic to anyone who wishes to understand them as are the phenomena of "faith." Psychologically they may be more proximate to contemporary consciousness or to the "contemporary mind." In no case, however, is either unbelief or faith to be "taken for granted" as readily identified or easily defined, nor does either phenomenon seem to be fully comprehended in the categories presently available. Crude reductionisms employed (or implied) in certain modes of "objective" analysis fail to seize hold of the phenomena they purport to study in a manner which does justice either to the subtlety and complexity of the phenomena themselves or to the clearer understanding of these phenomena of which social science might be capable.

It is perhaps in this mood of still-searching inquiry into the nature of religion that we should approach the papers by David Bakan, Talcott Parsons, David Ruth, and Johannes Fabian on the symbolization process or on verbal and other "religious symbols," their sources and their use as guides to the phenomena of faith or as elements in communication about religion. All four authors eschew any attempt to "define" religion, electing rather to move directly toward the symbols or the symbolic expressions of "man seeking meaning" or of what Bakan in his paper has called "the religious mind." In no case is "religion-in-general" the object of scrutiny here. It is particular symbols and symbolic expression of human responses to human experiences—in one case in the Bible and in others in the Judaic-Christian or the Christian tradition—which are brought forward to be considered. All four papers are descriptive and analytical; all are respectful of the nature of faith as it is held by the faithful, though none, to be sure, accepts it in precisely the same terms as do the faithful. They are not reductionist; and they are not patronizing of belief or of believers—not disparaging or disdainful in any way. Rather, in the best tradition of science, they seek to be neutral as well as factually "concrete" so that their interpretations and findings can be studied by others. Interest in symbols is, of course, not new. The development of psychoanalytic perspectives on human behavior brought with it a special impetus to renewed interest in symbols several decades ago as Rollo May and others have pointed out (cf. May, 1960; Douglas, 1970). What is new is an enlarged and possibly deeper appreciation of the significant role of symbols in the "creation" of "reality."

The language and temper, as well as the styles, of the remaining papers in this collection are quite different from those of the earlier papers. The effort to concretize religion moves, in the papers by Donald Ploch and of Clark Roof, in the not unfamiliar direction of describing the phenomena of religion in specific and discrete dimensions which can be located operationally and measured with increasing exactness through various indicators that have been devised. A major point demonstrated by Ploch and by Roof is that there are available models and newer methods (such as path analysis) which open up possibilities for more accurate and detailed descriptions of inter-trait relationships—in Donald Ploch's paper more precise specification of differences between religious groups, in Clark Roof's the clearer identification of significant variables implicated in "religious commitment."

The "exploratory" report by two theological school professors, Clarence Snelling and Read Whitley, themselves strongly attracted by the methods and character of the social sciences, describe a study that is still in its initial stages. Conventional "participant observation" strategies are used to examine a hypothesis, emergent from the study itself, that "deviant life styles" can and do train their adherents in disciplines reminiscent of the "work ethic" (and what came to be regarded as "virtues") found in older traditions.

The concluding paper by David Moberg raises the perennial, often overlooked, question of how the activities and programs of religious organizations are to be "evaluated." It raises issues in a quite different key from those raised by many of the other contributors (Victor Turner, Talcott Parsons, Benjamin Nelson, Roland Robertson, or David Bakan, for example), but equally germane to the *total* spectrum of objective studies of religion.

NOTES

1. There is, as Bryan Wilson and others have pointed out, a latent tautology here.
2. And Alfred Schutz, Hans Vaihinger, and others before them.
3. Robert Bellah (1970: 40) has raised this issue, with unusual effectiveness. Equally firmly one would expect Claude Lévi-Strauss, Edmund Leach, Noam Chomsky, and others committed to the classic (European) conception of "structure" to resist.
4. Although they are not dealing specifically with these questions, both Bryan Wilson in his "Sociologist's Introduction" to a collection of essays, *Rationality* (1970), and Steven Lukes in "Some Problems About Rationality" (*ibid.*, 1970) give voice to related and equally basic issues.
5. After having written this, I discovered, to my delight, that Bryan Wilson had wrestled with this identical problem and had arrived at what I consider to be an eminently reasonable conclusion (1970: xvii).
6. Wilson also discusses the different sense in which social scientists *understand* (and describe) the intentions of actors with respect to action.
7. That this injunction is easier to state than it is to achieve in actual research practice is demonstrated very well in a recent paper by Thomas Robbins and Richard A. Anthony (1972).

REFERENCES

BELLAH, ROBERT N.

1970   *Beyond Belief.* New York: Harper & Row.

BERGER, PETER L.
LUCKMANN, THOMAS

1966   *The Social Construction of Reality.* Garden City, N.Y.: Doubleday.

BURKE, KENNETH

1961   *The Rhetoric of Religion.* Boston: Beacon Press.

COHN, WERNER

1964   "What is Religion? An Analysis of Cross-Cultural Comparisons." *Journal of Christian Education* 7: 116–138.

DOUGLAS, MARY

1966   *Purity and Danger.* London: Routledge and Kegan Paul.
1970   *Natural Symbols.* London: Barrie and Rockliffe (The Cresset Press).

DURKHEIM, EMILE

(1912)   *The Elementary Forms of the Religious Life.* New York:
1961   Collier Books.

GARFINKEL, HAROLD
SACKS, HARVEY

1970   "On Formal Structures and Practical Actions." Pp. 337–366 in J. C. McKinney and E. A. Tiryakian (eds.), *Theoretical Sociology*. New York: Appleton-Century-Crofts.

GEERTZ, CLIFFORD

1966   "Religion as a Cultural System." In M. Banton (ed.), *Anthropological Approaches to the Study of Religion*. London: Tavistock.

LEACH, EDMUND

1971   *Genesis as Myth and Other Essays*. London: Jonathan Cape.

LUKES, STEVEN

1970   "Some Problems About Rationality." Pp. 194–213 in B. Wilson (ed.), *Rationality*. Oxford: Blackwell.

MAY, ROLLO (ED.)

1960   *Symbolism in Religion and Literature*. New York: George Braziller.

ROBBINS, THOMAS
ANTHONY, RICHARD

1972   "Getting Straight with Meher Baba." *Journal for the Scientific Study of Religion* 11: 122–140.

SCHELER, MAX

1954   *The Nature of Sympathy*. Trans. by Peter Heath. New Haven: Yale University Press.

SCHUTZ, ALFRED

1962   *Collected Papers*. The Hague: Martinus Nijhoff.

VAIHINGER, HANS

1924   *The Philosophy of "As If,"* Trans. by C. K. Ogden. New York: Harcourt, Brace.

WEBER, MAX

1963   *The Sociology of Religion*. Trans. by E. Fischoff. Boston: Beacon Press.

WILSON, BRYAN R. (ED.)

1970   *Rationality*. Oxford: Blackwell.

ZAHN, GORDON

1970   "The Commitment Dimension." *Sociological Analysis* 31: 203–208.

Part One
Direction of Renewed Interest in the Study of Religion

Ralph Wendell Burhoe

MEADVILLE/LOMBARD THEOLOGICAL SCHOOL, CHICAGO

The Phenomenon of Religion
Seen Scientifically

Within the burgeoning of scientific symbol systems increasingly able to explain all kinds of events in human experience, where stands the scientific study of religion?

It could be said that the scientific study of religion is today in a more primitive state than was biology two centuries ago. We have not yet had our Darwin; we have hardly had our Linnaeus to sharpen our basic descriptive terms and their classifications; and we have not sufficiently utilized the tested conceptual or symbolic systems of other pertinent disciplines to help structure and order our data.

If the scientific study of religion is in a state comparable to that of biology a few centuries ago, perhaps we can look forward to a comparable future. After extensive, empirically confirmed classifications and comparative analyses in the eighteenth century, biologists in the nineteenth century profited from the pictures of the time scale of life that were emerging from geology to move on to the grand and unifying hypothesis of evolution. Today biology and its evolutionary theory are advancing even more rapidly as they profit from the findings of chemistry and physics.

The scientific study of medicine may be a good example for the scientific study of religion as to how much useful information for understanding human problems can be derived from physics, chemistry, biology, and other sciences in an interrelated net of scientific concepts. One can ask what chemistry can do in explaining or curing souls and societies as well as psyches, especially if one knows that chemistry is involved in genetic heritage, feelings, thinking, and the evolutionary process in general. Religion, a close relative of medicine as an institution for deliverance of man from evil, may be equally studied more effectively by involving more of the already established biophysical conceptual systems for understanding the phenomenon of man and his ultimate place in the scheme of things.

Several examples are available of the usefulness of applying to the scientific study of religion even such basic conceptual systems as thermodynamics. I cite only two of several significant approaches that on the whole have originated independently of one another but all of which cohere in their illumination of the nature of the phenomenon of religion in the light of energy systems and the second law of thermodynamics.

Howard T. Odum is a physical scientist concerned with describing several elements of the flow and control of energy and matter in the earth's ecosystem. He recognizes religion as an expected and necessary element in any arrangement for the proper distribution of power within human society. In *Environment, Power and Society* (1971), which contains a full chapter on religion, he states:

> In recent years studies of the energetics of ecological systems have suggested general means for applying basic laws of energy and matter to complex systems of nature and man. In this book, energy language is used to consider the pressing problem of survival in our time— the partnership of man in nature. An effort is made to show that energy analysis can help answer many of the questions of economics, law and *religion*, already stated in other languages. (Odum, 1971: vii—italics added)

> When human societies first evolved as a significant part of the systems of nature, man had to adapt to the food and fuel energy flows available to him, developing the now familiar patterns of human culture. Ethics, folkways, mores, *religious teachings* and social psychology guided the individual in his participation in the group and provided means for using energy sources effectively. (*Ibid.*: 1—italics added)

Odum pictures human systems of living as more complex extensions of simpler systems of prehuman life, just as the latter, in turn, evolved from the simpler preliving stability patterns in a general stream of energy flow. A hierarchy of feedbacks, or cybernetic control loops, exists in these systems at all levels from molecule to man. Using energy-flow diagrams, Odum identifies religious systems as energy-flow control loops providing partial regulation of a social system or of an individual to provide viability in the context of the ultimate controls of the ecosystem. "Faith in a religion that supports a way of life is necessary to the group's coherent survival and continued efficiency. The need and importance of religion thus have a hard energentic basis" (ibid.: 240–241). And Odum concludes his unusual chapter on religion with:

> The key program of a surviving pattern of nature and man is a subsystem of religious teaching which follows the laws of the energy ethic. Whereas the earlier tenets of religions were based on the simple energy realms of their time, the new sources and larger magnitudes of power require revisions of some of the mores and the personifications used in teaching them. We can teach energy truths through general science in the schools and teach the love of system and its requirements of us in the changing churches. System survival makes right and energy commandments guide the system to survival. The classical struggle between order and disorder, between angels and devils, is still with us. (*Ibid.*: 253)

While a physical scientist may be quickly led to some impressive insights about religion directly from energy theory, religious and sociological scholars may properly question Odum's scholarship in their realm. Hence our next example is an anthropologist whose book Margaret Mead called "the most brilliant and ambitious treatment of religion in this generation" (Mead, 1967: 431). A. F. C. Wallace in his *Religion, an Anthropological View* joins Odum in finding that religions have been the prime agency to orient men at psychosocial levels to continue what recent physics shows to be the distinctive task of living systems in the world: the enhancement of order in spite of entropy.

> In view of the near universality of religion among men, its antiquity and the multiple functions which it seems to serve, it would seem that we may speak of "the religious process" as a type of event which occurs among human beings under very widely varying conditions. The essential theme of the religious event is, nevertheless, definable: it is the dialectic of disorganization and organization. On the one hand men universally observe the increase of entropy (disorganiza-

tion) in familiar systems: metals rust and corrode, woods and fabrics rot, people sicken and die, personalities disintegrate, social groups splinter and disband. On the other hand, men universally experience the contrary process of organization: much energy is spent preventing rust, corrosion, decay, rot, sickness, death and dissolution, and indeed, at least locally, there may be an absolute gain of organization, a real growth or revitalization. This dialectic, the "struggle" (to use an easy metaphor) between entropy and organization, is what religion is all about. The most diverse creeds unite in the attempt to solve the sphinx-riddle of the relationship between life and death, between organization and disorganization; the ideas of the soul, of gods, of world cycles, of Nirvana, of spiritual salvation and rebirth, of progress—all are formal solutions to this problem, which is indeed felt intimately by all men. (Wallace, 1966: 38–39)

Here is a scientific generalization about religion, not just the Judeo-Christian tradition, but any of more than a hundred thousand species of religion which Wallace has estimated to have flourished during the past hundred thousand years. Here is a theory about religion capable of being empirically validated and tested. It also provides religion with structural ties to the top scientific views about the relation of living systems to the physical systems of the cosmos by grace of which they live, move, and have their being.

Explanation of life's seemingly anti-entropic character was pointed out by Schrödinger (1956: 75) in 1943. Others have worked on this intriguing paradox that living systems and their evolution seem to run counter to the universal generalization of the second law of thermodynamics. It has become clear that, although living systems maintain order and even move to higher levels of order, it is not because they in any sense defy the second law of thermodynamics but because they are *not closed* but *open* systems which are shaped and selected to evolve to higher levels of organized complexity by adaptations to changing circumstances inherent in the very nature of the cosmos of which they are a part [1].

If such accounts as those of Odum, Wallace, and others are valid in saying that religions have indeed been effectively carrying on, at the psychosocial level, significant aspects of a transcendently important function required of all life by a universal physical principle, then light from physics and biology, more than providing a transforming and integrating illumination of the nature of religions, might give them cosmic grounds as grandiose as their own myths and theologists have proclaimed, and also might presage a rosy picture for the future of religious institutions. However, there are several dark thorns around this rose that we had better take care of before grasping it.

Perhaps the major thorn is that, while it may indeed be true that religions have provided functions of major importance for human life in many cultures up until now, evidence in the twentieth century is overwhelmingly accumulating that the traditional religious beliefs and practices of the world are rapidly fading, and—quashing hope for help from science—fading largely to the degree that their populations encounter the world view of the modern sciences. Wallace himself has pointed out that "at least from the age of Pericles, religious belief has been repeatedly challenged by scientific knowledge and the rational habits of scientific thought. In these contests, whenever the battle is fully joined, and both parties commit themselves to the struggle, science *always* wins" (Wallace, 1966: 260–261).

Religions like scientific technologies are behavioral patterns that depend on beliefs informed by *more than common* sense. Because the new sciences have produced more credible and effective new myths of the nature of invisible reality beyond common sense knowledge and because little effective translation of the truths in the traditional religious myths has been made from an earlier metaphysic or world view to the scientific one now reigning, religions have become less credible and effective in contemporary culture. As a result, much recent scientific study of religion has become characterized as the study of the illusions of more primitive levels of human culture or of their vestiges in the contemporary world (Bellah, 1970: 234; Glock and Hammond, 1973: xiv et passim), a study of life by examining skeletons. The study of dead or sick forms is as important for religion as it is for medicine and biology. But a science of social and cultural patterns of life should not remain content merely to have discovered skeletons or ill-adapted and disappearing species, as might be implied by the report that "Less than 12 percent of the articles [on religion in 10 major sociological journals over 10 years] report data which reliably relate religion to some other variable" (Bouma, 1971: 63).

Not only is the optimistic vision of a religious revitalization by virtue of a union of religion and science dimmed by science's discrediting of traditional religious belief, but it seems to many that the sciences are forever debarred from helping religion. In spite of some religious characteristics of certain salvatory programs that have in the past century been generated from some aspects of the psychosocial sciences, such as Marxist socialism and Freudian psychotherapy, there is little conviction among scholars of religion that these in any adequate sense ever have or ever could replace traditional religions. Even the skeptical psychosocial scientists doubt it. Wallace is doubtful (Wallace, 1966: 264ff.). Clyde Kluckhohn, who is among those who have recognized the religious characteristics of Marxism, is at the same time one of the best critics of its failure as an adequate religion. Kluckhohn is a rare scholar in the twentieth century who dares, nevertheless, to suppose that "we can bring the scientific method and outlook to bear upon these problems" of "a new religion" (Kluckhohn, 1966. 233.) I return to this view later in my discussion. But it would appear that most of the psychosocial scientists have not shared this view either of the central function of religion in human society or of the possibility of science coming to the rescue of religion (Bellah, 1970: 250).

The secular humanities scholars seem to have accepted the defeat of religion by the sciences, and seem seldom to present and hope for traditional religion to save society today. Moreover they often excoriate science and technology as devilish enemies of humanity—for example, Theodore Roszak in *The Making of the Counter Culture* (1969) and *Where the Wasteland Ends* (1972). Thus, there seems little hope for either religion or science, together or separate, to do anything for human salvation.

The Freudian soteriology has penetrated Western religion's preaching and ritual, and Freudian and behavioral psychotherapies have become themselves a rapidly expanding mass of new cults that are propagating salvation doctrines and rituals and are widely replacing the traditional religions. Perry London's "Future of Psychotherapy" (1973) presents a picture of psychotherapy's rampant expansion, as well as some of its weaknesses. Thus far the psychotherapies have not been very successfully adapted to meet larger social problems. Religions have covered these in addition to the private needs of the individual. One could say that Marx took up one half of religion and Freud the other, and that neither half works well for long without the other. Whether liberation of individual fears and repressions are healthy even for the individual, to say nothing of the society, is doubtful (*ibid.*: 12). But here the point is that, while within (as well as alongside) the religious institutions the new psychotherapies have been welcomed as providing much desired practical elements of a salvation program with a seemingly more scientific realism or authority, the psychotherapeutic doctrines have seldom come near to being synthesized with either the theologies or the common religious beliefs of the great traditions (Burhoe, 1968a). Moreover, many scientists, even psychiatrists, have their doubts that most of the proffered psychotherapeutic programs qualify as being scientifically based. Hence there is considerable ambiguity as to whether this flourishing movement represents either a valid aid to religion or a gift really from the sciences, in spite of its partially religious functions and characteristics.

It is well known, of course, that the bulk of theological interpreters of Western religion during the past few centuries have been fighting the sciences as enemies rather than welcoming them as friends. Some of them have even held up their hands in surrender, capitulating that "God is dead." But the more conservative theologians have sought to deny either the authenticity or the relevance of the sciences for religion, as in the fundamentalist or in the liberal neoorthodox movements. In effect supporting the view of the traditional theologians that the sciences cannot touch religion, some of the most able social scientific students of religion have been pointing to a critical thorn that threatens forever any grasping of the rose of a synthesis of science and religion. One of the most significant statements is made by the very Wallace whom I have cited for his great insight that religion continues, at the psychological level, the ancient and central biological function of maintaining life's order against the disordering or life-destroying forces within and around it. For Wallace as for many others, religion is forever irreducible to science because religion "includes explicit supernaturalism (including *mana*) as an indispensable element. . . . The question of the evolutionary fate of religion is a question about the fate of supernaturalism. . . . Put this way, the evolutionary future of religion is extinction" (Wallace, 1966: 264).

In summary, it appears to few, perhaps least of all to the social scientific scholars of religion, that the sciences can do anything about explaining religion except to explain it away. Perhaps the recent psychosocial scientific study of religion may be viewed as a continuation of the warfare between science and religion, in which the psychosocial scientist—already convinced that religious claims to factuality about the world or man are impossible after the defeat of Christian beliefs by Galileo and Darwin— happily follow the lead of the "better developed" sciences and join in the attack on religion. To caricature, we could say that one branch of the social scientific study of religion began with Marx's suggestion that the suppression of one social class by another requires the religious opiate or deception promising a better life hereafter and elsewhere. Another branch began with Freud's suggestion that psychological needs and weaknesses generate the illusions of religion. After a century of social scientific study of religion, little remains to be done except to make surveys that further confirm the irrelevance of religious beliefs and values in human behavior and to measure the continued decline of religious institutions, perhaps confirming Freud's views on the future of an illusion. I do not imply that all psychosocial approaches to the study of religion are thus to be characterized.

As a matter of fact, I side with those few who have supposed that religions are not necessarily either fraudulent or illusory but are necessary and valid social institutions. However, my reasons are often different from the ones they abduce. I do not believe the psychosocial sciences alone are in any better position to explain the history and future of religion than they would be to explain transportation technology, without utilizing information from the hard sciences concerning the dynamics of sails and winds or rocket engines. To understand man's ultimate concerns or destiny, and his culturally transmitted symbol systems for orienting himself to them, requires a truly interdisciplinary battery of information.

An outstanding scholar of religion with whom I share the view that religion is necessary and "not necessarily fraudulent" is Robert Bellah, who in 1969 presented to the annual meeting of the Society for the Scientific Study of Religion a paper in which he said: "To put it bluntly, religion is true" (Bellah, 1970: 253). Bellah also shares with me the view that to understand religion one needs to have an extended scientific model or theory, such as the "cybernetic model" where the "basic terms are 'energy' and 'information' " (ibid: 11). Yet he has an ambivalence and ambiguity concerning the usefulness of the hard sciences which keeps cropping up in his writings so that it seems to me that he spoils his argument and loses his case. For instance, against the role of objective science in religion he says that we must no longer conceive of religion within the "objective cognitive bias that has dominated Western thought ever since the discovery of the scientific method in the seventeenth century" (ibid.: 251). "For religion is not really a kind of pseudogeology or pseudohistory but an imaginative statement about the truth of the totality of human experience" (ibid.: 244). We must also reject "the claims of the historical realist theologians, who are still working with a cognitive conception of religious belief that makes it parallel to objectivist scientific description" (ibid.: 253), which has led to rejection of a religion as false and fraudulent (ibid.: 247). Instead, "all reductionism must be abandoned" and we should turn to "symbolic realism [which] is the only adequate basis for the social scientific study of religion" (ibid.; 253). In "symbolism realism"

> . . . reality is seen to reside not just in the object but in the subject, and particularly in the relation between subject and object. The canons of empirical science apply primarily to symbols that attempt to express the nature of objects, but there are nonobjective symbols that express the feelings, values, and hopes of subjects, or that organize and regulate the flow of interaction between subjects and objects, or that attempt to sum up the whole subject-object complex or even point to the context or ground of that whole. These symbols, too, express reality and are not reducible to empirical propositions. This is the position of symbolic realism. (Ibid.: 252)

In his proposal for "symbolic realism" Bellah suggests that, since religion involves symbols that are nonobjective and not reducible to empirical propositions, religious symbol systems are noncognitive and cannot properly claim parallel objectivist scientific description or be properly studied by scientific canons. In my opinion this is an error by which he loses both his goals—to be scientific about religion and to find religion real.

Moreover, this seems contrary to another side of Bellah's writings. He correctly understands that the hard sciences themselves are also based on noncognitive, prerational knowing as in Polanyi's "implicit knowing" (*ibid.*: 253), and that "the great symbols that justify science itself rest on unprovable assumptions sustained at the deepest levels of our consciousness" (*ibid.*: 245). Bellah also proclaimed earlier the virtues of a "cybernetic model," which is a part of the physicalistic model of organic and cultural systems such as the one described by Odum. Bellah was warm toward the cybernetic model because the explanations of the human action system in terms of "autonomy, learning capacity, decision, and control . . . give the cybernetic model the ability, lacking in previous mechanistic and organic models, to assimilate the contributions of the humanistic disciplines—the *Geisteswissenschaften*—without abandoning an essentially scientific approach" (*ibid.*: 10). Bellah's book contains many paradoxical affirmations and rejections of objective science.

Because a mixture of faith in and fear of the hard sciences is shared by so many, and leads not only theologians but psychosocial scientists and even many natural scientists to suppose that religion can have no future in the light of objective science, I present in brief outline a view—taken from the very hardest of the hard scientists and philosophers of science— whose usefulness for illuminating religion is not yet widely understood, but which may become a most significant avenue not only for the future development of a scientific study of religion but also for the scientific enrichment and validation of religion.

First, I deal with four problems confusing to Bellah and others: (1) confusions raised by the terms "subjective" and "objective" and the belief that the hard sciences do not and cannot deal with "subjective" experiences; (2) the error in supposing the hard sciences dismiss the nonrational and unconscious sources of human experience and in any case cannot explain them; (3) the supposition that "reductionism" is the wrong direction for understanding religion; and (4) the role of hard sciences in understanding "feelings, values, and hopes." I then deal with the seeming impossibility of relating the allegedly "transcendent," "other-wordly," religious concepts to those of the physical sciences; and finally I suggest how the new physical-science views of evolutionary theory can enable both a respect for the "objective" reality of religious symbol systems thus far and the constructive development of religion, like medicine, under the full light of empirically validated propositions.

SUBJECTIVE AND OBJECTIVE

At least two great physicists of our time would go even further than Bellah in giving primacy to the "subjective" world, not only for providing the symbols of reality but for providing the whole basis for the superstructure of the ordered system of scientific symbols of the "objective world." P. W. Bridgman, a Nobel Prize-winning experimental physicist, wrote that "My reason for insisting on the importance of the role of the individual in science was that 'proof,' without which no science is possible, is entirely an affair of the individual and is therefore private. . . . Any 'ultimately true' account that I can give of the world has be be from myself as center." Bridgman even had to defend himself against charges of solipsism (Bridgman, 1969: v, 217, 246). Erwin Schrödinger, another Nobel Prize-winning physicist, wrote: "The reason why our sentient, percipient, and thinking ego is met nowhere within our scientific world picture can easily be indicated in seven words: because it is itself that world picture" (Schrödinger, 1959: 52).

Back in 1885 the physicist Ernst Mach impressed upon his colleagues in science that the "reality" with which science deals was the phenomenal world of sensations or "certain denotations of direct sensations of the form: I see blue, I feel cold, etc." But "for certain complexes of sensations whose coherence proves to be vitally important, denotations like 'body,' 'substance,' 'thing,' etc. have been introduced" (Mises, 1951: 85–87). The "objective" world may be said to be a set of invariances found in the "subjective" world.

Great physical scientists and philosophers of science have, for a century at least, recognized that the "hard facts" of science itself are only new arrangements to provide order and meaning for symbols already inside the head. Of course most scientists prefer to establish themselves in the very useful ritual of using "objective" language, speaking of the objectivity of scientific knowledge and the worthlessness of subjective opinion. Even in psychology, a "good" scientist tries to emulate the "objectivity" of other fields. Because of the paradoxical or self-contradictory dilemmas that one gets caught in when utilizing our presently inherited symbols that divide the world of human experience into "object" and "subject," a careful psychologist like B. F. Skinner elected to keep clean by avoiding "subjective" language in his study of human "behavior." Ross Ashby in his *Design for a Brain* expressed the problem this way:

> . . . the fact of the existence of consciousness is prior to all other facts. If I perceive—am aware of—a chair, I may later be persuaded, by other evidence, that the appearance was produced only by a trick

of lighting; I may be persuaded that it occurred in a dream, or even that it was an hallucination; but there is no evidence in existence that could persuade me that my awareness itself was mistaken—that I had not really been aware at all. This knowledge of personal awareness, therefore, is prior to all other forms of knowledge.

If consciousness is the most fundamental fact of all, why is it not used in this book? The answer, in my opinion, is that Science deals, and can deal, only with what one man can *demonstrate* to another. Vivid though consciousness may be to its possessor, there is as yet no method known by which he can demonstrate his experience to another. And until such a method, or its equivalent, is found, the facts of consciousness cannot be used in scientific method. (Ashby, 1960: 11–12)

Because science is a part of linguistically transmitted information, its communicability requires "objective" language, and private experience is of no use except to the investigator himself. Bridgman would assert the uniqueness of subjective experience for the investigator, although he understands Skinner's and others' use of "objective" language. He suggests that he can use either language and that the paradoxes and problems of the "subject-object complex" are essentially problems of inexact linguistic usage (Bridgman, 1959, especially 215–219).

Many are familiar with the fact that the "objectivity" and the "outside" dimension of the world of our experience are established in part by the correlations that we make prior to language. As infants we make correlations between the outcomes of two or more separate routes to experiencing a ball. We experience it by seeing a round blob of color, but we also experience it by the tactual and kinesthetic feeling in our hands and arms. By such multiple correlations of experiences from many perspectives, certain preverbal patterns or symbols in our experiences become "objective realities" out there in the world (Bridgman, 1959: 45ff.). Language soon enters to supplement and congeal our preverbal symbols, as with the name "ball" (cf. Mises, 1951: 80–100). Jean Piaget's *The Child's Concept of the World* is valuable background in these matters.

A physicist develops objectivity in the same general way. When he wishes to assert that something is real, true, or objective, all he really needs to say is that several independent experiences have confirmed that some relationship or correlation among events remains unchanged. Bridgman has called this process one of finding "different routes to the same terminus." He and others do not stop with their own private experience, however. The term "objective" is enhanced when it is found that others performing the same or similar operations report essentially equivalent results, at least insofar as words or other cultural symbols can communicate "equivalent" experiencing from one individual to another (Bridgman, 1959: 52ff.). Another physicist who has carefully examined the problem of knowing and of physical science, Margenau (1960), has provided a very helpful analysis of how scientific conceptual systems that portray the objective world are built up from the private "plane of perceptual experiences," which are the data or the givens of subjective experience.

THE UNCONSCIOUS AND PRERATIONAL

Hard scientists are already aware of what Bellah wants to assert—namely, that the most basic elements of human experience originate not from conscious reasoning but from unconscious mechanisms. It is not clear, however, whether Bellah recognizes the extent to which the hitherto unconscious, cybernetic machinery and programs inside the head have recently, in the heads of some workers in the physical and biological sciences at least, become conscious. We can approach the task of understanding the unconscious in the pre-Freudian manner by enjoying or fearing the *primitive data* as they appear from out of the machinery in our head (of which we are not conscious) as the sensations, perceptions, symbols, dreams, or fantasies of which we are now aware. Freud already noted that these phenomena did not necessarily appear rational, and made some rough hypotheses concerning their sources. But perhaps the best route to understanding the unconscious sources of "subjective" experience today is exactly through a hierarchy of abstract propositions of the hard sciences that are everywhere in principle reducible to empirically testable, "objective" machinery.

A number of investigators of the workings of the brain during the past few decades have found this to be the case, and have studied the machinery of the brain by electrical, chemical, anatomical, neurophysiological, surgical, and other means—including comparative phenomena not only in other animals but in such utterly different mechanisms for doing similar things as computers. J. Z. Young portrayed "the brain as the computer of a homeostat" (Young, 1964: 14). His picture, like that of many other students of life, is that living systems are cybernetically self-controlled dynamic patterns adapted to maintain themselves in particular kinds of environments by their having information that allows them to take the right sort of action. Brains are such control centers structured by genetically and culturally transmitted information.

As a sample of the kinds of confirmation available by the "objective science" route to the same terminus I cite Benson E. Ginsburg (1963), who, writing on the phylogeny of symbolic behavior, noted the probability of genetic (that is, biochemical) grounds for species specific symbol forms in higher animals as well as men. This confirms Jung's finding more than a half century ago that there may be species-wide "archetypes" in men's dreams and symbols. For a note on understanding "symbols" in both subjective and objective language, see my "Editorial Note on Symbols" (Burhoe, 1968b). Bellah also recognizes the species-wide recurrence of patterns in his "nonobjective" symbols, but his exclusion of empiricism and objectivity from this realm would, if taken seriously, prevent the kinds of confirmation and illumination the hard sciences can give.

We have today very convincing evidence that all biological creatures are flows or streams of matter, shaped or patterned in *behavior* as well as structure by two interacting systems of information: *genetic* information (DNA structures) and the information structures *supplied by the environment.* I have already pointed out how physicists beginning at least a hundred years ago, as well as investigators of the brain recently, have provided grounds for understanding basic human perceptions and feelings as the product of complex learning processes (at unconscious as well as conscious levels) which involve the genetically guided operations of a brain in reacting to sensory data that are stimulated from inside the organism as well as from the environment. In the human case there is a very special and immediate layer of environment, saturated with the social heritage of accumulated information that shapes the patterns of human living. This heritage is closely related to what anthropologists have called *culture.* This cultural information, jointly with genetic information, operates to structure molecular arrangements inside the brain during the process of "enculturation." In the learning processes that take place as a child interacts with environing events, such as the language and other characteristic behavior patterns provided by the culture, his brain encodes this information in molecular and neural patterns.

Much of the information thus communicated to a brain does not directly enter consciousness. While *some* of this process takes place at levels of awareness—for example, at the time of originally learning to ride a bicycle, perform religious rituals, and so on—even this becomes habitual and largely operates unconsciously. Even in the preliminary learning processes, most of the underlying associating and integrating mechanisms of the brain do not ever directly enter consciousness—at least until some scientific research uncovers them in relatively high levels of scientific symbol systems. But it is exactly these physical events hidden in the brain that *are* the "unconscious mechanisms" that shape our conscious experiences. More than a decade ago Young pointed out that "the supposition that 'things of the spirit' are necessarily dealt with in another language [than that of the scientist] has persisted only because we have not yet been able to extend our scientific treatment to the brain" (Young, 1960: 8). Sperry recently wrote that "the accumulating evidence in neuroscience builds up overwhelmingly today to the conviction that conscious mental awareness is a property of, and inseparably tied to, the living brain" (Sperry, 1972: 126).

Thus, symbols, including religious symbols, depend both on genetic information and on information derived from the environment, including especially the cultural environment. Both sources of information are interwoven in the operating patterns of the nervous system. The result is that a large mass of unconscious information, structured in materials inside the head, sorted and categorized according to processes supplied by the genetic information, then becomes the unconscious background from which the sensations, perceptions, or symbols of our conscious experience of ourselves and of our world arise. When new inputs from the outside world are processed by the brain, the resulting conscious states are special representations in our particular response patterns of our relations to that *objective* world *outside* of our bodies. When the inputs to the brain are from the sensory mechanisms inside our gut or other parts of our bodies, we call these representations of states of the real world *inside* our bodies by such terms as *subjective* feelings, pleasures, pains, wishes, and so forth. When the representations of self and world are produced from concoctions projected from the brain's memories, and are not immediate processings of sensory inputs, we may call them dreams, artistic and technical imaginings, thinking, or scientific hypotheses—depending on their nature. Religious experiences may involve all of these together

Consciousness and memory cannot appear at birth, but require a period of months and years of assimilation of and learning from inputs into the brain from the various external and internal sensing mechanisms, both culturally patterned and raw. Consciousness of some things does not arise until we have matured for many years and lived in a high intellectual or scientific culture. Many people have never become conscious that they "speak prose," as Molière put it, or use grammar. Most people are not even conscious of *what* they are *really* doing, or *why*, when they engage in bisexual procreation—not until some advanced enculturation informs them of the evolution of the genetic strategy of sexual recombination for increasing the amount of viable variation within the gene pool.

The conscious level of personal human experience is where science begins and ends, according to this new "epistemological and ontological metaphysics," flowing out of recent physics and biopsychology. This "metaphysics" suggests that we can say, reciprocally, that the "subjective" world is a particularistic representation of some invariances extracted by a brain from the "objective" world; and, that the "objective" world is a set of invariances found in the "subjective" world. The two worlds are the same. We are confused when language reifies the difference between "objective" or "material" (that portion of our awareness to which we can point or touch in the world outside our bodies and get verbal or related symbols of agreement from others confirming what we say about it) and "subjective" or "mental" (that portion of our awareness which is privy to our internal states and hidden from others).

REDUCTIONISM

The terms "reduction" and "reductionism" similarly pose a problem for Bellah and many others. First, it should be clear from the above that "scientific reductionism" is not properly conceived of as reducing the subjective world to the objective world, if they are both aspects of the same world. Understanding "reduction" may be helped by using a better term introduced by Mises (1951: 69)—"connectibility." In human communication, symbols have to be connected with one another and with nonverbal experiences in ways that make sense. Science is for Mises as for Bridgman and many others simply a specialized extension of the unconsciously evolved inherited symbol system of communication called language. For them, one special requirement of the scientific language is that the connections of verbal and other artificial symbols must end in experiences that arise in awareness prior to and independently of words. These are often called the empirical data, the givens, of conscious experience. We now know they are phenomena produced by interactions of genes and environments, particularly in the unconscious machinery of the brain.

From Mach to Bridgman and others, the connections we make from verbal symbols to the preverbal symbols or "elements" of consciousness are called "reductions" to sensations and perceptions, the "protocols," the "operational definitions," or "rules of correspondence," etc. In this sense Bellah's noncognitive symbols that express reality, indeed, are not *reducible* to such preverbal and prelogical empirical givens of conscious experience, for they *are themselves* exactly what these physicists mean by empirical data. Certainly they are not reducible to anything else, if we are speaking of a reduction or connectibility going in the direction of what is ultimately given to and unanalyzed in consciousness.

But there is also another direction of connectibility and of reduction that is equally significant in the sciences, such as the hypothecated "reducibility of all physics to the laws of Newtonian mechanics" (*ibid.*: 97). Here connection or reduction is operating in the reverse direction, the direction pictured by Margenau (1960) and others when they indicate that

successive levels of conceptual symbols in a pyramidal hierarchy of conceptual levels above the plane of perceptual experiences successively abstract and symbolically represent a whole class of characteristics of the
level below them. The single symbol "dog" covers Fido and each and all
of a multitude of other four-legged creatures that bark or have certain
other characteristics. The Newtonian symbol $F = ma$ is a reduction to a
single statement of an invariant or universal relation in an indefinitely
large number of cases of the phenomena of motion, useful alike in explaining or predicting the motions of the moon, a falling apple, a basket-
ball player, or the particles of a gas that determine its temperature.

Far beyond the capacities of any participating individual to fully analyze them, human cultures have erected level after level of articulated
systems of linguistic and other symbols that are carefully organized to
reduce the millions of data given in perception to a manageable size, so
as to enable very finite brains effectively to anticipate and operate very
complex organisms viably within a very complex world. Each higher level
in a hierarchy of "reductions" contains symbols that embrace whole categories of symbols in the layer below. It is the culture that transmits the
information that above the level of the word Fido is the level of "dog," in
which Fido plays a part, and so on. There are, of course, many different
dimensions and kinds of systems for connecting symbols and for *reducing*
them to relatively simple, stable, or invariant schemes which can be managed in a brain and in the consciousness the brain produces.

Thus, when Bellah says that "religion is a reality *sui generis*," we can
all agree. But his statement that this means that "all reductionism must
be abandoned," overlooks this other and more important meaning of reductionism, a mistake that would frustrate Bellah's own wish to make it
possible for "theologian and secular intellectual [to] speak the same language" (Bellah, 1970: 253). To say that the world or anything in it is *sui
generis* does not mean that we cannot *reduce* to some more effective order
or scientific scheme our first levels of impressions, perceptions, or symbols
of it. In fact, if we want to *understand* phenomena, rather than merely be
immersed in them, we *must* reduce them to symbolic structures manageable by our genetic and cultural machinery for rational handling. Bellah's
arbitrary isolation of religion within a "symbolic realism" disconnected
from scientific realism would prevent religion's reality from being related
or integrated into the larger context of meaning. For it is the hard sciences
today that have pioneered in cultural evolution's most rapidly expanding
network of useful and simplifying codifications or reductions of linguistic
or other conceptual symbol systems to provide better explanation, to make
more sense, or to enhance understanding. (See Bridgman, 1959: Chapters 2
and 3; Mises, 1951: Part 1.)

This paper has only sketched some of the new epistemology coming out of the sciences. But it should help make clear why Bellah's suggestion that we move back toward basic or *sui generis* data, that is, toward unreduced or unanalyzed symbols in experience, is not a move toward the more "real," "objective," and powerful symbols by which the sciences are expanding man's knowledge of his world and himself. Science is not the data of empirical experience, but is the reduction of the relative chaos of those *sui generis* data to a system of organized symbolic relations that provides meaning and manageability.

FEELINGS, VALUES, AND HOPES

It should be clear from the above that man's feelings, values, and hopes do arise into conscious awareness from unconscious mechanisms, and that the genetic and cultural as well as wider environmental sources of brain patterns are what shape them. The hard sciences that describe the chemistry of the DNA of genetics and the new biopsychology and neurosciences are making great strides toward explaining them in terms of brain patterns operating at unconscious levels as well as at the levels of both preverbalized and verbalized symbols that are experienced consciously. These include the phenomena Bellah calls noncognitive symbols and religious experience, even if we can show how they are now "reducible to empirical propositions."

Religion is nevertheless indeed a very intangible and difficult-to-discern pattern. It lies inside the brains of the population. It is indeed "inner." Feelings of awe and the sacred, as well as convictions about the reality of unseen spirits and god concepts, *arise* from as far below the surface of the *perceived* external world and of the *perceived* inner self as do all the rest of the patterns of our conscious experience: in the "unconscious" complexities of the brain. But the "objective reality" of these elements of religious experience and symbols is best established in the ways we establish the reality of the invisible and intangible entities of chemical, biological, and cultural evolution.

We can in this chapter only sketch and not fully document the grounds for our hypotheses concerning the capacities of the hard sciences to deal with religiously significant aspects of inner subjectivity including feelings, emotions, hopes, and fears. With respect to psychological and social aspects of religious values as illumined by the harder sciences I have written a good deal and given more details on the various scientific sources on which I have drawn (Burhoe, 1967, 1969, 1971a, 1971b, 1971c, 1972a, 1972b, 1973a, and 1973d).

THE TRANSCENDENT AND SUPERNATURAL

I promised to return to what Wallace saw as the impossibility of belief in the supernatural if one believes in science.

Let us grant that belief in a system of power transcendent over both a man and mankind as well as over all events in the cosmic system is a primary—if not essential—characteristic of religion. Let us also grant it is man's sense of relation to such a transcendent power that provides his own identity, his sense of meaning, his sense of what is of ultimate concern and sacred, and that human motivation, hopes, and fears depend upon how man conceives his relation to the powers over him. It may be a professional perspective that many in the psychosocial sciences do not see as readily as do biologists and physicists the fact of man's utter dependence upon a larger system of power and reality in which man is infinitesimal. In my quotation from Odum, it was clear that a physical scientist recognized man's dependence upon and necessity to adapt to the ecosystem and *its requirements of us.* I have elsewhere suggested that physicists have today become the best revealers of the elusive but sovereign entities and forces, not immediately apparent to common sense, that do in fact far transcend human powers, that did create life and human life and do ordain human destiny. I suggested that it is to such real, superhuman, and ultimately insuperable powers and conditions of the cosmos—however primitively envisaged—to which the gods or supernatural powers of prior cultures referred rather than to nonexistent beings. "Supernatural" refers not to their unreality but rather to both the *hiddenness* of their reality from our commonsense view and also to their *prior reality* as a more ultimate source and ground of the more apparent or "natural" phenomena. The supernatural powers transcended the "nature" of classical common sense, even if such unseen powers are today a part of the "nature" with which modern physics deals (Burhoe, 1966: and 1973b: 423–24). In the concepts emerging today from the several dozen interlinked systems of scientific symbols, there is being revealed a cosmic system which is utterly transcendent to man, an interrelated whole or ecosystem of which man is a creature and in which man by the total system has been ordained to play a significant role as a cocreator of living systems at the top of the evolutionary hierarchy of life on earth so long as he continues to adapt to or obey the immutable and insuperable requirements laid out by this superordinate system in which human values, hopes, and fears can be said ultimately to rest, at least so far as we can see things today in the scientific view.

In *Beyond Belief* Bellah defines "religion as that symbol system that serves to evoke . . . the totality that includes subject and object and provides the context in which life and action finally have meaning" (Bellah, 1970: 252–53). He also quotes with approval Clifford Geertz's definition:

> Religion is a system of symbols which acts to establish powerful, pervasive, and long-lasting moods and motivations in men by formulating conceptions of a general order of existence and clothing these conceptions with such an aura of factuality that the moods and motivations seem uniquely realistic. (Ibid.: 12)

If a student of religion, who had already discerned its reality and significance in human psyches and societies, wanted to find a credible, factual, real, supersocial, transcendent, superordinate symbol system to explain or justify social norms as well as to provide meaning and hope for personal life, perhaps his best bet would be the network of concepts or "objective" symbols spreading out from the physical sciences and providing a comprehensive and reliable model of the sovereign realities of the "objective"—the reliably enduring "subjective"—world. For the greatest "aura of factuality" today is possessed by the conceptual schemes of the hard sciences.

There are some interdisciplinary communities of scholars who have been for more than a quarter of a century exploring ways of translating religious symbol systems into scientific conceptual systems, seeking possible integrations. I have described two of these in some detail (Burhoe, 1954; 1972d; and 1973c). My own efforts to translate between some of the new scientific languages and the traditional religious superordinate symbol systems are found in several papers, including especially (Burhoe, 1960, 1971b, 1972c, 1973b). In these papers there are references to many others working on this problem. In the pages of *Zygon: Journal of Religion and Science,* one can find a wide variety of efforts in this direction.

The above sketch of how to relate the scientific symbol system to the religious symbols of a transcendent and supernatural world is too brief to persuade many, and undoubtedly such a relationship will be as puzzling and unacceptable as was quantum mechanics 50 years ago or even the view of 500 years ago that the obviously flat earth is really shaped like a ball and that there are people at the antipodes who do not fall down into space but walk around upsidedown. It is just as upsidedown to say that "supernatural" in commonsense language becomes "natural" in physics. Let me simply suggest that I believe sooner or later that the problem posed by Wallace (and by many others, too) will be resolved in some such fashion. Among the more sophisticated we can have our transcendent and supernatural world mixed in with our best science without

logical contradiction. Others will come to accept it and not be afraid
to ship to Australia or the new world.

THE FUTURE OF THE SCIENTIFIC STUDY OF RELIGION

I promised to treat briefly one other topic: the advancement of religion
by its scientific study. This may also seem paradoxical in view of the fact
I have suggested that I agree with a number of able scholars of religion
who find even the great Marxist and Freudian attempts to supersede
traditional faiths to be inadequate. Moreover, I have suggested that the
religious traditions contain a great reservoir of wisdom or truth for regu-
lating human psychosocial patterns which no scientific analysis yet fully
comprehends. I would even say that it would be as foolish to suppose we
could produce a synthetic religion today any more adequately than we
could replace the naturally and unconsciously evolved processes of agri-
culture by chemical synthesis of our food supply. But it is exactly this
new scientific understanding of how *wisdom for life* is evolved, both unconsciously as well as consciously, that makes the difference between the
man entering the scientific study of religion today and one entering it
before the selective processes operating in the shaping of events evolving
throughout the range from chemistry to human cultures was beginning
to be understood.

This new area of scientific understanding of information theory and
the evolution of complex hierarchies of living systems derives from electrical engineering, thermodynamics, and utilizes elements from many of
the increasingly overlapping realms of the scientific conceptual network
or symbol system. For an important creative view I commend Herbert
Simon, especially (1969: 90–113).

An excellent review of the new approach to understanding cultural
evolution was given by Donald T. Campbell (1965). Campbell has also
pioneered in a significant analysis of the relation between cultural and biological evolution and his conclusion accents the reality and the necessity
of religion:

> Man is more similar to the social insects than to the wolf and the
> chimpanzee in complex social coordination, division of labor, and
> self-sacrificial altruism. In the social insects the behavioral disposi-
> tions involved are genetically determined, an evolution made possible
> by the absence of genetic competition among the cooperators. In man
> genetic competition precludes the evolution of such genetic altruism.
> The behavioral dispositions which produce complex social interde-
> pendence and self-sacrificial altruism must instead be products of

culturally evolved indoctrination, which has had to counter the self-serving genetic tendencies. (Campbell, 1972: 35)

I have presented religious implications of many aspects of these new understandings of the evolution of complex systems including the new views of psychosocial and cultural phylogeny and ontogeny, especially in Burhoe (1967, 1971b, 1972a–c, 1973a,b, and d). I share Campbell's strong statement that

> On evolutionary grounds . . . it is just as rational to follow well winnowed religious traditions which one does not understand as it is rational to continue breathing air before one understands the role of oxygen in body metabolism. I will argue that if modern psychology and social science disagree with religious tradition on ways of living, one should, on rational and scientific grounds, choose the traditional recipes for life, for these are the better tested. (in Burhoe, 1971b: 144)

But I must immediately point out that it is exactly this new understanding of and respect for religions as very real and objective social institutions containing a vast body of evolved wisdom of a kind ultimately necessary for the cybernetics of man's long-range values in the world ecosystem (Forrester, 1972) or man's ultimate concerns that makes it both *possible* and *necessary* for religion even more than medicine to be interpreted and advanced scientifically. Paradoxical as it may seem to some, I predict a relation of the sciences to a dawning new worldwide "theological" movement which will relate to, reform, and revitalize local religious practices in the next few decades in the ways that the sciences have done for medical theory and practices around the world in the past ten decades. This will require a theology (or cosmology and anthropology) shaped by the physical sciences as well as by the more traditional kinds of psychosocial arts and sciences, including the scholars and practitioners within the existing religious traditions. The cooperative and fruitful interchange among these several disciplines may be envisioned as evolving in ways similar to what has developed in the teaching hospitals at universities where biological, chemical, and physical scientists are teamed with clinical professors and professionals. When this begins to happen a little more fully, there will not only be a firm science of religion but also a living religion within high scientific culture to be scientific about, just as is the case for the equally ancient art of medicine.

The social scientific study of religion will then no longer be confined to archaic or obsolescent patterns irrelevant to contemporary life.

NOTES

1. In my opinion, one of the best accounts for the general reader of how the relation of life to the physics of entropy and the nonliving world can be understood is that of Bronowski (1970). Another account that carries the thermodynamics of living systems further with more detail is that of Katchalsky-Katzir (1971). A recent popular account is that of Prigogine (1973). An excellent extension of the thermodynamic picture to the dynamics of human psychological and sociocultural phenomena is presented by one of Wallace's students, Solomon Katz (1973).

REFERENCES

ASHBY, W. ROSS

1960   *Design for a Brain, the Origin of Adaptive Behavior*, 2nd rev. ed. New York: Wiley.

BELLAH, ROBERT N.

1970   *Beyond Belief*. New York: Harper and Row.

BOUMA, GARY D.

1971   "Assessing the Impact of Religion: A Critical Review." *Zygon* 6: 55–64.

BRIDGMAN, P. W.

1959   *The Way Things Are*. Cambridge, Mass.: Harvard University Press.

BRONOWSKI, J.

1970   "New Concepts in the Evolution of Complexity: Stratified Stability and Unbounded Plans." *Zygon* 5: 18-35.

BURHOE, RALPH W.

1954   "Religion in an Age of Science." *Science* 120: 522–24.

1960   "Salvation in the Twentieth Century." In Harlow Shapley (ed.), *Science Ponders Religion*. New York: Appleton-Century-Crofts.

1966   "Commentary on Theological Resources from the Social Sciences." *Zygon* 1: 93–96.

1967   "Five Steps in the Evolution of Man's Knowledge of Good and Evil." *Zygon* 2: 77-96.

1968a   "Bridging the Gap between Psychiatry and Theology." *Journal of Religion and Health* 7: 215–226.

1968b   "Editorial Note on Symbols." *Zygon* 3: 137.

1969 "Values via Science." *Zygon* 4: 65–99.

1971a "Introduction to the Symposium on Science and Human Values." *Zygon* 6: 82–98.

1971b *Science and Human Values in the 21st Century.* Philadelphia: Westminster Press.

1971c "What Specifies the Values of the Man-Made Man?" *Zygon* 6: 224–246:

1972a "The Control of Behavior." *Journal of Environmental Health* 35: 247–58.

1972b "Evolving Cybernetic Machinery and Human Values." *Zygon* 7: 188–209.

1972c "Natural Selection and Code." *Zygon* 7: 30–63.

1972d "Proposal to Establish an Independent Center for Advanced Study in Religion and Science." 7: 168–184.

1973a "Civilization of the Future: Ideals and Possibility." *Philosophy Forum*, 11.

1973b "The Concepts of God and Soul in a Scientific View of Human Purpose." *Zygon* 8: 443–482.

1973c "The Institute on Religion in an Age of Science: A 20-Year View." *Zygon* 8: 59–80.

1973d "The World System and Human Values." Pp. 161&187 in Ervin Laszlo (ed.), *The World System: Models, Norms, Applications.* New York: Braziller.

CAMPBELL, DONALD T.

1965 "Variation and Selective Retention in Socio-Cultural Evolution." In H. R. Barringer, G. I. Blanksten, and R. W. Mack (eds.), *Social Changes in Developing Areas: A Reinterpretation of Evolutionary Theory.* Cambridge, Mass.: Schenckman.

1972 "On the Genetics of Altruism and the Counter-Hedonic Components in Human Culture." *Journal of Social Issues* 28: 21–37.

FORRESTER, JAY W.

1972 "Churches at the Transition between Growth and World Equilibrium," *Zygon* 7: 145–167.

GINSBURG, BENSON E.

1963 "Genetics and Personality." In Joseph M. Wepman and Ralph W. Heine (eds.), *Concepts of Personality.* Chicago: Aldine.

GLOCK, CHARLES Y.
HAMMOND, PHILLIP E.

1973   *Beyond the Classics?* New York: Harper and Row.

KATCHALSKY, A.

1971   "Thermodynamics of Flow and Biological Organization."
                       Zygon 6: 99–125.

KATZ, SOLOMON H.

1973   "Evolutionary Perspectives on Purpose and Man." *Zygon*
                       8: 325–340.

KLUCKHOHN, CLYDE

1966   "The Scientific Study of Values and Contemporary Civili-
                       zation." *Zygon* 1: 230–243. [Reprinted from *Proc. Am.
                       Philos. Soc.* 102 (1958).]

KUHN, THOMAS

1962   *The Structure of Scientific Revolutions.* Chicago: Uni-
                       versity of Chicago Press.

LONDON, PERRY

1973   "The Future of Psychotherapy." *Hastings Center Report*
                       3 (6): 10–13.

MARGENAU, HENRY

1960   "Truth in Science and Religion." Pp. 100–116 in Harlow
                       Shapley (ed.), *Science Ponders Religion.* New York:
                       Appleton-Century-Crofts.

MEAD, MARGARET

1967   Review of *Religion: An Anthropological View. Zygon* 2:
                       418–431.

MISES, RICHARD VON

1951   *Positivism, a Study in Human Understanding.* Cam-
                       bridge, Mass.: Harvard University Press.

ODUM, HOWARD T.

1971   *Environment, Power and Society.* New York: Wiley.

PRIGOGINE, ILYA

1973   "Can Thermodynamics Explain Biological Order?" *Im-
                       pact of Science on Society* 23: 159–179.

ROSZAK, THEODORE

1969   *The Making of a Counter Culture.* New York: Double-
                             day.

1972   *Where the Wasteland Ends.* New York: Doubleday.

SCHRÖDINGER, ERWIN

1956   *What Is Life?* Garden City, N.Y.: Doubleday. (Originally
                             published in 1944 by the Cambridge University Press.)

1959   *Mind and Matter.* Cambridge: Cambridge University
                             Press.

SIMON, HERBERT A.

1969   *The Sciences of the Artificial.* Cambridge, Mass.: The
                             M.I.T. Press.

SPERRY, R. W.

1972   "Science and the Problem of Values." *Perspectives in
                             Biology and Medicine* 16: 115–130; also reprinted in
                             Zygon 9 (March, 1974).

WALLACE, ANTHONY F. C.

1966   *Religion: An Anthropological View.* New York: Random
                             House.

WEIZSÄCKER, C. F. VON

1954   *The Relevance of Science.* New York: Harper and Row.

YOUNG, J. Z.

1964   *A Model of the Brain.* London: Oxford University Press.

Roland Robertson

UNIVERSITY OF PITTSBURGH

Religious and Sociological Factors in the Analysis of Secularization

I

It is becoming increasingly commonplace to point to the intriguing relationship between social-scientific observation of religious decline and the striking upsurge of intellectual interest in religious phenomena (Robertson, 1969: esp. 11–14). In this paper I consider one aspect of this circumstance: the responses of "concerned" sociologists to the debate about secularization. I will interpret the category "sociologist" rather loosely

at some points in the discussion, in order to include within my perspective all those who self-consciously invoke social and cultural factors in
analyzing religious change.

Discussion of the social-scientific analysis of religious phenomena, then,
has become just as interesting, important, and challenging as has the
direct analysis of religion itself. There are undoubtedly some sociologists
who regret this tendency—those who would argue that our attention is
thereby diverted from more important tasks of analyzing changes in the
"real world," or that it is a form of unwarranted self-indulgence, a classic
example of sociologists taking themselves too seriously. But, like many
intellectual discussions, it is not simply a matter of a few individuals
choosing to study a problem which others think on rational grounds to
be inappropriate, but rather that the problems I wish to tackle in this
paper have become so evident that one simply cannot argue them away.
Sociologists of religion have become deeply involved in debates and
disputes about secularization, and of those who have entered the arena
protesting that the concept is meaningless and/or that the empirical
data fail to warrant the employment of the term, few, if any, have been
able to divert much attention from the idea of secularization as a major
sociological problem.

It is beyond the scope of this paper to trace the course which has led
so much of contemporary sociology to revolve around issues lying in
the area conventionally known as the sociology of knowledge. The
many subdisciplinary domains which have in one way or another arrived
at that area include the study of deviancy; the study of the future; political sociology; of course, the study of religion; and, not least, the study
of the sociological enterprise itself. In general terms, this development
represents an expansion of the self-consciousness of sociologists in respect
of their work—a tendency to inquire into the purposes and consequences
of their intellectual endeavors, the cultural and political relevance of
sociology, and so on (see Robertson, 1972; Gouldner, 1970; Friedrichs,
1970).

There has always been within sociology a tendency to argue that sociology *is* the sociology of knowledge—although that tradition has been
most conspicuously and continuously preserved outside of the main sphere
of the development of sociology, namely the U.S.A. The fact that in one
guise or another this tendency has become established in the American
context during the past few years is of particular importance; reflecting,
undoubtedly, the intensity and range of self-consciousness so apparent
in American society at the cultural level at the present time. The notion
of a sociology of sociology has become almost inexorably a key element
of the sociological scene; although it is interesting to observe the respects

in which particular sociologists fall just short of going in for such an enterprise in a truly comprehensive manner [1].

Traditionally, the sociology of knowledge has been bound up with the central issue of the relationship between social-scientific knowledge and other kinds of knowledge—between the ways in which beliefs, values, and so on, are generated and sustained in the phenomenal world, on the one hand, and the generation of sociological concepts, propositions and paradigms, on the other. This may not often have been its ostensible concern—although clearly in Mannheim's case it was, which is precisely why Mannheim is often regarded as the last of the classical sociologists of knowledge. The new sociology of knowledge has concerned itself much more with the elemental processes of so-called reality construction—and yet it too has tended recently to arrive at dilemmas similar to those apparent in varying respects in the work of such important sociological figures as Marx, Durkheim, Weber, and Mannheim. The critical difference between the two phases is that whereas Mannheim's approach issued in a triumphal call for the superiority of the sociological enterprise, the ensuing movement, which might be called "Bergerism" (for Peter Berger has been the central figure in the new sociology of knowledge), has resulted in virtually the opposite. Berger has emphatically called for a revitalization of sociology from a religious perspective; and although his has been the most visibly presented case, other sociological students of religion have, it seems, become skeptical of the cultural value of sociology on broadly similar grounds (see Berger, 1969; Bellah, 1970).

The modern condition of the sociology of religion and I include under this rubric much of the work of contemporary anthropology) has, at the most general level, much in common with the kinds of problem which beset the development of sociology in the nineteenth century and the early part of the twentieth century. Both Comte and Marx in the earliest part of this period saw the scientific study of society as impaired by religious culture—both, that is, saw religious belief and sociological belief as rivals. By the time Durkheim and Weber came to write about religion, the intellectual climate had undoubtedly changed in this respect. But the kinds of *problem* which Comte, Marx, and many others had confronted before them were still clearly central to the work of both Durkheim and Weber. In their different ways, both of the latter placed the study of religion in its broadest sense at the very heart of their analyses of sociocultural life. Both were concerned, analytically and "metaphysically" about the *relationship between* their respective diagnoses of the significance of religion in industrial societies and the sociological perspective itself.

The present revival of interest in the sociology of knowledge; the steps taken toward establishing a serious, as opposed to half-hearted and inter-mittent, sociology of sociology; and the revival of a healthy sociology of religion are, I believe, very closely related developments. They signal two important features of modern sociology; first, that the sociological enterprise is in the process of being recast; second, and in close connec-tion with this, that an identity crisis is developing in the sociological community—affecting sociologists as individuals and the sociocultural system of sociology as a (be it all fuzzily defined) collectivity. The secu-larization debate constitutes a crucial site upon which the identity crisis of the sociologists is being experienced.

None of these characteristics of the contemporary sociological situation ought to surprise us. As I have remarked, the early development of soci-ology was characterized by problems revolving around the relationship between the major cultural control agency in human societies—namely religion—and the scientific orientation which, by its very cognitive stance and its claim to comprehend sociocultural life, seemed to violate the diagnosis which stressed the cultural priority and paramountcy of religion. This orientation was, of course, the developing sociological one. Of all the early and classical sociologists, it was Durkheim who certainly saw this problem most clearly. Durkheim, having supported and elaborated in detail the proposition that it was through religious practice and belief that man first came to think about society—to be cognitively reflexive —had also to confront the problem that it was sociological culture which was becoming the major locus of societal reflexiveness in modern societies.

Luckmann has cogently stated that Durkheim, Weber, and their lesser contemporaries in the sociology of religion bound their inquiries into religious phenomena with such critical sociological themes as personal identity, meaningfulness, normfulness, and so on (Luckmann, 1967). In presenting his own theoretical interpretations of modern religious situa-tions, Luckmann has remained faithful to that perspective (an intensity of faithfulness about which I have some rather stringent reservations) Robertson, 1970: 34ff.). Thus Luckmann, together with Peter Berger (although they diverge on some central points), have been largely respon-sible within the strictly sociological community for the preesnt re-linking of the study of religion to the general concerns of sociology. However, having got this far, it now seems encumbent upon us to go further sociologically in the exploration of the relationships between phenomena lying in the domain of religion in the broadest sense and sociology itself. It should quickly be added that some individuals have indeed taken steps in this direction—including, of course, Berger himself. Berger's idea that social science could be regarded as a "profane auxiliary to the Christian faith" is an example of this, as is his more recent and apparently contrary view that sociology suffers from relativizing worldly encapsulation. Others, such as Bellah, Glock, Stark, and Martin have ventured conspicuously into this area of discussion; while Gouldner has vigorously explored some of the more general aspects of the issue, with special reference to the functionalist perspective in modern sociology. Indeed, of the many general overviews of the state of the sociology of religion published in the last five years or so, very few authors have failed to give the relationship between sociology and religion some attention— if only, in some cases, to argue that the relationship *ought not* to be significant or troublesome.

Thus the secularization debate is a manifestation of some of the more general problems of contemporary sociology. It is a case of sociologists grounding their analyses on deeply held views about the *raison d'être* of human life. Although many sociologists have used Tillich's "ultimacy approach" ostensibly as a"scientific" definitional base line for their subsequent analysis of religious phenomena, it seems clear that the secularization debate touches also at the heart of those same sociologists' attitudes toward (and beliefs about) the "ultimate" in a very direct sense. That is, definitions of religion—which lie at the very core of any discussion of secularization—in themselves expose metaphysical preferences. Some sociologists of religion have been explicit about this—others less so. Berger, to take a major example, has sustained an ongoing public dialogue *with himself* in this matter. In contrast—and at the risk of being invidious —Yinger has consistently argued in favour of a functional, "ultimacy" definition, which in his terms makes discussion of secularization virtually impossible. Yinger can, however, through extended argument claim that even though all comprehensive belief systems are by definition religious, a "scientific" approach to the study of religion shows Communism to be a deficient religion (Yinger, 1970: 508ff.).

The dilemmas are, as I have said, old ones. But, given the current fluidity of modern sociology and the almost consensually acknowledged view that modern societies are in some kind of cultural crisis, the fact that the dilemmas are old is no reason for not exploring them. At the moment we are witnessing some sociologists retreating from their sociological commitments because they feel that such commitments undermine what they believe (sometimes on sociological grounds!) to constitute the very pivot of personal and collective life. Others believe that sociology can help to shore up certain key elements of the religiosity which they discern to be pivotal and essential. Still others—"extended kin" of that group—believe, as Bellah seems to do, that sociology can assist in the development of new religious options. A less visible group believe that religion ought to be subjected to some kind of sociological critique, which does not necessarily mean attack. This latter orientation has probably been most visible among theologians lying outside the professionally demarcated domain of sociology—for example, some adherents to Death-of-God theology and the Theology-of-Hope. The fact that the position is less visible within the "official" sociological community evidently arises in large part because many sociologists have not typically thought the sociology of religion to be sufficiently interesting or challenging. Sociologists of religion themselves have on the whole tended to be in one way or another religious, or at least sympathetic to religious belief and practice. Outside the subdiscipline the view has been widespread that the study of religion is basically a "soft" area, concerned with phenomena which are not worthy of prestigious, or aspirantly prestigious, social scientists (see Sociology Panel of the Behavioral Sciences Survey 1969: 101–104) [2].

The upshot of much of what has been said so far is that (in functional-definitional terms) we have become increasingly "religious about religion." The sociology of religion is not unique in this. To take but one example, the sociological study of deviancy has become increasingly deviant in Britain and the U.S.A. during the past few years. Many of its younger practitioners are "deviant about deviancy"—their analytic orientations have become synchronized in a major respect with the orientations to be found in the sociocultural category which they focus upon (see Matza, 1964; 1969) [3]. In the present context at least, I shall make only one comment on such developments; if we are to preserve some kind of sociological, as opposed to metaphysical or "religious," basis for discussion—if we are, that is, to continue to practice a *sociology* of religion —then the very least that should be undertaken is the explication of the analytic parameters of the problem of secularization, its major internal axes of dispute, and, perhaps more ambitiously, the erection of some kind of logically shaped discussion framework.

I have no intention of tackling such problems in all their complexity here. What I seek at this stage is to set out some ground rules for reflecting upon just what the secularization debate has involved during the past few years.

II

I suggest that there are two major axes of debate: first, whether secularization is occurring at all; and, second, whether the perceived direction of religious change is approved of or not. In these terms it is possible, theoretically, to locate all relevant participants in the debate within a property space defined by the two axes shown in the figure.

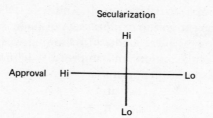

It might be thought that my depiction implies that diagnosis of the degree of secularization is prior to evaluation of it—that degree of approval follows such diagnosis. This is not my intention. I regard the two kinds of judgments as empirically interpenetrative—although in some cases more weight will be given to one side of the issue than in others. For example, a sociologist may not like the idea of secularization on sociological grounds—he or she judges it to be bad for the society in question, or perhaps for any society—in which case there may be a thrust toward finding evidence of lack of secularization or invoking theoretical arguments to deny the usefulness of the concept of secularization—or, indeed, both of these.

In view of this example, we have also to propose that the criteria in terms of which these judgments are made will vary also. In both axes there appear to have been two major such criteria. In the case of the assessment of secularization, these are, respectively theoretical and empirical arguments. In the case of degree of approval, they are religious/metaphysical and sociological arguments. (Here again, forms of judgment will be interpenetrative.) By dichotomizing the secularization and approval variable and introducing the criteria in terms of which judgments about these have been reached, we arrive at the following:

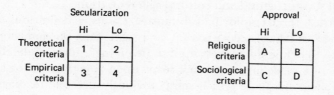

With respect to standards for assessing secularization and/or approval, any individual may combine theoretical and empirical criteria, and religious and sociological criteria, respectively; but I will here assume that one particular criterion is given more emphasis than the other. The presentation indicates that there are sixteen possible orientations to the idea of contemporary secularization. It would be laborious in this (and probably any other) context to explore each of these with examples. Thus I shall elaborate some typical modes of reasoning with respect to the two main variables (secularization and approval) delineating within these variable categories some salient criteria.

SECULARIZATION

Theoretical Criteria. When confined to the theoretical sphere, arguments about whether secularization is or is not occurring and, indeed, whether it is a meaningful concept at all, hinge very much on problems of definition and analytic delineation. The main dispute here is between those advocating functional, inclusive definitions, and those advocating substantive, exclusive definitions (see Robertson 1970). I do not argue that functional definitions have to be inclusive, or that substantive ones are always exclusive. I am merely generalizing that this seems to be the case empirically. I also leave largely on one side the ramifications of the point that functional definitions have to be made substantive in empirical research. For example, the functionalist use of the ultimacy definition of religion must issue in an operationalization of ultimacy if it is systematically applied to empirical and historical circumstances.

As I have indicated, some sociologists employing functional definitions try to avoid this problem by making their definitions of religious phenomena so inclusive and general that it becomes impossible to speak of secularization in any sense having to do with a society becoming "dereligionized." They can only speak of different *forms* of religion, or of religion as changing its *relation* to the sociocultural system (or systems) in question. This, broadly speaking, is the case with those who have argued that what is frequently called secularization is "merely" a twofold process of sociostructural and cultural differentiation.

In contrast, those employing substantive, exclusive definitions are more constrained to regard secularization as a significant phenomenon of the world and to define the process itself as involving a form of dereligionization. The use of definitions which focus upon supernatural or superempirical beliefs are those which most obviously precipitate diagnoses of secularization as a major sociocultural tendency in modern societies. (But this is not always the case, as will be seen in a moment.) Supernaturalistic definitions of religion fell steadily from grace during the present century, culminating in the great popularity of the "religion-as-ultimacy" definitional tendency (or variants thereof) in the 1950s. Increasing concern with methodological and theoretical precision was undoubtedly a major factor in precipitating the eventual fall from grace of the ultimacy approach—although some sociologists have managed (illogically) to interest themselves in the measurement of religiosity, while at the same time holding that all human beings are religious (for example, Lenski, 1961; cf. Yinger 1967).

There can, of course, be no such thing as a purely technical-theoretical judgment on these issues, for all sociological work entails what Gouldner calls background and domain assumptions (Gouldner, 1970)—which in terms of the schema being employed here means that approval factors, particularly of a religious-metaphysical kind, penetrate theoretical decisions. This feature of sociological analysis is not, however, denied by the insistence that the definitional problem comprises the core of the theoretical dispute about secularization (Robertson, 1970). Nor does this insistence mean that the theoretical debate has been scholastic, in the pejorative sense of quibbling in the name of science over meanings of terms. The work of, *inter alia,* Stark, Glock, Berger and Fenn attests to this (see Berger, 1967; Stark and Glock, 1968; Fenn, 1970). Among the more important of the largely theoretical-procedural problems which are central to discussions of secularization I would mention: *the level of analysis problem*—whether one analyzes at the level of individual religiosity or at the emergent societal, or other collectivity, level; *the dimensional problem*—which indicators of degrees of religiosity one elects to use and, not least, the basis upon which these are chosen; and *the historical-comparative problem*—a relatively neglected area of inquiry but one which clearly bears very much on the issue of the degree of significance which we attach to the idea of secularization. Each of these, and others which could be elaborated, hinges and also feeds back upon the definitional problem.

Empirical Criteria. Empirical questions are not divorced from theoretical and conceptual issues, but there are nevertheless those who erect arguments about whether secularization is or is not occurring on primarily empirical grounds. Much depends here upon choice of data or the mode of generating data. As in other branches of sociological inquiry, different patterns of religious commitment can be obtained through relying upon different data sources. Greeley, in reference to public opinion polls and certain survey data, can demonstrate fairly convincingly—in terms of belief in conventional appurtenances of religion—that religious commitment is not undergoing decline in contemporary America (Greeley, 1969), while Stark and Glock claim, on the basis of their data, that there are within American religious denominations patterns of changing commitment which indicate increasing detachment along what they regard as the major dimensions of religiosity (Stark and Glock, 1968). Martin claims in part that secularization is not a significant process in the contemporary world by pointing at the extent to which superstitious and associated beliefs remain remarkably presistent (Martin, 1967; 1969). Variants of the latter kind of empirical argument include attempts to refute the secularization thesis by seeing evidence of the vitality of supernatural beliefs in the apparent rise in popularity of astrology and occultic beliefs. This approach is an example of a substantive, although not very exclusive, definition being used to *deny* secularization—a special case which I have previously hinted at. The argument typically involved is that insofar as some form of supernaturalism and "irrationality" persists, it is inappropriate to speak of secularization. While obviously drawing on a variety of criteria, such a view must focus strongly on purely empirical evidence. This observation applies equally to that kind of argument which denies secularization on the basis of evidence—systematically or impressionistically collected (usually the latter)—about the "soul-searching" and quest for meaning evidenced in the young of the modern period.

A type of empirical argument related to the previously mentioned historical-comparative problem is one which points to evidence about the mythical distortion of the religiosity of societies in the past. By producing data, or at least empirical cues, relating to irreligiosity or areligiosity in the historical past, some sociologists claim to have thrown doubts on the viability of the secularization thesis as it applies to the modern situation. [4]. A variant of this approach is to argue in empirical terms that, in spite of episodic changes in the pattern of commitment, religious adherence remains stable over long periods of time—in other words, that if secularization is evident at this point of time, it is an *ephemeral* phenomenon.

Whereas we were able to pinpoint a core *theoretical* problem—that of definition—there is no single point of departure for arguments of an empirical kind. This was to be expected, since there is inevitably a marked eclecticism and discreteness about solely empirical arguments.

APPROVAL/DISAPPROVAL

Religious Criteria. Use of the term "religious criteria" raises a problem, for it implies a definition of religious phenomena. Thus, if one tends to adhere to a relatively exclusive, supernaturalistic definition of religious phenomena (as I do), then only a criterion which actually was premised upon belief in a supernatural realm or agency could appropriately be labeled "religious." This would, of course, severely restrict the category. Thus, for present purposes, I will rely on a subjectivist and internal definitional stance—realizing that there is a slight element of inconsistency involved, an inconsistency which is constructively attenuated by the use of the term "metaphysical" in conjunction with "religious."

A particularly interesting point emerges from this kind of consideration. If a sociologist adheres to a diffusely functional definition of religious phenomena, he can hardly escape being labeled "religious." Some, like Lenski, could not really complain of this. Lenski defines religious commitment so broadly that all human beings are religious. Luckmann, too, when he views religion as consisting in man's transcending of his biological givenness, would have to concede even more clearly that sociologists are religious *par excellence* (Lenski, 1961; Luckmann, 1967) [5]. Gouldner has recently argued, with the backing of empirical evidence, that there is an intimate connection between favoring the functionalist perspective generally and being religiously inclined (Gouldner, 1970) [6]. While I have severe reservations about Gouldner's treatment of functionalism, particularly with respect to its Parsonian form, it would seem that those who most strongly believe religion to be the central feature of socio-cultural life—as many described as functionalists do—are most prone to become "religious about religion."

Arguments of a religious kind about processes of secularization tend to revolve around normative judgments as to what to be religious means —they are often bound in concrete instances to theoretical arguments of a definitional and conceptual kind. Just as the ultimacy definition had been theologically inspired, the move toward more circumscribed and substantive definitions was theologically facilitated. In the 1960s, theological debate raised again the relevance of the substantive-supernaturalistic approach to definition, and, in simultaneously rejecting supernatural definitions and embracing the diagnosed processes of secularization (defined theologically as a shift away from supernaturalism) theologians brought, be it all slowly, issues to the attention of the sociological community of which the latter had been either unaware or too embarrassed to tackle. For some sociologists with relatively strong religious commitments of one kind or another the situation was particularly complex.

As is well known, Cox can happily approve of secularization because the process as he sees it opens up definite religious possibilities—a position which is in varying degrees rejected by those who hold to more transcendental conceptions of religious belief. In fact the issue of transcendentalism versus immanentism is crucial to the whole debate about secularization, but particularly in respect of religious criteria (for further discussions see Robertson, 1970: esp. 93–95, 215–218, 236–239).

Those who adhere to an immanentist view tend to accept the secularization thesis but not worry about it on religious grounds. Transcendentalists present a wider variety of standpoints. They may accept that secularization is occurring in the face of evidence of religious decline in the world at large and regret the "fact"; or they may point to new forms of "inner transcendence" as a correlate of secularization and therefore welcome it (cf. Richardson and Cutler, 1969; Moltmann, 1969; Bellah, part 3). (This latter view is one which sometimes shades into a *sociological* value judg-ment concerning the merits or demerits of secularization.) They may also, as we have seen briefly in mentioning superstition, astrology, and the like, base their evaluations upon highly diffuse conceptions of trans-cendence.

An important form of religious appraisal of the secularization thesis is that which views all major cultural motifs as being historical trans-missions of *religiously* based beliefs (see in particular Martin, 1969; Par-sons, 1963). Thus, secular beliefs—such as political ideologies—are seen as being in a significant sense religious. Belief systems such a ideological Marxism, existentialism, and indeed commonsense beliefs and symbols of "everyday life" can, in this view, be regarded as manifesting cognitive, evaluative, and expressive seeds sown in a more ostensibly religious past. Of course this standpoint shades into theoretical decisions about the *validity* of the secularization thesis; but it can be employed as a relatively independent criterion for evaluating other forms of more directly empiri-cal evidence about secularization. Evidence of secularization will tend to be greeted ambivalently: on the one hand, the secularization process may be regarded as "merely" a debased form of religion; on the other hand, the evidence may be used as a way of upholding the view that all cultural change is an emanation of *religious* culture, and *is* religious in a substantive respect.

Sociological Criteria. We are concerned in this category with modes of evaluation of secularization which are based on primarily sociological grounds, that is, judgments about the sociocultural advantages and dis-advantages of the diagnosed degree of secularization. Nisbet has suc-cinctly traced the changing sociological views during the nineteenth century in respect of the alleged centrality or otherwise of religion in human societies—pinpointing in particular the shift from early and mid-century arguments that religion was being overcome, and that it was the role of the social scientist to assist the process—to the late nineteenth century view that religion was a more durable and certainly more de-sirable feature of sociocultural life (Nisbet, 1966: 221–263). Witness the contrast between Marx's view that religion is an indicator and a mani-festation of man's lack of adequate sociality and Durkheim's thesis that religion is an indicator and a manifestation of precisely that sociality. Thus Durkheim was constrained to search for and advocate new modes of sacredness in modern societies which seemed to be rejecting conventionally recognized religious beliefs.

It has, of course, been the question of the functional necessity of a sacred religious "center" which has dominated purely sociological discussions of secularization. Recently, however, a new turn has been taken in the form of an increasing interest in the theme of symbolization and symbolic meaning. Whereas the necessity to provide sources of ultimate meaning has for long been embedded in the functionalist concern about religion, the relatively new interest in symbolization *per se* revolves more specifically around the role of social science in assisting in the development of forms of symbolization which allow men to *communicate* their ultimate and sacred sentiments and to cope with the exigencies of social structure and the human condition generally. Within this problem area, we can discern two main schools. There are, first, those like Bellah who are most closely concerned with *nonreferential* forms of symbolization—that is, with conveying sentiments and feelings as such. Of central importance here is the idea that man cannot manage without erecting meaningful symbolizations—not symbolizations *of* something but expressions of autonomous sentiment, desires, and so on which provide and convey meaning and experience as such. This is the position of symbolic realism (Bellah, 1970) [7]. In contrast, there are those like Mary Douglas, who directly relate the study of symbols and symbolic communication to social-structural patterns (Douglas, 1970a; 1966; 1970b. Here the concern is, within the Durkheimian tradition, to search for relationships between social circumstances and symbolic culture. This approach is largely, but not unambiguously, of the symbolic reductionist type.

Both of these approaches—but particularly as developed in the work of Bellah and Douglas—have involved giving advice about the structuring of religious belief, ritual, and so on; that is, they are sociologically prescriptive. And although it is easy to say that there is a religious motivation at work—notably in Bellah's case—the explicit point of departure is in the main sociological.

Discussion of symbolization has, of course, been important in strictly theological circles as well. The name of Tillich stands out in this connection. Robinson's *Honest to God* rested considerably upon arguments about the psychological, social, and cultural viability of different forms of Christian symbolization. But it would seem that modern theologians using sociological modes of reasoning to supplement their religious theses tend to rely more directly upon the examination of *trajectories of socio-cultural change,* as opposed to the principles governing symbolic communication. That is, they are concerned to adapt theology and religion to what they perceive to be the major sociocultural tendencies of our time and the extrapolations which one can distill from empirical trends. Variation in this respect is to be seen between those who "lock" religion into "things as they are"—that is, they simply advocate adaptation—and those who, like Moltmann and the "new" Cox, erect socioreligious *aspirations* on the basis of knowledge derived in a loose sense from social science (Cox, 1968; cf. Robertson, 1971; and in particular, Marty and Peerman, 1968). The latter may constrain and limit, but it also establishes a basis for realistic choice.

III

The rapid upsurge of interest in the theme of secularization during the 1960s can hardly be attributed to any startling new empirical evidence. I have already noted that a relatively autonomous social-scientific interest in problems of conceptualizing and dimensionalizing religiosity, and religious commitment in part, facilitated the debate. It is also worth remembering that discussions of a methodological kind about the dimensions of religiosity were in some cases inspired by the desire to comprehend the degree to which there had been a religious *revival* in post–Second World War America. In a major respect the sociological discussion about secularization is simply a response to a culmination and popularization in the 1960s of a long-drawn-out debate within the confines of theological circles. In other words, the pattern I am projecting is one of sociologists responding to a crisis in a different intellectual domain (cf. Fenn, 1968), and then constructing analytic tools and substantive, empirical propositions on the basis of the ensuing relationship between sociology and theology. Perceived theological change resonated in the minds of sociologists interested in religion who were themselves in a state of confusion.

I have attempted here only to sketch in some of the considerations which go into discussing the centerpiece of the current analysis—the *concept* of secularization. These considerations have in a number of respects hinged upon the relationship between religious commitment, particularly in its theological form, and the sociological enterprise, particularly in its sociology-of-religion specialism, I wish to conclude by highlighting the structure of this complex of problems concerning the religion-sociology relationship.

The two main aspects of this controversy are: first, whether one perspective can or should—logically or metaphysically—inform the other; and, second, whether *empirically* the two *do* influence each other. About the second of these there can be little doubt; one has only to open the pages of recent writings by such people as Cox, Berger, Bellah, Martin, to name but a very few, to see this clearly. The first dimension is more difficult, for it is there that problems arise in respect of the degree to which sociology—or social science generally—impinges on problems of cultural meaning. There is apparently some resistance—even among sections of the sociological community itself, to the idea that the social sciences constitute major cultural systems in modern societies [8].

I said earlier in this paper that the secularization debate was a particularly good example of the current identity crisis which afflicts many practitioners of modern sociology (see Robertson, 1971), and I wish to establish that my contribution is as much a symptom of that crisis as a diagnosis of it—a mode of self-expression which has been employed appropriately by Bellah in his analysis of religious evolution (Bellah, 1970: 20–45) [9]. But unlike Bellah I see no good reason for regarding this crisis automatically as a religious one. What I have called the identity crisis of many sociologists of religion can be expressed in terms of a number of options for interpreting the contemporary religious situation in the light of available sociological tools of analysis and substantive viewpoints.

1. *Segmentation* of sociological and religious commitments. That is, the individual may regard sociology and the religious standpoint as potentially—and, indeed, in principle—in some kind of relationship of rivalry and yet try to achieve a personal separation of each sphere. Such a tack very probably involves setting limits on both sociological and religious potentialities.

2. *Auxiliaration* of the sociological commitment to the religious one— as is suggested by Berger's comment about social science being a profane auxiliary of the Christian faith (Berger, 1961: 204). In this conception sociological insight and knowledge are used to supplement and perhaps suggest adjustments in religious orientation. But sociological commitment is secondary to religious commitment; and sociological praxis is predicated upon the background assumptions of the particular religious position. Historically, this stance has been maintained most consistently, continuously, and visibly by Catholic *religious sociologists*—but there are many Protestant adherents to the principle involved.

3. *Auxiliaration* of religious orientation to the sociological one. Here religious beliefs and prescriptions are mounted on the basis of what are regarded from a sociological standpoint as necessary or desirable features of sociocultural life. This stance is particularly well evidenced in the structural-functional tradition (see, for example, Bellah 1970).

4. *Compounding* of religious and sociological views into one generalized sociotheological role. This constitutes a *self-consciously fostered sociotheology*. The best individual examples of this perspective are some of the so-called radical theologians (see Robertson, 1970: 194–234; Bellah, 1970: 191–259).

There are two further options, one of which need not detain us here. This is the case in which the religious viewpoint is regarded as paramount and sociology or social science generally is seen as a total rival to religion. Since sociological perspectives are not constructively involved, this stance is in no way relevant to the concerns of this essay. In great contrast, there is the circumstance in which sociology (or social science) dissolves and supersedes theology and perhaps eventually religion itself. This is, of course, the view which was put strongly by Comte and was echoed on different grounds and in very different ways by Marx. There is a significant degree of overlap between this stance and that of the "sociotheologians."

IV

My major intention has been to make explicit the terms of the secularization debate and to link the latter to some more general aspects of current sociology. In the main, I have eschewed concern with the correctness or persuasiveness of the stances which have been pointed up. However, a brief discussion of one major strand of the discussion as it bears prescriptively on the religion-sociology problem is warranted.

It is rather misleading for those who object to sociology setting itself critically against religious standpoints or offering radical critiques to argue that their opponents claim that sociology, or indeed any or all of the social sciences synthetically, could provide for society in the same way that religion does. Those who have offered sociological critiques of theology or, more significantly, of religious belief and practice, have rarely in the modern period made such comprehensive claims. Sociology has been criticized for being unable to provide sufficient transcendence— for indeed being antitranscendental—by both Berger and Martin (although their worries about this are somewhat different in nature). But this appears to be a judgment on the present state of social science, as opposed to what it *could be*. It need not be purely technical in its social implications, nor purely therapeutic—or whatever negative characterization may be offered. Thus, some of those who have tended to opt for religious-theological superiority vis-à-vis sociology are open to the charge of *idealizing* the first and characterizing the second in terms of how it *actually* is.

The central point in the present climax is whether a "concerned sociology" or a "critical sociology" can both be respectful of the historic significance of religion in human societies and at the same time be daring enough to offer considered prescriptions about the viability of specific socioculture possibilities. There is much in recent sociology which suggests that a critical *sociology of the possible,* which subsumes the *sociology of the necessary,* is becoming increasingly feasible. Certainly it has become more popular. A lot of what has been said here leads, I think, to the conclusion that the sociology of religion has, in its confrontation with the secularization controversy, regained for itself much of its former centrality in the discipline as a whole. This restoration is not coincidentally or fortuitously related to the tentative reemergence of sociology as a critical discipline [10].

One of the major points of this essay has been that the idea of secularization is as much, if not more, of an artifact of a section of the intelligentsia as it is a feature of the "real world" [11]. But unlike some who have sought to disqualify, on such grounds, elaborate discussion of the issues raised by the secularization controversy, I think we should embrace the problems for what they are—manifestations of a loss of confidence and direction among sociologists; a fear of repeating nineteenth century mistakes; and a too easy characterization of social science as inevitably remaining as it has been for the past forty years or so. In a sense, what I have said here backs up what Berger and Luckmann argued some years ago about the relationship between the sociology and religion and the sociology of knowledge (see Berger and Luckmann, 1963). It is perhaps a comprehensive pursuit of the sociology of *culture* which will best alleviate the pains attendant upon discussion of the secularization thesis. Along these lines we might well explore again the possibility of a world without religion—although of course "hard" functionalists will always be able to spot elements of religiosity in any such projected sociological image.

NOTES

1. This is a criticism which I would make of both Gouldner, and, even more, of Friedrichs.

2. I think the report underestimates the degree of the theoretical and methodological refinement which has been recently obtained.

3. The latter is in many ways an exercise in the sociology of knowledge and has, I believe, some important implications for the sociology of religion, particularly in the much neglected field of religious conversion.

4. See the suggestions about the historical ubiquity of secularization in Nisbet, 1970: 387.

5. Further light is thrown on this kind of problem by dissection of ethnomethodolgists' attacks on what they call "constructive," as opposed to "indexical" analysis. See particularly Garfinkel and Sacks, 1970.

6. Of course, Parsons has often been accused of *positivistic anti-religiosity*; see, for example, O'Dea, 1970: ch. 12.

7. This article was completed before Bellah's important collection of essays was made available to the author.

8. I use the term cultural system as it is employed by Talcott Parsons et al., in *Theories of Society*, 1965: sp. 963–993.

9. The "confessional" nature of Bellah's *Beyond Belief* is in many ways its most striking feature.

10. Points in this paragraph are elaborated·in Robertson, 1971: 109–126.

11. This is a point which Martin has argued very strongly, as in Martin, 1969.

REFERENCES

BELLAH, ROBERT N.

1970   *Beyond Belief*. New York: Harper and Row.

BERGER, PETER L.

1961   *The Precarious Vision*. Garden City, N.Y.: Doubleday.

1967   "A Sociological View of the Secularization of Theology." *Journal for the Scientific Study of Religion* 6: 3–16.

1969   *A Rumor of Angels*. Garden City, N.Y. Doubleday.

BERGER, PETER
LUCKMANN, THOMAS

1963   "Sociology of Religion and Sociology of Knowledge." *Sociology and Social Research* 47: 417–427.

COX, HARVEY

1966   *The Secular City*. Revised edition. New York: Macmillan.

1968   "Ernst Bloch and 'The Pull of the Future.' " Pp. 191–203 in Martin E. Marty and Dean G. Peerman (eds.), *New Theology*, No. 5. New York: Macmillan.

DOUGLAS, MARY

1966   *Purity and Danger*. London: Routledge and Kegan Paul.

1970a   *Natural Symbols*. London: Barrie and Rockliffe (The Cresset Press).

1970b   "Environments at Risk." *Times Literary Supplement*, October 30, pp. 1273–1275.

FENN, RICHARD K.

1968   "The Death of God: An Analysis of Ideological Crisis."
        Review of Religious Research **9**: 171–181.

1970   "The Process of Secularization: A Post-Parsonian View."
        Journal for the Scientific Study of Religion **9**: 117–136.

FRIEDRICHS, ROBERT W.

1970   *A Sociology of Sociology.* New York: Free Press.

GARFINKEL, HAROLD
SACKS, HARVEY

1970   "On Formal Structures and Practical Actions." Pp. 337–
        366 in John C. McKinney and Edward A. Tiryakian
        (eds.), *Theoretical Sociology.* New York: Appleton-
        Century-Crofts.

GOULDNER, ALVIN W.

1970   *The Coming Crisis of Western Sociology.* New York:
        Basic Books.

GREELEY, ANDREW M.

1969   *Religion in the Year 2000.* New York: Sheed and Ward.

LENSKI, GERHARD

(1961) *The Religious Factor.* Garden City, N.Y.: Doubleday
1963   (Anchor Books).

LUCKMANN, THOMAS

1967   *The Invisible Religion.* New York: Macmillan.

MARTIN, DAVID A.

1967   *A Sociology of English Religion.* London: SCM Press.

1969   *The Religious and the Secular.* London: Routledge and
        Kegan, Paul.

MARTY, MARTIN E.
PEERMAN, DEAN G.

1968   *New Theology,* No. 5. New York: Macmillan.

MATZA, DAVID

1964   *Delinquency and Drift.* New York: Wiley.
1969   *Becoming Deviant.* Englewood Cliffs, N.J.: Prentice-Hall.

MOLTMANN, JURGEN

1969   *Religion, Revolution, and the Future.* New York: Scrib-
        ner.

NISBET, ROBERT

1966   *The Sociological Tradition.* New York: Basic Books.
1970   *The Social Bond.* New York: Knopf.
O'DEA, THOMAS F.

1970   *Sociology and the Study of Religion.* New York: Basic Books.

PARSONS, TALCOTT

1963   "Christianity and Modern Industrial Society." Pp. 33–70 in Edward A. Tiryakian (ed.), *Sociological Theory, Values and Sociocultural Change.* New York: Free Press.

PARSONS, TALCOTT, ET AL

                       Theories of Society. New York: Free Press.
RICHARDSON, HERBERT W.
CUTLER, DONALD

1969   *Transcendence.* Boston: Beacon Press.
ROBERTSON, ROLAND

1969   *The Sociology of Religion: Selected Readings.* Harmondsworth, England: Penguin.
1970   *The Sociological Interpretation of Religion.* New York: Schocken.
1971   "The Sociology of Religion: Problems and Desiderata." *Religion* 1: 109–126.
1972   "The Sociocultural Implications of Sociology: A Reconnaissance." Pp. 59–95 in T. J. Nossiter, A. H. Hanson, and S. Rokkan (eds.), *Imagination and Precision in the Social Sciences.* London: Faber and Faber.

SOCIOLOGY PANEL OF THE
BEHAVIORAL SCIENCE
SURVEY

1969   Neil J. Smelser and James A. Davis (eds.). *Sociology.* Englewood Cliffs, N.J.: Prentice-Hall.

STARK, RODNEY
GLOCK, CHARLES Y.

1968   *American Piety: The Nature of Religious Commitment.* Berkeley: University of California Press.

YINGER, J. MILTON
1967   "Pluralism, Religion and Secularism." *Journal for the Scientific Study of Religion* 6: 17–28.
1970   *The Scientific Study of Religion.* New York: Macmillan.

Part Two
Liminality in Religious Institutions and Culture

Victor Turner

UNIVERSITY OF CHICAGO

Metaphors of Anti-structure
in Religious Culture

In my book, *The Ritual Process,* I posited a difference between society as "structure" and society as "anti-structure." Perhaps I was wrong, as some reviewers have suggested, to make the overworked term "structure" work again in yet another capacity; but I consider that its traditional connotations make it an effective operative word in the argument.

By "structure" I meant, roughly, "social structure," as most British and many American anthropologists and sociologists have defined the term—that is, as a more or less distinctive arrangement of mutually dependent institutions and the institutional organization of social positions and/or actors they imply. "Class structures" are one species of structures so defined—and a measure of "alienation" may be said to adhere to all structures, including so-called "tribal structures," insofar as all tend to produce distance, inequality, and so on.

I have used the term "anti-structure" in the title of this paper; but I would like to make clear that the "anti-" is here used only strategically and does not imply radical negativity. When I speak of "anti-structure" or astructure I am really talking of something positive. I do not seek the eradication of matter by form, as some of my French-inspired colleagues have tried to do in recent years, but am supposing a matter from which forms may be "unpacked," so to speak, as men seek to know and communicate.

"Structure" has been the theoretical point of departure of so many anthropological studies that it has acquired not only a positive connotation but also the connotation of being the center of substance of a system of social relations or ideas. I prefer to regard "structure" rather as the "outward bound or circumference," as Blake might have said.

Roughly, the concepts of *liminality* and *communitas* define what I mean by anti-structure. *Liminality*—a term borrowed from Van Gennep's formulation of the processual structure of ritual in *The Rites of Passage* —occurs in the middle phase of the rites that mark changes in an individual's social status and/or cultural or psychological state in many societies, past and present. Rites of this phase characteristically begin with ritual metaphors of killing or of death marking the separation of the subject from ordinary secular relationships (in which status-role behavior tends to prevail even in informal situations) and conclude with a symbolic rebirth or reincorporation into society as shaped by the law and moral code. The biological order of birth and death is reversed in rites of passage—and there one dies to "become a little child." The intervening liminal phase is thus "betwixt-and-between" the categories of ordinary social life. Symbols and metaphors found in abundance in liminality represent various dangerous ambiguities of this ritual stage, since the classifications on which order normally depends are annulled or obscured; other symbols designate temporary antinomic liberation from behavioral norms and cognitive rules. The theme of danger requiring control is reflected in the paradox that in liminality extreme authority of elders over juniors often coexists with scenes and episodes indicative of the utmost behavioral freedom and speculative license. Liminality is usually a sacred condition protected against secularity by taboos and in turn prevented by them from disrupting secular order. It is a movement between fixed points and is essentially ambiguous, unsettled, and unsettling. In liminality, communitas tends to characterize relations between those jointly undergoing ritual transition. The bonds of communities are "anti"-structural in the sense that they are undifferentiated, egalitarian, direct, extant, nonrational, "existential," I–Thou (in Feuerbach's and Buber's sense) relations. Communitas is spontaneous, immediate, concrete —it is not shaped by norms, it is not institutionalized, it is not abstract. Communitas differs from the "camaraderie" found often in everyday life, which, though informal and egalitarian, still falls within the general domain of "structure"—which may include "interaction rituals." Communitas, to borrow a phrase of Durkheim's, is *de la vie sérieuse,* part of the "serious life." It tends to ignore, reverse, cut across, or occur outside of structural relationships.

In human history, I see a continuous tension between structure and communitas, at all levels of scale and complexity. Structure, or all that which holds people apart, defines their differences, and constrains their actions, is one pole in a charged field, for which the opposite pole is communitas, or anti-structure—the egalitarian "sentiment for humanity" of which David Hume speaks, representing the desire for a total, unmediated relation between person and person, a relation which nevertheless does not submerge one in the other but safeguards their uniqueness in the very act of realizing their commonness.

Communitas does not *merge* identities; it liberates them from conformity to general norms, though this is necessarily a transient condition if society is to continue to operate in an orderly fashion. I have discussed elsewhere (Turner, 1969; 99–106) how, among the Ndembu people of Zambia, in the liminal phase of their rites of passage, communitas is both metaphorically represented and actually engendered by ritual leveling and humiliation. Other societies exhibit similar features.

In more pronouncedly hierarchical societies with what Professor Nelson, interpreting Weber, might call "sacro-magical structures of consciousness," communitas is frequently affirmed by periodic rituals in which the lowly and the mighty reverse social roles. In such societies, too—and here I have drawn examples from European and Indian history—the religious ideology of the structurally powerful tends to idealize humility; orders of religious specialists undertake ascetic lives, while cult groups among those of low status ritually play with symbols of power. These contrary processes go on in the *same* religious field, modifying, opposing, and being transformed into one another as time goes on.

I would like here to give some examples of how such processes operate in the religious field of India, drawing on the work of two Indian colleagues and friends.

The first example is taken from a paper by Professor J. Singh Uberoi of Delhi University, "Sikhism and Indian Society" (Uberoi, 1967). Uberoi opens with the proposition that the Hindu system of caste relations (using the term "caste" to include both *varna,* the all-India classification, and *jati*, the localized sub-caste classification) is, in fact, only half of Hinduism. Here, of course, he parts company with Max Weber, who regarded caste (and particularly the position of Brahmins) as "the fundamental institution of Hinduism." The whole Hindu *dharma*—literally "law," "justice," sometimes "religion," and which might perhaps be paraphrased in this context as "religio-moral field"—is often described by the term *varnashramdharma*. That is, we have, in addition to caste (*varna*), the institution of the four stages or statuses (*ashramas*)—student, householder, forest dweller, and homeless medicant—through which high-caste Hindus were traditionally supposed to pass. If social anthropologists have tended to focus on the institution of caste to the exclusion of the *ashram* system, it is probably because until quite recently they have preferred to work with stable, localized systems of social relations and positions bound up in easily isolable customary regularities, rather than with processual models. But, as Uberoi points out, the social system of caste seems always to have been surrounded by a "penumbral region" of non-caste, or even anti-caste, where there throve the renunciatory religious orders whose principles repudiated the ascribed statuses resting on caste and birth. And, indeed, the fourth *ashram* or stage, that known as *sannyas*, the state of being a holy man or ascetic who has dedicated himself completely to the quest for *moksha* or "salvation," was always a metaphorical door through which the individual was recommended by sages and teachers to pass from the world of caste to that of its negation—from structure to anti-structure, one might say, for there is a moment when the *sannyasi* divests himself of all structural ties and is even recommended to erase from his memory all kinship connections.

As Uberoi argues, "the mutual relation of the two worlds, caste and anti-caste, seems to be of the greatest significance to a broad understanding of either." For there is a social and corporate aspect of the *ashrama* system. *Sannyas* is not only a stage in an *individual* life cycle but may represent a religious order of renunciation. Uberoi considers that the total structure of medieval India could be split into three main segments—even if this involves for historians an exercise in gross oversimplification. There was a division between (1) the rulers (the world of *rajya*); (2) the caste system (*varna*, with an emphasis here also on the *ashram* of the "householder," *grihasta*); and (3) the orders of renunciation (*sannyas*). The interrelations of these features would seem to define a sociocultural field in the medieval period, each part of which achieves its full significance only in terms of its relation to all the others.

In this field, Uberoi continues, there were many orders which rejected caste initially or broke pollution rules, regarding nothing as common or unclean—he instances the Sanyogis of the Punjab. In the course of time, many of these orders came back from mendicancy to householding again. Uberoi suggests that we can resolve this apparent contradiction by regarding both these conditions as forming the different stages or phases of a single development cycle. From this standpoint, any specific order or sub-order that once renounced caste with all its social rights and duties, and its notions of sacred space and time, and "walked out through the open front door of *sannyas* into the ascetic wilderness, could later become disheartened or lose the point of its protest, and even end by seeking to reenter the house of caste by the backdoor." In so doing, it would reverse the individual's institutionalized life path from householder to world renouncer; but, then, groups do not move irreversibly deathwards as individuals do. They tend to find that after a few generations they still confront the same old problems under approximately the same old conditions, and that what seemed a grand climactic gesture of world renunciation was, in fact, no climax at all, possibly an evasion, and certainly not a solution.

What seems to have happened in medieval India was that as a particular order or section fell back, so to speak, from the frontier of asceticism, and abandoned its nonprocreative, propertyless, occupationless, liminal existence, its function within the total field of *varnashrandharma* would be fulfilled by some other order or section. For the ascetic impulse—we may venture to say "protestant" impulse—itself remaained a constant feature. If we were making an extended case study of the genesis of a new order we might use Professor Marc Swartz's term and say that the *sannyas* principle was a perduring "arena-characteristic" of that field of *varnashrandharma*. Parallels with the modern American and West European "alternative" or "counter-culture" may be inaccurate and superficial here, but it does appear that the frontier of protest of "straight" or "establishment" Western culture is occupied by different types of groups every two or three years. For example, some specific groups have transformed themselves from "ghetto family" to city "commune" to manufactory or farm commune in a way that suggests broad parallels with the return from *sannyas* to *grihasta*. Western *askesis* (though this may have Near Eastern roots) parallels *sannyas* here—and the other major counter-structural modality, sexual community, has an affinity with certain Tantric notions—often the Eastern and Western notions converge in syncretic metaphors. Paperbacks and travel have brought Eastern religion into many Western milieux. But in the West the tempo is much more rapid under conditions of large-scale industrialism and urbanism and multiple communications media, and the results of the more rapid tempo might be compared with the differential effects of sun and incubator. The processual form is similar, though the transformations are speedier and more blurred.

Reverting to medieval India, Uberoi suggests that "during an order's ascetic period it may occupy one or the other of two positions, or pass through both successively. . . . it may either adopt a theory and practice completely opposed to that of caste and be for that reason regarded as heterodox and esoteric; or it might remain within the fold and link itself to the caste system through the normal sectarian affiliations of caste people." It could be said that a "heterodox or antinomian sect is one opposed to caste as its living shadow, while an "orthodox" sect is complementary to the caste system, being its other half *within* Hinduism.

Uberoi was interested in the special position of the Sikhs, being one himself and having problems about it. In his view, the Sikhs barred the door to asceticism, but did not return to the orthodox citadel of caste. What they tried to do, he thought, was to "annihilate the categorical partitions, intellectual and social, of the Indian medieval world," to liquidate its formal structure, one might say. Sikhism rejected the orthodox opposition between the states of common citizen or householder and renouncer, and of the ruler vis-à-vis both of these, refusing to acknowledge them as separate and distinct modes of existence, let alone stages in a developmental cycle.

The Sikhs did acknowledge the powers or qualities inhering in the domains of *rajya, sannyas,* and *grihasta,* but sought to invest their virtues conjointly in a single body of faith and conduct, like some Protestant sects during the European Reformation, who took the virtues of monasticism into the world, as Weber has shown so cogently. Nevertheless, Sikhism did not make for the internalization of conscience in the individual; corporate values were highly stressed even to the point of militancy. The Sikhs, in fact, renounced renunciation, and Uberoi goes on to show how this renunciation of renunciation is expressed in detail in the cultural symbolism of the five K's, the *kes* (= "long hair," or acceptance of "nature"), *kangha* (= "comb," to control the "natural" hair), *kara* (= "steel arm band," to control the sword arm), *kripan* (= "sword," directed aggression), and *katsh* (= "short drawers that end above the knee," to control the genitalia). I will not go into his analysis here, except to say that he argues that all these symbols imply both a recognition of natural processes and forces and simultaneously their religio-cultural control, a nice synthesis of asceticism and acceptance of natural urges. Sikh antistructure became in time counter-structure, as the gurus succeeded one another from Nanak (1469–1539) to Govind Singh (1675–1708), but remained outside Hindu structure (Macauliffe 1909).

My second illustration of how processes of structure, anti-structure, counter-structure, and restructuring can coexist and modify one another continuously over time in the same ritual field, and how field properties influence the metaphors in which religious experiences within it are expressed, is taken from a valuable paper by my colleague at the University of Chicago, Professor A. K. Ramanujan, on the religious literature of Vīraśaiva saints of the tenth to the twelfth centuries in South India.

The Vīraśaivas, though not ascetics, followed a ddifferent path to *moksha*, or salvation, from that taken by orthodox Hindus. They stressed devotion, love, and faith rather than the scrupulous performance of caste duties and rituals. Yet their "way" has become one of the three recognized ways of attaining salvation in Hinduism, alongside (1) complex and exacting performance of ritual, and (2) knowledge through meditation or Yoga. Nevertheless the Vīraśaiva movement was in its inception in the Kannada-speaking regions "a social upheaval by and for the poor, the lowcaste and the outcaste against the rich and the privileged; it was a rising of the unlettered against the literate pundit, flesh and blood against stone" (Ramanujan, 1973: 4).

Ramanujan suggests that, like other *bhakti* religions, Vīraśaivism is an Indian analogue to European Protestant movements. The Indian and European movements have in common such characteristics as:

> protest against mediators like priest, ritual, temples, social hierarchy, in the name of direct, individual, original experience; a religious movement of and for the underdog, including saints of all castes and trades (like Bunyan, the tinker) speaking the sub-standard dialect of the region, producing often the first authentic regional expressions and translations of inaccessible Sanskritic texts (like the translations of the Bible in Europe); a religion of arbitrary grace, with a doctrine of the mystically chosen elect, replacing a social hierarchy-by-birth with a mystical hierarchy-by-experience; doctrines of work as worship leading to a puritan ethic; monotheism and evangelism, a mixture of intolerance and humanism harsh and tender. (*Ibid*.: 40)

Dr. Ramanujan had written his paper for a *Seminar on Aspects of Religion in South Asia* at the School of Oriental and African Languages, University of London, in the spring of 1971, before he read my book *The Ritual Process: Structure and Anti-Structure*. He was so much struck by the resemblance between the opposition indicated in its subtitle and that which he had noticed in the Indian data that he made it the title of his own paper, "Structure and Anti-Structure: The Vīraśaiva Example." This was because the strategic thrust of his paper centered on an attempt "to unpack the meaning of a single 'binary opposition' in Vīraśaivism, i.e. *Sthāvara (stasis)* and *Jaṅgama (dynamis)* . . . and show how it organizes attitudes towards religion, society, language, metrical form, imagery, etc. . . . as seen in the *vacanas* (the body of religious lyric poetry produced by the early saints of the movement)."

Since I am now dealing with "metaphors" of anti-structure I can hardly do better than present in some detail Ramanujan's exegesis of a poem written by Basavaṇṇa, the Vīraśaiva leader, which exemplifies the opposition Sthāvara and Jaṅgama—an opposition which, stripped of its Indian integument, I hold to be cross-cultural and universal. The metaphorical opposition, too, draws much of its significance from its function within the South Indian religio-moral field of *varnashramdharma*. Here is Basavaṇṇa's poem:

> The rich
> will make temples for Siva.
> What shall I,
> a poor man,
> do?
> My legs are pillars,
> the body the shrine,
> the head a cupola
> of gold.
> Listen, O Lord of the meeting rivers,
> things standing shall fall,
> but the moving ever shall stay.

According to Ramanujan this poem "dramatizes several of the themes and oppositions characteristic of Viraśaiva protest" (*ibid.*: 2). Thus, Indian temples are "built traditionally in the image of the human body" (just as European Gothic cathedrals represent in many cases the crucified Christ, even to the extent that the hanging head is symbolized by a slight curvature of the building beyond the altar at the east end).

> The ritual for building a temple begins with digging in the earth and planting a pot of seed. The temple is said to rise from the implanted seed, like a human. The different parts of a temple are named after body parts. The two sides are called the hands or wings, the *hasta*. The top of the temple is the head, the *śikhara*. The shrine, the innermost and the darkest sanctum of the temple is a *garbhagrha*, the womb-house. The temple thus carries out in brick and stone the primordial blueprint of the human body.
> But in history the human metaphor fades. The model, the meaning, is submerged. The temple becomes a static standing thing that has

forgotten its moving originals. Basavaṇṇa's poem calls for a return to the original of all temples, preferring the body to the embodiment. The poems . . . suggest a cycle of transformation—temple into body into temple, on a circle of identities—a temple is a body is a temple.

(I am tempted here to see this also as a metaphor for the process whereby communitas becomes structure and then communitas again, and for the ultimate identification of both modalities as human sociality.)

Ramanujan points out that the poem draws a distinction between *making* and *being*.

The rich can only make *temples*. They may not *be* or become temples by what they do. Further what is made is a mortal artifact, but what one *is* is immortal ("things standing shall fall,/but the moving ever shall stay").

This opposition, the standing *vs.* the moving, *sthāvara vs. jaṅgama*, is at the heart of Vīraśaivism. The Sanskrit word *sthāvara* is cognate with the Indo-European words in English like *stand*, *state* (estate), *stature*, *static*, *status*, *stay*, and carries connotations of these related words. *Jaṅgama* contains a cognate of English go. Sthāvara is that which stands, a piece of property, a thing inanimate. *Jaṅgama* is moving, moveable, anything given to going and coming. Especially in Vīraśaiva religion a *Jaṅgama* is a religious man who has renounced world and home, moving from village to village, representing god to the devoted, a god incarnate. *Sthāvara* could mean any static symbol or idol of god, a temple, or a *liṅga* worshipped in a temple. Thus the two words carry a constrast between two opposed conceptions of god and of worship. Basavaṇṇa . . . prefers the original to the symbol, the body that remembers to the temple that forgets, the poor, though living, moving *jangama* to the rich petrified temple, the *sthāvara*, standing out there (*Ibid.*: 40).

I would like to cite Ramanujan's exegesis further, but time does not permit. As Ramanujan indicates, "the polarities are lined up and judged:

the rich	: the poor
temple	: body
make	: be
the standing (*sthāvara*)	: the moving (jangama)."

There is an evalutional asymmetry here: *jangama* is "better" than *sthāvara*. Here, too, evangelism begins.

Metaphors in other religious cultures make similar oppositions, but do not take sides. For example, the *Analects of Confucius* distinguish between the concepts *li* and *jen* but regard them both as necessary to a virtuous human social life. According to D. Howard Smith (1971: 40) the character *li* originally was closely associated with the sacrificial cult by which the names of the ancestors and the gods and spirits were worshiped and honored. In Confucius' day it had come to represent the "unwritten customary usages which regulated all the various relationships of society and family." It has been variously translated as "propriety, rites, ceremonies, ritual." The character *jen* has been variously translated as "love, goodness, benevolence, humaneness, man-to-man-ness" (*ibid.*: 42). A few quotations from the *Analects* (see Soothill, 1937) will indicate its operational meaning.

> Fan Ch'ih asked the meaning of *jen*. The master said, "love men." (*Ibid.*: 12:21).
>
> There may be a noble man who failed in *jen*, but never was there a mean man who possessed *jen*. (14:7).
>
> A man who possesses *jen* will not seek to preserve his life at the expense of *jen*. There are those who through death bring their *jen* to perfection." (15:8).

Jen is reconciled with *li* in the following:

> *Jen* is self denial and a return to *li* (propriety, ritual). For by self-denial and return to *li* the whole world would return to *jen*. (12:1).

Here Confucius sees the extremes as touching. I think that it would be possible to translate *jen* as "the sentiment of human kindness or for humanity," and its social expression as communitas, while *li* is not so far from what I have called "structure." Confucius seems to be saying that if men operated within and according to the norms of the structure without seeking to subvert those norms to their own self-interest or factional goals, then the result in terms of peaceful, just, social coexistence would be similar to those produced by spontaneous, existential communitas— the position which his critics down the ages have called "conservative."

This position implies, on the one hand, a bonding of individuals by "ritual" or "propriety," and, on the other, a safeguarding of each individual's independence with the general interdependence. Here distancing is not constraint, but the safeguarding of each person's dignity. To be perfectly fair, the Viraśaivas, too, sometimes saw that *sthāvara* and *jaṅgama* were ultimately one. Ramanujan writes: "The Viraśaiva trinity consists of *guru, liṅga*, and *jaṅgama*—the spiritual teacher, the symbolic stone-emblem of Siva, i.e., the structural signs of the cult, its incipient *sthāvara*, and his wandering mendicant representative. They are three yet one. Basavaṇṇa insists, in another poem, 'sthāvara and jaṅgama are one' to the truly worshipful spirit. Yet if a devotee prefer external worship of the stone liṅga (sthāvara) to serving a human jaṅgama, he would be worthy of scorn" (Ramanujan, 1973: 5).

This identification of the moving and the standing, the speaking and the spoken, man-to-man-ness and ritual, together with the process of their mutual recognition, forms a metaphorical triple classification found not infrequently in religious culture. The social correlates of these may be termed, in my view, anti-structure, structure, and societas, the process whereby anti-structure is periodically transformed into structure and structure into anti-structure.

You will have noticed, perhaps, that I have here stressed opposition not between communitas and structure but between anti-structure or "astructure" and structure. This is because the Vīraśaivas have elected to stress liminality, and the Confucians communitas, as the essential contrary to structure. For while li has a marked affinity to sthāvara, both being translatable without forcing as "structure"; jaṅgama, "the moving," is closer to liminality, and jen, "humanness," to communitas, than either is to the other. One archmetaphor for that which is outside structure, between structures, a dissolvent of structures, is "movement," "nomadism," "transience"—it is this aspect that concerns me in my current research on comparative pilgrimage processes past and present. Jaṅgama, "anything given to going and coming," fits well with this notion. In passing, we would seem to be in a period of history when "jaṅgama" values occupy a considerable place in public attention—exemplified, for instance, despite their manipulation for box-office purposes, by such films as Five Easy Pieces, Easy Rider, and other "road" movies and literature of "moving" people who, unable to "belong" to any institutionalized group, any "sthāvara" status, must needs travel from place to place, bed to bed, class to class, but may never stay anywhere long: in brief, the "hang-loose ethic" people.

In The Ritual Process, I suggested that history itself seems to have its discernable "liminal" periods, which share certain distinctive features, between relatively stabilized configurations of social relations and cultural values. Ours may well be one of them. One difference between East and West here, though, may lie in the sadness of Stoicism of the Western wanderers, and the gladness and faith of the Eastern. The former are positively negative, the latter negatively positive. Thereby hangs a tale it would take volumes even to begin to tell.

Liminality often provides favorable conditions for communitas, but it may have the reverse effect, either a Hobbesian war of all against all, or an existentialist anarchy of individuals each "doing his or her own thing." This is clearly not what Confucius had in mind when he dichotomized *li* and *jen*. Love of one's fellows could go very well, he thought, with "propriety," or the maintenance of those structures which depend upon the proper fulfillment of customary obligations (*li*). Thus for him there was no essential opposition between *li* and *jen*— *jen* was *li's* inner dynamic.

Yet traces of communitas adhere to *jangama* in Vīraśaiva thought. In his protest against traditional structural dichotomies, the poet Dāsimayya, for example, rejects the differences between man and woman as superficial, stressing their fundamental unity, thereby anticipating certain modern Western trends by nine centuries.

> If they see
> breasts and long hair coming
> they call it woman,
> if beard and whiskers
> they call it man:
> but, look, the self that hovers
> in between
> is neither man
> nor woman
> O Rāmanatha. (Ramanujan, 1973: 11)

Note here the *jangama* metaphors, "coming," "hovers," "in-between," "neither-nor," coupled with the communitas metaphor, the single "self" underlying cultural differences.

In connection with the Sikh illustration, I mentioned the sequence "structure/anti-structure/counter-structure/restructuring" as characterizing in India the fate of protest movements. Remanujan gives further examples of this. For him, the division made by Redfield between "great" and "little" traditions in Indian civilization, or between such similar antitheses as popular/learned, folk/classical, folk/elite, low/high, parochial/universal, peasant/aristocratic, lay/hieratic, is of little importance to the founders of protest religious movements such as Vaishnavism. Great and little traditions were rejected alike as the "establishment," as structure, and what was stressed was religious experience, *kṛpa* or "grace."

"The religious poems distinguish between *anubhāva*, "experience," and *anubhāva*, "the Experience." The latter is "a search for the unmediated vision, the unconditioned act, the unpredictable experience. Living in history, time, and cliché, one lives in a world of the preestablished, through the received (*śruti*) and the remembered (*smṛti*). But the Experience, when it comes, comes like a storm to all such husks and labels. . . . The grace of the Lord is nothing a devotee can invoke or wheedle by prayer, rule, ritual, mystical word, or sacrificial offering. A mystical opportunist can only wait for It, be prepared to catch It as it passes" (*ibid.*: 15–16). One is irresistibly reminded here of William Blake's: "He who catches the Winged Joy as it flies, Lives in Eternity's sunrise."

For Ramanujan, "structure" includes cognitive, linguistic, and ideological, as well as physical and social structures; it is, in brief, that which confers order and regularity on phenomena or assumes that these will be found in the relations among phenomena. It does so even as it breaks the continuity of the world into "sign" and "signified," "code" and "codified," in order to make that "external reality" intelligible and communicate knowledge of it.

Here we have the perennial problem of resolving the contradiction between distinction, or discontinuity (briefly, "structure"), and connection, or continuity; of experiencing unity while knowing it by means of contrasts. The Experience—what is often in Hinduism called *samādhi*, a state in which all distinction between subject and object is lost—appears to obliterate all structure, cognitive or communicational. In it, not only is the distinction between subject and object felt to be lost, but all is experienced either as One Self or as formless void. This is sometimes represented in Hindu mythology and ritual metaphor by the apparently amoral, capricious, yet creative acts of the major deities, who transcend the laws and limitations of men. In *anubhāva*, the Vīraśaiva devotee "needs nothing, he is Nothing," writes Ramanujan, "for to be someone, or something, is to be differentiated and separate from God. When he is one with Him, he is the Nothing without names" (*ibid.*: 17).

Structure depends upon binary oppositions in the last analysis—or so some of our French colleagues would have it. But anti-structure abolishes all divisiveness, all discriminations, binary, serial, or graduated. This creative moment of rejection of structures social, philosophical, and theological —what Ramanujan calls "this fierce rebellion against petrification" (*ibid.*) in the name of the "moving" of "grace"—tended, however, in practice and in Indian social history, to be merely a rebellion against *what Hindus were currently doing.*

It was not only an assertion of the value of interior experience against outward forms; it was simultaneously an attempt to *legitimate* such experience by having recourse to what were felt to be "pure" ancient traditions that were no different from true and present experience. The originally enunciated Truth, the "deposit of faith," was just such as the devotee had personally experienced.

Since these traditions had become part of "structure," the structure of both Great and Little traditions, the paradox existed that rejection of structure was legitimated by recourse to structure. In the same way, in Europe the Protestants appealed to the simple, communitarian Church of the founding fathers as their paradigm for rejection of the Catholic pharisaical formalism intervening between the pristine and contemporary states of Christianity. But once this has been done we cannot speak any more of "anti-" structure, but only of "counter-" structure.

Ancient Hindu scriptures were cited by Vīraśaivas to support a return to immediate experience. "Alienation from the immediate environment can mean continuity with an older ideal. Protest can take place in the very name of one's opponents' ideals" (ibid.: 18). The danger in doing this is, of course, that one thereby already puts one's foot on the first step of the structural escalator. Liminality is terminating; the return to the structural fold has begun.

Ramanujan, since he is at once a professor of linguistics and a literary critic, saw the Vīraśaiva return to structure via counter-structure in terms of the rhetorical structure of their literary output. I will not enter its technical dimension here, except to echo his conclusion that "spontaneity has its own rhetorical structure; no free verse is truly free," and that "without a repertoire of structures to rely on, there can be no spontaneity" (ibid.: 21). The common Hindu stock of similes, analogies, and metaphors is drawn upon in the Vīraśaiva poetry although used in new and startling ways—while the apparently inspirational poems can be shown to have a consistent metrical structure, characterized by what Roman Jakobson has called "grammatical parallelism," as well as other major symmetries and patterns. In the American tradition the poetry of Walt Whitman might provide an apt analogy.

To summarize drastically: Vīraśaiva protest mysticism initially collapses and rejects both all-India and regional structures and traditions and stresses mystical experience as the basic source of human meaning and social bondedness: in its developing group-expression it becomes counter-structural socially and culturally and ransacks past traditions to validate immediate experience; for analyzing the next stage Redfield's distinction between Great and Little traditions becomes useful again. For, as Ramanujan writes: "In course of time the (Vaisnava) heretics are canonized; temples are erected to them, Sanscrit hagiographies are composed about them. Not only local legend and ritual, but an elaborate theology assimilating various 'great tradition' elements may grow around them. They become, in retrospect, founders of a new caste, and are defied in turn by new egalitarian movements"—as the Jains, originally a Hindu heresy, were defied by the first Vīraśaivas (ibid.: 19). Anthropologists should take note from all this that a scientific study of any component of Indian religion, from jati-system to Jain ideology, at a given point in history, should take into account and represent by appropriate constructs the total field of Indian religion as context.

It is now time to look more closely at the structure of metaphor in these religious contexts. We have already seen how "the body" is stated as being in relation to what Vīraśaiva poets call *Jaṅgama*, "the moving"; and "the temple," to *Sthāvara*, "the standing." Although each of these terms is what I would call a multivocal symbol, there is sufficient similarity and analogy between the various referents of each symbol for it to represent fairly well the ensemble of referents.

One approach to the study of metaphor, which draws somewhat on Lévi-Strauss, Jakobson, and Chomsky, is Elli Köngäs Maranda's discussion in her recent article "The Logic of Riddles" (Miranda, 1971: 193–194). She relates metaphors to the concepts analogy and metonymy, accepting Aristotle's definition of the first: "There is an analogy wherever there are four terms such that the relation between the second and the first is similar to that between the fourth and the third," for example, A/B = C/D.

Analogy is a technique of reasoning, resting on two kinds of contrast between phenomena: similarity and contiguity, in other words "metaphor" and "metonymy." In the analogy formula, therefore, two members in the same structural position (A and C) constitute a sign, a metaphor in which one of them (A) is the *signans*, or the "signifier," and the other (C) is the *signatum*, or the "signified." The members on one side of the equation mark are in a metonymic relation to each other (A and B). In the analogy, metaphor, and metonymy are interrelated in the same picture:

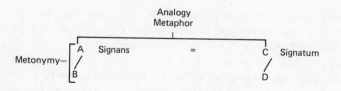

Metonymy is thus the *relation* of two terms; metaphor, the *equation* of two terms. In the Vaisnava poem translated by Ramanujan an analogy is constructed in the following terms: Temple/*Sthāvara* (Standing) = Body/*Jaṅgama* (Moving). The relation between Sthāvara to Temple is similar to that between *Jaṅgama* and Body. This analogy is then subjected to evaluation. In the abstract it may be true that the relation between stasis and temple is similar to the relation between Dynamis and the body, but the context of the poem introduces the paradox that "things standing *shall* but the moving shall ever *stay*" (my italics).

While the temple begins as a metaphor of the body, the poem suggests that in reality, even in eternity, there is no temple, only body (shades of the Christian doctrine of the resurrection of the *body*), but that the body has in it the holiness which is only metaphorically ascribed to the temple: "the body the shrine," as Basavaṇṇa puts it.

I would posit another metaphorical relationship here: *sthāvara:jang-ama*:: structure:anti-structure (communitas + liminality). *Sthāvara* is to *jangama* as structure is to communitas. For *sthāvara*, as Ramanujan writes, has such social structural connotations as "status, estate, a piece of property." And *jangama*, like the transitional period in rites of passage, represents "moving, anything given to going and coming."

The *jangam* in Vīraśaiva religion represents a permanently liminal man, a "religious man who has renounced world and home, moving from village to village." Even those who did not wander physically did not feel themselves bound by the strict rules of caste or kinship. Ramanujan stresses that the "Vīraśaiva movement was a social upheaval by and for the poor, the lowcaste and the outcaste against the rich and the privileged," a communitas based on the dissolution of caste ties in favor of immediate experience. For the Vaisnavas—"the Lord of the meeting rivers," which regularly appears as the refrain of the poems—does not refer to the personal Siva of the Hindu pantheon, but rather to the experience of *samādhi*, in which such distinctions as I-Thou, God-human, subject-object, become unimportant, and all seems to be one or nothing, in the sense that language has nothing positive to say about such an experience.

This position, common to both Eastern and Western mysticism, is perhaps most clearly formulated by the great scholar of Zen religion D. T. Suzuki, when he writes:

> Our language is the product of a world of numbers and individuals of todays and yesterdays and tomorrows, and is most usefully applicable to this world (known as *loka* in Indian *Mahayana*).
>
> But our experiences have it that our world extends beyond that *loka*, that there is another called by Buddhists *loka-uttara*, a "transcendental world," and that when language is forced to be used for things of this world, it becomes warped and assumes all kinds of crookedness: oxymora ("figures of speech with pointed conjunction of seeming contradictories, e.g., 'faith unfaithful kept him falsely true,' " OED), paradoxes, contradictions, contortions, absurdities, oddities, ambiguities, and irrationalities. Language itself is not to be blamed for it. It is we ourselves who, ignorant of its proper functions, try to apply it to that for which it was never intended. (*Suzuki*, 1968: 241)

In my view it is no accident that this *jangama*, or "mystical" rhetoric, charged with oxymora and metaphors, is very often characteristic of movements of egalitarian, popular protest during liminal periods of history when social, economic, and intellectual structures that have shown great stability and consistency over long periods of time begin to show signs of breaking up and become objects of questioning both in structural and anti-structural terms. We have been accustomed to thinking of mystical utterance as characterizing solitary individuals meditating or contemplating in mountain, desert, or monastic cell, and to see in it almost anything but a "social fact."

But the continuous operational conjunction of such language with movements of a communitas type, the Friends of God or the Rhineland mystics, for example, leads me to think that at least something of what is being uttered refers metaphorically to extant social relations. "Withdrawal" there is; "detachment," "disinterest," there is, to mention terms common to the mystical lexicon of many cultures; but this withdrawal is not from humanity but from structure when it has become too long petrified in a specific shape.

Here it is not merely a question of one component of the social structure, a class or caste or ethnic group, seeking to better its circumstances within a total structural system, nor is it a matter of making a new structural system free from the exploitative tendencies inherent in the structure of its predecessor. What is being sought is the emancipation of men together from *all* structural limitations, to make a mystical "desert" outside structure itself in which all can be one, *ein bloss niht,* "a pure nothingness," as the Western mystic Eckhart once wrote—though this "nothingness" has to be seen as standing in metaphorical opposition to the "somethingness" of a historically derived structure. It has as yet content but no manifest structure, only explosively stated anti-structure. History will of course unpack its latent structure, especially as experience encounters traditional structures of culture and thought. Those who have had the *Experience* now have to confront the establishments both of Great and Little traditions as they try to realize their vision in social relational terms. Now vision becomes *sect,* then *church,* then in some cases dominant political system or a prop for one—until communitas resurges once more against it from the liminal "spaces" and "instants" that every structure is forced by its nature to provide, since structure depends on distance and discontinuity between its units, and these interstitial spaces provide homes for anti-structural visions, thoughts, and ultimately behaviors.

Complex societies, too, provide a multiplicity of structural subsystems, manifest or latent, forming a field propitious for the growth of counterstructures, as individuals pass between subsystems. Society is a process which embraces the visions and reflections, the words and work, of religious and political mendicants, exiles and isolated prophets, as much as the activities of crowds and masses, the ceremonies of the forum and marketplace, and the deeds of legislators, judges, and priests. If we can see it as having such seemingly solitary or withdrawn purifiers, and "minuses" and "zeros" as well as pluses, in its central developments, anti-structure as well as structure, and if we see that there is a constant interplay between these on various levels and in various sectors of sociocultural fields, then we will begin to avoid some of the difficulties inherent in systems of thought which recognize only structurally positive values, rules, and components; and these are only "positive" because they are the rules recognized as legitimate by the political and intellectual elites at a given time.

Such systems throw out at least one-half of human sociality, the creative (and also destructive) half which insists on active, extant, vital unity, and upon novelty and extemporization in styles of human interrelations. But it should also be observed that fanaticism and intolerance tend to characterize movements that stress communitas as the counter-structural negation of structure. Iconoclasts, evangelists, Roundheads, as well as mystics, poets, and saints, abound in their ranks. The Vīraśaivas were fierce evangelists; the symbol of the Sikhs, the *khanda*—two curved swords, a double-edged dagger, and a discus—symbolizes martial virtue as well as spiritual power. "Liberty, fraternity, and equality" were shouts that drove Bonaparte on to an imperial crown.

Societies which stress structure—and establish mystiques of hierarchy and status, setting unalterable divisions and distance between categories and groups of human beings—become equally fanatical in the eradication of communitas values and the liquidation of groups which outstandingly exemplify them. Often we find "communitarians" unforgivingly arrayed against "structuralists," and vice versa. The basic cleavage in social man finds frequent historical expression. Those religions or humanistic systems which preach "love" as a major ethical principle—and all so-called "universal" religions profess this value as central—beam out some version of the Confucian reconciliation between *li* and *jen*, "ceremony" and "man-to-man-ness," this reconciliation being broadly what is meant by "love." The great religious systems harmonize rather than oppose structure and communitas, and call the resultant total field the "body" of the faithful, the *umma* ("country") of Islam, or some similar term which reconciles "love" with "law," communitas with structure. In fact, neither "law" nor "love" can *be* such when they are implacably opposed; both are then "hate"; all the more so, when masked as moral excellence.

Space does not allow me to develop fully the last section of this paper. In it I wanted to stress that both structure and anti-structure are represented in the concrete imageries and acts of the ritual process in tribal and peasant societies. Such societies are no less Man than we are, and their nonverbal symbols may even afford swifter access to the human matter than sophistries and apologetics. There structure and anti-structure have not become as yet generalized into opposed ideological positions, well adapted to political manipulation, but the metaphors of iconoclasm exist *within* the texture of ceremonies heavily endowed with icons. The construction and destruction of images are moments of a single ritual process. Most descriptions, since they have been made by alien observers, fail to describe adequately the communitas aspect of anti-structural metaphorical actions and their symbolic components in tribal ritual, but this will be increasingly remedied as literate members of these cultures describe what it has meant to them to participate collectively in ritual of an anti-structural tenor. Here novels, plays, and poetry currently being published in the new nations form an important body of data; personal documents that give us what Znaniecki calls the "humanistic coefficient" of a social analysis.

An analogous instance may be helpful here. In my current study of pilgrimage processes in historical religions such as Christianity, Islam and Judaism, Hinduism and Buddhism, I am beginning to accumulate evidence from pilgrim's narratives that experiences of a communitas type are often the subjective correlates of constellations of symbols and metaphors objectively indicative of anti-structure. Nevertheless, despite this grave *lacuna* about the presence of communitas in tribal limina, I would like to draw your attention to one example out of many that may be cited from studies of tribal ritual of the deliberate effacement or destruction of complex symbol structures, each of which is a semantic system of great complexity.

These instances of orthodox and permitted iconoclasm always take place in the liminal or "marginal" phase of major rites of passage, in the portion of institutionalized time assigned to the portrayal of anti-structure. Sometimes they are associated with an act of sacrifice, but often they occur independently of such an act though they have a sacrificial character. One of the best examples of the metaphorical destruction of "structure" that I know is given in Audrey Richard's account of the Bemba girl's initiation ceremony at puberty, *Chisungu* (Richards, 1956: 13–162 *passim*). Among the Bemba of north-eastern Zambia the *chisungu* is a long, elaborate sequence of ritual acts—which include miming, singing, dancing, and the handling of sacred objects—preceding the marriage of a young girl. It is also an "integral part of the series of ceremonies by which a bridegroom [is] united to the family group of his bride, in a tribe in which descent is reckoned through the woman and not the man, and in which a man comes to live with his wife's relatives at marriage rather than a woman with her husband's"(*ibid.*: 17). One of the distinctive features of this ceremony is the elaborate modeling of figurines in clay (Richards counted forty-two in one performance she studied) over several days of the protracted ritual, which lasted twenty-three days and in the past may have been longer, with many symbolic actions taking place each day. These pottery figurines or "emblems," as Richards calls them, known as *mbusa* (the mistress of ceremonies, is known as *nachimbusa*, or "mother" of the emblems) are suddenly pulled to pieces two hours after the ensemble of emblems is completed. The emblems are used to teach the girl-novice the duties, norms, values, and typical cultural settings of her coming structural position as wife and mother. Each has a specific ritual name, a cryptic song attached to it, and is interpreted to the girl for her social benefit by the senior ladies present, especially by the senior "mother of the emblems." Dr. Richards and Fr. E. Labreque, of the Missionary White Fathers, have collected much material on these didactic exegeses. Richards's appendix to *Chisungu*, giving informants' interpretations of *mbusa*, is particularly valuable. In brief, they add up to a fairly full account of a mature woman's structural fate in a matrilineal society, such as that of the Bemba, with many of its structural problems and tensions also represented—as I have indicated in my book *The Forest of Symbols* (1967: 193–194). Richards shows how the emblems refer, *inter alia*, to domestic duties, agricultural duties, the obligations of husband and wife, obligations to other relatives, the duties and circumstances of legitimate motherhood, the authority of chiefs, and to the general ethics incumbent upon mature Bemba. In Richards's words,

> In terms of time spent, the ritual handling and presentation of the sacred emblems probably occupied more hours than any other part of the rite. The handling, preparation and presentation of the pottery emblems and the collection of the woodland and domestic *mbusa* cost the organizers much time and energy. . . . The long day's work on the pottery emblems in the [novice's] hut has been described and it will be remembered that this long day's work was destroyed at the end of the very same day. . . . Apart from the making and finding of *mbusa*, their presentation by the different women in order of rank seemed, to me at least, the most interminable part of the *chisungu* rite since it involved the singing of every doggerel rhyme (interpreting the meaning of each *mbusa*) some twenty times or more. (Richards, 1956: 138)

The swift destruction of images and emblems laboriously constructed is not precisely comparable to the demolition of religious statues, paintings, and icons by Byzantine iconoclasts, Moguls in Banaras, Henry VIII's commissioners, Cromwell's Roundheads, or Scottish Covenanters. But behind it lies perhaps the same human impulse to assert the contrary value to "structure," that distances and distinguishes man from man and man from Absolute reality, describing the continuous in discontinuous terms. The important thing for those who use metaphorical means is to build up as elaborately as they may a structure of ideas, embodied in symbols, and a structure of social positions, symbolically expressed, which will keep chaos at bay and create a mapped area of security. Elaboration may, as in Chinese cosmological schemes, become obsessional in character. Then a metaphorical statement is made of what lies at once between the categories of structure ("inner space") and outside the total system ("outer space"). Here words prove useless, exegesis fails, and there is nothing left to do but to express a positive experience by a negative metaphorical act, to destroy the elaborate structure one has made and admit transcendence— transcendence, that is, over all that one's culture has been able to *say* about the experience of those who bear or have borne it to its present point in time. Actually, what is conceptually transcendent may well be experientially immanent—communitas itself. Only those who know how to build know how to collapse what has been built. Mere literal destruction is not the metaphorical destruction illustrated in ritual. Here the metaphor of destruction is a nonverbal way of expressing a positive continuous aspect of social reality which tends to escape the discontinuous character of most codes of communication, including linguistic codes. Perhaps this is because man may still be an *evolving* species; his future is in his present, but as yet unarticulated, for articulation is the presence of the past. This state Western thinkers share with the aborigines, and both of us reveal the dilemma in our nonverbal symbols, in our metaphors. *Chisunga*, we might say in conclusion, presents ritual and anti-ritual, in a relation of complementarity rather than contradiction. Structure and anti-structure are not Cain and Abel, to use a metaphor familiar to ourselves; they are rather Blake's Contraries that must be "redeemed by destroying the Negation." Otherwise we must all perish, for behind specific historical and cultural developments, East versus West, hierarchical versus egalitarian systems, individualism versus communism, lies the simple fact that man is both a structural and an anti-structural entity, who *grows* through anti-structure and *conserves* through structure.

REFERENCES

CONFUCIUS   (see Soothill, 1937)

DURKHEIM, EMILE

(1912)   *The Elementary Forms of the Religious Life.* New York:
1961   Collier Books.

GENNEP, ARNOLD VAN

(1909)
1960
The Rites of Passage. Trans. by M. Vikedom and G. Caffee. Chicago: University of Chicago Press.

MACAULIFFE, M. J.

1909
The Sikh Religion. 6 vols. Oxford: Oxford University Press.

MARANDA, ELLI KONGAS

1971
"The Logic of Riddles." Pp. 193–194 in P. Maranda and E. K. Maranda (eds.), *Structural Analysis of Oral Tradition.* Philadelphia: University of Pennsylvania Press.

RAMANUJAN, A. K.

1973
"Structure and Anti-Structure: The Virasaiva Example." In *Speaking of Shiva.* Harmondsworth, England: Penguin.

RICHARDS, AUDREY

1956
Chisungu. London: Faber and Faber.

SMITH, D. HOWARD

1971
Chinese Religions from 1000 B.C. to the Present Day. New York: Holt, Rinehart and Winston.

SOOTHILL, W. E. (ED.)

(1910)
1937
The Analects of Confucius. Oxford: Oxford University Press.

SUZUKI, D. T.

1968
On Indian Mahayana Buddhism. Ed. with an introduction by E. Conze. New York: Harper and Row.

TURNER, VICTOR W.

1967
The Forest of Symbols. Ithaca, N.Y. Cornell University Press.

1969
The Ritual Process: Structure and Anti-Structure. Chicago: Aldine.

UBEROI, J. SINGH

1967
"Sikhism and Indian Society," In *Transactions of the Indian Institute of Advanced Study,* Vol. 4. Simla.

Benjamin Nelson

GRADUATE FACULTY OF THE NEW SCHOOL FOR SOCIAL RESEARCH, NEW YORK

Eros, Logos, Nomos, Polis:
Their Changing Balances
and the Vicissitudes of
Communities and Civilizations

Elsewhere I have sought to distinguish several principal types of "structures of consciousness" illustrated in the histories of the areas which have been the cradles and homes of the world religions (Nelson, 1973a, b). Here I hope to throw light on the shifting blends and mixes in the crucibles of men's myriad histories of *eros, logos, nomos, polis*—central elements of sociocultural process (Nelson, 1962a; 1972a). I continue to be spurred forward in these efforts by the sense that once again today in both the so-called "East" and the so-called "West" decisive shifts are occurring in the shapes of *civilizational contents* and the balances of *intercivilizational ascendencies* (Nelson, 1973a).

A key notion in this context is the changing fortunes of societies and of men's sense of their fruitions; both prove to be in their most equable situations when hopes for the realization of vital balances of *eros, logos, nomos* and *polis* are not (wholly) unavailing (cf. Merton, 1938; ed. 1970; Nelson, 1961, 1964). In the absence of such options, received structures of rule and assurance as often as not break down. The needs for fresh expression in the ways of *eros, caritas,* resentment, defiance, alienation, or withdrawal course through society (Marcuse, 1955; 1964). Where apathy does not come to prevail there are thrusts to fresh actualizations of *eros,* of *diké,* of *charisma.*

Unhappily, many who have written on these themes have been insufficiently attentive to modalities and gradations. Simple polarizations such as those offered by Herbert Marcuse (1955, 1964) and Norman O. Brown (1959, 1966) will not suffice (cf. Nelson, 1961).

Throughout this paper, I shall be citing many illustrations from the twelfth and thirteenth centuries. My reasons for choosing that era are two—both weighty ones. The more one ponders these two centuries, the more one becomes convinced that *they constituted prime seedbeds of the institutional and cultural developments of the Western world* (Clagett et al., 1961; Haskins, 1927; Nordström, 1933). Indeed, I would take the next step and say that when these centuries are considered in intercivilizational perspective, they prove to have been *a watershed in the international history of the world* (see Bozeman, 1966; Barker, 1948; ICHSCDM, 1963–70).

To make this point clear, I adopt to my purpose an incisive observation by Whitehead. From the wider cross-cultural point of view, Whitehead explained, the great turning point in the history of Western civilization was the Scientific Revolution of the seventeenth century rather than the Protestant Reformation. The latter, he remarked, was in many critical respects an episode in the *domestic history* of the European people (Whitehead, 1968). The position taken in these pages rests upon the notion which Whitehead shared with others that there is no way of truly understanding the seventeenth century without truly appreciating the roots of those developments in the twelfth and thirteenth centuries.

The twelfth and thirteenth centuries are the decisive era in which the initiatives in all spheres shifted from the Middle East to the West. It is the era in which there occurred the reception of the new Aristotle, the reception of Roman law, the development of the canon law, the renewal of Greek political philosophy, the emergence of the universities, the development of scholastic philosophy, natural theology, natural science, the crystallization of critical logics associated with the "court of conscience" in all spheres of act and thought, and so on (Haskins, 1927; Clagett, 1961; Vinogradoff, 1967; Nelson, 1968; Chenu, 1969).

My second reason for selecting the twelfth and thirteenth centuries is that within this era, more clearly than in any time before our own, we are able to witness the struggles both to fuse and to defuse blends of *eros, logos, nomos,* and *polis.* This was the era in which the decisive break occurred in the emergence of incorporated cities (Weber, 1921; Pirenne, 1936), an institution with few parallels or precedents in non-Western history; a free self-governing citizenry; differentiation of occupations in handicrafts, manufacture, trade, shipping, with organized groups of artisans, merchants, moneylenders, financiers, professional philosophers, lawyers, doctors, notaries, mathematicians and so on.

The changes which occurred in all spheres during that era—in economy, polity, society, culture—were truly extraordinary. It was an era of decisive thrust of the so-called "West" to recover the Mediterranean as a European lake and the route to the East—Far and Near East alike; it was the era of the change of fortunes in the struggle with Islam (Davison, 1926; Thode, 1904); it was an era of the establishment of the cities, new institutions of communes of various sorts, intentional communities of almost every type, surges toward hierarchical political structures and countervailing surges against every type of nomistic control restraining the free flow of *eros* (Douie, 1932; Morrison, 1969).

A history of European social and religious developments from the beginning of the tenth to the middle of the fourteenth century offers supreme illustrations of the sorts of struggles we are again witnessing today. I refer to decisive struggles over the way in which the social fabric should be threaded, struggles over the ways in which the structures of consciousness should be formed. At no time so much as in that era and in our own can we see the convulsions which derived from the civil wars in the structures of consciousness. The battle ranges between the existential structure of "faith-consciousness" and the more objective "rationalized-structures" of consciousness (Nelson, 1973).

In the main, the twelfth and thirteenth centuries witnessed the spread of the rationalized-structures at the expense of the faith-structures. Today we are seeing the reversal of that trend. In short, from the point of view of a comparative historical sociology informed by a strong interest in the shapes of civilizational complexes and intercivilizational encounters, our twentieth-century days since the outbreak of the First World War need to be viewed against the backgrounds of wider horizons which include reference to the twelfth and thirteenth centuries (Nelson, 1972b; 1973).

Before entering into the main highway of my present story, I first need to make two brief detours in the hope of clarifying its comparative historical and "anthroposociological" horizons. The particular relevance of some suggestions of Feuerbach will be considered in the second of these prefatory turns.

I

This essay is written in the conviction that *sociology* and history—and one must add, *anthropology* and history—have a relation to one another like that which Kant ascribes to concepts and percepts. Anthropology and sociology—one wishes one would have available a broadened expression, *anthroposociology*—prove to be empty without history just as concepts are empty without percepts. And history without anthroposociology is blind just as percepts are blind without concepts. It is on these assumptions that I will feel free to refer here to matters historical as well as matters anthropological and sociological (Nelson, 1972 c).

Nor do I suppose that so-called past events have occurred once and for all. I am convinced that many pasts live again today; also, that many of the extraordinary features of the tumultuous sociocultural processes of the twentieth century are best understood as the *re*-presentations of what had been assumed to be extinct.

Thus, in my view, anthropology and sociology are strongly rooted in depth-historical understandings of structures of existence, experience and expression. We are hardly likely to range beyond *schematic* histories if we do not come into close contact with the actualities of existence; the myriad strivings to realize hopes, dreams, myths, in social and symbolic forms of various sorts; if we do not somehow see the meshes and mixes of *eros, logos, polis, nomos,* in wider civilizational and even intercivilizational perspectives. *Schematic* histories are exceedingly weak bases from which to plan creative new moves into as yet unknown future (*ibid.*).

II

I must now speak about Feuerbach, whose insights prove to have wider implications for our theme than have yet been clearly set down (Feuerbach, 1957; 1967).

In his *Essence of Christianity* (1841), which Marx and many others called a masterwork of their century—and which in my view remains a critical source for all interested in the study of sociocultural process —Feuerbach sought to explain the relations between the structures of men's existences and experiences, and the structures of their religious consciousness and theologies; and, as some readers may recall, after a rather systematic analysis of the doctrines of Christianity, he came to the view that "the key to theology was *anthropology*"—that is, the understanding of man's "nature," man's "essence," man's—"experience"—was the key to the understanding of theology (*ibid.*).

If Feuerbach's theses be true in some sense, if it be the case that man has indeed secreted his "essence" into his theology, if men have painted themselves and their histories into their faith, then it behooves us to look very carefully at men's theologies. Apparently in order to recover men's histories, and the understandings of their natures and their characters as persons, we must go by way of their theologies. This way of looking at the matter has not received the attention which is its due.

Before all else, it has to be perceived that men do not naturally know their own natures, any more than they naturally know their own histories. Men's natures and histories are in no sense immediately accessible, tangible, palpable, available; men have to continue, as it were, to seek to discover their natures through tenacious efforts, and they have to find some sort of terms in which to express the structures of their own *existences*, the characteristics of their *experiences*. They have got to look at their *expressions*. And since their theologies are a foremost form of their expressions, they must look intently at their theologies as well.

For this reason among others, as I have already indicated, I shall be placing strong stress here on the vicissitudes of men, institutions, cultural forms, theologies in the twelfth and thirteenth centuries. It is these very centuries which witnessed the systematic codification of great theologies —*scholastic* as well as *monastic* (Leclerq, 1945; Chenu, 1957; Bertola, 1970), *natural* as well as *moral* and *mystical*; it is these very centuries which now have to be designated as the seedbeds of the central structures of Western social and cultural organization. In fact, these centuries witness the constitution of what may be called the groundplan of Western civilization in a sense more technical than a familiar one.

If we be allowed to extend Feuerbach's thesis with the help of Durkheim and Mauss, we must be prepared for a surprising outcome: the existences and experiences which have found their way into the theology will *re*-present themselves to us in ways we never expected. Irresistibly as we assay the civilizational process of that era from the point of view of the shifting blends of *eros, logos, nomos, polis*, we will find strong evidence that men did, in fact, discover themselves in their theologies during the twelfth century. In making these discoveries, we also discover that the twelfth and thirteenth centuries are the era in which the notions —your notions and my notions—of Western man were recovered (Gilson, 1940a; Knowles, 1964; Peter Abelard, Luscombe, 1971; Murray, 1967). The distinctive characteristics which define the image of man, of society, and of civilization were uncovered or discovered in the twelfth century. If anyone would suppose that in the eighth or ninth centuries there was accessible to any great number of persons images of man, society, community, civilization, that were comparable to such images after the twelfth century, he would simply be mistaken. The history of the structures of consciousness or conscience is neither continuous nor consecutive, nor is there any consecutive or continuous understanding or awareness of man as an agent in all modalities of his personhood and existence. How, then, did men of the twelfth and thirteenth centuries find the ways in which to express their new experience of themselves?

I shall have to ask readers to join me in looking closely at the facts: if the data attest to anything, they attest to very critical transformations in the structures of consciousness and conscience. Why so? Where can this best be seen.

III

No setting presents the stirring changes of the twelfth century so strikingly as the confrontations of St. Bernard of Clairvaux (Knowles, 1964; Kneale, 1962) and Abelard (Williams, 1935)—confrontations which, in my view, were to have extraordinary political, sociological, cultural, and civilizational and intercivilizational consequences. These encounters offer us a paradigmatic instance of the passage from what I have elsewhere described as the faith-structures of consciousness to the rationalized-structures of consciousness (Nelson, 1972).

I will talk first of Bernard, then of Abelard.

Bernard felt himself called to devote his life to the recovery for man of the meaning and experience of love, God's love for man in Christ, man's love of God through Christ.

Hoping to enjoy a state of mystical union with the Godhead, wishing to be suffused with the word of God, eager to be possessed by the structures of faith-consciousness, Bernard meditated upon the Trinity (Williams, 1935). He meditated upon the mysteries which were involved in the relations and separate distinctions of persons in a single essence; he meditated the distinctions and yet sameness of the divine nature; and he also continued to meditate on the actual human existence of Christ [1]. In the process, Bernard discovered something that had not been fully disclosed or fully acknowledged before in Western theology. He discovered the Christ-*Man* as Everyman's Perfect Friend [2].

It was to be anticipated that one who meditated on the Trinity and Christ with the stark intensity and conviction of a Bernard—such a one would discover the man-God. The reasoning runs as follows: man had been put into the Trinity, into Christ, when the doctrines of the Trinity and the hypostatic union of two natures was developed. Whoever troubles to study the relations between Christian doctrine and the shapes and images of man and society and community and relations, and power and purpose and sequences of causality, and grace and spirit and all of these other notions—whoever pursues this path must not be surprised to discover that when the time for reappropriation occurs, what proves preeminently available for recovery is what had been secreted into theology.

Now, what Bernard strove to reappropriate was the incarnate son within the divine-human exemplar, the imitation of whom was the way of light, life, and truth. Bernard's discovery was one of the ultimate points in the history of Western culture. All images of *eros, logos, nomos, polis* which were Bernardine in inspiration represent a fundamental form of the option again and again taken in the West in the form of faith-consciousness (Nelson, 1973).

At the very moment Bernard was giving ultimate shape to the *eros*-as-*logos* structure, the notions of person and truth were being recovered in other ways and were actually being elaborated with other intentions and other purposes. I refer to the work of Abelard and the scholastic—as distinguished from the monastic—theologians. Only a word may be allowed here about a critical step in the passage from the monastic to the scholastic thinkers.

The early scholastic writers, including Anselm, said that they believed in order to know. *Credo ut intelligam*; *fides quaerens intellectum*: such were their telling expressions. Those who apply these expressions often enough, those whose faith insistently seeks understanding, find themselves imperceptively shifting on their axes; they discover themselves passing from *wanting to know in order to believe* to *wanting to know for the sake of knowing* (Barth, 1960; Knowles, 1964; Kneale, 1962).

The passage from the first stance to the second stance occurred quickly and with immense effect; it occurred in a single generation, and, when it occurred, those that had believed in order that they might know were discovering that there were others who were intent upon knowing in order that they might believe, and they were both performing the same job. What led Bernard to oppose Abelard, to pursue him so relentlessly? Some find it hard to understand. Before facing this question directly, we must talk of the institutional expressions of love and friendship.

IV

Eros and friendship are to be found everywhere in the life and work of Bernard. He reveals a comprehensive theology of love; it hardly needs saying that all monks who were in any way influenced by him, all communities that were in any way inspired by him were grounded in a notion of love. The notions of love and friendship were ruling conceptions in the twelfth and thirteenth centuries, as one sees quickly by looking at the sociocultural structures of those centuries (Egenter, 1928; Bloch, 1961).

Different institutions need to be regarded from the point of view of the characters of the mixes and the strains which developed within each of these structures. *Eros*—in the form of *philia*—*logos, nomos, polis* were fused, blended in various ways in all of them.

In some settings, a pro-structural stress on *eros* was greater than the pro-structural stress on the expression of *logos*, (see, e.g., Jocelin of Brakelonde, (ed.) Butler, 1949; Christina of Markyate (ed.) Talbot, 1959).

To understand the nature of communities bound in one or another form of *eros*, or in sublimated *eros*, that is to say, in *amicitia* (friendship), especially *spiritual friendship* [3], we would do well to look closely at two institutions, feudalism and monasticism. The first may not instantly strike us as an outstanding illustration of the notion of friendship, but it is the case that the *pro-structural* stress on friendship undergirded the entire structure of the relations of "Religion" and the "World," at almost every level and function in the Middle Ages. Thus we must look for prime crystallizations of *friendship* structures in the feudal world as well as in the cloister.

Feudal relationships preeminently involved relations of trust and loyalties—individuals who were tied to one another were obliged to undergo risks of life and limb for one another, to stand hostage and surety for one another, to come to one another's aid in continuing conflicts over prerogative and place. The seriousness of this pledge is not reduced by the fact that there were limits to the amount of time in which the fullness of these services could be demanded; the absolutely ruling ethic was grounded in the idea of the friend-foe relation (Bloch, 1964; Nelson, 1949).

To miss the fact that invidious friendship was the base of the feudal ethic is to miss the passion as well as the pride of the medieval world, indeed, of the entire premodern era. All relationships, vertical as well as horizontal, rested on the same hinges; the name of these hinges were friend and foe [4].

Among friends everything was common, especially enemies. All members of the nobility without exception were conceived and conceived themselves to be responsible to act in the spirit of the one example [4].

It is from the cloister that we receive perhaps the most critical underlying principle of the dualism of "Religion" and World, that is, the image of the Perfect Friend. In this era, Christ becomes the perfect friend. "Greater love hath no man than he lay down his life for a friend" (Gospel acc. to John, xv: 13). Christ laid down his life for all mankind. As the true and perfect friend he therefore represents a sort of exemplar—both for the nobility and for the clergy, notably the monastic clergy. And, indeed, Christ is presented to all as the model for all. It was in this spirit that it was possible for the church to preach the crusades, and to draw calculating nobles into acts of supererogation and acts of sacrifice beyond the line of duty.

Too few seem to know that the medieval era produced vast numbers of treatises on the subject of friendship, especially "spiritual friendship." The notion of friendship was, of course, not invented in the Middle Ages; *amicitia* is a classical ideal and it has its counterparts in many other societies and civilizations (Butler, 1922), which are not distinctly Greek or Roman—a very critical conception, but it does have notable variations in the institutional and cultural forms that were in crystallization in the medieval era.

It is odd that so little has been made of the fact that there is no other way by which great numbers, pledged to the triple vow of chastity, poverty, and obedience, could retain threads of communion which bound them in spiritual affections. As brothers and sisters in monastic houses and convents dare not love one another in the flesh, they nonetheless are pledged to love one another in the spirit and to express their love in the conjoint imitation of the example of the Perfect Friend (Nelson, 1939–44).

Each has one paradigm—Christ—who gave his life and his love for all mankind. Each is expected to make his or her own life a perfect imitation of the divine example. Each is expected to keep his or her own bridal chamber stainless and ready. For, as Meister Eckhart and so many others reminded their contemporaries, "Behold the Bridegroom cometh!" (Eckhart, tr. Blakney, 1957). None will have such occasion to lament as the foolish virgins unprepared for the holy matrimony.

Those who have talked about the Protestant ethic existing in the Middle Ages entirely miss the immense authority of these structures of consciousness and sensibility. One must remember that each of the monasteries and convents and each of the new religious groups were the centers of circles from which there radiated the structures of *eros* and sublimated *eros*. Whoever wishes to understand the development of the church must see that it is a community bound together in love and by love, a love that is bound together beyond a secular expression of desire and affection. Unless this ethic had persisted the church could not have continued at all.

The cracks of the medieval structure came from two sides—the routinization of the charismatic and the sacralization of the profane—which recur in different measures at various times. One of the most challenging tasks for anyone who has an historical interest in sociocultural process is to study the vicissitudes of these blends and relationhips of *eros, logos,* and civilization. No set of circumstances so powerfully illustrates these changes of phase as the main changes that occurred between the Cluniac Reform and the beginning of the so-called Babylonian Captivity of the Church.

I allow myself some comments at this point, which may perhaps be not as familiar as they might be, in reference to the notion of friendship as a structural principle for modern society.

Too few seem to perceive that in the medieval world and in the early modern world—prior, actually, to the Puritans—a full religious sacralization of the family or of family property did not exist. There did, indeed, not occur the sacralization of what might be called the special friendship with one's own wife. In the "world," the notion of temporal friendship was regularly conceived as friendship between two who had an almost blood-brotherhood relation, where they were altogether possessed of a single soul while they had bodies twain (Mills, 1937).

Now, how did the change occur? That is, how did the premodern—the classical, medieval, Renaissance notion of friendship—become the modern ethic of impersonal service on behalf of an impersonal goal? If there was anything at all about the earlier medieval ethic, it was stubbornly interpersonal. Now, how did we get our contemporary view?

Throughout antiquity and the Middle Ages friendship was conceived as the union that transcended all calculation and egotism whether of family or of person. From at least the time of Plato forward, the moralists and novelists insisted on preeminence of friendship, going so far as to deny that one's wife or members of one's own family could truly be friends in the highest sense. The stress on Christ as the perfect and true friend continued into the Renaissance, and the Elizabethan period in England. Interestingly, the first powerful assault on the idea of friendship was the Puritan attack on Elizabeth and the courtly style. Puritans correctly grasped that so long as friendship and friendship circles were held in the highest respect, there was no possibility of achieving sanctification of the special love within the family (Schücking, 1966).

It was the Puritans, above all, who mounted the attack on the ethos of friendship which prevailed in England until their day. The very idea that charity begins *at home* involves the sanctification of the home. It constitutes a very extraordinary extension of the notion *caritas incipit in se,* and it is, indeed, of course, something of an extension and elaboration of the notion that one is to love one's neighbor as oneself. Too few have noticed that such a sanctification goes far beyond the idea that we have to love ourselves as we love our neighbors. The new maxim, "charity begins *at home,*" is the sacralization of a collective egoism of the family and its property (Nelson, 1949, ed. 1969). It is the indispensible base of the newer structure which came into being with the Protestant ethic. Having elsewhere discussed some of the other facets of this story, I hasten to return to the vibrant twelfth century (Abelard, ed.; Luscombe, 1971; Landgraf, 1934).

V

To come back now to our briefly suspended confrontation. The second actor in our dialogue—Abelard—now demands to be heard.

I will address myself first to Abelard's own work and teaching; I will then turn to the activities of a number of notable scholastics and jurists, including some who were Abelard's students.

Throughout this discussion I will put the emphases on the changes in the structures of rationales which came to be elaborated as a result of the distinctively Abelardian notion that all activity had to be conceived as the action of individuals who were possessed *of consciences* which had a power to opt between alternatives of relative worth or of varying credibilities.

Doubtless, the idea of *conscientia* is to be found in antiquity; we can find it in Seneca, Cicero, and other authors, but the wider story which follows here has many surprises. The notion of conscience (*conscientia*) only comes to the fore with the breaking down of the structures of collective consciousness (Durkheim, 1955; Burckhardt, 1860; Nelson, 1965a) and the growing strength of the need to establish assessments of individual liability and individual responsibility, or individual blame. The more carefully we survey the historical developments, the more likely we are to find that it was not until the eleventh, twelfth, and thirteenth centuries that the term conscience came to undergo an extraordinary dialectical, logical, philosophical, religious, theological unfolding, (Lottin, 1942–60; Nelson, 1968). And it was set forth in very great detail, starting with Abelard's necessity to understand the contents of faith (Abelard, ed. Luscombe, 1971).

The more closely we scrutinize the documentary remains, the more we perceive the critical importance of notions of responsibility and guilt in the working out of the problems of intentionality [5]. We must not be surprised if we find the following among the questions most insistently put forward:

Who may be said to have been responsible in the case of the crucifixion (Abelard, ed. Luscombe, 1971; Nelson, 1947)? Are consent and knowledge prerequisites of sin? How shall the sinner make proper restitution (Abelard, ed. Luscombe, 1971)? How respond to the dictates of "conscience" (Nelson, 1968; 1949, ed. 1969)?

It is with Abelard that there begins the true unfolding of a variety of perspectives and logics which are connected with the analysis of the possibilities of conscience—conscience seeking to realize itself in the world here and now; seeking to make itself viable and operative, meaningful and fruitful in myriad ways.

There is, in fact, no possible activity which does not fall under the governance of conscience in this era. We are mistaken if we identify the notion of conscience exclusively with the sense of guilt or with retrospective remorse; the medieval conscience is mainly prospective [6].

An added word may be needed to explain how *opinions* fell under the governance of conscience. Abelard and others were convinced that every opinion had relative degrees of value as a truth-function or truth-claim. As time passed, the scholastic writers began to talk about the varying degrees of probability of opinion (Nelson, 1968; 1949, ed. 1969) relative to some particular logical object or state of affairs. It would not matter what the probability was, it was a relative probability of opinion in respect to the meaning of a moral norm or an opinion on the state of nature or anything else.

In short, Abelard and his followers present us with a twofold logic operating from the same hinge.

Two additional facts must be understood if we are to understand what came to be called the Court of Conscience. The complexities that must arise in the effort to administer so comprehensive a set of structures relating to so varied a range of predicaments are impossible to exaggerate.

A second point which needs to be recalled is that Abelard did a great deal more than evolve a philosophical schema. The institutions of the conscience were all predicated on the assumptions that all who were Christians were answerable. The notion of answerability was a paramount idea. There is no one, no pope, no king, no one who is not answerable to the tribunal of conscience—the king has his chancellor, who is the keeper of the king's conscience and from whose activity the entire law of equity is crystallized (Vinogradoff, 1967). And the Pope has his confessor.

All are answerable; there must therefore be an institution which reviews the case of the world in the light of conscience. The circumstances of the world being myriad, there is no single or direct move from any set of principles to a decision in all cases.

Now when everyone in Christendom was made responsible under the Fourth Lateran Council of 1215 to confess at least once a year, there was a need for highly elaborated moral theology in which all the cases of conscience were considered as they arose in the practical life of the times (Thompson, 1957; Michaud-Quantin, 1962). There was a period in which Christian moral theology and moral theologians made bold to consider every conceivable public issue in concrete terms. And they had the temerity to name the people who were engaged in the questionable activities at the very highest level of functions, and judge them publicly for all to read about [7].

The high point of this morality of prophetic witness covers a period roughly from 1170 to 1230. Stephen Langton was such a witness, (Nelson, 1933; Baldwin, 1970). Another man of the highest importance in this development was Cardinal Robert de Curzon (Nelson, 1933; 1949), who is often known as Robert de Courcon, the Cardinal-Legate of Pope Innocent III in France and author of an extraordinary *Summa* with an almost unique treatise on usury. I did not know that at the time I was writing my master's thesis on the theme many years ago that the tradition that Robert represented in such an extraordinary way was to have an early end as many good traditions do.

Even before the first half of the century had ended, reference to great public questions passed out of fashion in the *summae* of cases of conscience; instead, a sort of split occurred. The moral theologians moved ever closer to the very profound and yet more rarified atmosphere of advanced moral metatheology, or meta-moral-theology, and they did not deal with any of the cases except in a very general sense. And at the lower level, there were those who became experts in developing a kind of highly routinized, rationalized analysis of the predicaments and circumstances and worked them all out alphabetically. By the end of the thirteenth century, those deputed to serve official roles as judicial officers and physicians of the soul in the Courts Christian, in the confessional, could just do it "by the book." The mighty effort of society of the High Middle Ages to achieve a public moral governance of itself ground to a near halt. So far, at least as this horizon was concerned, "prophecy" gave way to "routine" (Nelson, 1949).

VI

Abelard and Bernard were not at infinite removes from one another. Both men put their faith in the virtuous imitation of a divine exemplar. Both placed profound stress on intentionality. But, in the words of a recent writer, Abelard was preeminently devoted to elucidating the *logic* of love—divine and human alike—the logic of willing, consenting, sinning, indeed of existing and acting in all the dimensions of experience.

Abelard needed *to know* what he believed. He needed to know who shared in the guilt of Christ's crucifixion; how to speak of the nature and persons of the Trinity; how to interpret the Faith to make it invulnerable to attack from whatever quarter; how best to ground moral obligation and argument.

By pursuing these issues relentlessly, Abelard became the foremost twelfth-century architect of structures of the rational consciousness [8]. Abelard worked out a logic of intentions. Without him there is no possibility of understanding the separation of subject and object as we understand them here. It is this separation which constitutes the logical crux of the foundations of Western civilization (Nelson, 1968; 1969; 1973).

In brief: I am saying that all the axial structures changed dramatically in the twelfth to the thirteenth centuries. Collective consciousness apparently gave ground to individual consciousness, and around these there developed comprehensive logics of opinion, belief, action, and so on; these treatises on human action, conscience, and cases provide a setting for the proliferation of highly developed structures and decision-matrices of all of the moralities of thought and action.

To oppose *eros* and *logos* as absolutely antagonistic principles is to miss the point; this view has turned the whole question of the future into *a one-dimensional prospect* which seems to characterize the projections of some of the millenarian thinkers named above. We have no recourse against one-dimensionality as prospect if we see one-dimensionality as constituting the total retrospect.

EPILOGUE

Rarely have so much social innovation and new culture come with such dramatic impact as in the period we have been discussing. The twelfth century witnesses extraordinarily dramatic fusion and institutionalizations of *eros, logos, nomos,* and *polis.* Vast funds of new passion pour into new polities. Prior structures suited for an earlier age now give ground to new collectivities—cities, guilds, universities, monastic communities, popular religious movements [9].

It is no wonder that the great confrontations between the faith-structures of consciousness and the rationalized-structures of consciousness occurred at that time. As we have observed above, transformative thrusts toward the advanced structures of the rationalized consciousness and rationales in the canon law, theology, and the public life gathered great momentum throughout the twelfth century. It is against these settings that it seemed best for our purposes to explore the historic encounter between St. Bernard of Clairvaux and Abelard.

Already by the third quarter of the twelfth century there are signs of tension within the newly rationalized sectors and structures. Insurgent mass movements, coming from below the surface, declare their will to reform the church and restore it to its mission as the exemplar and protector of the poor. The prime symbol of the new time is Peter Waldo—in his rejection of the profits of trade for the life of *a*cosmic love [10]. From this point forward there is an insistent recurrence of movements to blend the commitment to poverty and reform.

Peter Waldo is the harbinger of St. Francis of Assisi. It is not by chance that St. Francis sought to rededicate his movement to poverty and the life of simple faith. His followers were to own nothing either collectively or individually, were not to pursue learning, were not to mingle in governance.

The most decisive struggles of the thirteenth century were those which raged among the Spiritual and Conventual Franciscans—struggles which were deeply influenced by the eschatological visions of Joachim of Fiore. We must not be surprised that the crisis in the Franciscan order and the struggles over Joachism came to a peak in the Pontificates of Innocent III and Gregory IX.

Although many view the thirteenth century as the era of the full crystallization of Gothic Art and Scholasticism, there is as much warrant for another perspective, in which the Christian rationalized civilization that was developed in the twelfth century is seen to be undergoing mighty hammer blows from which it is never fully to recover. By the end of the century there had occurred the ultimate attempt of spiritualism to effect charismatic renewal of the church through the person of Celestine V. The rulers of territorial states had entered upon a civil war against the popes. Boniface VIII had undergone humiliation at Anagni and the Babylonian captivity of the church had begun.

Only one group failed to triumph in the midst of these debacles, the Spiritual Franciscans. For a time, it did appear as though the Spirituals would attain the heights of their hopes. With such leaders and champions as Peter John Olivi and William of Occam they hoped to humble the papacy. They did not succeed. In this very critical hour the popes were able to count upon the support of the lay estate and the patricians in the Italian cities. The Spiritual Franciscans were hunted down and persecuted. The middle of the fourteenth century initiates a new era in the life of Christian civilization, an era which was not ended until the Reformation.

We offer these evidences as proofs that developments of European society and Western civilization involved hectic changes in the mixes and blends of *eros, logos, nomos, polis.* Now, as then, issues of the fusions and conflicts of these elements are felt to be of peak religious and civilizational significance (see, e.g., Walter of St. Victor, ed. Glorieux, 1953; also see Turner, 1968) [11].

Few readers who have accompanied us thus far in our journey are likely to escape the feeling that the profound turnings of institutions and sensibilities we have just reported for the twelfth and thirteenth centuries seem to have a decidedly contemporary ring.

Then, as now, religious, theological and political antagonists insisted on pitting *eros* and *logos* against one another in the conviction that lasting truth, justice, and happiness could be realized only by the conquest of one by the other (Walter of St. Victor, post 1179, cf. ed. Glorieux, 1953; Marcuse, 1964, 1966; Brown, 1966, 1970; Roszak, 1969). Our effort to be faithful to the vicissitudes, changing balances, and realizable hopes of the cities, communities, and civilizations of this world has here led us to project a fourfold (actually, a $4+n$) "dialectic" of the mixes in sociocultural process. We have been unable to suppress the memory that a dialectic of two opposed terms all too often ends by forgetting the "social-reality principle" (Nelson, 1962b, 1964; cf. Turner, 1968).

NOTES

1. An especially helpful statement of these issues and links will be found in Mother Adele Fiske's two-part essay on St. Bernard's exploraton of the idea of friendship. Mother Adele writes: "To St. Bernard, all love is rooted in the love of God and therefore is an 'affection,' not a contract: 'Affectus est, non contractus.' This affection of love is, if not the equivalent, at least analogous to the vision of bodies. God is 'sensible' to the heart that loves; love then is a vision. For Bernard, knowledge is based entirely on a likeness of the subject knowing to the object known. For man to know himself is to see the image of God; he is miserable, for he is nothing of himself, and the 'likeness' has been lost by sin, but he is also great, for the

image remains, though defaced *curva*, bowed to the earth. The image for Bernard is in the will, in freedom. This is the bedrock of Cistercian mysticism, and it may be perceived behind all that St. Bernard thought and felt about friendship." (cf. essay just cited, pp. 1–2, in Fiske, 1970; the exceptionally interesting formulations *ibid.*, pp. 3–4, 15).

2. Many readers will detect the relation of the argument of these lines to the work of Henry Thode on St. Francis. It is therefore necessary to make clear that, so far as the structure of sensibility and image associated with St. Francis in the powerful pages of Thode are concerned, Bernard is here presented as a critical precursor rather than a full crystallization. Particularly interesting insights into this will be found in an essay by J. M. Déchanet entitled "On the Christology of St. Bernard." Déchanet makes two observations central to our theme. He notes how profoundly Bernard prepares the way for Francis. Thus he writes: "On a beaucoup insisté—beaucoup trop peut-être—sur ce côté sensible et quelque peu sentimental de la Christologie bernardine. On n'a pas assez remarqué et fait remarquer que les choses n'en restent pas là et qu'après avoir orienté—un des premiers semble-t-il—la dévotion chrétienne vers une attitude qui trouvera dans un saint François d'Assise son expression la plus aiguë, et son orientation définitive dans la Dévotion Moderne, saint Bernard est revenu à l'antique tradition de l'Eglise." However, one must not overlook the fact that Bernard's Christology does allow for a sharp distinction in a double approach to Christ through a double love and a double knowledge "selon le chair et selon l'esprit-libre" in accordance with the text (as Déchanet reminds us) of St. Paul.

The full context of this passage is of central importance for the argument of this essay. See Déchanet (1955: 65).

For extended evidences on the central importance of friend and friendship in the twelfth and thirteenth centuries, see Egenter (1928); Mills (1937); Nelson (1949, ed. 1969).

3. Mother Adele M. Fiske, RSCJ, has published many learned and valuable essays on this theme which are now published in the CIDOC Series at Cuernavaca, Mexico. The most interesting of these essays from the point of view of the present paper are listed in the References.

4. Certain insight into this theme, albeit from a special point of view, will be found in the writings of Carl Schmitt (1927; 1934). Cf. the work by Schmitz (1965); also cf. Fijalkowski (1968).

5. Abelard (tr. Luscombe, 1971). A fuller understanding of the varying experiences of guilt and systems of imputation of liability is a major desideratum of present-day comparative historical sociology. Some suggestions along these lines will be found in Nelson (1973). As the latter essay implies, Nietzsche and Freud have not spoken the last word on the matters above. A great deal remains to be derived from Durkheim and the Durkheimians; cf., e.g., Glotz (1904), Fauconnet (1928), Harrison (1912), Murray (1925), Cornford (1934, 1912).

6. Too few authors have given due weight to this critical fact. Studies and texts on the developments of the idea of conscience will be found in the following: Kirk (1927); Lottin (1940–60), esp. Vol. III, Pt. 2, 1949, 103–468; Hofmann (1941); Walter of Bruges (ed. Longpré, 1928); Nelson (1965a).

7. I made this point many years ago in my master's thesis at Columbia (1933); my *Idea of Usury* (1949). The point is not given due stress in recent studies of moral theology in the twelfth and thirteenth centuries. See, e.g., Baldwin (1970); Michaud-Quantin (1962).

8. For appreciations of Abelard's role here, see Knowles (1964); Kneale (1962); Jolivet (1969).

9. Pirenne (1936); Le Goff (1957); also see many excellent articles to be found in *Cambridge Medieval History*, Vols. 5–8; cf. esp. the chapters by A. H. Thompson, H. D. Hazeltine, E. A. Armstrong, G. Mollat, C. Roth, E. Power, E. Underhill, H. Pirenne; see also Southern (1953); Previté-Orton (1951); Boase (1933).

10. For Waldo, see Wakefield and Evans (1969), pp. 200–210 and *passim*; also Davison (1926); Thode (1904).

11. I am bound to report that as I was completing the last draft of this paper, there came to hand an eloquent essay by Father M. D. Chenu (O.P.) which paralleled the emphasis of the present essay on the critical importance of the twelfth-century developments for the history of the transformations of conscience and consciousness. See Chenu (1969). A glimmering of a related idea will be found in A. V. Murray (1967).

REFERENCES

ABELARD   (see Luscombe.)

ANCIAUX, PAUL

1949   *La théologie du Sacrament de Pénitence au XIIe siècle.* Louvain/Gembloux: E. Nauwelaerts et J. Duculot.

BALDWIN, JOHN W.

1970   *Master, Princes and Merchants: The Social Views of Peter the Chanter and His Circle.* 2 vols. Princeton: Princeton University Press.

BARKER, ERNEST

1948   *Traditions of Civility.* Cambridge: Cambridge University Press.

BARTH, KARL

1960   *Anselm: Fides quaerens intellectum (Anselm's Proof of the Existence of God in the Context of His Theological Scheme).* Richmond, Va.: John Knox.

BERTOLA, ERMENEGILDO

1970   *Il Problema dell concienza nella teologia monastica del XII secolo.* Padua: Il Pensiero Medievale (Collana di storia della filosofia, Ser. 2, Vol. 1).

BLAKNEY, R.

1957   *Meister Eckhardt: A Modern Translation.* New York: Harper Torchbooks.

BLOCH, MARC

(1961)   *Feudal Society.* Trans. by L. A. Manyon. 2 vols. Chicago:
1964   University of Chicago Press.

BOASE, T. S. R.

1933   *Boniface VIII.* London: Constable.

BOZEMAN, ADDA B.

(1960)   *Politics and Culture in International History.* Princeton:
1966   Princeton University Press.

BROWN, NORMAN O.

(1959)   *Life Against Death.* Middletown, Conn. Wesleyan Uni-
1970   versity Press.

1966   *Love's Body.* New York: Random House.

BURCKHARDT, JACOB

(1860)   *The Civilization of the Renaissance in Italy.* Trans. by
1958   S. Middlemore. 2 vols. New York: Harper Torchbooks.

BUTLER, DOM CUTHBERT

(1922)
1966   *Western Mysticism.* New York: Harper Torchbooks.

BUTLER, H. E. (TRANS.)

1949   *The Chronicles of Jocelin of Brakeland (Concerning the Acts of Samson, Abbott of the Monastery of St. Edmund).* New York: Oxford University Press.

CHENU, M. D., O.P.

(1957)   *Nature, Man and Society in the Twelfth Century.* Trans-
1968   lated from the French by J. Taylor and L. K. Little. Chicago: University of Chicago Press.

1969   *L'éveil de la conscience dans la civilisation médiévale.* (Conference Albert 'Le-Grand 1968). Montreal: Institut d'études médiévales; Paris: Librairie J. Vrin.

CHRISTINA OF MARKYATE (see Talbot, 1959.)

CLAGETT, MARSHALL
ET AL. (EDS.)

1961   *Twelfth-Century Europe and the Foundations of Modern Society*. Madison: University of Wisconsin Press.

CORNFORD, F. M.

1934   *Origins of Attic Comedy*. Cambridge: Cambridge University Press.

(1912)   *From Religion to Philosophy: A Study in the Origins of*
1968   *Western Speculation*. New York: Harper Torchbooks.

DAVISON, E. S.

1926   *Forerunners of St. Francis and Other Studies*. London: J. Cape.

DECHANET, DOM J. M.

1955   "La Christologie de Saint Bernard". *Bernard von Clairvaux, Mönch und Mystiker*. Ed. with an introduction by J. Lortz. Wiesbaden: F. Steiner Verlag.

DOUIE, DECIMA

1932   *The Nature and Effect of the Fraticelli Heresy*. Manchester: Manchester University Press.

DURKHEIM, EMILE

(1893)   *On the Division of Labor in Society*. Translated by G.
1933   Simpson. New York: Macmillan.

1955   *Pragmatisme et sociologie*. Paris: J. Vrin.

ECKHART, MEISTER   (See Blackney.)

EGENTER, R.

1928   *Gottesfreundschaft: Die Lehre von der Gottesfreundschaft in der Scholastik und Mystik des 12. und 13 Jahrhunderts*. Augsburg: B. Filser.

FAUCONNET, PAUL

1928   *La Responsabilité: Etude de sociologie*. New York: Stechert-Hafner.

FEUERBACH, LUDWIG

(1841)   *The Essence of Christianity*. Trans. by G. Eliot. Edited
1957   by B. Nelson. New York: Harper Torchbooks.

(1844)   *The Essence of Faith According to Luther*. Trans. by M.
1967   Cherno. New York: Harper and Row.

FIJALKOWSKI, JURGEN

1968   "Carl Schmitt." Pp. 58–60 in D. L. Sills (ed.), *International Encyclopaedia of the Social Sciences,* Vol. 14. New York: Free Press.

FISKE, MOTHER ADELE, RCSJ

(1955)
1970   *The Survival and Development of the Ancient Concept of Friendship in the Early Middle Ages.* Ph.D. Diss., 1955. Now published under the title *Friends and Friendship in the Monastic Tradition,* CIDOC Cuaderno No. 51, Cuernavaca, Mexico: Central Intercultural de Documentation. The main chapters drawn on here are:
     "St. Augustine and Friendship"
     "Aelred of Rievaulx/Idea of Friendship and Love"
     "Saint Anselm and Friendship"
     *"St. Bernard of Clairvaux and Friendship" (2 Parts)
     "William of St. Thierry and Friendship"

1965   "Paradisus Homo Amicus." *Speculum* **40**: 436–459.

GERBER, UWE

1970   *Disputatio als Sprache des Glaubens* . . . Zurich, EVZ-Verlag.

GILSON, ETIENNE

1940a   *The Mystical Theology of St. Bernard of Clairvaux.* Trans. by A. H. C. Downes. New York: Sheed and Ward.
1940b   *The Spirit of Medieval Philosophy.* New York: Scribner.

GLORIEUX, P. (ED.)

1953   "Walter of St. Victor's 'Contra Quattuor Labyrinthos Franciae.'" *Archives d'histoire doctrinale et littéraire du Moyen Age* **19**: 187–355.

GLOTZ, GUSTAVE

1904   *La solidarité de la famille dans le droit criminel en Grèce.* Paris: Fontemoing.

HARRISON, JANE

1912   *Themis.* Cambridge: Cambridge University Press.

HASKINS, C. H.

(1927)
1961   *The Renaissance of the 12th Century.* New York: Meridian.

HOFMANN, R.

1941   *Die Gewissenslehre des Walter von Brugge, O.F.M., und die Entwicklung der Gewissenslehre in der Hochscholas-*

tik. Münster: Aschendorffsche Verlagsbuchhandlung BGPTM.

ICHSCDM

1963–70   (International Commission for a History of the Scientific and Cultural Development of Mankind.) *History of Mankind: Cultural and Scientific Development.* 6 vols. New York: Harper and Row.

JOCELIN DE BRAKELAND   (see Butler, 1949)

JOLIVET, JEAN

1969   *Arts du langage et théologie chez Abelard.* Paris: J. Vrin

KIRK, KENNETH E.

(1927)   *Conscience and Its Problems: An Introduction to Casuistry.* London: Longmans, Green.
1948

KNEALE, WILLIAM
KNEALE, MARTHA

1962   *The Development of Logic.* Oxford: Clarendon Press.

KNOWLES, DAVID

1964   *The Evolution of Medieval Thought.* New York: Vintage

LANDGRAF, ARTHUR

1934   *Ecrits théologiques de l'école d'Abelard.* Louvain: Spicilegium sacrum Louvaniense.

LEA, H. C.

(1887)   *A History of the Inquisition of the Middle Ages.* 3 vols. New York: Harbor Press.
1955

LECLERQ, JEAN

1945   "L'amitié dans les lettres au moyen âge: Autour d'un manuscript de la bibliothèque de Pétrarque." *Revue du moyen-âge latin* 1: 391–410.

1960   *The Love of Learning and the Desire for God: A Study of Monastic Culture.* Trans. by C. Misrachi. New York Columbia University Press.

LE GOFF, JACQUES

1957   *Les intellectuels au moyen âge.* Paris: Editions du Séuil

LONGPRE, E. (ED.)

1928   *Quaestiones disputatae du Gauthier de Bruges* (Les philosophes belges, Vol. 10). Louvain: E. Nauwelaerts.

LOTTIN, DOM O.

1940–60   *Psychologie et morale aux douzième et treizième siècles.* 6 vols. Louvain: Abbaye do Mont César.

LUSCOMBE, D. E.
(ED. AND TRANS.)

1971   *Peter Abelard's Ethics.* Oxford: Clarendon Press.

MARCUSE, HERBERT

(1955)
1966   *Eros and Civilization.* New York: Vintage.

1964   *One-Dimensional Man.* Boston: Beacon Press.

MAUSS, MARCEL

1954   *The Gift.* Trans. by Ian Cunnison. Glencoe, Ill. Free Press.

MERTON, R. K.

(1938)
1970   *Science, Technology and Society in Seventeenth Century England.* With a new introduction by the author. New York: Harper Torchbook, 1970.

MICHAUD-QUANTIN, PIERRE

1962   *Sommes de casuistique et manuels de confession au moyen-âge.* Montreal: Librairie Dominicaine.

MILLS, LAURENS J.

1937   *One Soul in Bodies Twain: Friendship in Tudor Literature and Stuart Drama.* Bloomington, Ind. Indiana University Press.

MORRISON, KARL F.

1969   *Tradition and Authority in the Western Church, 300–1140.* Princeton, N.J.: Princeton University Press.

MURRAY, ALBERT V.

1967   *Abelard and St. Bernard: A Study in Twelfth Century "Modernism."* Manchester: Manchester University Press.

MURRAY, GILBERT

1925   *Five Stages of Greek Religion.* Oxford: Clarendon Press.

NELSON, BENJAMIN

1933   "Robert de Curzon's Campaign against Usury." Unpublished M.A. Thesis, Columbia University Library.

1939–44   (with Joshua Starr) "The Legend of the Divine Surety and the Jewish Moneylender." *Annuaire de l'institut de philologie et d'histoire orientales et slaves* 7: 289–338.

1947

"The Usurer and the Merchant Prince: Italian Businessmen and the Ecclesiastical Law of Restitution. 1100–1550." *Journal of Economic History* 7: 104–122.

(1949)
1969

The Idea of Usury: From Tribal Brotherhood to Universal Otherhood, 2nd edition. Chicago: University of Chicago Press.

1961

"Social Structure, Cultural Process, Personality System: Boundary Paradigms." Unpublished manuscript.

1962a

"Phenomenological Psychiatry, Daseinsanalyse and American Existential Analysis." *Psychoanalysis and the Psycho-Analytic Review* 48: 3–23.

1962b

"Sociology and Psychoanalysis on Trial: An Epilogue." *Psychoanalysis and the Psychoanalytic Review* 49: 2, 144–160.

1964

"Actors, Directors, Roles, Cues, Meanings, Identities: Further Thoughts on 'Anomie.' " *Psychoanalytic Review* 51: 135–160.

1965a

"Probablists, Anti-Probablists, and the Quest for Certitude in the 16th and 17th Centuries." *Actes du Xme Congrès internationale d'histoire des sciences (Proceedings of the Xth International Congress for the History of Science)* 1: 102–107, Paris: Herrman.

1965b

"Self-Images and Systems of Spiritual Direction in the History of European Civilization." Pp. 49–103 in S. Z. Klausner (ed.), *The Quest for Self-Control*. New York: Free Press.

(1965c)

"Discussion on Herbert Marcuse: 'Industrialization and Capitalism.' " In O. Stammer (ed.), *Max Weber und die Soziologie heute*. Verhändlung des 15. deutschen Soziologientages. Tübingen, J. C. B. Mohr. Trans. *Max Weber and Sociology Today*. New York. Harper & Row. Pp. 161–171.

1968

"Scholastic Rationales of 'Conscience,' Early Modern Crises of Credibility and the Scientific Technological Revolutions of the 17th and 20th Centuries." *Journal for the Scientific Study of Religion* 7: 155–177.

1969

"Conscience and the Making of Early Modern Cultures: The Protestant Ethic Beyond Max Weber." *Social Research* 36: 4–21.

1971

"The Medieval Canon Law of Contracts, Renaissance 'Spirit of Capitalism,' and the Reformation 'Conscience': A Vote *For* Max Weber." Pp. 525–548 in *Philomathes: Studies and Essays in the Humanities in Honor of Philip Merlan*. The Hague: Nijhoff. Translated into French and published in *Archives de Sociologie des religions* 4: 3–23, 1972.

(1970)
1972a
"The Omnipresence of the Grotesque." Pp. 172–185 in S. Sears and G. W. Lord (eds.), *The Discontinuous Universe*. New York: Basic Books.

1972b
" 'Communities,' 'Societies,' 'Civilizations': Post-Millennial Views on the Masks and Faces of Change." Pp. 105–133 in M. Stanley (ed.), *Social Development: Critical Perspectives*. New York: Basic Books.

1972c
"The Turnings of Men's Societies, Histories, Futures. In Memory of Copernicus, 1473–1543." Unpublished paper delivered at a Symposium on "Man, Nature and Society," Monmouth College, West Long Branch, N.J., April 27, 1972.

1973a
"Civilizational Complexes and Intercivilizational Encounters." *Sociological Analysis* 34: 2, 79–105.

1973b
"Weber's *Protestant Ethic*: Its Origins, Wanderings and Foreseeable Futures." Pp. 71–130 in C. Y. Glock and P. Hammond (eds.) *Beyond the Classics*. New York: Harper Torchbooks.

NORDSTRÖM, JOHAN

1933
Moyen Âge et Renaissance, Essai Historique. Trans. by T. Hammer. Paris: Stock.

PIRENNE, HENRI

(1936)
1956
The Economic and Social History of Medieval Europe. New York: Harcourt, Brace.

PREVITE-ORTON, C. W.

(1937)
1951
A History of Europe, 1198–1378. New York: Barnes and Noble.

ROSZAK, THEODORE

1969
The Making of a Counter Culture: Reflections on the Technocratic Society and its Youthful Opposition. Garden City, N.Y.: Doubleday-Anchor.

SCHMITT, CARL

(1927)
1963
Der Begriff des Politischen. Berlin: Duncker und Humblot.

1934
Politische Theologie, 2nd. edition. Munich: Duncker und Humblot.

SCHMITZ, MATHIAS

1965
Die Freund-Feind-Theorie in der politischen Philosophie Carl Schmitts. Cologne/Opladen: Westdeutscher Verlag.

SCHUCKING, LEVIN J.

(1929)   *The Puritan Family*. Trans. by Brian Battershaw. New York: Schocken.

SOUTHERN, R. W.

(1953)   *The Making of the Middle Ages*. New Haven: Yale Uni-
1959   versity Press.

TALBOT, C. H.
(ED. AND TRANS.)

1959   *The Life of Christina of Markyate: A Twelfth Century Recluse*. Oxford: Clarendon Press.

TANNER, J. R.
ET AL. (EDS.)

1957–59   *Cambridge Medieval History*. 8 vols. Cambridge: Cambridge University Press.

TEGGART, FREDERICK J.

1918   *The Processes of History*. New Haven: Yale University Press.

THODE, HENRY

1904   *Franz von Assisi und die Anfänge der Kunst der Renaissance in Italien*. Berlin: G. Frote.

THOMPSON, A. H.

1957   "Medieval Doctrine to the Lateran Council of 1215." Pp. 634–698 in *The Cambridge Medieval History*, Vol. 6. Cambridge: Cambridge University Press.

TURNER, VICTOR W.

1968   *The Ritual Process: Structure and Anti-Structure*. Chicago: Aldine.

VINOGRADOFF, PAUL

1967   *Roman Law in Medieval Europe*. New York: Barnes and Noble.

WAKEFIELD, W. L.
EVANS, AUSTIN P.
(EDS. AND TRANS.)

1969   *Heresies of the High Middle Ages*. 2 vols. New York: Columbia University Press.

WALTER OF BRUGES   (see Longpré, 1928)

WALTER OF ST. VICTOR   (see Glorieux, 1953)

WEBER, MAX

1956
1968

Economy and Society. Ed. and trans. by G. Roth and C. Wittich. 3 vols. Totowa, N.J.: Bedminster Press.

(1921)
1958

The City. Trans. by G. Neuwirth and D. Martindale. Glencoe, Ill.: Free Press.

WEINGART, RICHARD E.

1970

The Logic of Divine Love. Oxford: Clarendon Press.

WHITEHEAD, ALFRED N.

1968

Science and the Modern World. New York: New American Library. (Lowell Lectures of 1925.)

WILLIAMS, WATKIN W.

1935

Saint Bernard of Clairvaux. Manchester: Manchester University Press.

Part Three
Societal Functions
of Religion Reexamined

Phillip E. Hammond

UNIVERSITY OF ARIZONA, TUCSON

Religious Pluralism and
Durkheim's Integration Thesis*

It is fair to say that Emile Durkheim, more than any other classical sociologist, created a problem for the sociology of religion. The richness of
his offering has always been mixed with a serving of confusion, a state of
affairs he presumably would have corrected had he lived longer. The
richness, of course, comes in his insistence on the essential, "sacred" element in all social relationships, an insistence which helped alert sociology
to the binding potential in all social institutions. The confusion arises,
however, because, though such a religious component can be quite easily

* Revised version of a paper presented at the 1971 meeting of the Society for the
  Scientific Study of Religion. I am indebted to Robert A. Nisbet for his helpful
  advice.

identified in primitive society where social institutions are not sharply differentiated, its elusiveness is all too great in modern settings.

Durkheim's "mechanical" society (i.e., a society integrated by religio-moral homogeneity), identified in his *Division of Labor in Society* (1933), is exemplified by the Arunta and other primitives he analyzed in *The Elementary Forms of the Religious Life* (1961). There he could use his now infamous definition of religion: "a unified system of beliefs and practices relative to sacred things . . . which unite into one single moral community called a church all those who adhere to them" (1961:62). But because he never conducted an analysis of religion in modern society (i.e., "organic" society, integrated by functional interdependence), sociologists of religion are left with an incomplete account of Durkheim's understanding of religion. Though calling a "church" the religious system among the Arunta, he very likely did *not* mean to equate their religion—its theology, ritual, and meager organization—with the Roman Catholic Church of his day, say, or with Jewish Synagogues. United into "one single moral community" people of a modern society may be, but if they are, churches as commonly understood have little or nothing to do with it. And therein lies the problem bequeathed us by Durkheim. If religion is so important an ingredient in the integration of society, and if in primitive societies this relationship can be seen, where and what are the corresponding religions of modern societies? Catholics, Jews, Protestants, Humanists, and Atheists in a single society are hardly united by their Catholicism, Judaism, and so forth. In short, what happens to Durkheim's integration thesis in societies marked by religious pluralism?

Generally speaking, Durkheim's integration thesis has been interpreted as saying that a society is integrated to the degree that its members possess a common religion. Granted, such an interpretation is understandable in one who reads Durkheim's definition of religion (that *"which unites into one single moral community"*). And other statements in *The Elementary Forms* are just as conducive to that interpretation (e.g., *"rites are means by which* the social group reaffirms itself periodically" 1961: 432.)

But it is the fact of unity more than the fact of religion with which Durkheim begins. Religion is more the *expression* of an integrated society than it is the *source* of a society's integration. "Men who feel themselves united, partially by bonds of blood, but still more by a community of interest and tradition, assemble and become conscious of their moral unity," Durkheim goes on. "They are led to represent this unity" (1961: 432). Here is the key passage. It is in this kind of reasoning that Durkheim connects religion and integration—not that religion produces the cohesive society, but rather that the phenomenon of cohesion has a religious quality.

Now this argument is not at all unknown. In 1937 Talcott Parsons had observed that the real significance of Durkheim's work on primitive religion lay in his recognition not that "religion is a social phenomenon" but that "society is a religious phenomenon" (1937: 427). In other words, the very existence of society—the fact of stable social interaction itself—implies religion. The question is whether and how it is expressed.

Durkheim, of course, found religion expressed in the totemistic practices of the Arunta. The persuasiveness of his argument (where it *is* persuasive; see Demereth and Hammond, 1968: Ch. 1, for criticisms of Durkheim) lies in the rather direct link between the *experiences* of unity allegedly felt by the Arunta and their theological and ritualistic *expressions* of that unity. But Durkheim did not mean his theory to rest on the directness of this link. ("We cannot repeat too frequently that the importance which we attach to totemism is absolutely independent of whether it was ever universal or not" [1961: 114]). Hence, the implication of my opening paragraphs was that had Durkheim lived longer he very likely would have pursued the religious significance of societal integration in a modern context. When he asked rhetorically, "What essential difference is there between an assembly of Christians celebrating the principal dates of the life of Christ . . . and a reunion of citizens commemorating . . . some great event in the national life?" (1961: 475), he was hinting at this issue certainly. But it was only a hint. Was he noting that Christianity is no longer the language by which unity is expressed? Did he believe he could identify the "religions" which express for modern societies what totemism expressed for the Arunta?

Answers to these questions are not at all easy to come by. The interest in recent years in civil religion (Cherry, 1971) gives evidence of one rather direct approach to Durkheim's thesis—that of expecting in the modern society a reasonably close analogue to totemism. This work in civil religion, however, fails to deal with the "linkage" that totemism so conveniently provided. Why should a people, *dis*united by denominationalism and multiple traditions, be led to represent their unity anyway? Around what are they unified? Finding *a* religion present in a contemporary, religiously pluralistic society is a sizable task, but discovering why there is a religion—and how it came about—is an even larger task.

This essay makes no claim to resolving the larger task, of course, but it does attempt to outline two related issues: (1) How has a uniting religion emerged out of the variety of Christian groups in the Western world? (2) Is this religion simply "there," to be expressed by those who choose to do so, or are there structural settings (analogous to the "effervescent" phases in Durkheim's Arunta) where its enunciation is, so to speak, fostered, even compelled?

The commoner interpretation of Durkheim's thesis—that a society is integrated to the degree it possesses a common religion—is therefore given two twists in what follows: First, the major terms in the thesis are reversed and taken as saying that to the degree a society is integrated, the expression of its integration will occur in ways that can be called religious. And second, because conflict obviously endangers societal integration, wherever resolution of conflict occurs is a likely scene for the expression of this religion. In the religiously plural society, churches do not resolve conflicts, thus they need not express the common religion. On the other hand, legal institutions *are* called upon to resolve conflicts, and it is they which become a major channel for expression of the common religion [1].

In developing this argument I shall (1) take a close look at the notion of religious pluralism, finding it to mean much more than mere multiplicity of groups defined by ecclesiastical characteristics; (2) look at the historical form taken by pluralism in the Western world as a set of pressures to which responses were required; and (3) identify the "religiousness" of legal institutions. In so doing, I am attempting to extrapolate Durkheim's integration thesis into religiously plural societies.

RELIGIOUS PLURALISM: THE TERM

The term "pluralism" is widely used today by social scientists. At a minimal level it refers simply to heterogeneity, though in the hands of political scientists, authropologists, and political sociologists it stirs up such arguments as whether pluralism impedes or secures democratic government. Others refer to "cultural" versus "structural" pluralism, to "sociological" versus "political" pluralism. Theorists differ in their understanding of how pluralism works—whether it provides multiple channels to power-holders or supplies group anchorage for would-be alienated individuals. And there is the intricate argument that pluralism permits multiple—but contradictory—group memberships, thus making political conflict erupt more often within an individual or a group than between contending political factions [2].

For all of the specifications of "pluralism," however, the concept as used in political analysis almost always refers to heterogeneity of *groups*. And, since modern societies commonly contain several religious groups, the notion of religious pluralism has been seen as analogous to—or even synonymous with—racial or ethnic pluralism (see, e.g., Coleman, 1956).

There is, of course, nothing incorrect in this usage. Methodists *are* a different group from Presbyterians, just as Catholics are different from Protestants, Christians from Jews. Still, the incompleteness of this understanding of religious pluralism is better seen in the context not of denominational differences but of historico-cultural differences: the Judeo-Christian tradition versus the Islamic tradition, a Western versus an Oriental religious outlook, a mystical versus an ascetic perspective. What can religious pluralism mean if reference is not to denominational or group heterogeneity, but to a multiplicity of whole nonempirical belief systems? Understood this second way, religious pluralism builds on the classical understanding of religion in sociology and therefore requires fuller discussion.

Whether formulated by Durkheim (a system of beliefs and practices related to sacred things), or by Weber (that which finally makes events meaningful), or by Tillich (whatever is of ultimate concern), religion in its "classical" sense refers not so much to labels on a church building as to the imagery (myth, theology, etc.) by which people make sense of their lives—their "moral architecture," if you will. (Berger and Luckmann, 1966b, refer to "sacred comprehensive meanings for everyday life.") That human beings differ in their sensitivity to, and success in, this matter of "establishing meaning" there can be no doubt. Moreover, people certainly differ in the degree to which they regard historic, institutionalized formulations as personally satisfactory. Thus, some are churchgoers, some are not; some would change the prevailing theology or ritual, others would not. Societies might be said to differ in whether they offer only one or more than one system for bestowing ultimate meaning.

Teggart asserted that social change results from "the collision of groups from widely different habitats and hence of different idea-systems" (1918: 118). And if Teggart assumed that human history records few stable "pluralistic" situations, (i.e., single habitats with multiple idea-systems), he was very likely correct. The word "religion" in its plural form does not even enter the language of the West until the mid-seventeenth century and does not become common until the eighteenth. Closely related words —piety, obedience, reverence, worship—never do develop plural forms (Smith, 1963: 43).

Religious pluralism (in the sense "religion" is used here) is not equivalent to a choice between Rotary and Kiwanis, the Cubs or the White Sox, the Methodists or the Presbyterians. Rather, as Teggart notes, the consequence for the individual of confronting competing idea-systems is liberation from "traditional group constraints" and "enhanced autonomy" (1918: 118). Correlatively Smith observes that the word "religions" (plural form) comes into use only as one "contemplates from the outside, and abstracts, depersonalizes, and reifies the various systems of other people of which one does not oneself see the meaning or appreciate the point, let alone accept the validity" (1963: 43). In other words, though religious pluralism can mean the existence simply of religious differences, it can also refer to a situation qualitatively different from other pluralisms: when one meaning system confronts another meaning system, the very meaning of "meaning system" changes.

In the Western world, this change is most readily seen in the separation of church from state—the explicit differentiation at the structural level of religion and polity. But, as MacIntyre (1967: 54), referring to British society, contends: "it is not the case that men first stopped believing in God and in the authority of the Church, and then subsequently started behaving differently. It seems clear that men first of all lost any over-all social agreement as to the right ways to live together. . . ." The accuracy of this time sequence determines the viability of the notion of religious pluralism being presented here: if the separation of church and state is regarded as only a political event, then churches are seen as voluntary associations, and pluralism indicates merely the presence of multiple religious groupings. Alternatively, if the separation of church and state arises from a situation of competing meaning systems (i.e., is essentially a political response to a *religious* state of affairs), then the existence of multiple churches indicates something far more profound than simply a choice of religious groups. [3]. Needless to say, this latter interpretation of religious pluralism is the one used here [4].

THE GENERAL NATURE OF RELIGIOUS PLURALISM

It should be clear that the above comments are no mere attempt to legislate the use of terms in sociological discourse. They mean to suggest that, viewed in a certain way, the concept of religious pluralism can have new theoretical importance.

John Courtney Murray (1964: 27ff.), in discussing the "civilization of pluralist society," uses the notion of religious pluralism in both the senses outlined above. First, religious pluralism implies different people's different histories—here Murray is, in essence, merely relabeling those differences. Second, because discussion of concrete affairs goes on in abstract terms—in "realms of some theoretical generality"—pluralism implies the existence of different sets of terms, different realms. Discourse, Murray says, thus becomes "incommensurable" and confused.

Compare MacIntyre's analysis:

> If I tell you that "You ought to do this," . . . I present you with a claim which by the very use of these words implies a greater authority behind it than the expression of my feelings. . . . I claim, that is, that I could point to a criterion . . . you too ought to recognize. . . . It is

obvious that this activity of appealing to impersonal and independent criteria only makes sense within a community of discourse in which such criteria are established, are shared. (1967: 52)

Kingsley Davis says it more succinctly yet:

As between two different groups holding an entirely different set of common-ultimate ends, there is no recourse.

Religious pluralism need not imply entirely different sets of "common-ultimate ends," of "impersonal and independent criteria," or of "moral architectures." Even so, it may still be argued that *some* level of sharedness must exist for institutions to exist, and religious pluralism would appear to reduce that sharedness.

But does it? Once a society permits multiple meaning systems to exist side by side, does it cease to *be* a society? Doubtless that can happen, but it is more normal for a society to work toward a new, more generalized, common, meaning system. It is easier to form a social contract than for all to go to war against all. Still, as is now recognized, "mere" social agreement, a rationally derived document, is insufficient. Commitment to its rightness is also required. Every contract has its noncontractual element, Durkheim said; every legal order possesses its charismatic quality, noted Weber. And that noncontractual element, that charismatic quality, that commitment is articulated finally in terms which are (by definition) "religious." In a single society, then, can more than one set of religious terms exist? And, if they do coexist, can they continue to function as they are thought to function in a society with a religious monopoly [5]?

Obviously individuals do not generally confront each other's "moral architectures" in any direct fashion. Such situations do arise, of course, but manifestations of moral commitment more often occur as institutional conflicts and conflict resolution. The city government decides between road improvement and welfare payments. The corporation chooses to reward longevity or quality of service. The church elects to immerse or sprinkle. The citizenry is ordered to stop plowing and go to war. In all such instances (assuming the absence of sheer coercion), persons feel—or can come to feel—an *obligation* to justify their behavior. But this is not because of any prerecognized specific norm; there is no detailed prescription for every conceivable act. Rather the obligation is in "realms of some theoretical generality," to use Murray's phrase. It is, as Talcott Parsons (1969: 445) notes, a "generalized obligation" which is morally binding. A person or an institution demonstrates integrity not only by choosing right from wrong in a concrete situation but by maintaining a "commitment to the pattern over a wide range of different actual and potential decisions, in differing situations, with differing consequences and levels of predictability of such consequences."

Such commitment—in any but the simplest, thoroughly ascribed society—must be to a "generalized symbolic medium," not to specific norms (*ibid*: 455). Given the integrative potential of such a generalized symbolic medium—of action to action, policy to policy, person to person—the question can be raised whether, in a single society, more than one such medium can exist. Or, if "pluralism" exists, can any one medium command the same commitment it might in a monopolistic situation?

The relation between a "generalized symbolic medium of values" and what earlier was referred to as "moral architecture" or "set of religious terms" is quite clear and has long been recognized. The "primary moral leadership in many societies," Parsons writes (*ibid*.: 452), "has been grounded in religious bodies, especially their professional elements such as priesthoods."

THE PRESSURES OF PLURALISM

Religious pluralism, as just interpreted, clearly has enormous impact on those institutions designated as religious before pluralization: churches, clergy, theology, and so forth. In some sense they become "less" religious if they no longer enjoy a monopoly in articulating the ideology by which ultimate meaning is bestowed. Reduction in ecclesiastical power, the transformation of ritual into a "leisure" time activity, and the "privatizing" in general of theology into pastoral counseling or religious "preferences"—all reflect this altered status [6].

If churches become less religious in some ways, however, some other place in the social structure may be said to become *more* religious. If pressures are great in a society for a single generalized symbolic medium, a single reality-defining agency—and churches no longer can receive those pressures—then the pressures will be exerted elsewhere. It is my contention that *legal* institutions feel those pressures greatly, that portrayal of the sacred or articulation of the charismatic tends to be expected of them. In this special sense, the law becomes more "religious." In the pages that follow, then, I attempt (1) to show how a "common religion" emerged out of religious pluralism, and (2) to illustrate how current legal institutions express that common religion. I believe that in this effort a new meaning can be placed on Durkheim's integration thesis.

Puritanism and the Common Law. The impact of Puritanism on the common law is now widely acknowledged (Pound, 1910, 1921). More recently the close connections between Puritan theology and early seventeenth-century common law have been traced by David Little (1968). Considering the volatility of the seventeenth century, it is hardly surprising that religious and legal reformation shared common elements. But tracing out those elements in detail is, as Little shows, an exceedingly difficult task. For example, the codifying common lawyer, Sir Edward Coke, remained a loyal Anglican all his life, paying no special attention to Puritan theological debates going on at the time. And yet, in the jurisdictional struggle between church courts and common law courts, Coke not only claimed the latter's superiority but justified the claim by reference to common law tradition (Little, 1969: 185). In so doing he effectively sided with Puritanism in its struggle against Anglican traditionalism.

Pound's assertion of Puritanism's "impact" (1921) is not well documented. It does little more than show how "individualism" in the common law had analogues in Puritanism, but as Pound himself makes clear, this individualism in the common law has many other roots. Moreover, Puritanism may have contributed (or did contribute) as much to a renewed interest in "collectivism" in the law, considering the stress it placed on the covenant, on the "contractualism" it posited between man and God or man and man [7]. David Little claims that "explicit Puritan influence on the particulars of the common law was nil" (1969: 239). Nevertheless, he continues:

> It is my contention that the concurrence of important tensions and changes in legal and religious outlook toward the end of the sixteenth and at the beginning of the seventeenth centuries is more than coincidence. In this I believe I am not far from Pound's interest . . . [in his effort] to understand how a system of law comes to embody and perpetuate a general way of looking at social life—a special system of values. (*Ibid.*: 240)

The argument by which Little so carefully weaves together these two entities—Puritanism and common law—does not follow Pound, then, in method. He does not see a *direct* impact of one on the other. Nor does he follow Eusden (1958), who argues that the close alliance between Puritans and common lawyers of the period came chiefly from their shared distaste for royal domination, not from any mutual intellectual heritage, purpose, or set of values. Instead, Little argues, the common law was in a fluid state at the time, seeking principles of legal interpretation for frequent new activities and conflicts. Where might such principles be found? More accurately, perhaps, how might they be articulated? Little's answer is twofold: first, that the religious revolution of the seventeenth century—a revolution that defined new "order" in the church, in the parish, in the "priesthood of all believers," and in social life generally—provided an ideologically parallel case; and, second, that Calvinistic and, later, English theological conceptions found outlet in the common law's articulation of its principles.

> Obviously, the crown and the courts could not work together indefinitely so long as each was making the kind of claims to authority it was. A solution had to be found, but it would have to come from sources other than the old English order [i.e., the "ancient realm or the Anglican tradition"]. . . . The deep-seated tensions of early seventeenth-century English society had to be solved by some rather novel rearrangements of political and legal institutions. (*Ibid.*: 225)

In other words, Puritanism was an "ordering" ideology *available* to a common law seeking solid foundation.

What is underplayed in this approach, however, is the additional role Puritan theology played in *legitimizing* religious pluralism. Calvinism, Anabaptism, and subsequent "Protestantisms" contributed a new interpretation of order; but *they also provided a theological rationale for ending church monopolies on articulating that order*, thus forcing legal institutions into the attempt themselves. As the historian of nationalism puts it:

> The Protestant Revolution, by disrupting the Catholic Church and subjecting the Christian community to national variations of form and substance, dissolved much of the intellectual and moral cement which had long held European peoples together. At the same time it gave religious sanction to the notion, already latent, that each people, and each alone, possessed a pure faith and a divine mission. (Hayes, 1960: 36)

Puritanism, then, did more than offer an alternative articulation of social values for seventeenth-century England, even as it did more than provide parallel support to common lawyers in their fight against traditionalism. In addition—though not all at once, of course—Puritanism forced onto society's agenda the item of pluralism, the question of "religious liberty," the separation of church and state, the matter of "intellectual and moral cement." In so doing, it left legal systems, especially the common law tradition, the task of formulating a new religion, so to speak. This process is most clearly evidenced in the activity surrounding the U.S. Supreme Court, to which we turn presently. First, however, two intermediate steps.

Step One: The Doctrine of Religious Liberty. It has just been argued that Protestantism provided a theological rationale for ending church monopoly. Any doctrine of religious liberty will lead to the separation of civil authority from matters of faith, hence possibly to pluralism. But inasmuch as Zwingli's Zurich, Calvin's Geneva, or Puritan New England, are normally regarded as having been religiously intolerant, the task of tracing the establishment of religious liberty is a critical one.

The first *idea* of religious freedom is, of course, lost to history, but it may be accurate to suggest 1523 as a significant date in the *social structuring* of the idea in the West. For it was in October of that year that Conrad Grebel and others (who "became" the Anabaptist movement) challenged Zwingli's use of civil power to enforce religious conformity. Bender highlights it thus:

> Here is where the first break in the Reformation occurred that led inevitably to the founding of Anabaptism. In 1523–25, at Zurich, are the crossroads from which two roads lead down through history: the road of the free church of committed Christians separated from the state with full religious liberty, and the road of the state church, territorially fixed, depending on state support, and forcibly suppressing all divergence, the road of intolerance and persecution. (1953: 8)

The "logic" of religious toleration was established, then, even though occasions of reneging were obviously frequent. Thus, Geneva must be considered a theocracy by all accounts, but Calvinism's English counterparts, the Presbyterians, really had no rebuttal for their "leftist Puritan" challenger, Henry Robinson. A real commitment to the doctrine of predestination, he said, precluded religious persecution. Those not elected by God could not possibly be saved; "uniformity of profession" cannot be confused with "certainty of grace" (Little, 1969: 255–256). A doctrine of religious liberty and therefore of pluralism was clearly implied here, even if its widespread institutionalization was a long time in coming.

Soon after Henry Robinson came another Robinson—this one the Reverend John—who also symbolizes the Protestant theology of pluralism. As spiritual leader of what became the Mayflower Pilgrims (though he remained in Leydon, never coming to Massachusetts), John Robinson is remembered today as the author of the phrase, "The Lord hath more truth and light yet to break forth" [8]. One does not have to believe that the Massachusetts colonists *wanted* to be religiously tolerant; it is enough merely to acknowledge that a theology allowing religious liberty (or legitimating pluralism) was being clearly enunciated, however long before it became socially structured [9].

Step Two: Law and Authority in Colonial America. Not surprisingly, without many of the traditional encumbrances, the emerging American society was freer than old societies to manifest religious pluralism and its consequences. This is especially true with respect to the articulation by legal institutions in the American case most noticeably by the Supreme Court—of the newly emerging "common" religion. As will presently be shown, the history of the Court can be interpreted as a halting, hesitant, but "inevitable" effort to perform for American society the religious task of providing a common moral understanding. Before attention is given to that dependent variable, however, a second intermediate step must be taken—this time into colonial history, another arena where sociologists can fear to tread.

American colonial life has been highly romanticized. With respect to the subject at hand, should one remember witch hunts or Roger Williams? Was Massachusetts Bay a theocracy or the fount of town meeting democracy? Judgments by historians on these questions may vary, but it seems important to the thesis here to maintain that the pressures of pluralism and their impact on legal institutions did not wait for the Revolution and Constitution-making. Is there evidence in colonial America, then, that these pressures were felt from the beginning?

C. K. Shipton points out that "there never was an established church in Massachusetts, there was no agreed-upon body of dogma, and serious moral deviation was punished by the state, not the church. . . . Many of the normal functions of the established churches in Europe were here transferred to the state" (1965: 137). Towns maintained a minister at public expense, it is true, but all inhabitants, including vocal Quakers, Baptists, and Presbyterians, participated in his selection "with the result that the minister's theological difficulties were usually with the civil body rather than with the church" (Shipton, 1965: 138) [10]. Meanwhile, the civil body—township or colony—was able to escape the "chaotic confusion of laws" in England by administering them "in one tribunal," according to Howe. "Ecclesiastical, maritime, statutory, and equitable" laws were subsumed under the common law, which Bay colonists recognized "as a set of unchanging principles of public law, principles which our usage would describe as 'constitutional' " (Howe, 1965: 14–15) [11].

It may have been an intensely moralistic atmosphere, therefore, but churches had no monopoly in defining what was moral. Anticipating the distinction between "professed doctrines of religious belief" and "actions" as it arose in *Reynolds* v. *United States* (98 US 145 [1879]—a case resulting in the prohibition of plural marriage—a number of persons came to see that religious "liberty" would become behavioral license unless the "obligations between man and man shall be subject to the jurisdiction of man's tribunal" [12]. By mid-eighteenth century in New Haven, William Livingston rephrased a "Puritan principle" to read:

> The civil Power hath no jurisdiction over the Sentiments or Opinions of the subject, till such Opinions break out into Actions prejudicial to the Community, and then it is not the Opinion but the Action that is the Object of our Punishment. (Shipton, 1965: 143)

Shipton suggests that this principle of freedom of thought, often believed to be state policy first in Virginia, whence it entered the U.S. Constitution as a "natural right," may have been borrowed from Puritan New England. If, as Rossel (1970) suggests, the revivalistic Great Awakening (1730–1745) was a last ditch effort to reinstate the "old order" against the onslaught of the coming denominational pluralism, it would be accurate to say that the cause was hopeless. The Puritan "old order" itself quite clearly contained the ideas which had already destroyed its ordering capability.

But "ordering" could not be avoided. "Natural rights mean simply interests which we think ought to be secured" (Pound, 1921: 92), but it is clear that legal institutions increasingly had the task not only of securing those rights but of defining them as well. Laws, that is to say, not only would inform citizens what to do and what not to do but would have to serve as well to assess the *morality* of what they did [13]. The common law as influenced by Puritanism in England, then, was transferred to America, but in the transfer its moral-architectural ("religious") features stand out because the pressures of pluralism also stand out. To a degree hitherto unknown in the West, people were free to adopt any religion. The consequence, however, was that the simultaneously emerging common law was forced to take up the slack, giving it, as Pekelis insists, a "religious and moralistic character" (1950: 56). That is to say, the pressures for a single moral architecture (single "reality-defining" agency, single "generalized symbolic medium") were (and are) felt most in common law institutions. American society well illustrates the effect of those pressures.

LEGAL INSTITUTIONS AS RELIGION

> Indeed, the law for Coke is more than the measure of reason. It is, it would seem, the measure and source of virtue as well. (Little, 1969: 177)

> Another consequence [of the Puritan notion of covenant] was to make a moral question of everything, and yet in such a way as to make it a legal question. (Pound, 1921: 43)

Many of the fundamentals of criminal and civil law correspond to
religious injunctions. (Galanter, 1966: 223)

The institutions of the common law seem to have had a "religious"
flavor for a long time. Consider as one example the notion of "contempt
of court" as found in English and American law:

> The Anglo-American idea . . . means that the party who does not
> abide by certain specific decrees emanating from a judicial body is a
> contumacious person and may, as a rule, be held in contempt of
> court, . . . fined and jailed. . . . Now, this very concept of contempt
> simply does not belong to the world of ideas of a Latin lawyer. It
> just does not occur to him that the refusal of the defendent . . .
> may, as soon as a judicial order is issued, become a matter to a certain
> extent personal to the court, and that the court may feel hurt,
> insulted, "contemned. . . ." (Pekelis, 1950: 45-6)

Where the law is highly codified, where, so to speak, the law is asked
to specify duties—the situation more nearly found in "civil law" or Latin
cultures—the courts can act more administratively, less "judgmentally."
But where the task of justifying, articulating, or "interpreting" the law
is asked of the courts—where "aspirations" as well as "duties" Fuller,
1964) are at issue—then courts must take on a "religious" character. Only
in a sense, Pekelis reminds us, does the United States have a written constitution. "The great clauses of the Constitution, just as the more important provisions of our fundamental statutes, contain no more than an
appeal to the decency and wisdom of those with whom the responsibility
for their enforcement rests" (1950: 4). Whether courts are thought to
"interpret" or to "make" the law, the fact remains that common law
courts find and give *reasons* for their decisions. And in the act of reasoning
they do more than cite statutes: additionally they develop the single
symbolic moral universe—the moral architecture. The common law, then,
has a "collective" character quite as pronounced as the individualism
more often viewed as its distinctive feature. Any *concerted* effort to promote individual interests will yield a collective enterprise, needless to say.
But if religious liberty is among the promoted interests, the concerted
effort takes on an interpretative task on behalf of the collective.

> . . . We must say that the aspects of legal life in England and
> America . . . do not substantiate the contention of the individualistic
> character of the common-law technique. On the contrary, the strength
> of the enforcement devices, the clerical and moralistic character of
> the legal approach at large, the duty of disclosure, the close control

exercised by the community upon the individual and upon the law, if compared with the analogous legal institutions of the Latin countries, seem to disclose rather a more collectivistic than a more individualistic character of the common-law system. . . . It seems to us that what is generally considered as and taken for the individualistic aspect of American life is simply the existence and coexistence of a plurality of communities and—let's not be afraid of this quantitative element—of an extremely great number of communities of various types. (Pekelis, 1950: 66–67)

Though this essay's central notion, religious pluralism, is reduced by Pekelis to merely "communities of various types," the elements of the argument are all there by implication: (1) Plurality of religious systems requires redefinition of order but does not escape the need for order. (2) Legal institutions therefore are called upon not only to secure order but to give it a uniformly acceptable meaning as well. (3) The result is a set of legal institutions with a decided religio-moral character. The historical context of these forces in the West has led the common law to become their medium, the legal philosophy of the Enlightenment their symbols, and the U.S. Supreme Court most concretely their vehicle of expression. Only this last point will receive further elaboration.

The Religion of the Legal System: A Disappearing Rhetoric. Little documentation is needed for the claim of an expanding judiciary in American history [14]. The present thesis, however, contains a critical corollary less widely acknowledged—that with this expansion the judiciary has adopted the task of articulating the collective's moral architecture. Of course, many have spoken of "the nine high priests in their black robes" and of the sacredness imputed to the Constitution and other artifacts of the legal order [15]. But in keeping with Eugene V. Rostow's characterization of the contemporary Supreme Court as a "vital national seminar" (1952: 208), it is worth noting that the original charge to the Court was only that it render an aye or a nay. It quickly began handing down written opinions also, however, and, under Marshall, began the practice of trying for a single majority opinion, which gave "judicial pronouncements a forceful unity they had formerly lacked" (McCloskey, 1960: 40).

With the expansion of judicial *explanation* came the difficult problem of distinguishing human "actions" from religious "justifications." Reference has already been made to the *Reynolds* case in 1879, wherein Mormon polygamy was outlawed. "Can a man excuse his practices . . . because of his religious belief?" asked Mr. Chief Justice Waite. "To permit this would be to make the professed doctrines of religious belief superior to

130 SOCIETAL FUNCTIONS OF RELIGION REEXAMINED

the law of the land. . . ." Were "religious" exceptions to be made, the opinion held, "then those who do *not* make polygamy a part of their religious belief *may be found guilty* and punished" (98 US 145 [1879] italics added).

Here, in a single decision, is exemplified the paradox confronting legal institutions in religiously plural societies—a paradox which hands to them the erstwhile religious task of articulating a moral architecture. On the one hand, religious beliefs cannot be used by citizens to justify any and all actions. On the other hand, truly religious belief, it is thought, *ought* to be manifest in action; else why assume that in finding Reynolds innocent, society might find non-polygamists guilty? Protestantism enhanced the development of the concept of religious liberty and thus religious pluralism. But this in turn led, as Pound and others saw, to making evertyhing a moral question yet also a legal question. Courts, then, could not resolve legal questions without resorting to moral answers. But the rhetoric and imagery available for expressing these moral answers could decreasingly be drawn from the language of orthodox religion as the implications of religious pluralism became clearer. Instead, the rhetoric— if it was to have *general* meaning—had to be drawn from another sphere, but from a sphere no less religious in its functioning [16].

This change in rhetoric is readily illustrated in so-called church-state cases [17].

1. *Church of the Holy Trinity* v. *United States* 143 US 226 (1892). Events in our national life, wrote Mr. Justice Brewer, "affirm and reaffirm that this is a religious nation." Moreover, in holding that a statute prohibiting aliens to be imported for labor was not intended to prevent a church from hiring a foreign Christian minister, the Court quoted approvingly from two previous judicial opinions showing that "we are a Christian people, and the morality of the country is deeply ingrafted upon Christianity" and "the Christian religion is a part of the common law of Pennsylvania."

2. *United States* v. *Macintosh* 283 US 605 (1931). Forty years later the Court was faced with a question of whether citizenship could be denied a person because he held reservations about taking arms in defense of his country. It is evident, said Mr. Justice Sutherland, "that he means to make his own interpretation of the will of God the decisive test which shall conclude the government. . . . We are a Christian people, according to one another the equal right of religious freedom, and acknowledging with reverence the duty of obedience to the will of God. But, also, we are a nation with the duty to survive." Citizenship was denied.

3. *Zorach* v. *Clauson* 343 US 306 (1952). Two decades later, in its decision that released-time religious instruction is permitted provided that it occur off public school grounds, the Court asserted—in Mr. Justice Douglas' words—that "We are a religious people whose institutions presuppose a Supreme Being." This statement, as well as the result, drew the dissent of Mr. Justice Black, who claimed that "Before today, our judicial opinions have refrained from drawing invidious distinctions between those who believe in no religion and those who do believe."

4. *United States* v. *Seeger* 380 US 163 (1965). Here, in another conscientious objection case, the Court decided that "belief in relation to a Supreme Being," thus exemption, is to be determined by "whether a given belief that is sincere and meaningful occupies a place in the life of its possessor parallel to that filled by the orthodox belief in God of one who clearly qualifies for the exemption." More than monotheistic beliefs qualify—Mr. Justice Clark noting the "vast panoply of beliefs" prevalent [18]. Seeger's beliefs qualified, therefore, and he was exempted.

5. *Welsh* v. *United States* 398 US 333 (1970). The result in *Welsh* was identical with that in *Seeger*, the Court finding the facts to be the same, so that the legal application was the same. The opinion—by Mr. Justice Black—contained an even more expanded notion of religion, however. Exemption from Selective Service is to be allowed on "registrant's moral, ethical, or religious beliefs about what is right and wrong," provided "those beliefs be held with the strength of traditional religious convictions." Moreover, inasmuch as the Government had argued that Welsh's beliefs were less religious than Seeger's, the Court responded that this "places undue emphasis on the registrant's interpretation of his own beliefs. The Court's statement in *Seeger* that a registrant's characterization of his own belief as 'religious' should carry great weight . . . does not imply that his declaration that his views are nonreligious should be treated similarly . . . very few registrants are fully aware of the broad scope of the word 'religious' [as interpreted by law since *Seeger*]."

It is instructive to see what developed in the course of a century. In *Reynolds* the Court recognized that "religion" is not defined in the Constitution, but agreed that even if the state had no power over opinion, it was free to regulate actions. And polygamy, it said, has always been "odious" to Western nations, leading as it does to "stationary despotism." Therefore, though there is no implication that Mormon *opinion* is punishable by law, Mormon *action* clearly is. A few years later the Court can speak of the "Christianity" of the nation, of its people, and of its morality, which therefore permits a church (though not a secular employer) to import alien labor. Though a *church* is entitled to special exemption from a law for religious reasons, however, an *individual* is not. Even if "We are a Christian people," and even if Macintosh is a professor in a Christian seminary, the government's interest in self-preservation is greater than a person's right to religious free exercise.

In *Zorach* v. *Clausen* the remark that "We are a religious people" might be seen as gratuitous—this is the only case here involving the Establishment rather than the Free Exercise Clause—except that what is allowed by the Court is a *religious* program. Black, in dissent, wonders about the rights of *irreligious* people; are they protected by the First Amendment mention of "religion"? They might be, it would appear from the *Seeger* and *Welsh* cases, since what is "religion" gets an even broader interpretation, to the point in *Welsh* where Black says that the law may have to regard as religious something which persons themselves claim is non-religious.

At this point, it would seem, the definition of religion is so broad as to be meaningless in deciding cases—at least free exercise cases. From a time when the rhetoric used to justify a decision could be presumptively Christian, there arrives the occasion when it cannot even be presumptively religious. *Seeger* and *Welsh* set out a distinction—sincere and meaningful belief occupying a place parallel to that of orthodox belief—but as Harlan argues in his concurring opinion in *Welsh*:

> My own conclusion . . . is that the Free Exercise Clause does not require a State to conform a neutral secular program to the dictates of religious conscience of any group. . . . [A] state could constitutionally create exceptions to its program to accommodate religious scruples. That suggestion must, however, be qualified by the observation that any such exception in order to satisfy the Establishment Clause of the First Amendment, would have to be sufficiently broad to be religiously neutral. . . . This would require creating an exception for anyone who, as a matter of conscience, could not comply with the statute.

"Religion" for legal purposes becomes simply "conscience," and Congress, if it is to grant conscientious exemptions, "cannot draw the line between theistic or nontheistic beliefs on the one hand and secular beliefs on the other." For all intents, assuming the eventual "triumph" of Harlan's position or something like it, the law simply dispenses with the notion of religion as commonly understood. Having tried for a century to regard it on its own terms—as sacred, special, compelling—courts realize that the attempt is futile. All efforts to allow "free exercise" of religion *because it is religion* conflict with the requirement of "no establishment" or special treatment [19]. Religious pluralism requires that articulation of "highest obligation" be done not in orthodox religious language but otherwise. What form does this take?

The Religion of the Legal System: An Emerging Rhetoric. If the analysis here is correct, a new rhetoric is still in developing stages. Were this new "religion"—this new moral architecture—fully mature, it would be very much a part of the common culture.

Some clues to its development are available, however, one being Weber's discussion (1947: 342) of how "traditional" authority can be overcome on traditional grounds:

> Opposition is not directed against the system as such. It is impossible in the pure type of traditional authority for law or administrative rules to be deliberately created by legislation. What is actually new is thus claimed to have always been in force but only recently to have become known through the wisdom of the promulgator. The only documents which can play a part in the orientation of legal administration are the documents of tradition, namely precedents.

In the present terms, then, commitment to religious liberty (pluralism) makes impossible the documents (precedents, rhetoric) of any *one* religious tradition; so a new religion is found.

McCloskey's discussion of "due process" illustrates nicely how this new religion comes about. Entering the Constitution in Article IV as a doctrine of civility and procedure, the notion of due process eventuates as the center of the Fourteenth Amendment, becoming equivalent to justice itself, through "a process so subtle and complex that not even the craftsmen themselves would be fully aware of what was happening, and in the end both they and their observers could feel that the doctrine they applied was a familiar, indeed an immemorial, rule of law. Justice could be served, but the illusion of a changeless constitution need not be abandoned" (1960: McCloskey, 133). Such an event lends support to Parsons' contention (1966: 27) that the factor of procedure—"as distinguished from substantive precepts and standards"—becomes emphasized in "modern legal systems." This is so, however, not because *procedures* are uniquely required in modern (plural) societies—*all* societies require procedures—but because the *rhetoric* of procedure is required to justify outcomes between paties whose erstwhile religions are different. The rhetoric of procedure becomes the new, common religion or moral architecture.

It is in this context that the jurisprudence of Lon Fuller can best be understood. When he remarks on the impossibility of distinguishing the law that *is* from the law that *ought* to be (1966), or when he discusses the imperceptible line between the "morality of duty" and the "morality of aspiration" (1964), he is not—as Morris Raphael Cohen (1941), the realist, contends—denying an analytic distinction but only insisting that the law itself has concretely the task of portraying the ideal, whether it wants to or not. And, though Fuller has not included this point in his argument, it is argued here that the "law" takes on this task to the degree that "religion" is denied it as a result of pluralism. Thus, the "internal morality" of the law informs and guides a judge, even though the "external morality" (interests) of contending parties must remain of no concern to him (Fuller, 1964: 131–132). If Fuller finds a "natural law" rubric congenial for analyzing this process (Selznick, 1970), noting that the label "legal naturalism" would provide Fuller with less of a handicap), then it bespeaks even more the degree of transcendency that the law takes on as transcendent "religions" multiply.

Legal institutions do not take on the transcendent on moral architectural task single-handedly, of course. Public schools certainly play a critical role in socializing youngsters into the "transcendence" of the law (see Hammond, 1968; Herberg, 1961). As Kohlberg has framed the issue:

> It has been argued . . . that the Supreme Court's *Schempp* decision [prohibiting school sponsorship of prayer and Bible-reading] calls for the restraint of public school efforts at moral education since such education is equivalent to the state propagation of religion conceived as any articulated value system. The problems as to the legitimacy of moral education in the public schools disappear, however, if the proper content of moral education is recognized to be the values of justice which themselves prohibit the imposition of beliefs of one group upon another. . . . [This] does not mean that the schools are not to be "value-oriented." . . . The public school is as much committed to the maintenance of justice as is the court. (Kohlberg 1970: 67–68)

One can, however, usefully distinguish agencies for socialization into the ideology from agencies for articulating or elaborating it. Public schools are the new "Sunday schools," it might be said, whereas courts are the new pulpits.

Conclusion. The emerging theology of the legal system is probably most clearly seen in America's "civil religion," where its sacred literature, shrines, and saints are already institutionalized. Far from being merely the cheap patriotism of ignorant people, it is a vibrant ideology which is identifiable readily in Presidential inaugural addresses, as Bellah (1970: 168–186) demonstrates. Moreover, commitment to it does not preclude self-identification as religious in other, older ways as well. What is not so clear yet are the connections between the civil religion as theology and the parallel civil religion as moral architecture. How does "God," as portrayed in Presidential speech, relate to "due process," as portrayed in Supreme Court opinion? What is the equivalent of a Catholic, Protestant, or Jewish conscience? Will the moral architecture as developing in legal institutions and elsewhere ever be as general as, say, Catholicism in twelfth-century Europe, or is the new ideology incapable of "completion?"

These questions can be asked, it has been argued here, because of the consequences of religious pluralism. Representing not merely a choice of meaning systems, the creation of and legitimacy accorded religious pluralism changed entirely the role of competing meaning systems, and placed on legal institutions the task of articulating a new one.

The result is admittedly different from the totemistic beliefs and practices which united into one single moral community called a church all the Arunta. But just as there are unbelievers in modern societies' common symbol systems, so must there have been agnostics among the Arunta. And just as Arunta priests and rituals no doubt violated their own ideology on occasion, so do the legal institutions of today sometimes fail to live up to their ideals. There is no need in other words, to prove the purity of either the "church" or the congregation in order to argue its religious status. The American people, for example, cannot be said to "revere" their Supreme Court; most of them hardly know its makeup, and few keep track of its "sacred" work.

But Durkheim, it is contended, was not a fundamentalist. What he claimed to identify, after all, was religion in its *elementary* forms. To expect these elementary forms to appear also in complex, religiously plural societies is hardly in keeping with his argument. The effort here has been to suggest—remaining faithful to Durkheim's integration thesis —what some not-so-elementary forms might be.

NOTES

1. This is not to say that *only* legal institutions perform this task. The idea that governments adopt religious functions has been noted frequently. The burden of the present essay is to specify one way in which the frequently noted idea is true.

2. The work of S. M. Lipset (1960) is central to this kind of understanding of "pluralism." Good recent summary discussions are found in Arend Lijphart (1968: Ch. 1) and Leo Kuper and M. G. Smith (1969: Chs. 1–2).

3. In an essay which, in many respects, is theoretically analogous to this one, David Apter (1963: 74) writes, "The preoccupation with law in the West

was one of the important ingredients for the development of a community
that regarded the framework of law itself as the sole and ultimate commitment by which the community lived, breathed, and prospered. But it was
not the only factor relevant to the development of a reconciliation system
(i.e., pluralistic democracy). The second was the separation of church and
state. I shall try to show that the separation of church and state was in fact
an essential element in developing such a system and, as well, how the
notion of law was a necessary ingredient."

4. This argument should not be taken as a renewal of the realistic-idealistic
    quarrel so many have mistakenly read into Weber's work. Obviously the
    "competing meaning systems" of the sort we discuss here have social
    structural roots, investigated for example by G. E. Swanson (1967). The
    "Weberian" position, stated simply, is that social activities cannot be under-
    stood without reference to the "meaning" placed on their social structural
    roots.

5. In their discussion of "levels of legitimation," culminating in a "symbolic
    universe" or "matrix of all socially objectivated and subjectively real
    meanings," Peter Berger and Thomas Luckmann (1966a: 92ff.) are admir-
    ably clear but pay too little attention to the structural sources of this
    phenomenon (see Phillip E. Hammond (1969) for more systematic critique
    of this point.) Giving a *cognitive* emphasis to these "higher systems" allows
    a too ready assumption that differences, though awkward perhaps, are not
    disruptive of the social order. Moreover, Berger and Luckmann, in avoid-
    ing the functionalists' pitfall, go too far and see the "functions" being
    served by these symbolic universes as largely individual functions. While
    not adopting a doctrinaire, "societal prerequisite" stance, I believe that
    some minimal interpersonal or institutional sharing is required. Thus, at
    the least, *pressures* exist on prevailing institutions to adopt a single universe
    of meaning.

6. Peter Berger (1967a, Ch. 6, and his individual papers cited there) has
    attended to these matters in more detail and far more interestingly than
    anyone else.

7. Thus, as one example, late in the sixteenth century Thomas Cartwright, a
    Puritan theologian argued with Anglican theologian John Whitgift over
    the proper wording to be used in the communion service. The Anglican
    favored "take thou" (singular), the Puritan "take ye" (plural). For the
    Anglican, sacraments were "instruments of grace unto every particular man,"
    whereas for the Puritan "community was necessarily implied in communion
    with God." It should be clear legal institutions could have "borrowed" not
    individualism but collectivism from Puritanism (Little, 1969: 91 and 154).

8. It is worth noting that this is the same Robinson whom Pound (1921:
    42–43 quotes on at least two occasions as saying, "we are not over one
    another, but with one another." Pound is interested in finding the *sub-
    stance* in Puritan doctrine which yields the common law doctrine whereby

"the common-law judge tends to seek for some relation between the parties, . . . some duty of one to the other." And the convenantal nature of Puritanism qualifies, of course. As Little's study shows, however, the Puritan influence is a good deal more subtle than that. The new theology had effects it never anticipated.

9. This "Robinson" tradition continues into the twentieth century with the appearance of Bishop John Robinson's *Honest to God* (1963), the best-selling precursor of the death-of-god theology. Whatever else the movement is (was), it represents the final capitulation of "church" language and imagery to "secular" language and imagery. See Berger (1967b).

10. Of considerable interest at this point is J. J. Mol (1968). He shows that Dutch Reformed and German Lutheran clergy in early eighteenth-century America, to the degree they held Puritan (evangelical or Pietist) convictions, were favorable to religious "voluntarism," breaking with the mother church, adopting the English language in worship, and training clergy locally. Their orthodox-conservative counterparts opposed such "American" adjustments.

11. G. L. Haskins (1968: Ch. 10), goes further; the common law tradition was the "cornerstone," the Bible merely the "touchstone," of early Massachusetts. Haskins (1965) is a case study of his general thesis.

12. The phrase is Leo Pfeffer's (1958: 44) describing Roger Williams' conception of society. Williams had noted that the Ten Commandments came on two tablets, one specifying man's obligations to God, the other man's to man.

13. This, I take it, is Lon Fuller's distinction (1964) between "the morality of duty" and "the morality of aspiration," the latter the realm from which the law's "internal morality" is drawn. Fuller is discussed below.

14. "Actually, beween 1820 and 1890 the judges were already taking the initiative in lawmaking. Far anticipating the leadership of the executive or administrative arms, the courts built up the common law in the United States—a body of judge-made doctrine to govern people's public and private affairs" (Hurst, 1950: 85).

15. Most famously, perhaps, by Max Lerner (1937). See also Bickel (1962: esp. 29–33), but Bickel only touches on the context of the law. He does not take contextual change as problematic. The moral leadership role of the courts is analyzed more as the willful choice of individuals.

16. Thus, says Bickel (1962: 236–238) "The function of the Justices . . . is to immerse themselves in the tradition of our society and of kindred societies that have gone before, in history and in the sediment of history which is law, and . . . in the thought and the vision of the philosophers and the poets. The Justices will then be fit to extract 'fundamental presuppositions' from their deepest selves, but in fact from the evolving morality of our tradition. . . . The search for the deepest controlling sources, for the precise 'how' and the final 'whence' of the judgment . . . may, after all, end in the attempt to express the inexpressible. This is not to say that the duty to

judge the judgment might as well be abandoned. The inexpressible can be recognized, even though one is unable to parse it."
It would be difficult to find a better description of the "religious" task as it is outlined in classical sociology.

17. What follows is no systematic review. For a recent *legal* review of church-state cases, see Galanter (1966). An excellent sociological review is J. R. Burkholder (1969).

18. In a concurring opinion, Douglas went further in acknowledging how pluralism forces rhetorical change. Hawaii, he noted, at the time the Selective Service law was passed (1940), probably had more Buddhists than members of any other "faith," and how could a concept like Supreme Being be helpful in determining a Buddhist's eligibility for exemption? This from the Justice who thirteen years earlier could write that American institutions "presuppose" a Supreme Being.

19. From the perspective of this essay, a particularly interesting and poignant case was recently decided in the Wisconsin Supreme Court. As one in a series of "Amish" cases, *State of Wisconsin* v. *Yoder* 182 NW 2d. 539 (1971) differed from the others in permitting Amish children exemption from compulsory school after age 14. The majority opinion asserts that: (1) the Free Exercise Clause protects the *practice* of religion "which is binding in conscience" (i.e., action cannot be separated from belief), even though (2) the state clearly has the power to regulate compulsory education. (3) Therefore, the law weighs the "relative importance of the religious beliefs in issue"—which is judged here to be major—and the relative importance of the state's aims in making education compulsory—here judged to be minor—and then (4) decides. A dissenting opinion points out, however, that the famous school desegregation case, *Brown* v. *Board of Education* 347 US 483 (1954), asserted that "Today, education is perhaps the most important function of state and local governments." In other words, the "religiousness" which Amish attach to the question of public education is indistinguishable in the law from the "religiousness" which some may attach to education. At this writing, the U.S. Supreme Court has agreed to hear the Wisconsin case on appeal.

REFERENCES

APTER, DAVID

1963   "Political Religion in the New Nations." Pp. 57–104 in
                            Clifford Geertz (ed.), *Old Societies and New States*. New
                            York: Free Press.

BELLAH, ROBERT N.

1970   *Beyond Belief*. New York: Harper and Row.

BENDER, HAROLD S.

(1953)
1970
The Anabaptists and Religious Liberty in the Sixteenth Century. Philadelphia: Fortress Press.

BERGER, PETER L.

1967a
The Sacred Canopy: Elements of a Sociological Theory of Religion. Garden City, N.Y.: Doubleday.

1967b
"A Sociological View of the Secularization of Theology." Journal for the Scientific Study of Religion 6: 3–16.

BERGER, P. L.
LUCKMANN, THOMAS

(1966a)
1967
The Social Construction of Reality. Garden City, N.Y.: Doubleday Anchor.

1966b
"Secularization and Pluralism." Pp. 73–84 in Yearbook for the Sociology of Religion, Vol. 2, ed. by J. Matthes.

BICKEL, ALEXANDER

1962
The Least Dangerous Branch. Indianapolis: Bobbs-Merrill.

BURKHOLDER, J. R.

1969
"Religion in the First Amendment." Unpublished Ph.D. dissertation, Harvard University.

CHERRY, CONRAD

1971
God's New Israel: Religious Interpretations of American Destiny. Englewood Cliffs, N.J.: Prentice-Hall.

COHEN, MORRIS A.

1941
Review of Lon Fuller, The Law in Quest of Itself. Illinois Law Review 36: 239.

COLEMAN, JAMES S.

1956
"Social cleavage and religious conflict." Journal of Social Issues 12: 44–56.

DAVIS, KINGSLEY

1950
Human Society. New York: Macmillan.

DEMERATH, N. J.
HAMMOND, PHILLIP E.

1968
Religion in Social Context. New York: Random House.

DURKHEIM, EMILE

1961
Elementary Forms of Religious Life. New York: Collier. (Originally published in French in 1912).

EUSDEN, JOHN

1958   *Puritans, Lawyers and Politics.* New Haven: Yale University Press.

FULLER, LON

1964   *The Morality of Law.* New Haven: Yale University Press.

1966   *The Law in Quest of Itself.* Boston: Beacon Press.

GALANTER, MARC

1966   "Religious Freedoms in the United States: A Turning Point?" *Wisconsin Law Review,* 217–296.

HAMMOND, PHILLIP E.

1968   "Commentary." Pp. 381–388 in D. R. Cutler (ed.), *The Religious Situation.* Boston: Beacon Press.

1969   "Peter Berger's sociology of religion." *Soundings* 54 (Winter): 415–424.

HASKINS, G. L.

1965   "Reception of the common law in 17th Century Massachusetts." In G. A. Billias (ed.), *Law and Authority in Colonial America.* Barre, Mass.: Barre Publishers.

1968   *Law and Authority in Early Massachusetts.* Hamden, Conn.: Archon Books.

HAYES, C. J. H.

1960   *Nationalism: A Religion.* New York: Macmillan.

HERBERG, WILL

(1955)
1960   *Protestant-Catholic-Jew: An Essay in American Religious Society.* Garden City, N.Y.: Doubleday Anchor.

1961   "Religion and Education in America." In J. W. Smith and A. L. Jamison (eds.), *Religious Perspectives in American Culture.* Princeton: Princeton University Press.

HOWE, MARK DE W.

1965   "The Sources and Nature of Law in Colonial Massachusetts." In G. A. Billias (ed.), *Law and Authority in Colonial America.* Barre, Mass.: Barre Publishers.

HURST, J. WILLARD

1950   *The Growth of American Law.* Boston: Little, Brown.

KOHLBERG, LAWRENCE

1970   "Education for Justice: A Modern Statement of the Platonic View." In J. M. Gustafson et al., *Moral Education.* Cambridge, Mass.: Harvard University Press.

KUPER, LEO
SMITH, M. G. (EDS.)

1969   *Pluralism in Africa.* Berkeley: University of California Press.

LERNER, MAX

1937   "The Constitution and the Court as Symbols." *Yale Law Journal* 46: 1290–1319.

LIJPHART, AREND

1968   *The Politics of Accommodation.* Berkeley: University of California Press.

LIPSET, S. M.

1960   *Political Man.* Garden City, N.Y.: Doubleday.

LITTLE, DAVID

1969   *Religion, Order and Law.* New York: Harper and Row.

MACINTYRE, ALASDAIR

1967   *Secularization and Moral Change.* London: Oxford University Press.

MCCLOSKY, ROBERT

1960   *The American Supreme Court.* Chicago: University of Chicago Press.

MOL, J. J.

1968   *The Breaking of Traditions: Theological Convictions in Colonial America.* Berkeley: Glendessary.

MURRAY, JOHN COURTNEY

1964   *We Hold These Truths.* Garden City, N.Y.: Doubleday.

PARSONS, TALCOTT

1937   *Structure of Social Action.* New York: McGraw-Hill. *Societies: Evolutionary and Comparative Perspectives.* Englewood Cliffs, N.J.: Prentice-Hall.

1969   *Politics and Social Structure.* New York: Free Press.

PEKELIS, ALEXANDER

1950   *Law and Social Action.* Ithaca, N.Y.: Cornell University Press.

PFEFFER, LEO

1958   *Creeds in Competition.* New York: Harper.

POUND, ROSCOE

1910   "Law in Books and Law in Action." *American Law Review* **44**: 12–34.

1921   *The Spirit of the Common Law.* Francestown, N.H.: Marshall Jones.

ROSSELL, ROBERT D.

1970   "The Great Awakening: an historical analysis." *American Journal of Sociology* **75** (May): 907–925.

ROSTOW, EUGENE V.

1952   "The Democratic Character of Judicial Review." *Harvard Law Review* **66**: 193–224.

SELZNICK, PHILIP

1970   Review of Lon Fuller, *Anatomy of the Law. Harvard Law Review* **83**: 1474–1480.

SHIPTON, C. K.

1965   "The Locus of Authority in Colonial Massachusetts." In G. A. Billias (ed.), *Law and Authority in Colonial America.* Barre, Mass.: Barre Publishers.

SMITH, WILFRED CANTWELL

1963   *The Meaning and End of Religion.* New York: Macmillan.

SWANSON, GUY E.

1967   *Religion and Regime.* Ann Arbor: University of Michigan.

TEGGART, FREDRICK J.

1918   *The Processes of History.* New Haven: Yale University.

WEBER, MAX

(1922)   *Theory of Social and Economic Organization.* Trans. by
1947   A. M. Henderson and Talcott Parsons. Glencoe, Ill.: Free Press.

Richard K. Fenn

UNIVERSITY OF MAINE, ORONO

Religion and the Legitimation of Social Systems

A number of observers consider secularization a process in which religion loses some of its traditional functions to other institutions. It is widely accepted that the religious subsystem has been relieved of direct control over the political, economic, legal, welfare, and educational functions in the more modernized societies, with the result that religious institutions appear to "specialize" in expressive activities related to the maintenance of the kinship system, of families, and of individuals in search of personal meaning and social identification (Parsons, 1971: 99; Greeley, 1972: 70; Bellah, 1964). Observers appear to disagree, however, over the question whether the increasing autonomy of other subsystems from direct religious control represents the fulfillment or the reversal of the Judeo-Christian tradition. They differ also on the question whether the restriction of religion to expressive activities in the private sphere represents a purification of religious institutions from secondary functions or a secular "privatization" which reduces religion to the level of personal preference and individual idiosyncracy (cf. the points of view represented in Childress and Harned, 1970). Some of these differences of interpretation reflect differing assumptions concerning the normative relation of religion to society as well as problems in sociological theory and research. This paper, therefore, will not attempt to resolve the differences but rather to restate them as problems within a coherent conceptual framework.

One issue pertaining to the functional dimension of religion is of central concern here. The function in question is legitimation: the process by which one aspect of a social system confers sanctions on the society as a whole and on particular institutions within it. There is apparent agreement that religion today is not the only institution which exercises this function; legitimation requires as well the contributions of political, educational, and legal institutions in modern societies (Parsons, 1971: 99; Swanson, 1971: 161ff). There are those, however, who would appear to agree with Levy (1966: 616) or Bellah (1967) that religion is the ultimate source of legitimation for the polity even of modern societies, while others (cf. Etzioni, 1968) appear to ignore religion as a legitimating factor in the most advanced societies. The middle ground is occupied by those who assume that, although religion has lost *direct* control over the legitimation of modern societies and their several institutional subsystems, it still exercises an indirect influence (Parsons, 1963; Smelser, 1963: 32–34).

Since "modern" societies are at various stages of development, some propositions regarding the legitimating function of religion may be more appropriate to modernizing than to advanced societies. Again, some propositions may be directed toward the effect of religion on the macrosocial level or on one institution, such as the government, as opposed to the microsocial level or the individual himself. Similarly, legitimation may convey to one writer only the positive sanctioning of the status quo, whereas for another, legitimation may include positive support for social change.

The problem of whether religion functions to legitimate any aspect of modern social systems therefore needs to be stated somewhat more formally: Under what conditions does religion provide legitimation to modern societies? The answers to that question, of course, will not be found until a comprehensive theory has been developed which is capable both of integrating the already numerous empirical studies pertinent to the problem and of generating further research. All I am attempting here is to develop a theoretical framework which can be used for developing and testing propositions concerning religious legitimation. That framework, essentially social system theory, will consider the interrelations of four variables and their contribution to the probability that religious beliefs and values are of causal significance in the process of legitimation.

The independent variable will be the degree to which religious roles, organizations, and cultural systems become differentiated from the rest of a society. It will be argued that the influence of a differentiated religious system on the process of legitimation is mediated by three intervening variables. (1) The *autonomy* of the religious institutions influences the effectiveness of religion in the process of legitimation. Autonomy at the macrosocial level, as in the separation of church and state, may be inversely related to autonomy at the local level. The level at which autonomy is achieved may in turn affect the level at which religion exercises effective cultural sanctions. (2) Whether these sanctions are positive or negative depends on another variable: the degree to which the system of religious symbols is integrated with nonreligious elements in the culture. The less integration, the more likely it is that religious symbols will be a source of negative sanctions. (3) The effectiveness of the sanctions depends on the degree to which religious structures (roles, organizations, collectivities) are *interdependently* related to other structures in modern societies. To the extent that religious roles, for instance, occupy a different category from occupational roles, the less likely it is that religious sanctions will be effective in the process of legitimation outside the religious subsystem.

PARSONS AND DIFFERENTIATION

Every society depends for its existence on the tendency of most individuals to "take it for granted" most of the time. That is, a society cannot long survive in which the majority of individuals doubt that the society itself is morally or otherwise valuable, or consider it to be either transitory or an illusion of the senses. In fact, any society which constantly has to defend its basic principles is in a continual crisis of legitimacy. Societies, then, depend on an element of basic trust; or, to use Parsons' phrase, societies are constituted by generalized "value-commitments" which constitute a reserve of good faith on which each society can draw as it adapts to various internal and external exigencies (Parsons, 1968).

Parsons draws on economics for a metaphor to conceptualize the fluctuations in legitimacy which characterize societies in the process of change.

Parsons draws on economics for a metaphor to conceptualize the fluctuations in legitimacy which characterize societies in the process of change.

The inflationary case involves what is frequently called *overcommit-*

ment, at least in the value-implementation context. It occurs when a unit has made so many, so diverse, and such "serious" commitments that its capacity to implement them effectively must reasonably be called into question. . . . However, the common feature of all deflation is what we may call value *absolutism*. It is the assertion of sharp limitations on implementive flexibility, restricting the obligation to the most immediate, often most drastic, steps for implementing the pattern at the particular level of reference. Legitimation is thereby withdrawn from otherwise open ranges of flexibility with respect to more remote means of implementation or other subvalues within a larger system. (*Ibid.*: 153)

Inflation of trust, of "value-commitments," within a society therefore occurs when leaders or units entrusted with the responsibility for innovation are unable to implement the values in question in new social arrangements; conversely, deflation occurs when leaders or units are restricted to carefully prescribed forms of action in implementing the value-commitments.

An extension of trust may occur in a number of cases through the social system: when political leaders are enabled to propose new programs; when judges are enabled to apply the law to cases not covered by precedent or previously considered within their jurisdiction; when religious leaders are enabled to propose new forms of obligation; when influential persons are enabled to give information and exert influence; and when the monetary system enables exchange and investment without stringent requirements for hard assets underlying the exchanges. The extension of trust becomes inflationary when no requirements are effectively made for the implementation of the new legal, political, religious, or economic programs. If the ensuing crisis of legitimation is not successfully met, whether by appeal to shared values or by "success," a deflationary cycle is most likely to ensue which emphasizes strict construction in jurisprudence, the accountability of politicians, requirements that information be documented with reliable "facts," high levels of reserve assets in the economic system, and the "old time" religion (Parsons, 1968).

The concept of inflation may vary not only between societies but within a given society over relatively short spans of time. Further, Parsons' illustration suggests that social indicators may yet be developed which can measure, however crudely, the degree of legitimacy in a particular social system as a whole and in its several subsystems. His metaphor is doubly useful in pointing (if only by implication) to the exceedingly complex role of religion in the process of legitimation.

Parsons thus shows that religion can function in two ways: to limit the type of legitimate activity and organization within rather rigid prescriptions, or to provide legitimation for a much broader range of social action. This relatively commonsense observation is supported by Eisenstadt's studies of modernization, in which he observes a transition from the endowment of particular roles with "direct religious meaning" to a more generalized religious legitimation of worldly action (1968: 18–19). Etzioni appears to concur in his conceptualization that modernization is accompanied by a shift from "prescriptive" to "contextuating" types of social control (1968: 443).

Underlying the historical development in which societies, organizations, and individuals are enabled to take on a broader range of legitimate social action is the process of differentiation. Viewed horizontally, differentiation involves separating from one another the economy, the polity, the legal, and the religious subsystems of a society. Parsons appears to view the major revolutions of Western history as the stages by which the polity was differentiated first from the economy and then from such traditional sources of solidarity as ethnicity and religion. The latest stages of modernization have extended this process of differentiation still further: to the point at which the normative order and the informal sources of solidarity are "not grounded directly in religion. The educational revolution is a further step in this secularization" (Parsons, 1971: 101).

The key word here is "directly." Parsons (ibid.) has argued that, as major areas of a society separate from direct religious supervision, values become "generalized" to a much broader and more complex range of situations. A corollary of this cultural development is that institutions and individuals acquire more flexibility in adapting to the requirements of modernization. Although some societies have experienced regressions to more direct religious legitimation, as in situations where fundamentalist religious and political movements have prevailed, the direction of change is linear rather than cyclical.

One outcome, then, of the process of differentiation is a greatly attenuated process of religious legitimation. The linkages between religious ideas and values and actual, institutionalized patterns of organization in work and politics are loosened to the point that it is difficult, if not impossible, to determine whether certain values are in fact implemented within the society. The separation of the political and economic system from religious control is frequently more visible in the total society than at the regional or community level. If the process of differentiation proceeded at the same rate on the local level as it does at the level of the whole society, a major source of conflict in modern societies would be overcome. Fundamentalist pressures against the generalization of values, however, arise from strata in the population which expect religion to provide rather direct legitimation to politics and education. Populist protests against "Godless" communism or against taking God out of the public schools emerge from a social context in which religion is not markedly differentiated from educational or political institutions. Some of the pressures for deflation to which Parsons refers are undoubtedly based in segments of the population that are missed in purely macrosocial perspectives.

The process of differentiation makes it increasingly difficult for a society to mobilize the interests and loyalties of individuals and groups. As loyalties are extended from the family, for instance, to more inclusive social structures, standards frequently become stretched and values generalized to the point that they have no direct relationship to particular actions or social arrangements. Values become so "general" as to be emptied of specific content. It is next to impossible, for instance, to achieve consensus on what it would mean to implement the value of equality in educational or occupational institutions. It therefore becomes increasingly difficult to close the gap between myth and reality in modern societies. Political leaders who successfully manipulate the symbols of particular values generate inflationary pressures by mobilizing a high level of commitment of energy and trust to the larger society. The more nearly American society operates at full capacity to meet the requirements of its values, the more inflationary is the impact of these new commitments. And the more deflationary is the impact of the society's failure to fulfill the expectations thus generated.

In addition to the generality of value-systems already mentioned, the development of pluralistic cultures makes it possible for individuals to conceive of alternative directions for social change. The taken-for-granted character of a particular society is therefore more easily called into question. Secondly, the process of differentiation is seldom smooth. As I have noted, it may occur more rapidly on the macrosocial level than on the microsocial level of a society and thus generate deflationary pressures from groups and individuals who resist the demands of the larger society on their energy and loyalty. The process of differentiation therefore entails something of a paradox. Successful differentiation makes it possible for societies to adapt to new demands; yet the more highly differentiated a society becomes, the more subject it is to cycles in the inflation and deflation of commitments.

In this paper I am assuming that religion may still have important consequences in modern societies for the mobilization of individual energy and trust. Under what conditions, then, does religion affect the inflationary and deflationary aspects even of the most advanced societies? When does religion serve to inflate the level of trust in American society, for instance; and under what conditions does it have deflationary impact on legitimacy? In the rest of the paper I will outline a theoretical framework for sociological inquiry into precisely this question.

AUTONOMY, INTEGRATION, AND INTERDEPENDENCE:

At least one other metaphor, besides Parsons' image of inflation and deflation of commitments, attempts to express the peculiar cyclical dynamism of modernizing societies. Schermerhorn's metaphor of centripetal and centrifugal tendencies (1970: 85) is more fruitful because it implicitly refers to three variables which need to be considered in any theoretical discussion of religious legitimation.

> Centripetal tendencies refer both to cultural trends such as acceptance of common values, styles of life, etc., as well as structural featurs like participation in a common set of groups, associations, and institutions. . . . Conversely, centrifugal tendencies among subordinate groups are those that foster separation from the dominant group or from societal bonds in one respect or another. Culturally this most frequently means retention and preservation of the group's distinctive traditions in spheres like language, religion, recreation, etc., together with the particularistic values associated with them: Wirth's pluralism. But in order to protect these values, structural requirements are needed, so there are demands for endogamy, separate associations, and even at times a restricted range of occupations. (*Ibid*.: 81–82)

In an earlier context Schermerhorn notes that differences in the degree of cultural integration and of power (relative autonomy) are independently related to each other and are of direct significance in structuring conflicts over legitimacy (*ibid*.: 75). Centrifugal trends can therefore be conceptualized in part as the outcome of the attempts by various groups to enhance their autonomy and cultural distinctiveness.

It would appear from Schermerhorn's illustration (*ibid*.: 84) that centrifugal trends also include the variable of interdependence. French-speaking cantons in Switzerland maintain their cultural distinctiveness because they are granted high levels of autonomy by German-speaking superordinate groups; nonetheless, they are only "partly disengaged." Their interdependence with German-speaking cantons remains relatively high. The goals of black radicals in America during the 1960s also included the creation of "a separate community": a cultural integration, high autonomy, and a lower level of interdependence than the partial disengagement which French-speaking cantons in Switzerland have either sought or achieved.

Although Schermerhorn is interested in legitimation in general, the variables which both he and Parsons have identified as being of primary causal significance can be applied to the particular case of religious legitimation. Demerath and Hammond (1969) have made an excellent attempt to integrate a number of discrete empirical studies into a theoretical framework which uses differentiation, autonomy, integration, and, implicitly, interdependence as the primary variables for their analysis. Their contribution is particularly useful because it distinguishes between the macrolevel and the microlevel of analysis. For instance, in explaining the attempts of local churches to preserve their sources of organizational support, Demerath and Hammond state that these churches are operating under conditions of relatively low autonomy. That is, the parishes are dependent upon their constituency for money and support. Local parishes are therefore trying to "restore the unity that differentiation has threatened" (Demarath and Hammond, 1969: 222). In terms of Schermerhorn's metaphor, the local churches are centrifugal in that they seek to strengthen the solidarity and to support the particularistic values of local or ethnic groups. By way of contrast, nonparish clergy take advantage of the differentiation of regional or national religious organizations from other structures such as the family, achieve considerable autonomy from their constituencies, and are thus enabled to support norms and values which are "prophetic" in nature, (ibid.: 223). In terms of Schermerhorn's metaphor these clergy are "centripetal": they are storming the centers of public policy.

The Demerath and Hammond analysis sometimes becomes unclear. In speaking of Liston Pope's study of the relation between churches and textile mills in Gastonia, North Carolina, they explain their assertion that the churches were "unable to sustain a high degree of differentiation" by pointing out that the churches were obliged to support the mill owners against the striking workers (ibid.: 112–113). But by differentiation they here mean autonomy. They could more accurately have said that local churches were both lacking in autonomy and in differentiation from structures in the economic system. Again, Demerath and Hammond characterize the churches' lack of influence in social or political affairs as "differentiated autonomy," whereas they are actually describing a lack of interdependence between religion and political or social institutions, (ibid.: 113). Finally, it is sometimes unclear what the authors mean by "integration." Do they mean a function, or the extent of consensus between the church's values and those of its constituents (ibid: 223)? If integration is a function, then the church is clearly interdependent in its relations with other institutions in the society; as a variable referring to the degree of consensus, however, it refers to the extent of cultural integration between the church, its constituency, and the rest of the society.

A similar overlapping of meaning between the terms "integration" and "interdependence" appears in Swanson's analysis of the potential sources of religious legitimation in modern society (1968: 825ff). He notes the congruence between the ideology of professionalism and certain basic religious values, for example, in their mutual concern for persons and for the long-term effects of action on the whole society. His proposition, however, has to do with the integration, rather than the interdependence, of two value-systems or belief-systems. Furthermore, it is a proposition which is relevant to the relation of religion to particular organizations or collectivities rather than to the whole society. Bellah (1967), to take a different example, claims that religion provides legitimation to the total society through a symbolic system which he calls the civic religion. And a number of writers have made similar observations about the incorporation of secular values, such as activism and success, into the specifically religious system of values in American society. Like Swanson, they are concerned less with the process of legitimation than with the empirical integration of diffentiated value-systems. The advantage of such propositions is that they call for the use of such data as Presidential inaugural speeches and the sacred documents of the religious bodies in American society; and they are macrosocial in their level of reference. They nonetheless refer to integration rather than to interdependence. It is quite possible, for instance, that despite the integration of the *contents* of religious and political beliefs, the political system itself may remain largely immune to influences from the religious system. Under these conditions, it would be difficult to consider the two as in any way interdependent.

The relation between the several variables which we have considered in this discussion is diagramatically presented in Figure 1. A brief comment on each variable may serve to raise the more important theoretical and empirical questions implied by the diagram.

One could argue that the process of differentiation is a necessary, if not sufficient, cause of problems of legitimation. If there were no differentiation between culture and social structure, all institutional arrangements would appear exactly as they are prescribed by the beliefs, values, and norms of the culture. As I have already noted, differentiation introduces the possibility of some lack of consistency in the institutionalized pattern: conflicting values, for instance, or a lack of successful institutionalization of such values as justice and equality. Vertical differentiation—stratification of individuals whether on the basis of ascribed characteristics or achievement—inevitably introduces a gap between the ideal and the actual, between the myth and the reality.

This discussion undertakes to analyze only one relatively limited, although still complex, aspect of the process of differentiation: the separation of religious from other institutional areas of modern society. In this

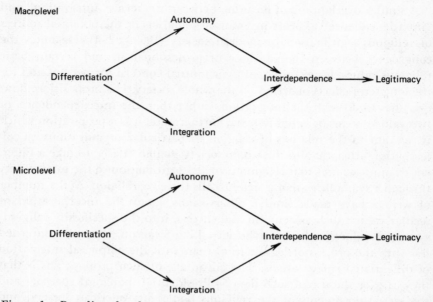

Figure 1. Paradigm for the analysis of relationships of institutionalized religion to the legitimation of modern societies, at two levels of the social system.

context, differentiation refers to the process by which religious roles, statuses, and organizations become separate from roles, statuses and organizations in political, educational, occupational, ethnic, or legal systems. Modernized societies are characterized by an increasingly elaborate set of roles which are clearly indentifiable as "religious," such as clergy, administrators, lay officers, teachers, etc. within such ecclesiastical institutions as school, churches, seminaries, and bureaucracies. Differentiation also refers to the development of special systems of religious symbols—to systems of doctrine, ethics, and dogma.

Differentiation may therefore be accompanied by a segmentation of religious roles and organizations from other parts of the society, but it also may be accompanied by an increase in mutual influence between religion and the social system. We can assume that in modern societies the organizations which are primarily responsible for the maintenance of the ultimate beliefs and values of the cultural system are separated from the organizations which are responsible for the formation of public policy. In a highly differentiated society, of course, these latter institutions are in turn separate from other structures which are responsible for the implementation of public policy, such as military institutions, corporations, and the educational system. To assume that the process of differentiation reduces the extent to which religion exercises a controlling or guiding function in the society, however, is to confuse differentiation with interdependdence. If Parsons and Greeley are right, religion in the United States is still highly interdependent with other institutions from which it is nonetheless clearly differentiated; its legitimating or guiding function is exercised as fully, however indirectly, as it is in less differentiated societies.

Finally, the process of differentiation needs to be specified both at the macrosocial and microsocial level. Societies may be compared, for instance, on the basis of how many differentiated religious institutions (and their associated symbolic systems) have a constituency in the society as a whole. Two relatively modern societies may contain within their territories an equal number of distinct religious subsystems. Of these two societies, however, the first may have only one religious subsystem which penetrates most of its regions or strata, whereas the second may have several. Or a society may have a large number of clearly differentiated religious subsystems, but with each region relatively homogeneous, as in the Protestant Reformation solution of *cuius regio, eius religio*. Finally, at the level of local communities, there may be a wide variation in the number of distinct religious subsystems. In each case, specifying the process of religious differentiation by ecological or socio-economic variables leads to different conclusions as to the potential for religious legitimation. The government of a country in which only one religion has macrosocial dimensions is far more likely to be legitimated by religious institutions than one in which several religious subsystems coexist at the macrosocial level.

The same qualifications, of course, apply to the other variables. As noted earlier, Demerath and Hammond made good use of difficult kinds of analysis in comparing the relative autonomy of officers in church bureaucracies with the lack of autonomy of the average parish clergyman on controversial issues. On the local level, then, autonomy means the ability of the religious organization, or of the incumbent of a particular religious role, to withstand pressures from his clients or customers. It is a variable which is frequently used in analyses of professionalization: the less able the professional is to withstand the demands of the client, the more suspect he becomes in the eyes of his colleagues. On the national level, of course, autonomy refers to what is usually called the separation of church and state: the freedom of the church from governmental sanctions.

The fact that autonomy on the local level may be quite different from autonomy on the national level may be the source of interesting comparative studies of the effects of establishment on the professionalization of religious practitioners. An impressionistic assessment of Anglican priests in England and Episcopal priests in the United States suggests that the less autonomy the church enjoys at the national level, the more likely the clergyman is to achieve relative autonomy at the local level in interacting with his parishioners; and vice versa.

The variable of cultural integration also needs to be specified at both the macro and microsocial levels. It is generally agreed that the official value-system of the major churches is more integrated into the dominant value-system of modern societies than is that of smaller, sectarian groups. The generalization may hold true, however, only at the macrosocial level. Churches at the local level frequently support particularistic values which conflict with those of the larger society, whereas sectarian groups may support the socialization of the individual into the values of the dominant society (cf. Campbell and Pettigrew, 1959; Johnson, 1961).

The degree of cultural integration is inevitably related not only to macrosocial factors but to other variables present at the local level. Greeley (1972: 124–125) notes that Polish and Italian Catholics, who are more influenced by socialization received from parents and parochial school. In view of Greeley's observation about the relative lack of church involvement among Italians, and the relatively greater conflict between Polish clergy and their congregations, when either group is compared with the Germans and Irish, it might be inferred that the German and Irish clergy enjoy a greater degree of autonomy at the local level than do the Polish or Italian clergy. This would account for the relative weakness of religious socialization among the Poles and Italians in comparison with the Germans and Irish. Conversely, Gans's study of the "peer group society" indicates the basis for the relatively greater communal involvement among younger Poles and Italians as compared with the German and Irish (Gans, 1962: 74ff). It therefore appears that cultural integration is complexly related to the degree of autonomy attained by local religious institutions and by the degree to which religious membership is differentiated from ethnic sources of identification.

The type of interdependence diagrammed in Figure 1 is structural rather than cultural. Structural interdependence refers to the degree to which religious affiliation is interrelated with ethnic, occupational, or political ties or with other sources of social location. It is what Wilensky called "the articulation of various role systems in society" in his brilliant study of the strength of communities based on workplace, occupation, and religion (1967: 561).

The degree of interdependence between religious and other structural factors varies according to the level of analysis. Wilensky's description of the larger society may be quite accurate: "We can best look at modern society as a loose collection of overlapping communities of work, religion, race, class, and locality held together mainly by economic interdependence, by legal, military, and political institutions, and by the mass media" (*ibid.*: 557). Wilensky's only reference to cultural integration in modern societies concerns the mass media rather than religion, and he makes no reference at all to religious legitimation. Nonetheless, Wilensky makes a notable contribution to the microsocial assessment of interdependence between religion and other sources of legitimacy (*ibid.*: 557). The article cited indicates that the extent of interdependence between religions is very low. Where interdependence between religion and profession does occur, it is contingent on the ethnicity of the individual, on whether or not he is upwardly mobile, and on the type and ethnic composition of workplace (academic, bureaucratic, or solo).

Interpreting Wilensky's findings is a much more difficult task than reporting them. At the very least, they appear to support Thomas Luckmann's thesis that religious orientations are thoroughly separated from occupational orientations in modern societies. That is, they neither support nor conflict with the individual's reference system in his occupational roles. The two are independently related because they are in fact in separate compartments. Religion acquires salience in an area of relatively limited scope; it interprets and organizes the individual's private sphere of family, friendship, and individual biography.

On the other hand, Wilensky offers little support for Swanson's suggestion that religious values reinforce professional commitments to an ideology of societal usefulness. To begin with, professionalism and religious identification as measured by Wilensky do not refer to the specific content of the ideology of either system, whereas Swanson explicitly relates the contents of a religious value-orientation to the norms of professionalism. Secondly, Swanson's generalizations pertain to the level of organizations and, perhaps, of total societies. It is on these two levels of analysis that the congruence of religious and professional ideologies may be relevant to Swanson's insistence that modern societies constitute a religiously supported moral order. Survey data of individual orientations, then, may not be at all relevant to tests of such intermediate or macrosocial hypotheses. Swanson is applying to organizations the notion, derived in sociology from Durkheim through Parsons, that modern societies base their normative order on the norms and values of the professionalized division of labor. To test this hypothesis on the level of individual orientations ignores the possibility that variables are differently related to each other at different levels of social organization.

To test functionalist propositions with survey data is hardly a novel approach. The weaknesses of the method, however, can be illustrated in Greeley's recent study of religion in American society. Greeley begins by affirming the "influence of religion" in contemporary society; at the very least, he sees little or no evidence in various surveys for a "long-range decline in the importance of religion" in American society (1972: 137). The survey data he cites, however, are generally inventories of religious beliefs, attitudes, and opinions. They are data on the individual level, which, while they may indicate the scope or the intensity of religious socialization, do not indicate the consequences of religiosity either for individual action, or for decision on the level of organizations, or for the legitimation of the whole society.

I am arguing, then, that propositions concerning the functional inter-dependence of religion with other subsystems, or with the whole society, are inherently causal. This means that they cannot adequately be tested with data which reflect the substantive strength or weakness of religious belief over time. Eisenstadt, for instance, notes that when a religious belief with a transformative potential, such as Protestantism, is held by a rela-tively small elite which is open to participation in the center, or by an active sect, it may have important consequences for the legitimation of social change (1968: 14–15). The beliefs may not be widely distributed; they may be of little scope insofar as their incidence in the population may be ascertained through survey research. Their consequences for social change, however, may be quite independent of the numbers who hold the beliefs. It is less important to know how many individuals hold these beliefs than to know their position in the social system. The same beliefs, held with the same intensity by the same number of people, will have different consequences for the legitimation of social change, depending on whether the adherents are an oligarchy in control of the society (as at Geneva), a suppressed minority, or an elite open to participation with other elites in the building of a new nation (ibid.: 22).

The present argument also holds that propositions regarding the inter-dependence of religion with the society as a whole cannot be tested with data which describe the content of the beliefs and values. Ideologies with different contents, such as democratic capitalism and socialism, may have quite similar consequences for the mobilization, integration, and legitima-tion of a society. Conversely, the same ideology might have quite different consequences in a different society or in the same society at a different time.

Another aspect of the present argument, and perhaps the most impor-tant, stresses the level of the social system at which propositions regarding the role of religion in the legitimation of modern societies are to be tested. It is possible that religion may be quite separated from occupa-tional or political affiliations in an individual role-set, whereas on the macrosocial level religion may serve important legitimating functions. Con-versely, the setting of religion in a separate category from politics or from education, while an important aspect of public policy at the macrosocial level, may run into strong resistance at the local level from groups which do not wish "to keep God out of the schools" or to separate God from country. Propositions about the differentiation and interdependence of religion in modern societies cannot be specified at one level and tested at another.

SUMMARY

The process of differentiation has the somewhat paradoxical impact of proliferating religious roles and organizations while at the same time making the effect of religion on the society more contingent and indirect. Religious influence is more indirect in highly differentiated societies because it is mediated through a complex set of roles and organizations. And such influence is more contingent because it depends on the operation of other variables in the religious system. The effectiveness of religious legitimation is dependent on the degree to which religious institutions are both independent of secular authorities and yet interdependent with them. Religious institutions which depend on secular sanctions at either the macrosocial or the microsocial level cannot exert independent influence, and even highly autonomous religious institutions cannot be effective if they are segmented from (rather than interdependent with) other role-systems, organizations, or collectives in the society. Similarly, whether religious institutions exert negative as well as positive sanctions depends on the degree to which the religious and secular aspects of the culture are relatively well integrated with each other. Integrated cultural systems, however, do not provide prima facie evidence of religious legitimation in the present; the evidence for such legitimation depends on the degree of interdependence between religious and secular institutions and symbolic systems.

There are a few obvious implications of this analysis for current sociological studies of religion. To begin with, content analysis of the culture, such as Bellah's argument for the presence of a civil religion, may simply be examining the evidence for past conflicts and supportive relations between religious and secular institutions. Current symbolization may be analogous to memory traces in the individual; although the cultural symbols are somewhat more accessible to analysis than is the more frequently suppressed individual memory of past conflict and growth, the symbols do not indicate present relations of either conflictive or harmonious interdependence. The symbols, like the memories, may acquire renewed salience to individuals and groups in the society in accordance with changed circumstances; they may come back with renewed vigor to define and interpret the experiences of particular strata even in modern societies. In themselves, however, the symbols do not indicate actual relations of interdependence between religious and other roles and organizations at any level of the society.

This paradigm can also be applied to analyses of differences between churches and sects. It has been argued, for instance, that as sects interact more successfully with their environments (achieve higher interdependence), their value-systems and beliefs become more consistent (integrated) with the secular elements of the culture (cf. Johnson, 1961). With longevity, sects may develop more differential role-systems, such as an ordained clergy, and an institutional apparatus which acquires relatively higher degrees of autonomy over local and national constituents and competitors. It is this process in which sects become more differentiated and autonomous that accounts for their initial successes in shaping their environment and for their eventual development into organizations concerned primarily with preserving gains. It is possible then, that this paradigm will contribute to meeting the need in church-sect studies for a method which breaks down "the multidimensional conglomerates which presently pass for *sect* or for *church* entirely into their potentially component variables or attributes and then construct[s] empirically-derived clusters of traits, with probabilities of combinations of various characteristics spelled out explicitly on the basis of observed instances of concurrent appearance, or other association, in various historical movements or organizations" (Eister, 1967: 86).

The residue of sectarian conflict may remain in the form of cultural symbols which are reappropriated by new groups or strata under particular conditions. Symbols of suffering and death, of birth and rebirth, generated through sectarian movements, acquire new significance to strata which are experiencing threats to their autonomy within the society. Similarly, strata which are emerging from a relatively undifferentiated social system, such as one in which familial and occupational role-systems are not separated, generate symbols as memories of this undifferentiated social condition which become part of the common property of the national culture. Under certain conditions, strata which are resisting the process of differentiation—for example, youth in modern societies—may utilize these symbols for the legitimation of their resistance. The symbolic memories become symbols of hope.

As the process of structural and cultural differentiation advances, however, it becomes increasingly unlikely that any single religious system can serve to legitimate an entire society. Internal differentiation within religious institutions generates potential conflicts of interest and of values between elites and laity. These potential conflicts become actualized as religious institutions seek to exercise influence on the national scale and are consequently subject to countervailing pressures from the local level.

Indeed, the very attempt to exercise religious influence on a macrosocial level may increase rather than decrease the difficulties of legitimation within a society. The universalistic orientation of religious elites may conflict with the values of laity, who—themselves in less differentiated settings —resist attempts to weaken their control over local areas and institutions. Local groups of laity may come to distrust national church leaders as well as racial leaders or union officials who exercise influence on the national level, with a concomitant further loss of trust in public officials. Secondly, the exercise of influence at the macrosocial level may serve to raise expectations which the society cannot fulfill, with a resultant deflation of hopes and commitments on the part of large segments of the population. The rise and fall of the churches' support for the civil right movement is perhaps the best recent example of conflict between religious elites and laity and of the consequence deflation of commitments.

The ideological tone of the debate over secularization is due in part to conflicting assumptions concerning the importance of religion to the order and survival of all societies. It is a debate heavily charged with unexamined background assumptions and personal commitments. If this paper assists in translating the issues of that controversy into the terms of sociological theory, it will have served its purpose. To this end, I have elaborated a paradigm which makes it possible to investigate the conditions under which religious culture can have a positive or negative impact on the institutions of a society. The shape of the paradigm reflects two of my background assumptions: that under conditions of advanced differentiation religious institutions are increasingly less able to provide any type of legitimation to the larger society. Furthermore, an uneven rate of differentiation at the macrosocial and microsocial levels makes it increasingly difficult for a religious elite to mobilize the commitment of individual trust and energy to the goals of the larger society. Whether these assumptions will be borne out by further inquiry remains to be seen.

REFERENCES

BELLAH, ROBERT N.

1967   "Civil Religion in America," *Daedalus* **96** (1) (Winter) 1–21.

BERGER, PETER L.
LUCKMANN, THOMAS

1966   *The Social Construction of Reality.* Garden City, N.Y.: Doubleday Anchor.

CAMPBELL, ERNEST Q.
PETTIGREW, THOMAS F.

1959   *Christians in Racial Crisis. A Study of Little Rock's Ministry.* Washington, D.C.: Public Affairs Press.

CHILDRESS, JAMES F.
HARNED, DAVID B. (EDS.)

1970   *Secularization and the Protestant Prospect.* Philadelphia: Westminster Press.

DEMERATH, N. J.
HAMMOND, PHILLIP R.

1969   *Religion in Social Context: Tradition and Transition.* New York: Random House.

EISENSTADT, S. N. (ED.)

1968   *The Protestant Ethic and Modernization.* New York: Basic Books.

EISTER, ALLAN W.

1967   "Toward a Radical Critique of Church-Sect Typologizing." *Journal for the Scientific Study of Religion* **6:** 85–90.

ETZIONI, AMITAI

1968   *The Active Society.* New York: Free Press.

GANS, HERBERT

1963   *The Urban Villagers.* New York: Free Press.

GLOCK, CHARLES Y.
STARK, RODNEY

1965   *Religion and Society in Tension.* Chicago: Rand McNally.

GOULDNER, ALVIN W.

1957   "Cosmopolitans and Locals." I. *Administrative Science Quarterly* **2:** 281–306.

GREELEY, ANDREW M.

1972   *The Denominational Society: A Sociological Approach to Religion in America.* Glenview, Ill.: Scott, Foresman.

HERBERG, WILL

1955   *Protestant-Catholic-Jew: An Essay in American Religious Sociology.* Garden City, N.J.: Doubleday.

HUNT, RICHARD
KING, MORTON L.

1971   "The Intrinsic-Extensic Concept: A Review and Evaluation." *Journal for the Scientific Study of Religion* **10:** 339–356.

JOHNSON, BENTON

1961   "Do Holiness Sects Socialize in Dominant Values?" *Social Forces* **39**: 309–316.

1971   "Church-Sect Revisited." *Journal for the Scientific Study of Religion* **10**: 124–137.

LEVY, MARION J., JR.

1966   *Modernization and the Structure of Societies.* Princeton, N.J.: Princeton University Press.

MERTON, ROBERT K.

1957   *Social Theory and Social Structure.* New York: Free Press.

PARSONS, TALCOTT

1963   "Christianity and Modern Industrial Society." Pp. 33–70 in E. A. Tiryakian (ed.), *Sociological Theory, Values and Sociocultural Change.* New York: Free Press.

1968   "On the Concept of Value-Commitments." *Sociological Inquiry* (Spring).

1971   "Belief, Unbelief and Disbelief," Pp. 207–245 in R. Caporale and A. Grumelli (eds.), *The Culture of Unbelief.* Berkeley: University of California Press.

1971   *The System of Modern Societies.* Englewood Cliffs, N.J.: Prentice-Hall.

SCHERMERHORN, R. A.

1970   *Comparative Relations: A Framework for Theory and Research.* New York: Random House.

SMELSER, NEIL J.

1963   "Mechanisms of Change and Adjustment to Change." In B. Hoselitz and Wilbur E. Moore (eds.), *Industrialization and Society.* The Hague: Mouton, UNESCO.

SWANSON, GUY E.

1968   "Modern Secularity: Its Meaning, Sources & Interpretation." Pp. 801–834 in Donald Cutler (ed.), *The Religious Situation.* Boston: Beacon Press.

WILENSKY, HAROLD L.
LADINSKY, JACK

1967   "From Religious Community to Occupational Group: Structural Assimilation among Professor, Lawyers, and Engineers." *American Sociological Review* **32** (4): 541–561.

Part Four
Belief and Unbelief:
Problems of Definition
of "Religion" and "Faith"

Ward H. Goodenough

UNIVERSITY OF PENNSYLVANIA, PHILADELPHIA

Toward an Anthropologically
Useful Definition of Religion

The late Erwin Goodenough used to say that if we wish to understand what religion is about, we must study man praying, not what he is praying to. Like most epigrams, this one obviously oversimplifies. But it underscores what has been a major problem in the study of religion: a primary focus on the content of belief and relatively little concern with the believer. Dissatisfaction with this emphasis has been expressed more than once, going back a long way. But little more has come of it than definitions of religion as man's response to his fear of the unknown. Sociological and psychoanalytical interpretations, again, have sought to explain religion rather than to define it in a way that allows us to identify what we are to recognize as religion in cultures radically different from our own or, for that matter, in the lives of men in our own society who disclaim affiliation with any estatblished church, sect, or "divinely inspired" cult group.

In anthropology, the definition of religion in terms of the content of belief has been questioned by Gerlach and Hine (1970: xix) and eschewed by La Barre (1970), but it has been continued by Anthony Wallace, who gives the following as his basis for recognizing what is religion in other societies:

> It is the premise of every religion—and this premise is religion's refining characteristic—that souls, supernatural beings, and supernatural forces exist. Furthermore, there are certain minimal categories of behaviors, in the context of the *supernatural premise*, are always found in association with one another and which are the substance of religion itself. (1966: 52)

By this definition, we have not significantly moved away from E. B. Tylor's "belief in spiritual beings," which Wallace regards as a "still respectable minimum definition of religion" (1966: 5). Nor is it much altered by Spiro's otherwise sensible substitution of "superhuman" for supernatural (1966: 91).

The difficulties with such a definition are apparent when we look at the categories of behavior that Wallace says are to be found "in the context of the *supernatural* premise" and that make up the substance of religion. The fact is that these behaviors are frequently found in other contexts as well. Rituals, for example, are often highly elaborated in relation to social status without reference to anything that our culture classes as "supernatural." Furthermore, people may believe in the existence of what we see as spirits or supernatural beings without associating with them any of Wallace's categories of religious behavior, as Frake (1964) has elegantly demonstrated for the Subanun in the Philippines. The kinds of behavior that are Wallace's "substance of religion" are distributed among individuals and human activities in ways that overlap, but by no means coincide with, a belief in the supernatural. We cannot logically define religion in terms of belief and go on to treat it in terms of behavior.

We may seriously ask, therefore, whether we wish to define religion as some kind of belief (with associated behavior) or even as an attitude or commitment to something transcending the self, or whether we wish, in the spirit of Erwin Goodenough's epigram, to define it in relation to certain problems of human existence—problems that may be expressed by particular kinds of belief and attitude but that may be expressed in other ways as well, including the manipulation of symbols that are in no way associated with a "supernatural premise."

The latter approach has advantages for anthropology, at least so it seems to me. It makes the domain of religion a true complement of the domains of economics, politics, recreation, and so forth, a complementarity we often assume in practice, as when we identify institutions as economic, political, and religious. We recognize that the economic domain is defined by problems relating to the availability for consumption of valued commodities. Every custom and institution is economic to the extent that it pertains to the management of these problems. The same institutions are political, to the extent that they pertain to the management of political problems, such as the making and administering of collectively binding decisions and the allocation of power. Complementarily, then, every custom, institution, and belief is religious to the extent that it pertains to the management of religious problems.

From this viewpoint, the problem of definition becomes one of deciding what kinds of human problems are to be regarded as religious. I expect there are some on which we can fairly readily agree, at least, in theory. Dealing with the "tremendum" (E. Goodenough, 1965: 6) or with the "ultimate problems of human life" (Yinger, 1970: 7) may be among them. There are others, of course, on which we will be likely to disagree— disagree as to whether they are real problems at all or, agreeing that they are prolems, disagree as to whether they should be included in the domain of religious problems. But if that is where our disagreement lies, we shall already be ahead of where we are now.

Because of its intimate association with Christianity and with what we all accept as religious movements, I regard the packet of problems to which the term "salvation" refers as one none of us would exclude from the domain of religion. I shall use it as a starting point to illustrate how our conception of religion and how our understanding of our fellow men as religious beings may be affected by a problem-oriented approach.

For this discussion, I shall take salvation to mean the achievement of an idealized state of being—whether that achievement is associated with the human condition before or after death. Thus salvation involves goals for the self.

Self-goals take two forms: avoidance of undesired states—such as sickness, pain, and anxiety—and the achievement of desired states. The avoidance of some states and the achievement of others constitute ends in themselves. We wish to be free from pain just to be free from it, not necessarily as a means to accomplishing something else. Similarly we may wish to feel perfectly cared for or to feel in harmony with the universe for the sake of the feeling itself. It is out of transitory experiences of euphoria that such ultimate goals for the self are forged. Other goals for the self appear to be instrumental—not ends in themselves, but prerequisites to whatever our ends are. Sometimes our ultimate self-goals are inadmissible, as when adults continue to yearn for states of being that were idealized in childhood or infancy, yearnings whose existence they suppress from conscious awareness. At the same time, they magnify to themselves goals that seem instrumental to or symbolic of the one they suppress.

Thus what we are to mean by salvation becomes immediately complicated by the distinction between states of being people wish to maintain as against those they wish to achieve, and by the distinction between those whose maintenance or achievement is an end in itself and those whose maintenance or achievement is instrumental to them. A state of being, like good health, may be an end in itself and at the same time be instrumental to other desired states. If we define salvation as the achievement of idealized states, we must recognize that its complements—the maintenance of such states and the avoidance of or deliverance from undesired states—are closely related concerns, no one being fully separable from the others. And if we see salvation as pertaining to states of being that are valued as ends in themselves, we must recognize that the problem of achieving salvation is to bring into being the conditions—including other states of being—that are considered necessary to achieving the ultimate states. Human concern with salvation most often has to do with finding "the way."

The problem of salvation, then, is simultaneously one of a definition of what are the means to achieve those ends. Both definitions must be at once intellectually and emotionally acceptable. Among people whose cosmology includes ancestral spirits or anthropomorphic beings endowed with superhuman powers, intellectually and emotionally acceptable definitions may have to take account of such beings. For people whose cosmology allows for the existence of nothing that is unconfirmed by or inconsistent with empirical observation, intellectually and emotionally acceptable definitions of salvation and means to salvation must *exclude* any reference to such spiritual or superhuman beings. If concern with salvation is a religious concern, then I cannot dismiss Marxist definitions of it from the domain of religion because they eschew reference to spirits. In other respects, I often find it hard to distinguish behaviorally between those of my acquaintances who are ardent Marxists and those who are ardent Fundamentalists.

We should note, further, that people may be thoroughly devoted to the achievement of self-goals that are disapproved by their fellows—such as the acquisition of political or economic power. A particular conception of salvation may be more or less difficult to hold depending on how it is publicly evaluated; but we would not disqualify the early Christian view of it, for example, because its profession was for a while outlawed by Roman officialdom and anathema to the majority of people in imperial Roman society.

Furthermore, people may conceive of salvation in more than one way and with reference to different aspects of being and to different onto-genetic phases of their existence. The same individual may simultaneously idealize a state in which he is perfectly cared for by an all-nurturing mother and one in which he is omnipotent. He may be torn between incompatible goals for the self, some infantile and some adult, between former idealizations he does not wish to give up and new ones to which he aspires. Freedom from such conflict may become the focus of a new conception of salvation, conceived as the achievement of a resolution of the conflict and internal harmony or as escape from the warring parts of the self, even by loss of the self entirely through its absorption into the ultimate, integrating order of the cosmos. But I would not confine the definition of salvation to such transcendent conceptions of it. Rather I see it as a meaningful question for research to try to discover the conditions that promote the kinds of problems of self that lead people to such transcendent conceptions of salvation. The apparent association of such conceptions with complex social and cultural milieus is suggestive.

Consideration of salvation, then, leads us to a body of problems relating to the definition and achievement of goals for the self. From the point of view expressed at the beginning of this paper, we may say that whatever else the domain of religion includes, it has to do with the human handling of these problems. Whatever these problems are, they presumably arise out of the kinds of experiences of self that people have in their social dealings with one another and in their dealings with the rest of their environment. Dealings with the nonhuman features of environment may play a very important role in the definition of these problems in small hunting societies of the arctic forest and tundra, whereas they may be insignificant in congested urban populations. Clearly, however, the cultural ordering of social relationships plays a crucial role in how people are likely to experience themselves at the hands of others.

Anthropologists have already paid considerable attention to customary procedures in child-rearing and their effects on adult personality. The importance of such practices in helping to shape predominant ego concerns is now widely recognized. But ego concerns are continually being shaped and reshaped as the individual progresses through life. He must go through a series of changes in his social identity, from infancy to childhood to adolescence to adulthood to old age; from the single state to the married one and then to parenthood; from being well to being ill and back to being well again; and from ordinary citizen to the holder of political office.

The necessity of a series of such identity changes—imposed by the maturation and socialization process, if by nothing else—gives to life a progression of the self. There are publicly approved progressions, however, that are socially reinforced. Failure to progress in the approved manner is a source of concern to parents and kin, and their continual communication of their concern is likely to make it a serious ego-problem for the individual at fault. In an earlier work I have already dealt at some length with the problems that accompany the process of identity change in connection with the social psychology of social and cultural change and of social movements—including "religious" ones (W. Goodenough, 1963). I shall not review them now, but wish only to call attention to some of the ego-needs that arise as a consequence of the progression of identities.

An obvious consequence is that people become concerned with what the progression is supposed to be toward and why. Thence come social definitions of the state of being toward which people should strive—definitions of what they should be trying to make of themselves—minimally as responsible, socially acceptable adults and optimally as paragons of what is publicly esteemed as the ideal, whether it be the ideal king or queen, the ideal father or mother, the ideal warrior or courtesan, or the ideal servant. Another obvious consequence is that people have to come to terms with themselves as being less than what they and their fellows hope they will be. They have to find ways of coping with their feelings of shame, guilt, and inadequacy. They also have to find ways of handling their other ego-needs that stand in the way of their being the kinds of persons they would like to be—infantile yearnings that interfere with their ability to exercise responsibility, perhaps. All of us have problems of this kind, and we are clinically classed as "neurotic" to the extent that our ways of handling them involve compulsive behaviors that limit our freedom to play the social roles appropriate to our stations in life. Most societies provide publicly acceptable ways of expressing these compulsions, especially in connection with problems that are widely shared.

Successful transition to new social identities is realized in performance of the social roles associated with them, and successful performance requires the development of behavioral skills and confidence in one's ability to perform satisfactorily. To promote such learning people have institutionalized ways of rehearsing the roles that they aspire to play.

In this regard, the work of Roberts and Sutton-Smith (1962) is particularly revealing. Seeing games as media for rehearsing different kinds of social roles, they found a significant association between three basic types of games—physical skill, strategy, and chance—and three types of roles—competitive or achievement oriented roles, obedience roles, and responsibility roles respectively. In societies where competitive roles are stressed, for example, games of physical skill are more prevalent than in societies where such roles are not stressed. Furthermore, where there is indication of high anxiety regarding a given kind of role, corresponding kinds of games or combinations of games are likely to be elaborated and widely played. Roberts and Sutton-Smith indicate the possibility of similar associations between group pastimes (as distinct from games) and independence, between playing with models (such as dolls and doll houses) and nurturance, and between performance of stunts and self-reliance.

Of special interest here is that addiction to certain kinds of games is indicative of emotional conflict relating to the kind of role indicated—for example, compulsive playing of bingo or of slot machines reflects emotional concern with or "hangups" about responsibility. We may generalize this finding and offer as a working hypothesis that people tend to be unable to leave alone what is symbolic or expressive of their emotional conflicts—what is expressive or symbolic, that is, of their major ego concerns. Being unable to leave such things alone, being compulsively drawn to them, people tend to elaborate them and to keep coming back to them over and over again [1].

So we come inevitably to ritual. Ritual can be seen as developing around situations and involving objects that are associated directly and symbolically with matters about which people are in emotional conflict—things that their ego-problems make it hard for them to leave alone. The compulsion may take one of several forms. It may be a frequently repeated return to a simple rite, like saying a prayer or touching a fetish. It may be expressed in less frequent but more extended spates of activity whose ritual elaborations reflect the compelling force of concern. And again, it may take the form of elaborations of fantasies, expressed and indulged through the telling of myths and tales, the reading of particular kinds of popular novels, attendance at certain kinds of motion pictures, or even devotedly following professional football or baseball. The standard Western novel and Western movie, for example, is a kind of morality play, whose basic theme varies little. It is told over and over again to a large audience that cannot leave it alone, an audience I would surmise that is in emotional conflict about physical courage in a society where the role of an adult man requires him to give his life, if necessary, in order to demonstrate his identity as a man of honor and hence as a "real" man, while at the same time he is not very well prepared to do so. It is, perhaps, no accident that the principal audience for Western movies and novels is in the southern states and among youths about to move into the age group where this aspect of their manhood is most likely to be tested. There is a kind of cult here, which like most cults is aimed at a specific ego-problem and has a correspondingly limited group of devotees.

With these thoughts in mind we may find it instructive to examine the subject matter of ritual elaboration in Truk, an island complex in Micronesia.

My first exposure to Truk was twenty-five years ago, when, as a member of a five-man research team, it was my job to collect information on pre-Christian religious practices there, some still practiced and the rest still vivid in the memories of Truk's older inhabitants. At the same time, Thomas Gladwin collected individual life-histories and a body of psychological test materials, using the Rorschach and Thematic Apperception Tests, from a representative sample of people in the community in which I also worked. We did our work independently, however, and Gladwin published the findings resulting from the test materials without reference to my still unpublished material on traditional religious practices (Gladwin and Sarason, 1953). The test materials, therefore, serve as an independent measure of what seem to be the principal emotional preoccupations of Trukese. Before recounting these, however, I should say something briefly about the more relevant features of Trukese social organization (W. Goodenough, 1951).

The community studied was organized into several matrilineal lineages, each a corporate body holding title to an estate. Sublineages within the larger ones might have estates of their own, also; and individuals, too, held some property in their own names. The interests of the individuals and sublineages, however, were supposed to be subordinate to the interests of the lineage. Siblings were the principal solidarity group, their obligations to one another taking priority over those between parents and children, which took priority in turn over the mutual obligations and interests of husband and wife. The women of each lineage or segment of lineage lived together, if they possibly could, in a single household on land belonging to their lineage or donated to them and their children by one of their husbands. Sisters were subject to the authority of their brothers and were supposed to accede to their brothers' wishes in all things. Similarly, younger brothers were subject to the authority of older brothers, and younger sisters to the authority of older sisters. Lineage headship was based on two principles of seniority working simultaneously: seniority of line within the lineage and seniority by simple order of birth. The eldest son of the eldest woman in the senior female line within the lineage was its symbolic head, whereas the eldest man by order of birth was its executive head. Often the two forms of headship were combined in the same person.

A local political district consisted of several lineages whose estates were derived from grants by male ancestors who had been members of the founding lineage of the district. Members of the founding lineage, or of the lineage that had acquired the right to call itself the founding lineage, together with the children of its male members, were of chiefly rank. All others in the district were commoners. Commoners had the duty of making presentations of food to the district chief in recognition of his eminent domain rights over their estates, held in grant for his lineage. Similarly, the members of a lineage had to provide food on order of the lineage head to meet their lineage's obligations to the chief. People who held grants of trees or land from their father's lineage owed the head of that lineage presentations of food harvested from the land or trees thus received.

Each person was totally dependent on his lineage, his father's lineage, and other kin (in that order of priority) for the necessities of life. He had rights only where he had kin, and he could be a citizen only of the district in which his lineage held an estate. Though he lived with other kin elsewhere, he could not ever change his citizenship. Here was no opportunity for independence, for making one's own way apart from one's family. It followed that one could not marry without one's family's consent nor successfully defy the wishes of one's senior kin, for to be disowned by them was to be in a truly precarious state. The opportunities for individual achievement were confined to skill in war, to being attractive to the opposite sex, and to the practice of specialized skills to which a person had accession by right of kinship. The ideal for both men and women centered on sexual adequacy, on physical bravery and stoicism, on responsibly carrying out their duties to their lineage and kinsmen, on cheerfully and willingly acceding to the demands of those of their kin who had authority over them, and, very importantly, on proving themselves to be responsible adults by the nurturing care they provided for their children. Indeed, children were necessary in order to validate one's status as a responsible adult—especially for men, whose duty it was to prepare and cook the staple breadfruit and taro in bulk for their household (R. Goodenough, 1970).

Within this social context, infants were given a great deal of close human contact for the first two to three years of life. They were continually held by someone within the extended kin—men as well as women. They were never left alone. They were nursed largely on demand. Their toilet training was easy and untraumatic. Weaning, however, was abrupt. At the age of about one year, children were given to a grandparent or similar older relative for a couple of weeks, so that weaning from the breast was accompanied by physical separation from the mother. The pattern of preparing food in bulk every few days worked in practice to mean that food was often gone before the men mobilized to gather and prepare more. There were also seasons of the year when food was relatively scarce, though few starved. The result for small children was that they had to put up with unrequited hunger at unpredictable intervals. In the end, they got fed, but it was by no means certain that there would be something available for them when they were hungry. As children grew older, they were liable to be punished by having food withheld.

When a child reached the age of three or four, it was subjected to a fairly severe dependency weaning. Before, if it cried or was unhappy, it was rocked or dandled or sung to or given food. Now, it was ignored and expected to cope with his own minor hurts and frustrations without a fuss. Tantrums were common at this age.

Subsequently, childhood for boys and girls, but especially for boys, was a period of considerable freedom. Children were not seriously expected to observe the social tabus and obligations in force among adults. Older siblings, however, especially girls, were expected to help look after younger ones, early being given responsibility in this respect, and girls were expected to accompany and assist their mothers in domestic tasks.

At adolescence another dramatic change occurred. Girls at onset of menstruation and boys at acquisition of their first loincloth in the early ones, early being given responsibility in this respect, and girls were expected to observe the social taboos and obligations. Moreover, they were youngest in their lineage's age hierarchies and hence at the beck and call of their seniors, girls being subject to the orders of senior relatives of both sexes. Until their early to middle thirties, however, young men and women continued to be regarded as fairly irresponsible and unreliable. They perfected their physical skills in various tasks, but they were not regarded as ready to be practitioners of the specialized arts and crafts, whose practice often required sexual continence for long periods of time. It was in their forties and fifties, then, as experienced parents, as emerging seniors in their lineage pecking orders, and as now acknowledged practitioners of specialized arts and crafts, that men and women could achieve recognition as persons of account in their lineage and community.

The foregoing description suggests a number of plausible inferences about the emotional life of at least many Trukese. We might expect:

1.   Considerable frustration at the hands of senior relatives in authority, especially among younger people.

2.   Considerable feeling of anger and aggrievement toward the frustrating elders.

3.   Strong feelings of dependency on kin coupled with uncertainty about dependency desires being met and a resulting anxiety over possible neglect or outright rejection by one's kin.

4.   Consequent anxiety about expressing one's feelings of hostility toward one's kin, such expression being grounds for rejection by them.

5. Consequent suppression of overt expression of anger in favor of covert and symbolic expression.

6. Anxiety that one's kin may harbor hostility toward oneself and be expressing it covertly.

7. A tendency to view sickness and personal misfortune as a consequence of hostile activity toward the self—either by human agency (sorcery) or by superhuman agency.

8. Great concern over exhibiting correct form in one's behavior, so as not to give offense, and, in particular, strong feelings about the importance of meeting one's kin obligations.

9. Anxiety about taking independent action on one's own initiative and a corresponding concern to have one's actions and decisions sanctioned by authority.

10. Anxiety about having enough to eat.

11. Tendency to be preoccupied with one's own wants.

12. Consequent tendencies to self-indulgence when opportunties arise and finding it difficult to give of oneself to others consistently and for sustained periods.

13. Consequent emotional conflict between one's desires for self-indulgence and passive dependency on others and one's fear of rejection and disapproval by others for failure to be dutiful and responsible.

14. An accompanying tendency to narcissism and a concern to be admired and found desirable as a person.

15. Consequent anxiety about personal adequacy in relation to those aspects of the self to which social value attaches: physical bravery, sexual adequacy, correctness of behavior, and responsibility.

If these inferences represented no more than a reasoning back from the data on religion in order to arrive at a good fit between emotional concerns and topics of ritual elaboration, what I have to say in this regard would be suspect, indeed. It is crucial, therefore, that the inferences I have just outlined are in very close accord with the conclusions to which Sarason came from his "blind" analysis of Gladwin's psychological test materials (Gladwin and Sarason, 1953) [2].

His conclusions about Trukese personality included the following:

1. Lack of intellectual flexibility and difficulty with problem-solving situations.

2. Lack of self-confidence in decision-making situations.

3. Strong inhibition of hostile feelings.

4. Superficiality of personal relations and a tendency for them to be emotionally unsatisfying and hence a source of frustration.

5. Strong anxiety about sexual adequacy.

6. Tension between the sexes—men feeling the need of positive affec-

tional responses from women, and women feeling a need to be assertive over and subtly to aggress against men.

7.   Difficulty in being consistently giving and responsible as parents, leading to inconsistent treatment of children, to problems of self-confidence and self-acceptance in children, and to equations of food with security and love.

8.   Marked food anxiety.

9.   Marked separation anxiety, closely linked with food anxiety.

10.   A passive and self-indulgent orientation as against a self-assertive, self-denying one.

Thus, we have independent corroboration of our inferences. We can accept them as apparent facts about the emotional concerns and ego-problems of many Trukese. We expect these concerns and problems to be reflected in customary practices and beliefs. The reflection, as it turns out, is remarkable.

My own material relating to what I regarded as belonging to the domain of religion at the time I collected it, produced four major areas of ritual elaboration: (1) divination; (2) rites relating to insuring good harvests of breadfruit and fish; (3) rites relating to the diagnosis, treatment, and care of the sick; and (4) rites relating to spirits of the dead. I noted also a pantheon of heavenly gods, but found that they were not objects of direct worship nor foci of ritual, having more to do with the cosmological frame or background within which ritual practices were oriented and explained. The above four topics were not the only foci of ritual elaboration; but they are the ones that I saw as having something to do with the "supernatural" and which, according to convention, I therefore classified as pertaining to religion at the time of my study. So I shall discuss them first and thereby set the stage for the other rituals.

The Trukese had many forms of divination. Some were very simple and in class with our "She loves me, she loves me not." Others involved noting natural phenomena, the flight of birds, and the like. The most elaborate was a form of divination with knots, involving the 256 possible permutations of two sets of sixteen, each sixteen being based on the permultations of two sets of four. Every permutation had a name and a meaning that was adjustable to the nature of the question being divined. Specialists in the art, who had to pay a handsome fee to learn it, were consulted on all kinds of occasions to diagnose illness, to determine the duration of a state of affairs, and to determine the auspiciousness of every conceivable kind of undertaking. It is evident from their talk that people were frequent consultants of the diviner.

The thing about divination, of course, is not its reliability as a predictor but its serving as an authority that sanctions a decision. It relieves the decision maker from responsibility for the outcome of his decision; he acted, after all, on the best of authority. The regularity with which Trukese consulted the divinatory knots is in keeping with anxiety about responsibility. It is also in keeping with separation anxiety, for a person who is not responsible cannot be blamed for the outcome by those on whose affection and good will he is emotionally dependent.

Another specialty had to do with the performance of rites to insure a good breadfruit harvest. From the time just before the fruit began to form until it was ready to pick, the breadfruit summoner, on invitation by the district chief, performed a series of rites. They included the daily recitation of certain spells, making model canoes and holding model-canoe races, and offerings to the lord of the mythical southern homeland of breadfruit—all done, it was said, to insure that the spirits of breadfruit will come and infuse the local trees with fruitfulness. The rites were not necessarily performed every year. In response to my prodding, I was told that breadfruit did indeed grow anyway, but people felt a lot better about it if the rites were performed. Somewhat less elaborate rites to insure a good fish supply were held irregularly as there seemed to be need, Breadfruit in Truk, like bread in pre-potatoes Europe, is the staple food and hence the symbol of food generally. The elaborate ritual accompanying the growth of each year's crop is in keeping with anxiety about food and about all the food symbolizes.

The Trukese regarded illness as resulting from being "bitten" or "eaten" by a dangerous or evil spirit or by a ghost; from sorcery (which involved the use of such a spirit or ghost); from the anger of a heavenly god or good spirit of the dead; from the anger of the spirit of a dead kinsman, angry because his surviving kin had not conducted themselves as kinsmen should; from the breach of taboos pertaining to important specialists; or finally and less commonly from one's soul having departed from one's body and failed to return. In every case but the last, sickness is a consequence of having behaved incorrectly in some way, obviously in keeping with anxiety about behaving correctly. It is also in keeping with anxiety about covert hostile feelings by others toward oneself, especially the attribution of illness to sorcery, which was not uncommon. Treatment involved the use of medicines over which the appropriate spell had been recited. Some treatments were widely known—in a class with our own home remedies. Others required the services of specialists. Following a more serious illness, fairly elaborate rites were performed to insure against a relapse.

Sickness was a time when the kin were all supposed to rally around and be very supportive. Trukese people today often refuse to go to the hospital for treatment for fear of being separated from their kin—especially if they expect that they will not recover. Every Trukese man I have ever talked to about it has been insistent about wanting to die in the arms of his close female kinsmen, especially his sisters and sisters' daughters. And the one death that I have had occasion actually to witness was in their arms. We would expect sickness greatly to heighten dependency needs and separation anxiety. The ritual involvement of kinsmen is in keeping with such anxiety.

Rituals and beliefs relating to the spirits of the dead were also elaborate (W. Goodenough, 1963: 132–140). They turned on the idea that each individual was both a good and a bad soul. When a person died, his grave was watched for several nights in the hope that the good soul might possess a living relative, who would then become a spirit-medium through whom the good soul would subsequently communicate with the living. Usually such possession did not occur. In any case—regardless of the dead person's conduct in life—his good soul went to live in the sky world, where existence was much as on earth but benefited from the superhuman knowldge and powers of the sky deities who presided there. If the good soul possessed someone, it became a member of a special class of potentially helpful spirits that could diagnose some illnesses, retrieve lost souls, and foretell good fishing. Moreover, it might teach its medium new medicines and spells, acquired from the heavenly gods. However, such a spirit was easily offended; its desires for perfume, for delicacies to eat (through the body of the medium), and for entertainment in the form of elaborate dances needed to be indulged. The good soul was therefore a symbolic representation of the senior relatives on whom one was dependent. One could never be sure, but maybe this one would turn out to be a dependable spirit who, if properly catered to, would counsel, feed, succor, and impart life-giving knowledge to his junior dependent kin. It was to be expected, of course, that he would punish them for neglect or improper behavior by making them ill. All of this again is fully in keeping with the self-aspirations of people who see fulfillment through dependency on—and who at the same time fear rejection by—seniors who themselves tend to be in conflict about their responsibilities.

Beliefs about the bad soul were also in keeping with the psychological picture. Each person's bad soul invariably became a ghost, and ghosts were dangerous, fearsome things that eventually became indistinguishable from a class of evil spirits associated with the soil, whose bite was believed to cause elephantiasis, one of the more dread diseases. I have known people who have seen and experienced ghosts. Ghosts could be exorcised if they were too troublesome, but to perform the rite of exorcism was regarded as a terrifying thing. Here we have a projection of that other image of senior kinsmen as objects of one's hostility. They appear as dangerously inclined to satisfy their own needs by feeding, as it were, on their junior kinsmen. All of this is again in keeping with a pattern of covert hostility toward senior relatives. As a symbolic act of hostility toward those to whom one dares not show hostility directly, the rite of exorcising ghosts must seem terrifyingly dangerous indeed.

When I came back from Truk with my data on religion, all I had was material for a description of ritual and belief. I could not say what it meant to the Trukese; I could not say why they should want to hold to such ritual and belief. The psychological analysis by Gladwin and Sarason provided the information that began to make it intelligible to me. But it also forced me to ask about the other ego-problems that were *not* reflected in the four bodies of ritual I had recorded as Trukese religion. Were there other bodies of ritual that I had excluded from Trukese religion because they did not appear to be associated with supernatural beings or with supernatural power? Indeed there were—rituals that not only gave expression to the missing areas of concern but gave further expression to the areas already covered by the so-called "religious" rituals. In other words, if ego-problems are to be our point of reference, my sticking to the supernatural was providing an incomplete picture of the Trukese religious life.

Extramarital love affairs were widely, indeed compulsively, pursued by younger men and women (W. Goodenough, 1949; Gladwin and Sarason, 1953). The game was elaborately ritualized, with changing fads as to the manner of its ritualization. Go-betweens, standardized signaling systems, highly stylized modes of speaking, mutual scarifications, the use of magic, and in recent years secretly transmitted love letters were all parts of the rituals of love. It was a Trukese saying that everyone wants to marry his sweetheart, but once he marries her, she cannot be his sweetheart any more. The point of the saying is that in marriage, the mutual interests of husband and wife were subordinate to their duties to their respective sets of siblings and parents. The husband was caught up in a system of obligations to his in-laws that could be onerous; and it was his wife's duty to take their part against him if he complained. To be important and loved for oneself alone or at least to have the illusion of being thus important and loved, young men and women had to go outside the public system of social relationships to a private, secret world of their own, where the risks of being caught in adultery provided testimony of how much they meant to one another. That the same protestations of eternal love might get made to someone else a few months later reveals that it was the game that mattered, a game to which many people were addicted and which they elaborately codified and recodified. It fits well the psychological test findings of anxiety about sexual adequacy [3] and frustration in emotionally satisfying social relationships.

Also ritualized were the behaviors to be shown by junior to senior relatives, by commoners to chiefs, and by laymen to the more prestigious categories of learned specialists. These were the people on whom others were most dependent for their welfare and whose disfavor was most to be feared. Where separation anxiety and control of hostility led to a concern with formally correct behavior, we should expect this concern to have produced a ritualization of correct forms in those relationships where concern was most heavily felt. Another by-product of concern with correct behavior was the fairly heavy emphasis on taboo—not with the idea that violation resulted in ritual pollution, but with the idea that violation was offensive, either to spirits or to other and more powerful human beings, and hence bound to lead to failure in whatever undertaking the taboos were associated with.

At least several times a year, people were obligated to make presentations of food to their district chief. These presentations were accompanied by considerable ceremony. Each lineage carried the great bowls of food it had prepared on special frames and marched to the chief's meeting house, chanting songs special to the occasion. There the food was piled high. The object at feasts generally, and these were no exception, was for each lineage to strive to outdo the others in the production of food and to allow everyone to wallow in abundance. As one Trukese said to me as he and I surveyed such abundance at a feast, "There is nothing more beautiful than to see a great pile of food, to know that you can eat all you want, that everybody else can eat all he wants, and that, when all have finished eating, there will still be a great pile of food left." These occasions were reaffirmations of their loyalty to the chief and of his being one on whom they could depend as provider and nurturer of all. He took a share of the food presented and divided the bulk of it up among the people to take back home, thus affirming his obligations as their patron, as custodian of their welfare. The chief's duty to oversee the general welfare, his duty to ask the breadfruit summoner to perform for the community, and the original meaning of the word for chief, "big father," these along with other things indicate that the relation of father to dependent child. The rituals of dependency in the relations of the living to the good souls of the dead were reenacted in slightly altered form in the relations between commoners and chiefs.

The psychological concerns I have enumerated were also expressed in organized community dancing under the direction of the chief—occasions for narcissistic indulgence and so treated. They continue to be expressed in the widespread modern addiction to the game of bingo and other games of pure chance. They were and continue to be expressed in folk-tales, many of which involved either bad or inadequate older brothers as against meticulously correct and clever younger ones or, more often, cannibalistic evil spirits or ogres who are outwitted by a clever youngest brother. The concerns that could not be left alone in ritual dealings with the supernatural could not be left alone in folktales, either. If rituals relating to the dead were religious activities, then the telling of folktales that gave expression to and provided relief from the same concerns must be regarded as religious activities, also.

It should be clear by now how inextricably intertwined in their expression the problems of ego-maintenance and of ego-fulfillment can become. So much so that one might understandably ask whether the Trukese traditionally had a conception of salvation at all. I think they did, though not in the sense of freedom from sin and release from guilt, so common among Christian views of salvation. The most important view of salvation for most Trukese seems to have been dependency on a reliably feeding and nurturing parental figure. Its achievement was the longed-for dream. It was looked for among the spirits of the dead and it was looked for among the chiefs. In modern times, it has been looked for in the Christian churches and in the administering colonial powers. Indeed, it tends to be looked for in social relationships generally. Very recently I witnessed a Trukese businessman in his thirties, mellowed with drink in a restaurant, turn his chair so that he could recline in the arms of his former American high school teacher, calling him "father," as he sought his advice regarding a financial problem.

What I have been saying should not be confused with the kinds of psychological analyses of religious practices and beliefs that are aimed at explaining religion away by reducing it to the language of psycho-pathology in order explicitly or implicitly to discredit traditional, cher-ished beliefs as crutches for neurotic souls. The knowing ones ever thus belittle the myths and rites of others without recognizing their own dependence on ,other myths and rituals, such as myths of the soul put forward in the name of science and the many rituals of self-testing—from athletics to reading papers at scholarly or scientific meetings—in which som any of us compulsively engage. If I here use the language of ego-psychology, it is because it is the only language I have for talking about the universal human concern with self-maintenance and self-realization. I am not seeking to debunk religion, but to delimit its subject matter.

To some the approach to religion taken here may appear to be incom-patible with that taken by Durkheim and his followers in sociology and anthropology, but I do not think it is. If I have defined religion differently, my definition includes within its sphere of relevance such things as human concern with the moral authority of society. Problems of ego-maintenance and ego-fulfillment of the kind I have discussed are intimately bound up with social expectations and with the moral authority that sanctions those expectations. Nor is my approach inconsistent with the idea that people tend to anthropomorphize forces that impinge upon them in ways consistent with social experience (Swanson, 1960). It assumes that people will conceive the problems in ways that reflect those experiences. Nor do I exclude from the domain of ego-concerns the need to feel cognitively oriented, the kind of need that has been emphasized by Geertz (1966). I am merely saying that if we take the problems, not the ways they are conceptualized, as delimiting the cross-culturally (and cross-personally) common ground of religion, we shall be better able to develop a satisfying theory of religious behavior.

To this end I am suggesting that we take seriously the view that people's major emotional preoccupations, especially their concerns with the cultivation and maintenance of the self in the social and symbolic milieus in which they live, are the stuff from which the phenomenon of religion arises. To describe how people express these preoccupations and how they try to deal with them is to describe their religious life. Particularly attractive to me as an anthropologist is that, in this view, there is no man without a religious life, without religious concerns, and without some ways of expressing them and dealing with them that together constitute something we can consider to be his religion. We may not always find it personally attractive, but that is beside the point.

It may seem that the approach to religion taken here opens the door too wide, so that almost everything becomes religion. If that is so, does the concept of religion lose its value for social and behavioral science by becoming too general? That religious concerns pervade much of human activity seems to me no more troublesome in this regard than the well accepted idea that economic concerns do so also. Given our habits of mind, anthropologists may feel more comfortable to confine the term religion to publicly approved customary practices and professions of belief that have to do with ego-concerns of the kind I have discussed. In doing so, however, we must recognize that we are dealing with a phenomenon resembling an iceberg. Our understanding of the phenomenon requires that we consider its totality, not just the small portion that shows above water or that is publicly approved and institutionalized.

It is not startlingly new to define religion in terms of human problems of being, in a psychological (i.e., spiritual) as distinct from a material sense. The problem is that anthropologists have not followed out the logical implications of such definition. But by doing just this, it seems to me, we can put the comparative study of religion on a firmer foundation than will ever be possible as long as we continue to take the content of professed belief about supernatural beings (or about anything else) as our defining criterion.

NOTES

1. This conclusion is consistent with the finding by Whiting and Child (1935) that "negative fixations" resulting from child-rearing practices are significantly associated with the content of at least some projective systems, such as beliefs relating to the causes of illness.
2. "Blind" refers to Sarason's having based his analysis on the test materials alone without prior knowledge of Trukese social organization and child-rearing practices.
3. That sexual and, by extension, personal adequacy was very much involved is demonstrated by the common view of sexual intercourse as a "contest" in which the one who experienced orgasm sooner "lost" to the other.

REFERENCES

FRAKE, CHARLES O.

1964   "A Structural Description of Subanun 'Religious Behavior.' " Pp. 111–130 in W. H. Goodenough (ed.), *Explorations in Cultural Anthropology*. New York: McGraw-Hill.

GEERTZ, CLIFFORD

1966   "Religion as Cultural System." Pp. 1–46 in M. Banton (ed.), *Anthropological Approaches to the Study of Religion*. London: Tavistock.

GERLACH, LUTHER
HINE, VIRGINIA H.

1970   *People, Power, Change: Movements of Social Transformation*. Indianapolis: Bobbs-Merrill.

GLADWIN, THOMAS
SARASON, SEYMOUR B.

1953   *Truk: Man in Paradise*. Viking Fund Publications in Anthropology No. 20. New York: Wenner-Gren Foundation.

GOODENOUGH, ERWIN R.

1965   *The Psychology of Religious Experience*. New York: Basic Books.

GOODENOUGH, RUTH G.

1970   "Adoption on Romonum, Truk." Pp. 314–340 in V. Car-
                    rol (ed.), *Adoption in Eastern Oceania*. Honolulu: Uni-
                    versity of Hawaii Press.

GOODENOUGH, WARD H.

1949   "Premarital Freedom on Truk: Theory and Practice."
                    American Anthropologist 51: 615–620.
1951   *Property, Kin and Community on Truk*. Yale University
                    Publications in Anthropology No. 46. New Haven: Yale
                    University Press.
1963   *Cooperation in Change*. New York: Russell Sage Foun-
                    dation.

LA BARRE, WESTON

1970   *The Ghost Dance*. Garden City, N.Y.: Doubleday.

ROBERTS, JOHN M.
SUTTON-SMITH, BRIAN

1962   "Child Training and Game Involvement." *Ethnology*
                    1: 166–185.

SPIRO, MELFORD E.

1966   "Religion: Problems of Definition and Explanation." Pp.
                    85–126 in M. Banton (ed.), *Anthropological Approaches
                    to the Study of Religion*. London: Tavistock.

SWANSON, GUY E.

1960   *The Birth of the Gods*. Ann Arbor: University of Michi-
                    gan Press.

WALLACE, ANTHONY F. C.

1966   *Religion, an Anthropological View*. New York: Random
                    House.

WHITING, JOHN W. M.
CHILD, IRVING

1953   *Child Training and Personality*. New Haven: Yale Uni-
                    versity Press.

YINGER, J. MILTON

1970   *The Scientific Study of Religion*. New York: Macmillan.

Paul W. Pruyser

THE MENNINGER FOUNDATION, TOPEKA

Problems of Definition and Conception in the Psychological Study of Religious Unbelief

1

Definitions of belief and unbelief change with the times. Biblical writers had much to say about true believers and idolaters, but hardly knew of unbelievers. They had, however, a pungent statement about lukewarm people, whom God would "spew out of his mouth." Tertullian considered the human soul not only religious by nature, but *naturaliter Christiana.* During the Crusades a sizable portion of mankind were called infidels; these happened to be Turks, who, as adherents of Islam, were ready to give their lives for their faith in holy wars. Slightly more liberal was the attitude of Francis Bacon: "It were better to have no opinion of God at all, than such an opinion as is unworthy of him: For the one is unbelief, the other is contumely" (Bacon, n.d.: 69). These examples suffice to show the persistence of a *vantage point which makes belief (sometimes a particular belief) the norm and declares unbelief a deviant condition in need of a special explanation.* This vantage point is fixed by the linguistic structure of the word unbelief, which, as negation, takes belief as the normative state.

What time does to definitions of belief and unbelief is illustrated by modern examples. Kierkegaard's image of the "leap of faith" implies that unbelief is a more natural state than belief, and that the latter requires an explanation. At another level, this image is based on a sophisticated but partisan distinction between religious belief or religiosity in general, including membership in Christendom, and what Kierkegaard saw as authentic Christian faith. That same distinction is demonstrated in the fondness of many contemporary theologians for the neo-orthodox slogan that religion is unbelief. Around the turn of the century, William James wrote his celebrated essay *The Will to Believe* (1897) in an effort to make a state of belief understandable, if not acceptable, to intelligent people who were prone to take, as he put it, "a different option between propositions." Since James, far more has been written about the psychology of belief than the psychology of unbelief, but it would be rash to conclude that this meant that belief was taken as the normative condition. On the contrary, many writers, particularly the early psychoanalytic students, seemed surprised at the existence and persistence of belief in otherwise reasonable people and therefore found it worthy of special attention and special explanation. Thus, in modern times, at least for some people, the negative term unbelief is no longer a term of disapprobation. *The vantage point is shifting from belief to unbelief as the natural or normative condition.*

The psychology of religion cannot take either of these two points of view for granted. If it is to do justice to the phenomena both of religion and of irreligion, or of belief and of unbelief, it finds a better foothold in thought patterns that keep both terms in apposition. Apposition can take several forms. Kierkegaard regarded belief and unbelief, faith and doubt, religion and faith, dialectically. This means that every thesis elicits its antithesis and no proposition remains fixed. A simpler form of apposition is demonstrated in the intriguing Baconian phrase that "there is as superstition in avoiding superstition" (Bacon, n.d.: 71). In terms more amenable to investigation one could say that it takes a kind of faith to be an unbeliever of sorts. Browning stated the relation between the two vantage points poetically and with a touch of nostalgia in Bishop Blougram's Apology:

> All we have gained then by our unbelief
> Is a life of doubt diversified by faith,
> For one of faith diversified by doubt:
> We called the chess-board white—we call it black. (Browning, 1895: 351)

Whatever the particular formulation, the interactional point of view has the virtue of placing the state or process of belief as well as unbelief where it belongs: in the breast of each individual, in the bosom of each church, in the pattern of each culture. We can no longer indulge in the game of calling unbelievers all those who do not share our particular beliefs, or of pitying as naive believers all those who do not share our posture of self-confessed unbelief, doubt, skepticism, agnosticism, or atheism.

The interactional view also allows us to keep a good grasp on reality, which, inasmuch as it is interesting, is so precisely by its phenomenal messiness rather than any neatness. Reality presents such untidy facts as a gradual attrition of church membership in this country in the last fifty years, with a sudden upward spurt in the ten years following World War II; considerable dissent within denominations; acts of faith outside the congregational establishments and postures of unbelief within; the rise of new religions and belief systems or the reemergence of old ones such as astrology, witchcraft, or chauvinistic nationalism complete with creed and cult (Pruyser, 1971); renewed interest in the Cabala and drug-induced mysticisim; and the rise of underground churches which once more pitch faith against religion. Reality presents the brutal fact that many unchurched persons claim to be believers, not in religious fads or spiritual eccentricities, but in mainline Christian tenets. Reality offers the observation of the tremendous expansion of the religious book market in the last several decades, not solely in churches but in universities and on paperback racks.

Another and very important element of untidiness in any approach to the phenomena of unbelief is conceptual: whether belief and unbelief are apposed or opposed, much will depend on the underlying definition of religion. I myself regard the problem of defining religion insoluble, not because of any presumed elusiveness, spuriousness, or ephemerality of religion, but because religion is so tied up with thoughts of vastness and plenitude, capsuled in the German prefix Ur- and the Latin omni-. I rest my case with the following statement by Goodenough:

> Those who think they know most clearly, for disapproval or approval, what religion "is" seem to recognize least what amazingly dif-

ferent aspects of human life the term has legitimately indicated. We can, therefore, best approach religion by getting in mind the various experiences that men have called religion, rather than what we think should ideally be given the name. (Goodenough, 1965: 2)

Goodenough, like James, kept the *varieties* of religious experience in the picture because he saw variety itself as an essential feature of religion, much as the idea of art entails by necessity a multiplicity of media, forms, and schools.

Granting, then, that definitions of religion will affect any statement about the apposition or opposition of belief and unbelief, I would like to illustrate the inherent complexities of unbelief by reviewing selectively a few major psychological thinkers about religion in order to see where their thoughts would lead. Indeed, what I wish to emphasize is the immense variety of unbelief, and the tenuous status of the word "unbelief" in designating the whole span of phenomena. I will focus on authors whose works have proved to be seminal.

II

A very good starting point is Schleiermacher, not only because his major work from 1799 is now undergoing a kind of renaissance, but because he pitched his lectures on religion *an die Gebildeten unter ihren Verächtern* —to the sophisticates among its despisers (Schleiermacher, 1955). Here is no quick damnation or cheap denigration of unbelievers; on the contrary, there is the implied compliment that many unbelievers are eminently reasonable, cultured persons with impeccable ethics, an asset to their civilization. In essence, Schleiermacher asks them whether they realize their "utter dependency," that is, their contingency, and what they do with the feelings aroused by the human condition. Their heart is in reasoning, but do they know the reasonings of the heart?

Schleiermacher made the "feeling of utter dependency" central to his definition of religion, and even if we translate this feeling as *sentiment* or *awareness* in order to do him historical justice, it follows that, for him, unbelief is the failure to admit, realize, or come to terms with one's utter dependency and as a result, organize one's life around it. In modern terms, unbelief is in this view an intellectual attitude of narcissism in which the individual assumes more self-determination and greater ontological status than he actually has. This is, however, a meta-psychological and not a psychological statement, for Schleiermacher was well aware that most of his hearers were not more prone than anyone else to particular narcissistic symptoms. He assumed in his discourses that many of them were quite exemplary in their object relations, as we would say today, and he praised their high-mindedness. He even left the door open to the possibility that their expressed views of the self were not commensurate with their private feelings about the self.

In other words, Schleiermacher questioned the limits of enlightenment. An admirer of Spinoza and Schelling, he was quite enlightened himself, but struggled over the proper role of humility in an enlightened mind and culture. Obviously he felt that humility not only preserves a balanced perspective on a person's status in the cosmos but actually enriches his life and enhances his human potential. He spoke movingly of a sense and taste of the infinite, a sense of wonder, a longing of the heart, and an attitude of reverence. Trusting that the feelings of the heart are pathways to objective truth, he was bold enough in his other works to try to produce an empirical theology. And thus one can say that unbelievers are richer than believers in self-respect and dedication to reasoning, but depleted in humility and knowledge of that path to discovery that leads from feelings to thought.

It should be noted, however, that humility has ambiguous status as a condition of religious belief. Psychoanalytic investigators, noting how often religious belief is buttressed by speculations about individual immortality, and vice verse, have correctly pointed to a persistent core of grandiosity in some religious formulations of "life after death." Empirically, some people are humble enough not to demand immortality for themselves, and they may regard themselves irreligious; others, more likely to call themselves religious, humiliate themselves now before their gods in order to assure their eventual continuity after death.

Turning now to Otto (1912), by jumping over more than a century, we find religion defined as the exercise of a common human talent for dealing with the idea of the holy. The holy is a symbol for the *mysterium tremendum et fascinosum*, for the *wholly other*, for the numinosity that confronts man in situations of awe, terror, grandeur, and overwhelming power. In the later editions of his famous book, Otto assumed that human beings have a disposition or an *Anlage* for numinous experiences; that some people even have a talent for them (1936, 140, 204), and that stimulation and nurture are necessary to turn potentiality into actuality. In the stimulus conditions he included not only religious education, that is, all the obvious ways in which religion is taught, but also the phenomenal forms in which the holy appears—the theophanies of the spirit in nature, art, liturgy, myth, and mysticism.

The crucial implication of this definition of religion for unbelief lies in the notion of disposition or talent for numinosity. Are unbelievers simply less gifted? Are they poorly endowed with talent for the numinous?

Or have they been nurtured less by adequate educational experiences—perhaps starved of the Spirit's own theophanies? In either case, unbelief would seem to be a lack of something, resulting in statistical data which would show an uneven distribution, just as aesthetic talent and artistic sensitivity seem to be unevenly distributed in any population.

But Otto's thoughts on religion have prepared the soil for another conceptualization of unbelief. His *mysterium* has two dynamic parameters: it attracts and it repels, it causes feelings of bliss and awe. It produces not only an awareness of one's dependency, or even of Schleiermacher's *utter dependency*, but insight into one's creatureliness vis-à-vis the objectivity of the noncontingent, that is, the presence of the numinous. Unbelief, from this vantage point, is not merely a quantitative but a qualitative datum. It might consist in selective blunting of feelings in which the mystery is eliminated from the *mysterium*. One form of unbelief would be the condition of being lukewarm, of having selectively flat affect, with no room for bliss or awe. Another form of unbelief would consist in opting for only one of the *mysterium's* parameters: if bliss be the option pursued to the extreme, the end-product is the Pollyanna who is perfectly at ease with the whole universe because it is so friendly; if awe is the sole option, one ends up in a state of chronic depression and anxiety or in relentless gloom. Neither case elicits the holy; instead, one is either thrilled to death or haunted to death without having to reflect on the ambiguities of his creatureliness. Belief is hardly necessary in these conditions, for the cosmos presents no enigma, no puzzlement, no intrigue, no serious mystery. The individual leaps from his own dominant mood to the composition of the cosmos and finds the two identical, by a grand narcissistic projection, unthwarted by the exigencies of reality testing. Of course, the whole idea of creatureliness is foreign to this projection, for the self is endlessly expanded to the furthest reaches of the universe.

James regarded religion, for the purposes of his Gifford lectures, as consisting of "the feelings, acts, and experiences of individual men in their solitude, so far as they apprehend themselves to stand in relation to whatever they may consider the divine" (James, 1902: 31). It is a selective, yet lenient definition, and he used it magnificently in describing the varieties of religious experience. He emphasized the solemnity of reactions to the divine, stressed their enthusiastic quality, and imbued believers with a sense of reality for the unseen. He paid much attention to mysticism and conversion, and as a good pragmatist he tended to evaluate religion by its fruits rather than its origins, putting much stock in saintliness and zest.

James did address himself to the problem of unbelief in the last chapter of the *Varieties*, mainly by opposing science and religion. To him, those who shy away from traffic with the reality of the unseen either have no vision of the unseen, and thus lack imagination, or hesitate to attribute any reality to it, and thus in the spirit of positivism deny its validity. In either case unbelief derives from a narrow conception of the universe and a shallow response to its complexities. James also held that the impersonality of science makes it deal only with the symbols of reality, whereas private and personal phenomena make us deal with "realities in the completest sense of the term." Belief may be untidy, ad hoc, and concrete, but the bit of experience it deals with is "a solid bit as long as it lasts." Unbelief on positivistic grounds may be orderly, general, and abstract, but what it deals with are "but ideal pictures of something whose existence we do not inwardly possess" (James, 1902: 499). But James's great stress on motor activity would make him also say that in the end a man's beliefs appear in what he *does* (with all possible contradictions among his doings), rather than in the ephemeral accounts of his verbalized world view.

In *The Will to Believe* (James, 1897), which preceded the *Varieties* by several years, religious belief is defined as a momentous and a forced option between hypotheses, guided by the double law of knowing the truth and avoiding error. Belief here is seen as risk-taking, committing oneself, choosing, venturing, exercising the will; in a word, acting in accord with Pascal's wager argument. By implication, unbelief would be characterized at first blush by a lack of commitment and venturesomeness. But James indicated that one can, at time, passionately decide not to decide, be determined to "leave the question open," in which case one shoulders some risk of losing the truth. In other words, a deliberate and passionate agnosticism can be very close to religious belief, despite its surface appearance of unbelief. This commitment to open-endedness is is precisely what Rieff (1966) has singled out as the attitude of faith in classical psychoanalysis. We can thus complement Bacon's phrase that there is a *superstition in avoiding superstition* by the proposition that there can be a *faith in avoiding faith*. It seems to me that this particular kind of faith may account for some of the interesting data which Vernon found in his analytical study of the so-called "Religious Nones" (1968).

Before turning to Freud, it would be well to pay attention to Jones, who, although a minor psychoanalytic student of religion, formulated the strategically important thought that "what one wants to know about the divine purpose is its intention towards oneself" (Jones, 1951: Vol. 2: 203). Though not a definition of religion, this statement implies that a substantial element of belief for many people is thoroughly personalistic: the belief in a personal God, who has intentions toward his worshipers, whom he regards as individuals. In this conception, God and man engage in object relations, have mutual concerns and invest in each other; it is desirable that they are known to each other at the level of motives and intentions. The aspect of God correlated with this belief is known to theologians as providence.

In this perspective on belief, unbelief might consist of any balking at providence, any disinterest in the terms of one's own contingent destiny, any rejection of the mutual trust that is a necessary condition for engaging in object relations with the divine. Since Jones saw the divine personalities as an analogues of human family figures, conceived by projection, and since he considered the God-image essential to religion, unbelief can be a reasoned as well as an irrational or neurotic objection to the kind of object relations assumed in the providential model of belief. A reasoned objection might focus on the childish origins and the atavism of the cosmic projection of the family model and reject it, or it might denounce the public or doctrinal formulations of providence as myth. Neurotic objections may stem from personal distrust in any providential benevolence anywhere in the universe and thus lead to a depersonalization of any God-image.

In Freud's definitions of religion, the God-models most often used are the progenitor and the father-image of divine providence, whose power can make or break a man, but to whose power one seeks access as a possible aid in one's own felt helplessness. Constructing a phylogenetic sequence, Freud hinged much of his definition of religion on what people do with their infantile feelings of omnipotence. In the animistic stage, people are given to a frank use of omnipotent thinking, expressed in rituals and magical acts which exert power. In the religious stage, man cedes omnipotence to his gods but retains some of it for himself in order to influence these gods to act in his favor. In the scientific stage, man relinquishes his omnipotence and resigns himself to the superior forces of nature, except for that trace of it which undergirds his belief in the power of his mind to cope with reality.

Since phylogeny is repeated in ontogeny, religious beliefs is by definition a maturational or developmental phenomenon. It lies on the hitherside of that unwavering, cold-blooded reality testing which is the ideal of positivism, and of that sober resignation to the superior power of nature in the face of which one dare not ask for personal favors. By conjecture, some unbelief, then, is a rejection of childish propensities or an abandonment of natural wishes for protection and solace. This kind of unbelief requires self-scrutiny, intellectual honesty, and the courage of one's unpopular convictions.

But it is implied in Freud's approach to religion that many forms of unbelief can be at the same developmental level as belief itself. As a clinician, Freud (1907:14) knew of periods of doubting in the faithful;

he knew of the dynamic concomitance of faith and doubt as expressions of ambivalent feelings. Some of his patients engaged in compulsive blaspheming; others had obssesions about God and the Devil, or loving and hating their God. Some religious persons merge the image of their father with their image of God; others separate these two and split their positive and negative feelings between them. At this level, unbelief can be just as primitive, neurotic, and drive-determined as belief. In fact, it may lack the finish which adheres to a more consistent and integrated system of religious belief, particularly when the latter is so much in the public domain that subscribing to it has adaptive value.

There is a third ground for unbelief. Publicly upheld religion, buttressed by authoritative doctrinal formulations, exerts in Freud's view a peculiar form of thought control. Its propositions are held to be beyond scrutiny. Belief is close to taboos. Science, however, knows no taboos. Therefore, some unbelief, particularly if coupled with a positivistic spirit, can be appreciated as a liberation of the mind from the fetters of taboo. This kind of unbelief can have a certain nobility as well, for since taboo is feared precisely to the extent that the forbidden act against which the taboo is erected is also desired, such a liberation of the mind implies a disciplined overcoming of desire. Meditation, conversion, or self-education could enhance such a state, which in some ways resembles the ideals of Stoicism and whose outstanding features are clarity of mind and intellectual vigor.

Implicit in Freud's thought on religion is a fourth form of unbelief. Religion, like everything else, is subject to transformations. Freud recognized differences between primitive and sophisticated religion, both anthropologically and individually. He considered his friend Pfister an intriguingly sophisticated religionist. One could thus ask whether religious development can proceed to the point at which it eliminates itself or becomes something else, like a philosophy, an ethical stance, a *Weltanschauung,* or an existential posture, with creed and cult receding into the background (Pruyser, 1973). I think this is a fascinating problem, which puts some forms of unbelief in that special category of modern experience that some theologians have described as the post-Christian attitude. It may be linked with a God-is-dead theology, and it may even approximate that special state of faith which Kierkegaard saw as the overcoming of religion.

The last student of religion I turn to is Goodenough, whose work is deeply influenced by both Otto and Freud. From Otto he took the idea of the holy, especially its aspect of the *tremendum.* Edified by Freud's thoughts, he saw the *tremendum* not only as the external and cosmic *x,* chaotic in appearance, which controls the universe, but also as the internal and personal *x,* also chaotic, of our motives. childhood fixations, and sense of guilt controlling each of us from within. Both are equally mysterious and powerful—awe-inspiring in a very potent sense. Man defends himself against the terror of both *tremendums* by throwing protective blankets over them (the blanket of repression, the curtain that hides the holy of holies, the veil that covers the unrevealed, etc.), and paints on them, in concert with his fellow men, pictures of his beliefs about the hidden content. Myths, creeds, symbols, gods, doctrines, moral rules—these are all projections produced by the individual and his tradition, appearing as ideograms on the blankets.

Goodenough goes on to say that modern man tends to be more acceptant of the *tremendum* than his forebears, and has a penchant for inscribing his curtains with hypotheses instead of dogmas. His interest in meaning is coupled with running pragmatic tests of meaning, and he tends to answer questions with new questions rather than with definitive answers. He is at home with an agnostic stance: he may be aware of some ultimate in the sense of a substrate or order, but will not personalize it. Like the mystics who chose the *via negativa* he dwells on question after question, seeking an ever higher quality of questioning. He does not like closure on any question. The important point which Goodenough makes is that such an ever-questioning attitude need not be positivistic; it is, at least in some cases, a modern way to keeping sacred things sacred. "Prayer for modern man is replaced by eager search, which is a form of prayer itself (Goodenough, 1965:181).

It seems to me that Goodenough's ideas put appropriate strain on the definition of belief as well as that of unbelief, and in this sense fit the temper of our time. Some unbelief can be understood as disbelief in the validity or relevance of certain ideograms on the protective blankets; indeed, some ideograms are primitively pictographic. Some unbelief is skepticism whether an ideogram will ever fit the intangible ultimate whose essence is intuitively grasped and felt to be ineffable. Some unbelief takes the form of recognizing that there has always been a lively trade in blankets with various designs, but questioning whether blankets are necessary or useful at all.

Holding fast to this imagery of Goodenough, one can bring unbelief in interesting appositions to belief. For instance, one can now recognize that some belief may be little more than an aesthetic appreciation of some ideograms on some blankets. Some belief may consist in the conviction that certain ideograms match the hidden reality under the blanket—it is a belief in adequate matching and goodness of fit. Some belief can be understood as hanging on to the blanket itself, much as the toddler carries his security blanket with him while he is fully dressed and not cold. Some belief is reading and rereading the ideograms as intriguing puzzles to be deciphered. Some belief is a compulsion to invent new ideograms that are more meaningful or clarifying than the old ones. Some belief is playing the game of blankets, without any sense of a *tremendum* anywhere.

III

In the perspective gained thus far it is apparent that unbelief is at least as diversified as religious belief, and that Goodenough's warning about the dangers of rigidly defining belief would pertain to defining unbelief as well. To paraphrase Goodenough I thus propose that we can "best approach religious unbelief by getting in mind the various experiences that men have called unbelief or irreligion, rather than what we think should ideally be given those names." We don't know what unbelief *is*, just as we cannot pretend to know what religion *is*.

While such a position may be uncomfortable for any ontologist, it is no hindrance to the scientific study of unbelief. To me, scientific study of anything is perspectival: with an apparatus of concepts, words, theories, methods, and hypotheses, each organized discipline can throw its searchlight on the phenomena of belief or unbelief and analyze their qualities, relations, and transformations. What counts in such an endeavor is that the student remain true to the categories of his own science, basic or applied, and not sell out to the categories of religion. To be sure, the phenomena are not neat, if they are indeed what anyone calls belief and unbelief, and if anyone's experience is to be taken seriously. But these untidy phenomena can be ordered, clarified, and understood in terms of the categories that each discipline has to offer; and playful efforts at such ordering, clarifying, and understanding constitute precisely the fun of scholarly work.

The psychology of unbelief, then, is to be approached in psychological terms. The methodology can vary from large-scale statistical studies to the analysis of an individual case; it can be nomothetic or idiographic; it can be cross-sectional or longitudinal. The point of view can be nativistic or learning-oriented, Leibnitzian or Lockean, cognitive or behavioral, experimental or clinical. My own preference is for a combined psychodynamic and psychoeconomic approach (Pruyser, 1968), which places belief and unbelief in an adaptational framework, asking how one copes —through belief or unbelief—with the tasks, strains, and opportunities imposed by his self, nature, society, and culture, and what happens to the forms of belief and unbelief as one uses them. Important additional phenomena for each individual are the publicness, dissemination, and transmission of either belief or unbelief, which require that one also has to cope with the justifications for and consequences of the options between these two and their varieties, which is no mean stress.

It seems to me that the terms belief and unbelief, and their cognates, however one defines them, are quite empirical. Each of them has a long history, and in the history of civilization the two terms, as well as the experiences they stand for, are often transmitted alongside each other. They are clearly a pair, just as truth and falsehood, beauty and ugliness, the good and the bad are pairs. But are the members of the pair opposites? Are they positives and negatives? Are they presence and absence of something? Does each term in the pair have an independent status? Are they like two sides of a coin? Are they variable expressions of an unknown *tertium quid?* The answer to these meta-scientific questions will depend on one's meta-psychological posture toward all phenomena and data. Some minds stress the discontinuity of things and wallow in differences; other minds stress the continuity of things and wallow in similarities; still other minds recognize genotypical similarities while spotting phenotypical differences, and vice versa. As long as one makes clear to oneself and others what meta-psychological style one brings to his work, his psychology of religion or irreligion will not only be possible but plausible and viable.

At the psychological level, we will benefit from careful phenomenological description as a step toward dynamic understanding. For instance, in the kind of knowledge obtainable in psychotherapy there is reason to differentiate between certain forms of *un*belief which seem conflict-free or at any rate relatively uncathected, and states of *dis*belief engendered by a strong cathexis of the propositions of belief, with the scales tipped in a tantalizingly acute imbalance. In clinical work one can find expressions of unbelief in any god or any benevolent principle, coupled with a profound belief in devils, Satan, and other impersonations of malevolence, with much energy spent on maneuvers to ward off the evil influence. Henry Murray (1962) has argued that many of us scientists, wittingly or unwittingly, have found a working alliance with the Satanic. But whether we deal with gods or devils, the psychological study of belief and unbelief must come down from the height of global generalities to the untidy details of concrete experience, in order to produce that as yet unwritten tome: *The Varieties of Experiencing Irreligion.*

In pondering an appropriate title for a book on irreligion which would have the sweep of James's classic on religion, I find myself caught in snags which once more illustrate the nasty conceptual problems we are facing. Could one simply modify James's title into *The Varieties of Irreligious Experience* and then proceed to document such experience? I think not, for such a title could cover any experience, any facet of life as lived, minus those specific to religion. Such a work would be without focus. It would also be rather sloppy; for what do words like *irreligious, areligious,* or *nonreligious* mean when used adjectivally with experience?

They only designate a spurious exclusion. And yet history has shown that such an exclusion could leave us with some substance in the sense of recognizing describable alternatives to a religious point of view. Jaspers produced just such a work in 1919 under the title *Psychology of Waltenschauungen,* which amounts to a typology of philosophies of life.

Would a title speaking of *religious unbelief* be a better choice? Apart from the paradoxical juxtaposition of these two words, which superficially have contrary meanings, belief is only one aspect and not the whole of religion, so that unbelief would only exclude a cognitive portion of the life of a person who could plausibly maintain certain religious practices and habits. In fact, such a condition, which may be far more widespread than we are prone to think, would be a subject for any regular psychology of religion!

Right now I tend to think that irreligion, like religion, has a certain thickness, substance, content, style, structure, and function which qualify a person's total experience. Irreligion is not merely the absence of something, and certainly not simply the missing of something good, desirable, or pleasant. It is much closer to adopting an active stance or posture, involving the act of excluding another posture which, despite its popularity or naturalness, is deemed to be a poor fit in an acquired life style. Irreligion, like religion, can be zealous, militant, declarative, dogmatic, or persuasive. Like religion, it can be the product of training, existential decision-making, or drifting. And all too often it can be a product of religious instruction!

For the moment, then, let me leave you with the double challenge of writing a good, descriptive, or explanatory book and finding a correct and telling title that has overcome the hurdles which I posed.

REFERENCES

BACON, FRANCIS

n.d.   "Of Superstition." Essay 17 in *Essays or Counsel, Civil and Moral, of Francis, Lord Verulam.* Mount Vernon, N.Y.: Peter Pauper Press.

BROWNING, ROBERT   (see Scudder, 1895)

FREUD, SIGMUND

(1913)   "Totem and Taboo." *The Standard Edition of the Com-*
1955   *plete Psychological Works of Sigmund Freud.* James Strachey (ed.), London, Hogarth Press, dates according to volume. The date in parentheses is the date of original publication. Vol. 13.

(1919)
1955

"Psychoanalysis and Religious Origins." Preface to T. Reik, *Ritual: Psychoanalytic Studies. The Standard Edition of the Complete Psychological Works of Sigmund Freud.* James Strachey (ed.), London, Hogarth Press, dates according to volume. The date in parentheses is the date of original publication. Vol. 17.

(1918)
1955

"From the History of an Infantile Neurosis." *The Standard Edition of the Complete Psychological Works of Sigmund Freud.* James Strachey (ed.), London, Hogarth Press, dates according to volume. The date in parentheses is the date of original publication. Vol. 17.

(1909)
1955

"Notes Upon a Case of Obsessional Neurosis." *The Standard Edition of the Complete Psychological Works of Sigmund Freud.* James Strachey (ed.), London, Hogarth Press, dates according to volume. The date in parentheses is the date of original publication. Vol. 10.

(1911)
1958

"Psychoanalytic Notes on an Autobiographical Account of a Case of Paranoia (Dementia Paranoides)." *The Standard Edition of the Complete Psychological Works of Sigmund Freud.* James Strachey (ed.), London, Hogarth Press, dates according to volume. The date in parentheses is the date of original publication. Vol. 7.

(1907)
1959

"Obsessive Actions and Religious Practices." *The Standard Edition of the Complete Psychological Works of Sigmund Freud.* James Strachey (ed.), London, Hogarth Press, dates according to volume. The date in parentheses is the date of original publication.

(1927)
1961

"The Future of an Illusion." *The Standard Edition of the Complete Psychological Works of Sigmund Freud.* James Strachey (ed.), London, Hogarth Press, dates according to volume. The date in parentheses is the date of original publication. Vol. 21.

(1923)
1961

"A Seventeenth-Century Demonological Neurosis." *The Standard Edition of the Complete Psychological Works of Sigmund Freud.* James Strachey (ed.), London, Hogarth Press, dates according to volume. The date in parentheses is the date of original publication. Vol. 19.

(1928)
1961

"A Religious Experience." *The Standard Edition of the Complete Psychological Works of Sigmund Freud.* James Strachey (ed.), London, Hogarth Press, dates according to volume. The date in parentheses is the date of original publication. Vol. 21.

(1930)
1961

"Civilization and Its Discontents." *The Standard Edition of the Complete Psychological Works of Sigmund Freud.*

James Strachey (ed.), London, Hogarth Press, dates according to volume. The date in parentheses is the date of original publication. Vol. 21.

(1939)
1964   "Moses and Monotheism." *The Standard Edition of the Complete Psychological Works of Sigmund Freud.* James Strachey (ed.), London, Hogarth Press, dates according to volume. The date in parentheses is the date of original publication. Vol. 23.

GOODENOUGH, ERWIN

1965   *The Psychology of Religious Experience.* New York: Basic Books.

JAMES, WILLIAM

1897   *The Will to Believe and Other Essays in Popular Philosophy.* New York: Longmans, Green.

1902   *The Varieties of Religious Experience.* New York: Longmans, Green.

JASPERS, KARL

1919   *Psychologie der Weltanschauunger.* Berlin: Springer.

JONES, ERNEST

1951   "Psycho-analysis and the Christian Religion." In *Essays in Applied Psycho-Analysis.* London: Hogarth Press.

MURRAY, HENRY A.

1962   "The Personality and Career of Satan." *Journal of Social Issues* 18: 36–46.

OTTO, RUDOLF

(1912)
1924   *The Idea of the Holy.* Trans. by J. W. Harvey. New York: Oxford University Press.

1936   *Das Heilige.* 23–25 Auflage. Munich, C. H. Beck'sche Verlagsbuchhandlung.

PRUYSER, PAUL W.

1968   *A Dynamic Psychology of Religion.* New York: Harper and Row.

1971   "A Psychological View of Religion in the 1970's." *Bulletin of the Menninger Clinic* 35: 77–97.

1973   "Sigmund Freud and His Legacy: Psychoanalytic Psychology of Religion." Pp. 243–290 in C. Y. Glock and P. E. Hammond (eds.), *Beyond the Classics?* Essays in the Scientific Study of Religion. New York: Harper and Row.

RIEFF, PHILIP

1966   *The Triumph of the Therapeutic.* New York: Harper
                        and Row.

SCHLEIERMACHER, FRIEDRICH E.D.

(1799)   *On Religion.* Trans. by J. Oman. New York: Ungar.
1955

SCUDDER, H. E. (ED.)

1895   *The Complete Poetic and Dramatic Works of Robert
                        Browning.* Boston: Houghton Mifflin.

VERNON, GLENN

1968   "The Religions 'Nones,' a Neglected Category." *Journal
                        for the Scientific Study of Religion* 7: 219–229.

Part Five
The Symbolization Process
and Communication in Religion

David Bakan

YORK UNIVERSITY, TORONTO

Paternity in the
Judeo-Christian Tradition

I

In this essay I will deal with the notion and fact of paternity as major factors in the determination of the Judeo-Christian tradition. I will use the commonly available text of the Bible as a principal source of information.

Allow me first to make some prior observations on the methodological orientation of my task. I am a psychologist. There are many matters that should concern a psychologist under the rubric of "ultimate concern," whereby Paul Tillich defined the province of religion. As a psychologist, I am concerned with the mind of man. I choose the Bible as a source of information because it is perhaps the best single, available expression of the mind of man in Western civilization. It has survived the test of the social equivalent of natural selection. It has more regularly and more reliably been reaccepted by generation after generation than any other designable set of literary expressions. Its ideas and meanings have been critically involved in virtually every major cultural event in the history of our civilization.

It is axiomatic to me that nothing complex can be perceived which is not first conceived. As a psychologist, I take as the areas of my concern the thinking (cognition), the willing (volition), and the feeling (affection) of human beings. Since, with the single exception of what is available to me introspectively, these processes are not available to me directly, the method of psychology must, in my opinion, be interpretive and speculative. The necessity for interpretation and speculation is at once a major weakness and a major strength of an authentic psychology.

Language is the behavior of choice for understanding psychological processes. Thus, the Bible, as a linguistic product, qualifies excellently as an expression of mind.

But what mind? Certainly the Bible is not the expression of a single mind. The authors and editors of the Bible are multiple. The contributors range over time and space. If my aim were to identify psychological processes of individuals, psychological analysis of the Bible would be very difficult. The biblical mind is essentially transgenerational, and it expressed itself richly in the texts of the Bible which lie before us. Whereas the multiple authorship of the Bible would constitute an obstacle for individual psychology, it is an advantage in identifying transgenerational psychological characteristics, traits that abide beyond the duration of a single lifetime. I would point out, parenthetically, that contemporary social science is quite inadequate in dealing with transgenerational psychological characteristics.

Nor is the historical reality of biblical figures important for my purposes. It is of little consequence, for example, that there ever was a single real person called Abraham; or that it was his particular life experiences which were recounted in Genesis. Abraham might have been one person, a composite of several persons, or a fantasy of one or several authors, with little consequence for my approach. For—if I might take a liberty with Voltaire—even if Abraham or Moses or Jesus did not exist, the biblical mind would have found it necessary to invent them. What is important about these figures is not that they once had fleshly existence—man's yearning that his legendary heroes shall have had body and blood is an interesting problem in itself—but that they portray certain significant psychological features in personified form.

There is a valuable convergence between psychology and theology— between the Freudian psychological distinction of the latent from the manifest of human expression, and the Bultmannian distinction of kerygma from myth. I therefore put the question as What is the latent kerygma in the manifest myth?

As the last of these preliminary observations I would stress the anthropocentric rather than theocentric nature of my approach. I do not engage in theology. Indeed, from my point of view, theology, which involves making images of God, is sinful. The progressive feature of the history of religion is in the ever-growing realization that the properties of God are unspecifiable.

II

Paternity is one of the most frequent themes in both the Old and the New Testaments. One can hardly open the Bible at random without finding some allusion to the biological connectedness between male progenitors and their offspring, at the very least by the identification of the person as so-and-so the son of so-and-so. The authors of the Bible were extremely preoccupied with fatherhood. Indeed, so preoccupied were they with fatherhood that they even conceived of God as father. We presume that they projected onto God characteristics of their own which were of great moment to them. One may contrast the Bible with other great historical works such as, for example, those of Plato or Aristotle, in which paternity is clearly of far less concern to the authors.

Freud took the Oedipus complex as central in determining the nature of the human psyche, as the paradigmatic crisis in the life of man. To have taken the son in rebellion against the father as the paradigmatic life experience may be profoundly correct. Yet it is only partial. A more general formulation would be one that involves the relationship between father and son. There are not only filial but paternal aspects as well. There are crises associated not only with sonhood but with fatherhood. The myth to which Freud alludes refers not only to the son killing the father, but to a prior impulse of Laius to kill Oedipus. Maturation entails not only replacing the father, but also being the father. Not only are there the agonies of wishing to engage in, say, incest with the mother, but also those of being the father, of having sexual relations with the new mother, producing offspring, and assuming the burden and responsibility for their care.

The Bible is obviously the product of men—men who were, at the time of their participation in the authorship of the Bible, in their maturity. It was unlikely that this set of books was written either by women or by persons who were very young. It is rather the writing of persons who were fathers, or at least potential fathers.

My thesis can be stated rather simply: the Bible is a document which both expresses and depicts the crisis of paternalization. That crisis is both historical and ontogenetic. As historical, it corresponds to a period in history when the role of the male in conception was discovered and, more importantly, socially assimilated. Ontogentically, it is a crisis which is repeated in the life of each male who lives long enough to mature into the potentiality for parenthood. I venture to speculate that one of the reasons for the abiding tenacity of the Bible as a document of interest over history is that it touches on and expresses the psychological crisis that generation after generation of males must go through. Its appeal is to that part of the society—the mature men in it—which has characteristically held the major power in the total society. They had the power to guarantee that the documents would be maintained, and that there would be institutions to promulgate the ideas in them.

The Bible, then, expresses the historical crisis that accompanied the social assimilation of the discovery that men had a role in human procreation. We may presume that there was an early time when it was not known that men played a role in the birth of a child. The authors of the Bible allude repeatedly to the necessity of a male in procreation. Interestingly enough, however, they do not seem to know the duration of the gestation period, thus making authenticity of paternity a matter of particular concern. The Bible may be interpreted as a record of the effeminatization of the male, of how the male came to assume and share the archaic functions of the female in taking care of the children. In this sense "paternalization" is equally the "maternalization" of the male.

The biblical mind discovered that children could be created at will, as it were. In the biblical mind, men truly became as gods in this respect. Sexual intercourse was euphemistically referred to as knowledge—for it touched on the ultimate knowledge of the creation of man. The Bible may be regarded as a document of the shock of men when they realized that they were the willful creators of human beings, the shock of knowing that they were creators as they had imagined their gods to have been. The Bible is the record of the experience of man as he was making a giant step in answering the question of how man is created.

The projected onto God what must have appeared to them to be the matching right to that of creation: the right of destruction. This is expressed several times in the Bible, as for example: "And it repented the Lord that he had made man on the earth, and it grieved Him in his heart. And the Lord said, I will destroy man whom I have created from the face of the earth" (Genesis 6: 6–7).

The insight that men had the power to create other human beings at will was coupled to the awareness that the indefinite life of an individual was not a matter of his will. The biblical mind coupled these two insights into a possibility of achieving biological immortality by means of the willful creation of offspring. The biblical mind thus endowed God with a trait that men did not have: immortality. It is in the image of Abraham that the genius of the biblical mind expresses itself best, in the idea of the Covenant; which simply entails a God who would provide for Abraham's offspring a land for them to live in after Abraham died. This was to be a land of "milk and honey," food suitable for young children. Abraham's God was a primitive life insurance policy, designed to take care of the children when he himself was gone.

III

The identification of man with his offspring was, however, compromised by three things. First, the offspring might not be loyal, might not continue to provide, might not continue to obey, and might even kill their parents. Thus arises the obedience morality of the Bible. Indeed the only one of the ten commandments that indicates a consequence is that of honoring father and mother, which is followed by "that thy days may be-long" (Exodus 20: 12), suggesting that if parents are not honored, days might be short.

Second, the simple burdensomeness of raising children under conditions of shortages of resources was itself a threat. The sin alluded to in the story of the fall of man may indeed be the eating of the children. One interpretation of the story of the Garden of Eden is that since the tree was the tree of knowledge, which also means copulation, the sin of eating from that tree was the eating of one's own children. The covering of the genitalia following the eating also suggests that this might be the case; as does Eve's punishment of pain in having children, that she might be reminded that the product of her knowledge was not to be eaten; and Adam's labor, his acceptance of the burdensomeness of providing resources for the continued maintenance of Eve and children.

Third, the biblical mind was compromised by the possibility of lack of authentic paternity. The biblical mind had little difficulty in entertaining polygamy; but polyandry was intolerable. The biblical mind was especially uneasy about the first-born, because the first-born is ever of dubious paternity if the gestation period is not known. The Bible indeed suggests killing all first-born of women: "sanctify unto me all the first-born, whatsoever openeth the womb among the children of Israel . . . It is mine" (Exodus 13: 2).

The story of the binding of Isaac by Abraham is central for the ensuing development of both Judaism and Christianity. The text in this instance is remarkably suggestive of dubious paternity of Isaac; and would thus tell us the reason for Abraham's move to kill him. There are a number of features of the text, especially in the eighteenth chapter of Genesis, which suggest this. In this chapter Abraham has three visitors, and it is indicated that Sarah would have a child. Whereas Abraham instructs Sarah to bake cakes for the guests while he runs off to prepare a calf, leaving the guests with Sarah, the menu recited in the eighth verse conspicuously leaves out mention of the cakes. The meal is of "butter, and milk, and the calf which he had dressed." No mention of cakes, leaving doubt about her activity when she was supposed to be baking cakes. Whereas the story begins with three visitors, one of them magically disappears, with the next chapter beginning with the two angels. Sarah hears the prophecy in the tent door, and the text reads: *v'hoo acharav,* and he—whoever he was—behind it. Isaac's name, which means "one laughs," suggests the possibility that Isaac was the "joke," and Abraham the cuckold: Abraham, Father; and Isaac, Ha-ha. The biblical narrative made Sarah eminently attractive to men, with her winding up once in the harem of the Abimelech and once in the harem of Pharoah, while married to Abraham. The great Jewish commentator Rashi indicates that the scorners of the generation were suggesting that Abimelech was the father of Isaac, but the proof that Isaac was really the son of Abraham was that Isaac's facial features were similar to those of Abraham. To the latter "proof" there are two objections from the text. First, according to the text, Sarah had the same father as Abraham, which would explain a facial similarity. Second, there is nothing in the text to indicate that there was such a facial similarity. The facial similarity was invented by subsequent commentators who must equally have experienced the doubt suggested by the text. Indeed, even Paul may have had Isaac's dubious paternity on his mind: "Neither, because they are the seed of Abraham, are they all children: but, in Isaac shall thy seed be called" (Romans 9: 7). The dubious paternity theme is repeated in the story of Joseph, Mary, and Jesus.

The essence of Judaism and Christianity is the management of the infanticidal impulse resulting from these three factors, and a binding of the father against acting out the impulse.

One of the main historical functions of the Judeo-Christian tradition has been to counteract the infanticidal impulse which arises as a dialectical antithesis to the assumption of paternal responsibility on the part of men.

IV

I have indicated that the theme of paternity is one of the most frequent in the Bible. Let me now add the observation that another frequently mentioned theme—a theme central to the major events of the biblical narrative and to some of the most significant developments in Judaism and Christianity—is the killing of children. Moses is saved from a holocaust of infant slaughter. Jesus is saved from a holocaust of infant slaughter. The great historical crisis of Judaism is the almost-slaying of Isaac. The great historical moment of Christianity is when the son, Jesus, is slain.

It is not difficult to suppose that the temptation to kill children must have been real for it to have provoked the writers of the Bible to speak out against it. Ezekiel, for example, complained: "For when they had slain their children to their idols, then they came the same day into my sanctuary to profane it" (Ezekiel 23: 30). Isaiah scolded: "Enflaming yourselves with idols under every green tree, slaying the children in the valleys under the clifts of the rocks" (Isaiah 57: 5). The prophets railed against idolatry, which was associated with the sacrifice of children, and against adultery and whoredom, from which would arise children who were unwanted, who would not have identifiable and authentic paternity, and who would especially be targets for sacrifice.

V

One of the specific forms of injunction against child sacrifice was against Molech worship. Molech was a Semitic god, served by compelling children to pass through a burning furnace. The psychological remnants of child sacrifice are still present in the Bible in the assertion that the first-born child belongs to God, with the "belonging to god" being a euphemism for license to kill the child. The Canaanites evidently worshiped Molech. And the prophets were very concerned about the influence of this feature of Canaanite culture on the Israelites. However, the name Molech appears to be related to the Hebrew word *melech*, which means king; and this may be a thinly disguised way of suggesting what may have been one of the major functions of the king: to assume the responsibility and the guilt of the community for reducing population. According to II Kings 21: 6, King Manasseh (687–642 B.C.) introduced Molech worship. Although King Josiah, who followed him, abolished Molech worship, it was reintroduced by his son, Jehoiakim, who succeeded him. Pharoah, according to the biblical story, attempted a genocidal holocaust. Herod, of Jesus' time, killed all the children of Bethlehem that were under two years old. In the very recent history of the world, Adolf Hitler stepped into the traditional role of kings, setting up the pattern of historical Molech worship, furnaces and all. Hitler's genocide was in the tradition of Pharoah and Herod before him. In my opinion, it is hardly incidental to this that in Nazi Germany under Hitler there was intense opposition not only to Jews but to every manifestation of the Judeo-Christian tradition, and a reversion to more pagan forms of cultural expression.

As history developed, the right of kings to thin the population by frank infanticide was converted into the right of kings to decide to wage war on their own responsibility. Indeed, this remains one of the great dangers of modern times: that political leaders have the power to wage war on their own initiative, without necessary review or restraint.

The Judeo-Christian tradition has operated as a counter-force to the Molech tradition. It has countered the power of both parents and kings to have either their private or public holocausts of slaughter.

VI

The idea of the king as Molech is closely related to its opposite, the idea of the Messiah-king. The very idea of the Messiah in the history of the Judeo-Christian tradition is that the Messiah is the looked-for king. This new king was to be a different kind of king. He was to be a king who used his power not for slaying children but rather for delivering them. The kingdom of God is antithetical to, and yet dialectically related to, kingdoms in which the king had the right to dispose of human life at will. Evidence that this was on the minds of the people of biblical times is reflected in the Gospel story of the ironic play of the soldiers with Jesus:

> And they stripped him, and put on him a scarlet robe. And when they had plaited a crown of thorns, they put it upon his head, and a reed in his right hand; and they bowed the knee before him, and mocked him, saying Hail, King of the Jews! And when he was crucified they placed a sign on the cross over his head which read. THIS IS JESUS THE KING OF THE JEWS. (Matthew 27)

The very idea of the Messiah as another kind of king must be understood in terms of the history of the biblical land. Following the death of Solomon, the history was a stormy one. Population pressure in the land was great, in contrast to the nomadic origins, when children were assets rather than liabilities. Frequent reversions to the Molech tradition took place. In contrast there was always the promise of Abraham to be fulfilled, the promise which contained the words of God to Abraham: "That in blessing I will bless thee, and in multiplying I will multiply thy seed as the stars of the heaven, and as the sand which is upon the seashore" (Genesis 22:17).

The root psychological meaning of saving as this occurs in the messianic tradition is being saved from slaughter in infancy. The Messiah is indeed the savior, saving the child from nonexistence.

VII

The idea of the Messiah is closely related to the rite of baptism. Drowning is one of the most readily available ways of getting rid of unwanted children. Being saved from drowning can be regarded as a paradigmatic form of being saved from infanticide. Thus, in the story of Moses, we have Pharoah condemning the children to death by drowning in the Nile. Moses was saved from death in the Nile. He was named by that act of salvation. The biblical explanation of his name is that he is called Moses by the princess "Because I drew him out of the water." The verb *masah* (Moses) means to draw out. It is doubtful that the Egyptian princesss spoke Hebrew. Yet the meaning of the name to the biblical mind is unambiguous. The name Moses means that he was saved from drowning. Jesus is equally "saved" from drowning, as it were. It will be recalled that it is precisely at his baptism, that Jesus' messiahship is revealed to him:

> And it came to pass in these days, that Jesus came from Nazareth of Galilee, and was baptized of John in Jordan. And straightway coming up out of the water, he saw the heavens opened, and the Spirit like a dove descending upon him: And there came a voice from heaven, saying "Thou art my beloved Son, in whom I am well pleased." (Mark 1: 9–11)

Coming out of the water—that is, in this interpretation, in being saved from drowning—he receives an affirmation of his existence from the *father*, "Thou art my beloved son, in whom I am well pleased." What is the alternative? I am not pleased with you. You are not my son. And you may stay in the water!

In order to live there must be a *second* affirmation of existence. It is not enough to be born to have a claim upon existence. Being born is, of itself, merely the result of sexuality—in this sense, original sin. Baptism, as a second affirmation, by someone who will assume the responsibility of care, is essential. Not only is the child to be born, but someone must claim him, must acknowledge his right to live. There must be someone to draw him out of the water, as Moses was drawn out. The baptism still retains its meaning in that the baptized are thus identified as belonging to the church, as belonging to the extended family of man which the church represents. Infants who are baptized are pledged to the church by their parents; and thereby the parents are pledged to the child. This historical association between the idea of baptism and the solidarity of the family and church reflects an essential feature of the meaning of baptism.

VIII

Many of the meanings associated with baptism in Christianity are shared by circumcision in Judaism. Circumcision is essentially an affirmation of the child to the larger community, analogous to the Christian church. The main difference between circumcision and baptism is in the method of killing the child alluded to. In baptism it is drowning. In circumcision, it is being killed by a knife, an allusion to the way in which Isaac might have been killed by Abraham. The suggestion from the Bible is that the eighth day was the primitive day for the sacrifice to take place. It was the traditional day for the sacrifice of animals to God. Circumcision is equally performed on the eighth day.

Baptism and circumcision are each both substitutes for, and symbols of, the sacrifice of the child. As symbols they are substitutes, and are in this way redemptive. They are then in fact ceremonies of acceptance rather than of sacrifice.

One of the important features of these ceremonies is that they are associated with naming the child. Name, in the history of civilization, is very important. The right to a name is the right to life. The absence of a name is the absence of a right to a life. Granting a child his father's name constitutes a pledge on the part of the father to care for that child. In the circumcision ceremony the name which is granted to the child is not just one name but two names linked together. When Isaac receives a name at his circumcision it is not simply Isaac that he is called. He is given the name *Isaac the son of Abraham,* as Jesus is given the name *Jesus the son of Joseph.* A blood bond is established between father and son to remove all doubt of the existence of a prior blood bond. The ceremony establishes the right of the child to the father's care. It is essentially an assertion on the part of the father to the effect, "Thou art my son, in whom I am well pleased," the words that Jesus heard as he emerged from the Jordan river.

The dropping of the requirement of circumsion in the development of Christianity should be understood as a way of enlarging the opportunities for admission into the Christian faith. For one of the main features of Christianity is that it sought to place the acceptance of people, their deliverance, on a less contingent basis than acceptance just by one particular man. Thus, the dropping of circumcision as a requirement for admission to the Christian church constituted an affirmation of the right to life, independnent of the kinship origins first associated with that right in the biblical mind.

The Passover is of utmost importance to both Judaism and Christianity. For Judaism it commemorates the exodus from Egypt. For Christianity it is the occasion of the Last Supper, and is equally important as the Eucharist, the central sacramental rite of Christianity.

The main event of the Passover is the slaying, and the sparing, of children. It is, in part, Moses' delayed revenge on Pharoah for having killed the children of the Israelites at the time of his own infancy, an instance of the biblical *lex talionis*.

The biblical text depicts the God of the Israelites slaying the first-born children of the Egyptians. In preparation for this, God commands that

> they shall take to them every man a lamb. . . . Your lamb shall be without blemish, a male . . . and the whole assembly of the congregation of Israel shall kill it in the evening. And they shall take of the blood and strike it on the two side posts and on the upper door post of the houses, wherein they shall eat it. . . . For I will pass through the land of Egypt this night, and will smite all of the first-born in the land of Egypt, both man and beast. . . . And the blood shall be to you for a token upon the houses where ye are: and when I see the blood, I will pass over you, and the plague shall not be upon you. (Exodus 12: 3–13).

Here we have the root story of Christianity. In the New Testament, Jesus is referred to as the passover, "Christ our passover is sacrified." Jesus is referred to as the lamb, and his blood is the blood of the lamb whereby one is saved from the expression of the infanticidal impulse. In the history of Christianity, the bloody cross is taken as a protection against evil, against the infanticidal impulse in this interpretation. Just as we characteristically use a cross as an identifying mark, to indicate that some special treatment is appropriate, so is the Christian cross a similar mark.

Where there is the sign of the cross, the bloody cross, the cross marked with the blood of the lamb, the cross made with the blood of Jesus—there the infanticidal impulse will not come to rest. Jesus has thus become the "lamb without blemish" as he is referred to in the New Testament.

X

What took place at the Last Supper was essentially a renewal of the injunction against infanticide by Jesus. The time of Jesus was a time of great population density in the land. There was great suffering and deprivation. Some of the people had dedicated themselves to a life of chastity in order to bring no further human beings onto the earth. The Essenes, for example, abstained from sexual relations. Jesus, of course, refrained from marriage. And Paul allowed that marriage should take place only under the condition of "better to marry than to burn." The conditions were ripe for the rise of the infanticidal tendency: as indeed, we know was the case from the episode of Herod slaying the children of Bethlehem. There was a rejection of the earthly father, and a turning to the father in heaven. "And call no man your father upon the earth," Jesus says in Matthew (23: 9), for "the father shall deliver up . . . to death the child" (10: 21). And one should not seek life in the immediate family but rather should join the larger group which would function as a family but in which sexual relations would be taboo. Jesus welcomed those who could do without family life. "And every one that hath forsaken houses, or brethren, or sisters, or father, or mother, or wife, or children, or lands, for my name's sake, shall receive an hundredfold, and shall inherit everlasting life" (Matthew 19: 29). This was important. Because what Christianity did was offer a dignified and fulfilling life to all who could make the sacrifice of not being a part of a literal family. Christianity opened the door of dignity and righteousness to anyone who could somehow manage to suspend the sexual functions.

The passover meal, originally a meal associated with family living, was now expanded into the Eucharist, in which all could join who were willing to join. In that last meal, Jesus asked his disciples to eat the bread, as his body, and drink the wine, as his blood, clearly alluding to the cannibalistic feature associated with infanticide. Indeed, if we follow the version of this in John, we find that when he enjoined his disciples to eat his body and drink his blood, they "murmured at it," and "from that time many of his disciples went back and walked no more with him" (John 6: 66). It is my conviction that Jesus, or at least the authors of the texts, were aware of the infanticidal tendency to which I have been devoting my attention; and that it was his or their hope that the real or imagined ministry of Jesus would mitigate the infanticidal tendencies in man. Both the Jewish and the Christian traditions, each in their own way, have in fact worked to control that impulse throughout the centuries.

XI

If indeed I have been partially right in reading the kerygma or the latent meaning in the text, what implications does it have for our day? In my opinion, one of the most serious limitations of the contemporary versions of the Judeo-Christian tradition is the failure to draw out the significance of the paternity question for modern times. I would just indicate a few things about the nature of the contemporary world which bear on the matter.

1. In the past hundred years, with warfare having increasingly involved civilian populations as targets of destruction, children have become increasingly victimized.

2. One form of infanticide which our society has engaged in is the sending off of young men to fight in wars. I would observe, for example, that America's involvement in Vietnam coincided quite precisely with the maturation to military age of the first crop from the post-World War II baby boom.

3. The black problem in the United States is as much an age problem as it is a race problem. I would simply point out that the median age of the blacks in the United States is about twenty. That is, half the black population is under twenty years of age. The corresponding figure for the white population is around 27. The blacks in America are preponderantly children.

4. There has been an enlarging tendency to bring to bear police against youth, in the name of "law and order." I suggest that this is an active continuing form of the historical tendency to turn the infanticidal act over to the king.

5. I would point out that the infant mortality rate in America is extremely high for a modern urban industrial society; that there are many children who suffer nutritional diseases; and that there are many children who suffer from want of the ordinary kinds of benefits of a social nature that all children have a right to.

6. Finally, I would point out that there are daily occurrences of child abuse without appropriate protective or preventive measures being taken. Data collected on child abuse indicates that children are whipped with

leather belts, hung by ropes, bathed in ice water, pressed against steam pipes and electric pressing irons, exposed to severe outdoor temperatures, scalded with boiling water, forced to swallow urine, feces, alcohol, vinegar, and other odious material. The reports, says one reporter, read like the case-book of a concentration camp doctor. And public efforts to curb these activities, or even the research efforts whereby we might better understand this abuse of children, are negligible.*

---

* I have dealt with the problem of child abuse in greater detail in Bakan, D. *Slaughter of the Innocents*. San Francisco: Jossey-Bass, 1971; Toronto: Canadian Broadcasting Corporation, 1971.

Talcott Parsons

HARVARD UNIVERSITY

Religious Symbolization and Death*

In this paper I attempt to describe the framework of constitutive symbolism within which death is defined in cultures with a Judeo-Christian background. One might consider such a framework to be specifically related to the concept of *definition of the situation* as this has been used in recent theorizing at the level of the general system of action. My principal reference points will be the Old Testament, especially the Book of Genesis; the Christian development in its Roman Catholic version, especially as symbolized in Renaissance art; and some further changes from that position associated first with Protestantism and then with what some authors might call a "post-Protestant" phase.

* This paper is a slightly different draft version of the first part of the article "The 'Gift of Life' and its Reciprocation," of which the coauthors were Renée C. Fox and Victor M. Lidz and which was published in *Social Research*, Fall 1972.

217

My thesis is that the primary symbolism of death is part of a larger complex of constitutive symbolism—the complex which sociologists and anthropologists have come to call that of "age and sex." It concerns meanings of the human life cycle from conception and birth through the phases of earthly "living" to death and the problem of orientation to the possibility of any meaningful "after death."

The life cycle of the individual, however, is inseparable from the problems of reproduction and the succession of generations. No human individual is isolated in this respect. Cooperation of persons of opposite sex is an essential condition of reproduction, and one aspect of the meaningfulness of death is to "make room" for the succeeding generation and those yet to follow it.

The myth of the Garden of Eden, as stated in Genesis, portrays Adam as "the Lord of the creation" who has been created by God "in His own image," where the immortality of Adam is clearly presumed. The Tree of Life standing in the center of the Garden seems to be the symbol of this immortality. It is not clear whether immortality was to be extended to other living species. I presume not, because it is said of animals, before the creation of Adam, that "male and female created He them." The necessity for both sexes at the creation itself suggests reproduction and, of course, with it the mortality of the preceding generations.

However this may be, the myth says in an extremely interesting phrase that it was "not good for Adam to be alone"; so God created Eve. Her function in the Garden was presumably that of companionship rather than reproduction.

The existence of Adam and Eve in the Garden was not only free of the limitations of mortality, but was free of all responsibility—their every want was automatically and, one presumes, instantaneously satisfied. This literal "condition of paradise" was subject, however, to one prohibitory condition—the famous commandment, "Thou shalt not eat of the fruit of the tree of the knowledge of good and evil," with its accompanying warning that, if the commandment was disobeyed, "Thou shalt surely die." Eve, so the story goes, allowed herself to be seduced by the wily serpent, and she in turn seduced Adam. The divine reaction was to expel Adam and Eve from the Garden and to impose on them not only mortality as punishment but also the two extraordinary curses—on Eve that woman should bring forth in pain and travail, and on Adam that man should subsist "by the sweat of his brow," interesting in their dual reference to childbirth and to work. The French word *travail* usually rendered in English by "labor," has an interesting connotation, because in English the word "travail" suggests suffering in a rather strong way, even as contrasted with "labor." In other words, the "human condition" after expulsion from the garden was conceived as a condemnation to suffering and death with strongly negative valences attached to "this life."

If, however, human life was to be conceived as continuing from generation to generation, the reproductive function became essential, and the roles of Adam and Eve, were no longer simply those of companions but of partners in bringing about reproduction. It seems quite clear that the sin of Adam and Eve was a dual one. In the first instance it was that of disobedience. In the Garden they were subjected to one and only one prohibition: "eating the fruit." This is what Kenneth Burke refers to as the capacity for the negative on the part of man as a symbol-using animal, but there is a further connotation beyond mere disobedience as such. In presuming immortality and "knowledge" together—knowledge of the meaning of good and evil—Adam was presuming to act as if he were God. This, I feel, is the most fundamental meaning of original sin. The imposition of death is conceived as God's crucial assertion that man may not presume to be God but must accept his mortality and all the costs of living the life of a mortal. Another common Christian phrasing is that the fundamental sin was "idolatry of the flesh."

In the continuation of the myth, the divine anger seems to have been virtually unappeased, and culminated after a long time in God's decision to destroy his own creation of living beings on the earth, including humanity. God relented, however, in the case of Noah, Noah's wife, their sons, and the sons' families, and he instructed Noah to build the Ark to save his own extended family and the famous "animals two-by-two." In this connection Noah, who from the divine perspective was the only "good man" of his generation, became the recipient of the first covenant with Yahweh. On condition of giving faith and obedience to the divine commandments, Noah and his issue not only were permitted to exist after the recession of the great flood, but became the nucleus of Yahweh's chosen people, the vicissitudes of which are well known through the stages of Abraham and the new covenant with him, the exile, Moses, and the entry after Moses' death into the Promised Land.

The fate of the individual was, in classical ancient Judaism, in a sense absorbed in that of the people of Israel. The primary religious focus was on the people, including not only its existence and vicissitudes as a corporate entity but, above all, the Law, observance of which was the divine condition of continuance in divine favor. The people of Israel constituted a kin-based ethnic group, to which the members' descent from Noah was a primary symbol of belonging. This may be one main point of entry of the symbol blood into the Judeo-Christian story. Another particularly interesting feature of the myth with regard to the Promised

Land, is that it was the land of "milk and honey." Milk surely is a fundamental symbol of feminine nurturance which leads beyond the purely biological reproductive function assumed by Eve and her successors to one
of nurturant solicitude for the welfare of offspring and—since all members
of the people of Israel were "offspring" in this symbolic sense—for the
people generally. Honey has another symbolic connotation: it is a prototype of an unproduced food substance found in nature. The availability
of honey, then, is associated with the plenitude of life in the Garden of
Eden; it is something good, not a human product, to be found in the
natural environment. Indeed, the combination of milk and honey may be
considered to be a kind of prototype symbol of material well-being in a
human situation.

It is a big jump to the symbolism of the much later Christian development, but our concern is not primarily with cultural history, but with
the meaning structure of a symbolic complex. There is a crucial difference
between the relation of God to Adam on the one hand, to Jesus on the
other. God *created* Adam, but Jesus was "his only *begotten* son." We may
perhaps infer that, by the virtue of the series of covenants, God has committed himself to the continuance of the human species—particularly,
but presumably not exclusively, to that of his chosen people. His intervention in the human condition, therefore, could not, as in the case of
the flood and Noah, be for the purpose of continuing or destroying his
creation, but it had to be intervention in the affairs of humanity as "a
going concern." Mary and the myth of the Annunciation is the symbolic
focus of the divine recognition that "cooperation" with humanity is essential in order to carry out the grand plan. It is in this context that the
very critical symbol blood becomes central as referring to the continuity
of the succession of human generation, which, of course, assumes the death
of each individual person but the continuity of the population through
sexual reproduction—"begetting," to use the Old Testament term. The
"blood" of Jesus had therefore both a divine and a human component,
the latter being the blood of Mary.

Another crucial symbolic note is sounded in the Christ story. In Judaism
on the whole, though Jahweh treated the people of Israel as his chosen
people, and protected them and favored them in many ways, his primary
concern with respect to them was their obedience, that is, their observance
of the Law he had imposed upon them. In the Christian story the new
note is that of love. Perhaps the primary mythic statement is, "For God
so loved the world that He gave His only begotten Son." It is noteworthy,
of course, that God is said to have loved not only the people of Israel, but
"the world." This surely is a fundamental anchor point for the universalistic features of Christianity.

There was a new conception of the relation between the "eternal" and temporal orders, the divine and the human, in the New Testament. Through Mary's "Immaculate Conception," the divine became human. Jesus was conceived to be both God and man at the same time. This definition of the situation fundamentally altered the Judaic conception by its potential for upgrading the status of humanity. Again, in spite of certain tendencies within Hellenistic Judaism, I think we can correctly say that Judaism was not a religion of the salvation of the individual in the sense that Christianity has been. Burke has pointed out that the idea of a redeemer is implicit in the Genesis myth, but how the role of the redeemer should be conceived, and, in particular, what the relation of this role to the fate of the people of Israel should be, remained an open question.

The redemptive event, which was the founding event of Christianity, was mythologically, we may presume, the sacrificial death of Jesus by crucifixion. It has been basic to the Christian tradition that this was a real death; it was not, as would be common in Greek mythology, the disappearance of a divine personage who had chosen to spend a certain time on earth disguised as a mortal. Jesus, that is, really died on the cross and had to be "resurrected" in order to reenter the divine sphere of eternal life.

It is of course central that the meaning of Jesus' death was symbolized as *giving* his *blood*. Blood, it seems to me, symbolizes a special combination of two things. The first is what in another connection we may speak of as the *gift* of life, which is expressed in maternity. In the Christian myth Mary was the giver of life to Jesus, a specially symbolic case of the more general conception of a woman *giving* birth to her child. In ordinary usage the word "give" has not been stressed in this expression, but I think it is symbolically crucial. The human component of the blood of Christ, therefore, was a gift from Mary, who only in more extravagant phases of Catholic symbolization has herself been considered divine. This human component, however, was combined with the divine component originating from the begetting of Jesus by his divine father. In these circumstances Jesus' own death was relativized. The concept death applied only to the human component, not to the divine. The symbol blood is the primary focus of the unity of the divine and the human. And this unity is the focus of the Christian conception of the transcending of death.

In the act of dying—which was in a very important sense voluntary on Jesus' part, since Jesus might be said to have provoked the Roman authorities into crucifying him—there was another component which has Hebrew antecedents but was profoundly modified in the Christian phase. In the symbolism of the Last Supper, which was built into the basic sacramental ritual of Christianity—the Eucharist—not only the blood of Christ but also the "body" of Christ is symbolized by the bread of the Eucharist. The body of Christ, meaning of course the risen Christ, came to be the symbol for the church conceived as a supernatural entity, which came to have the "power of the keys," the capacity to elevate the fate of the individual human being from the limitations of mortality and the other "Adamic" features of the human condition.

I do not think it is too far-fetched to suggest that the church was symbolically meant to "identify," in a sense not very different from the psychoanalytic-sociological use of the word, the ordinary human being with Christ. As a member of the church, man became part of the "body of Christ." In dying he thus became capable of *giving* his life, symbolized by blood, in a sense parallel to that in which Jesus gave his blood in the crucifixion. There seems to be a deep duality of meaning here. Death is conceived, on the one hand, to be deeply traumatic, as symbolized by the suffering on the cross—a kind of a "supreme sacrifice." At the same time, the death of the human individual is conceived not merely as paving the way for his own entrance into "heaven" but as a sacrifice for the redemptive benefit of humanity in general. Quite apart from the metaphysical problems of what can possibly be meant by "survival" of the individual after death, I think that this second view of death is a kind of a sublimation, in the positive sense, of the grimly tragic view of the human condition as defined by the consequences of Adam's original sin. By the acceptance of the divine commandments and by the acceptance of Christ as the redeemer, man is not in principle totally expelled from the Garden, to be dominated by "sin and death," but has the opportunity to participate in the divine order and not to be in the Adamic sense only human. We can say that this represents a major upgrading of the religio-metaphysical status of man.

A theme in Western religious history which I have several times emphasized is that the biblical conception of God's making man in his own image and making him Lord of the creation was later transformed into the conception of a "kingdom of God on earth." This in turn implied that human society and personality could be permeated with a divine spirit and thus in some sense narrowed the gap between the divine order of things and "the things of this world." What I have called the relativizing of the meaning of death seems to me to be a central part of this development. Every human individual's death may thus be seen as a sacrifice on the one hand, a *gift* on the other.

The human individual's capacity to die in the role of giver of gifts —most explicit in the case of a soldier or martyr who "gives his life for his country" or "for a cause"—is dependent on three other crucial gifts having preceded his. The first of these was the gift on the part of God the Father of what sometimes religiously is called the "living Christ" to humanity—given, it should be noted, through the process of "begetting." Christ, after all, was God's only begotten son. And this was a gift to humanity *from* God, not a sacrifice *to* God on the part of some human group or individual. It was, moreover, a gift said to have been motivated by "love" of the world. The second was Mary's gift of life as a man, as a human being, to Jesus—a gift symbolized in the person of Mary. Thus, the Christian conception of the human feminine role focuses upon "Mary, Mother of God," who has given the human component of the blood which could be sacrificed for the redemption of humanity. The third gift was the sacrificial death of Jesus, which has frequently been symbolized as the *giving of his blood* for our redemption. Within this framework, then, the death of the human individual can be conceived as a sacrifice for others but also as a gift to others for the future of humanity.

The question now arises of what modifications of this predominantly Catholic definition of the situation should be introduced to take account of the Protestant development and more recent phases which are no longer predominantly Protestant.

Before discussing the Protestant phase and what has followed it, let me sum up what seem to me the four principal steps in the development from the Book of Genesis to full-fledged medieval Catholicism.

1. It is clear that the original meaning of death was as punishment for the disobedience of Adam and Eve in the Garden. The sin, however, was not merely disobedience but the pretention to the status of divinity, and mortality is the *primary* symbol of nondivinity. The imposition of death and the expulsion from the Garden were linked with the conception that this life should be burdened with travail.

2. With the development of the convenant relationship between Yahweh and his chosen people, death took on a new meaning. The biblical phrase is reception into "the bosom of Abraham," which may be interperted to mean that the dead achieve the honorific status of ancestors (as in traditional Chinese religion) in the transgenerational collectivity of the people. Mortality is accepted as part of the generalized human condition with all its limitations but with a note of special value emphasis on the concept of chosenness. The symbol blood emerges in the first instance as a symbol of ethnic belongingness, not only in one generation, but in the continuity of successive generations. This continuity in turn is linked with the special significance of the law, which was divinely ordained through Moses.

3. In the original Christian syndrome, a major shift took place. There

was a relative disassociation from an ethnic community, and both the spiritual and temporal fates of the individual acquired a new salience. Human life, with its continuities, is in a new sense conceived as given. The primary symbol here is the portrayal of Jesus as the only *begotten* son of God the Father. God's begetting of Jesus is quite different from His creation of Adam. It presumes the continuity of humanity and the human reproductive process. Mary gives Jesus the gift of life at the human level, and it is the synthesis of the divine element and the human as symbolized in the Annunciation which qualifies Jesus to be the redeemer of mankind. In his role as redeemer, by his sacrificial death, "He gave His blood" for the redemption of mankind. It must be remembered that blood in this sense was neither wholly divine nor wholly human but a special synthesis of the two, which transcended the stark dichotomy of divine and human in the Book of Genesis.

4.   It seems to be clear then that the primary symbolic effect of Jesus' sacrifice was the endowment of ordinary humans with the capacity to translate their lives into gifts which simultaneously express the love of other human beings and the love of God, reciprocating God's love for "the world." The sacrifice of Jesus by dying on the cross was therefore conceived in a generalized manner so that all human deaths could be conceived in sacrifices. The element of sacrifice, however, emphasizes the negative side, the cost side, of dying, which was so salient for the crucifixion because of its excruciating suffering. The positive side is the *gift,* not Mary's gift of the particular human life of Jesus, but the gift of his own life by the living, human Jesus. This seems to me to be the primary symbolic meaning of the Christian conception of death transcended. Death acquires a transbiological meaning because the paramount component of its meaning is the giving of a life, at the end of a particular life, to God. It is conceived as a perpetuated solidarity between the biohuman level, symbolized by the blood of Mary, and the divine level, symbolized by the blood of Christ. In the ideal Christian death, one came to participate in the blood of Christ at a new level.

In the Catholic system, the mutuality of giving as the expression of love was mediated by the sacramental system of the church and fragmented by particularized absolutions from time to time. In the Protestant version, however, the sacramental system no longer had this capacity. The "power of the keys" was eliminated, and the clergy became essentially spiritual leaders and teachers. Most important, the life of perfection—the life conceived to be both sacrifice and gift to God, namely, that of members of religious orders—lost its special status, and every human being, layman and clergyman alike, was placed on the same level. I think it legitimate, as Weber did, to see this as basically an upgrading of the status of the laity rather than a downgrading of that of the religious. As Weber put it, "Every man was to become a monk."

In one sense, the accent on life in this world was strengthened rather than otherwise. The Calvinistic thought that it was the mission of man to build the kingdom of God on earth. In this context the whole life of the human individual was considered a unity, and its basic meaning was that of contribution to the building of the kingdom, that is, insofar as the individual lived up to religious expectations. His death then was seen as consummatory, as signaling the completion of the task for which he was placed in this world. The consummatory aspect, of course, requires divine legitimation, but it also means that dying becomes in a sense a voluntary act, as it was for Jesus. It is, for example, striking that a sharp distinction is made between dying a natural death and being killed. Dying as consummation is beautifully symbolized in the phrase in the Episcopal funeral service, "His work is done" (also in "Well done, good and faithful servant"). The individual human being is brought into a special kind of partnership with God in the implementation of the divine plan for the world. One might say that the Genesis conception of the life of travail and its bitter ending by death followed expulsion from the Garden has been transformed into the conception of life in this world as a great opportunity to serve as an instrument of the divine will in the great task of building the kingdom. One of the marks of Protestantism is acceptance of worldly life as basically good and of death as the natural and divinely ordained consummation.

There is, however, an underlying conflict. This positive and, one might say, optimistic view of life and death is essentially conditional on fulfillment of the divine mandate, on actually *doing* God's will. Fulfillment, however, cannot be guaranteed. What Burke calls the element of the negative, the capacity to disobey, is just as characteristic of modern man as it was of Adam. Hence, the problem of what is to happen to the inveterate sinner cannot be avoided, because it cannot be guaranteed that sinners will cease to exist. The note of death as punishment and its symbolic aftermath is always a counterpoint note to the positive Protestant conception.

It seems to me that the same basic view of life and death has survived the often suggested abandonment of the traditional Judeo-Christian conceptions of the transcendental God. It has survived most conspicuously in Marxian socialism, which, at least in its Communist version, bears striking resemblances to early Calvanism. Here, clearly, the basic human assignment is the building of socialism. The fate of the individual "soul" after death is clearly thought of differently than in theistic Protestantism. But I think that the basic pattern is very similar, that is, mortality and the other fundamental features of the human condition are accepted, and, therefore, the completion of a total life in the ideal case gives death a consummatory meaning.

Recent movements suggest a shift from the Protestant Ethic emphasis on "work" to a communally organized regime of love, which, of course, links with the Christian traditions of love at both the divine and the human levels. It is not clear just how these movements are going to crystallize, if at all; but one thing is almost certain: that they will share with Puritan Protestantism and Marxian socialism the conception of the religious sanctification of life in this world.

We must not forget, however, that the early Christians were eschatalogically oriented: they looked forward to a second coming of Christ and, with it, the day of judgment and the end of the world as it had existed and been known. Those who were saved would then enter into a state of eternal life in a new paradise, in some respects resembling the Garden of Eden, yet different from it. The belief in some kind of preexistent paradise in which man participated has reverberated through the centuries, especially during the Enlightenment, in Rousseau's idea of the state of nature. A preexistent state of nature has been dynamically linked with the conception of a terminal state where all the problems of the tragic human condition are believed to have been solved. This kind of a utopia, of course, has been exceedingly prominent in the socialist movement, most notably in the idea of communism as the end state of socialist societies, guided by the communist vision of Marxism-Leninism.

Very similar orientations seem to be characteristic of the movement that I have elsewhere (1971) called the new "religion of love." Indeed, in its extreme versions it is suggested that the regime of total love can be set up in the immediate future. It will, however, have to be a terrestrial regime which cannot conceive "the end of the world" in the sense in which early Christians used that phrase. It would mean only the end of the evil parts of the world. A clear conception of the meaning of death has not yet emerged in these circles. But there is a fantasy of immortality —a feeling that death, as it has been known since the abandonment of Christian eschatological hopes, is somehow unreal—that is attributable to new understandings of the centralness of human life. It will be interesting to follow developments in this area.

REFERENCE

PARSONS, TALCOTT

1971   "Belief, Unbelief and Disbelief." Pp. 207–245 in R. Caporale and A. Grumelli (eds.), *The Culture of Unbelief*. Berkeley: University of California Press.

David N. Ruth

GEORGETOWN UNIVERSITY, WASHINGTON, D.C.

The Social Reference
of Body Symbols

---

*... all symbolism, even in the highest flights of
sublimation, remains body symbolism* (Brown, 1970: 1710)

Men have always studied symbols. The approach to the subject, however,
varies according to the historical climate surrounding human imagination and to the particular perspective of the individual investigator. Traditionally, the sociologist assesses the function of symbols in their
institutional setting, the anthropologist looks to symbols for insights into
prevailing cultural values, the historian for morphological structures, the
personality theorist and therapist for unconscious phenomena, the
theologian for liturgical reference, and so on [1].

Today, everyone knows—or claims to know—that many of our major cultural symbols are radically changing. Some familiar symbols seem to be dying; others are dead already. Some new symbols are being born; others holding their own. Yet social scientists seem peculiarly reluctant to study symbols at all. This is surprising, for symbols offer the social scientist empirical data without necessarily trapping him in quantitative trivia.

To discover the *strength* of a particular class of symbols in a given setting and time, the sociologist today needs to develop ways to measure the responses to new and old symbols while resisting the temptation to freeze their nonempirical referents into static analytical categories. Living symbols are like birds in flight. They cannot be "stopped" and remain what they essentially are.

The task of studying symbols is important because ours is an age that urgently needs to learn afresh which symbols are capable of helping us to find meanings in the larger world around us, and which are not. Do today's symbols connect the empirical with the nonempirical dimensions of reality? Do responses to symbols suggest that the "sacred canopy" of meaning (in the sense used by Peter Berger) is, or is not, holding. Two basic questions seem to be:

1. Do symbols refer to what they are traditionally proposed to refer?
2. To what do symbols refer, in the responses of the adherents within the symbol system itself?

Responses to symbols offer one way of determining a symbol's strength in a given social setting. In this initial study, the type of strength we shall examine is the social reference, especially of what are designated as body symbols [2]. What kinds of, and how many, "I" and "we" responses does a particular class of symbols elicit? The symbol is strong when it elicits the widest range of responses. The following list includes four "I" categories, four "we" categories, and two residual categories.

Individual reference: "I" responses
1. Body, e.g., *my* body, *my* feelings, the feeling "*I*" have.
2. Self . . .: "I" with no other reference.
3. Interpersonal . . .: "I" and "he" or "she" and the "other."
4. Plurality of Individuals . . .: "I" and "they"; "I" and "others."

Social reference: "we" responses
5. Small group, e.g., "we" as a group.
6. Society . . .: "we" as a society.
7. Culture . . .: "we" as part of a cultural heritage.
8. Supernatural . . .: "we" as part of a supernatural world.

No social response

9. Physical, i.e., physical description only.
10. No response, i.e., no *verbal* response.

In the absence of any existing topology of religious symbolism, and because of the immensity of the field, our area of investigation is limited to body symbols currently used within the Christian tradition. Symbols employing body metaphor were chosen for four reasons:

1. Western civilization today is fairly well body-oriented.
2. Christianity among the living religions has a highly developed corporal symbol system related to its doctrine of incarnation. Phrases like the "Word made flesh" or reference to the church as "the body of Christ" suggest that the body has always been a major empirical referent for Christian symbolism.
3. There has been an emergence of corporality in current writings of phenomenologists, existential sociologists, psychiatrists, psychologists, and philosophers, as well as an expanding consideration of the "body image" in much personality theory.
4. The author invites research in body symbolism; he believes that Christian symbolism, expressed in points of corporal contact, not only spans the widest range of religious experience but utilizes the best medium man has to express his very corporal existence.

It is assumed that a strong body symbol will evoke responses throughout all or many of the types of "I" and "we" categories. A weak or dying symbol will command only a small number of responses, or elicit only physical descriptions of the symbol, or evoke no response at all. I hope that empirical studies of this kind may lead eventually to theoretical clarification of the birth, death, and rebirth of meanings and symbols and their role in the current reshaping of our own culture.

THE METHOD

This is a descriptive study, using the phenomenological method. The temptation to try to discover why symbols got where they are or why they are there now is resisted. The goal is simpler—the discovery of what *is*.

The individuals whose verbal responses have been used in this study to assess the strength of Christian body symbols were drawn from two populations on the basis of "theoretical sampling"—one consisting of fifty schizophrenic hospitalized Christians, and the other of fifty mentally healthy, nonhospitalized Christians functioning as active members of a

Christian church. The two samples were matched on seven variables: religious affiliation, geographic location, age, sex, marital status, educational background, and race.

Psychotic persons were chosen to contrast with the healthy group because of their relative detachment from normal social interactions. It was assumed that a psychotic Christian, already withdrawn from "society" because residing in a mental hospital, would respond with contrasting degrees of "social reference" in comparison with a "healthy" group fully involved in social interactions in a normative sense.

Pictures focusing on particular bodies and body parts were selected and mounted on cards, which were then shown individually to the subjects [3]. The "test" consisted of presenting thirty cards and eliciting the associations which the pictures had for the various respondents. The responses to the cards were recorded *in situ*. Scoring was made on the basis of the number of "individual" and "social" references to the symbol itself, the number being determined by the content elicited.

THE RESULTS

In a sense, there can never be final results to a study on symbolism. The statistics may all be carefully added up, but they hardly equal the total effect of what happens when interviewees and interviewer meet for 263 hours in an attempt to assess the impact of Christian body symbols. To face a symbol alone is adventure enough. To have that adventure stretched by one hundred sensitive persons in sickness and in health is never to return to the land from which one started!

The results of this study are not thereby invalidated; but, rather, the symbol and the man, once in open interaction, experience in varying degrees of intensity a kind of natural metamorphosis. Objective conclusions as to dead symbols may be stated with statistical finality, but the values of living symbols are constantly expanding and contracting.

A total of 5,701 scoring decisions were made and recorded in the ten categories listed above. Table 1 summarizes the scores for all thirty symbol cards collectively.

The overall results of this study clearly suggest a severe lack of social reference in body symbols in the Christian tradition. "Individual references" total 64% in the schizophrenic group and 65% in the healthy group. In contrast, "social references" amount to only 21% for the schizophrenic and 22% for the healthy samples. Thus there is more than 3–1 ratio of "individual" over "social" references.

The "I" responses far outweigh the "we" responses in both samples.

TABLE 1.   STATISTICAL TOTALS OF
THE SOCIAL REFERENCE OF BODY SYMBOLS

Categories	Schizophrenic Group A		Healthy Group B		Total	
	Score	%	Score	%	Score	%
Individual ("I") references						
Body	184	6%	87	3%	271	5%
Self	844	29%	1,053	37%	1,897	33%
Interpersonal	109	4%	110	4%	219	4%
Plurality of individuals	713	25%	582	21%	1,295	23%
	1,850	64%	1,832	65%	3,682	65%
Social ("we") references						
Social group	66	2%	131	4%	197	3%
Society	50	2%	19	1%	69	1%
Culture	438	15%	428	15%	866	15%
Supernatural world	41	2%	46	2%	87	2%
	595	21%	624	22%	1,219	21%
Nonsocial references						
Physical	343	12%	328	12%	671	12%
No response	99	3%	30	1%	129	2%
	442	15%	358	13%	800	14%
Total scores	2,887		2,814		5,701	100%

The only social reference category to achieve any impressive total is "culture," in which responses generally referred to a value or norm which "we inherited." A sense of the symbol's relation to the issues of society, in which "we are all called upon to act, received only 69 of 5,701 scores, about 1%. The identity with a supernatural agent—the "supernatural world"—acting in behalf of a "we" group does little better, with a 2% total reference. Even the "my body" or "one-to-one" relationship categories equal only 5% and 4% of the "I" references. With 14% of the responses, the symbol elicits only physical descriptions or no response at all.

Not all of the thirty symbol cards elicited so few social reference scores. Six body symbols, in fact, achieved a wide range of scores, with sufficient social references to suggest signs of symbolic vitality.

Although six symbols showed relative "strength" in these terms—with the noncorporal symbol of *Light* strongly associated with Christian body symbols—the total set of body symbols, judged on the basis of our diagnosis of responses to the thirty included in this study, looks to be seriously ill! We review the symbols in six categories: "dead" "dying," "sick," "of indeterminate health," "in moderate health," and (so far as we can judge), "vital" or vibrant.

1. "Dead" Symbols. Two extremities of the body—*hair* and *feet*—are, in a sense, already dead. Demons as symbols appear also to have no "meaning"; they now only amuse.

The erstwhile strength of *hair* as symbolic has receded, probably irreversibly. A few strands of life still exist in the tonsured heads of cloistered Christians, as the following statement by a schizoid subject suggests; but even here it is cut off from any social reference:

> Rulers and kings wear crowns as an attractiveness on the head. That's why monks take hair off the top of the head; they're removing something very vital—it could be the animal. . . . That's why *we* wear hats in church—out of respect to our Lord."

Women generally, however, cover their changing hairdos in church with mounting indifference. While in some sectors of contemporary culture, there exists a growing erotic association of beards, whiskers, and hair on other parts of the body with virility, such ideas are politely ignored or deliberately pushed aside from any religious interpretation.

Washing of *feet* is another dead symbol. Although churches at opposite ends of the liturgical spectrum may annually respect this once-common symbol of humility, derived from an age of dirt roads and sandaled feet, the reported associations frequently reversed the original "meaning" as suggested in the following:

> *I* remember the Pope washing the feet of twelve priests on Holy Thursday. *He* had a gold basin and a gold cloth. You saw the priests take off their shoes and socks; but they were very carefully guarded so you couldn't see their feet. The Pope went around and splashed feet and sort of dipped them, but he didn't wash them. They probably washed, oiled and powdered their feet before they ever came to the Pope, so he really didn't wash them.

To be chosen to have your feet delicately splashed by anyone from Pope to Pentecostalist preacher could signify, in other words, special status.

Feet still retain some erotic connections; but in our frankly physical age, sex has moved up the leg. Although phrases like "foot-loose and fancy free" and the like still exist, Christian foot symbolism has generally foresaken the sensual aspects and appeals only to very old notions, if any. God and Satan once were reported to have "walked to and fro on the earth"; but the sounds of their footsteps are expected no more.

As symbols of Cosmic Evil, *demons* have lost out—indeed have become laughable, inciting no one to righteous indignation or to holy battle, it seems. Except perhaps in mental hospitals, the "Power of Evil" today largely goes nameless. "There's a little devil in all of us," one patient said, intending, apparently, to speak literally. But ordinarily demons appear chiefly on the labels of canned deviled ham or of additives to automobile engines and the like. Although "Powers of Darkness" remain, the specialized body of the demon has died. Now the symbol of Evil is as boundless and "free as a spirit."

2. "*Dying Symbols.* God's Eye as a symbol of an ever-watching, all-just, all-knowing Father has been painted out of most twentieth-century church ceilings. Its superhuman capacity to "peer into the very core" of a man's sould remains meaningful for some; but more often the Eye of God is displaced by the eye of the clergyman, the psychiatrist or a friend: "[This] . . . looks like my doctor's eye," said one hospitalized patient. "*I* notice his eyes. I consider him sort of saving my life." A "mentally healthy respondent'" commented on "the light of His Eye . . . it transmits a sense of creation. There is more to things than we grasp; we can just attempt. . . . It's a mystery, not in the sense of the obscure, but always there is something more to find out."

The *Eye of God,* however, has all but vanished with the stroke of a paint brush, peering into the sanctuary, if at all, only occasionally through church windows, referred to as "the Eye of God looking in." To restore a big godly eye to sanctuary walls or to the dome of the church would probably no longer suggest an all-seeing Creator to the modern Christian mind. Hope for this symbol may rest with its present association with Light entering the church through the soft colors of stained glass. Light coming through glass, however, appears to be more "individually comforting" than "socially challenging" and is often detached from any "supernatural vision." The worshiper seldom looks above the windows to the dome.

The *halo* seems to have become a spiritualized "hat" which the contemporary Christian is determined to remove. One respondent who likened haloes to "protective space helmets" may be merely reflecting the current glorified status of secular space heroes. As an identifying mark of a "saint" or of a "member of the Holy Family," the haloed head has solid, built-in cultural strength for many Christians. What identifies it, however, is a special status associated with the Middle Ages, not with contemporary life. Facetiously, one respondent commented: "Joseph doesn't have a halo. Did somebody goof—or did *he* goof?"

"*Praying hands*" is perhaps the weakest member of a trilogy of "hand symbols"—creating hands, blessing hands, and praying hands. While the placement of the hands in a prescribed position elicits many associations —for example, as a ritualistic aid for prayer—praying hands are linked most often with children or with clergy. The posture keeps children's hands out of their pockets and out of trouble; it puts the clergy into a position attributed to their role. But vitality in the symbol is apparently dying. Only when Light is attributed to praying hands ("which point up like burning flames" in the words of one subject) does there seem to be any association with energy, life, hope.

Those symbols which legitimize and sanctify sexual relations seem to have been devitalized by deadening appeal to conformity. Church *weddings* are still commonly preferred because they seem "holy," "nice," and/or "pretty"; the priestly pronouncement of marriage arouses memories of magical words, solemnly uttered; but as a vow of two people spoken in faith to God, witnessed and supported by a vital, organized community, the wedding ceremony itself has little symbolic "life." The modern double-ring ceremony does not seem to symbolize the union of male and female or of the pair into one broad communal circles but suggests as often that which "binds" or "brands" like slaves or like cattle. Marriage by the church is often little more than a civil ceremony with stained glass windows, yet "I must get married in church in order to make it [i.e., sexual relations] legal" was the representative response of one. *Sexual relations* symbolized for another "the love of God for us—that He would enable us to create another human being," but this is not frequently heard.

The *nude body* in Christian symbolism has little life or "associational freedom" but is quickly hidden by anything from a fig leaf to the vestments of clergymen and of the cloistered "religious" alike. Whenever a nude body was assigned a "meaning" by anyone in this study, the association assumed an "apple" and "the doctrine of the Fall." Despite assertions of many clergy to the contrary, the "apple" means sex and "the Fall" sexual intercourse. If the original sin of man is presently connected with "an apple, sex, and a fig leaf," one should not be surprised to find no social reference to the nude body as a symbol.

By contrast, in communism, man stands naked before a future in which freedom and social justice beckon all—or stands exposed to exploitation. The Christian promise of a fig leaf seems small by comparison, challenging few.

Generally the heavily *clothed body* of clergy and cloistered persons provokes rigid identification with "religion." The sight of clerical garb, in a test from which interdenominational biases were eliminated, still produced negative associations. The symbol is not dying because it lacks ritualistic interest but because what it elicits has little "health" in it. The clergy and the cloistered, by their clothes, represent not what they give by their service but what they "give up." Sometimes a particular vestment signifies "what my church has" and "your church has not."

Body size has shrunk in symbolic power. A long or attenuated shape still suggests saintliness for a few; and the fat man receives few kind words. In fact, the endomorph was alleged by one to be so fat that he "could never rise up to heaven: he'd just sink down to hell." The effete ectomorphic depiction of the Sunday school Christ seems unappealing to children and adults alike; and while the mesomorph represents the ideal for some, the comment of one respondent was, "What would a religious man want with muscles like that?"

Body position in worship varies according to liturgical customs, but the responses to the symbols involved are similar. Standing, sitting, and kneeling still maintain some "strength," but as a rule people stand "because everybody stands," sit because "you can't stand all the time," or knelt in prayer simply because "that's the way we pray—kneeling." The old formula, "kneel to pray; stand to praise God; sit to be instructed," no longer carries much weight of meaning.

Christians generally seem to ignore their corporality. The body functions like a machine—noticed only when it "fails" in some respect. Although there is a "slow leak" in the underlying symbol strength of the body position in worship, this may not be posing serious or immediate threat since there appears to be a gradual slackening in the felt need for spontaneous body movement, leading, possibly, toward breakdown in the capacity of the whole man to express his religious sentiments by bodily actions. In the meantime people "process" to the sanctuary—and recess from it—while "God gets carried in and out with the choir."

An empty cross near an empty tomb, which we have taken to symbolize historically the *abstract resurrected body,* is today almost devoid of symbol life. The empty cross is a *thing*, not a body. As a thing, it still challenges the eye when it is placed on top of a church steeple, embedded in gold on the cover of a bible, or traced in the air by pope, priest, or parishioner. As a thing, the cross may have lost its association with capital punishment, being now worn comfortably around the neck on a little gold chain.

Many Protestant churches have put heavy reliance upon the empty cross as a symbol of resurrection, but Protestants no less than Roman Catholics in the study appeared to find the empty cross "cold," "sterile," "too abstract" and so on. Only for those few with extensive doctrinal training was the idea of resurrection readily associated with an empty cross. A Protestant respondent expressed many less explicit ideas associated with the cross as an abstract resurrected body symbol:

> I don't think the Cross is going to go when the Orientals and colored races come into their own. The cross will remain . . . but somehow as an irrelevant outpost. . . . It will be irrelevant to what is going to take place in the new world. This is a greater indignity for [it] than chopping it down. . . The worst indignity for the cross is to live on . . . when it has lost any inward meaning."

The need for a symbolic form to express man's desire for life after body-death is by no means dead. But a thing, such as a cross, no longer meets that "symbol need." Only with an eerie blue Light above the empty tomb did a few see "heaven" and "life" in any form.

Angels appear to manifest a little more symbol vitality than do their "dead" demonic opposites—but not much. "I may have a guardian angel," was the opinion of a mentally ill respondent, "but I don't know her name. Where is she now, damn her?" Or, as another (mentally healthy) respondent explained, "Protestants and intellectuals have knocked the guts out of anything angels might have meant. They mean nothing to me."

The present place of angels seems dependent upon parochial school teaching and upon the skills of commercial artists. Apart from these, angels sometimes appear as "sweet" or "cute" praying creatures or jolly cherubs decorating Christmas cards. As symbolic guardians of the Good, angels might win out over demons but hardly over the larger, formless Cosmic Evil. Nor would they be thought of as assisting man against the "little evils" of daily existence; they are no longer enlisted, having folded their wings permanently in the Middle Ages.

3. *"Sick" symbols.* The intensity of association of *evil eye* symbolism came as a research surprise. A big red medical eye, pictured with a small white spot of reflected light reflected near the center, set off an explosion of fearsome responses. Both in and out of the mental hospital, "the big evil eye" came to life. For some, indeed, this ordinary medical picture became "the most evil eye I've ever sen: you saw my reaction."

"Evil eyes seem to be watching me," declared another, ". . . even the eyes on TV are watching eyes."

There was no mistaking the initial sense of fright which many subjects exhibited, as there was no mistaking the apology these twentieth-century persons felt required to add. Following some embarrassment, the response often turned to "little eyes" and away from individually held, often intense reactions to Cosmic Evil as being thus symbolized.

When the stylized painted "Eye of God" on one hand and the "Eye of the Evil One" on the other were brushed out of Christian symbolism, there occurred what may be an irreversible loss. What is needed, it would seem, is a radically revised symbol with both "Big Good" and "Cosmic Evil" associations if the lesser goods and evils of our society and of ourselves are to be "engaged." What is needed is a symbol or symbols strong enough to enlist men constructively in the never-ending struggle between these forces.

Only muffled sounds enter the symbolic *ear*. Even for individuals with paranoid schizophrenia, it is easier to imagine human or cosmic enemies listening with deadly acoustical accuracy to the spoken (and even unspoken) words of man than to believe that God either desires or is able to "tune in" humans. "The ear reminds me of something to listen to," said on schizophrenic, "But no one ever hears *me*."

While the "holy sound" of the altar bell is a ritualistic sign of warning to some and the clicking of rosary beads is a "happy sound" to some, most often these and other sounds disappear into general oblivion. An exception in ear symbolism seems to be the strong sound of the church organ. Associations are reported as swirling around the individuals engaged in pleasant reverie or caught up in a "consuming majesty" of power, eros, and drama. The sound of a pipe organ alone seems able to carry the entire ear symbolism toward a relatively strong "social reference" score. "The organ makes me float. . . . It really gets me trapped," said one. "I love the organ." As against this very personal response there is a sense of the sound of an organ swelling to fill whole cathedrals, enveloping all. This lopsidedness of "organ strength," however, spells "sickness" for the symbol as a whole.

The symbolism of the *mouth* provokes ideas, for some, about the comparative worth of the communications of prophets and preachers. "I don't pay much attention to the priest when he talks," one remarked. Another spoke, upon looking at the picture, of a "contrast between prophets and good preachers. There's Jeremiah; I'd like to hear one of those for a change."

The urgency and challenge of a Jeremiah are sharply contrasted with the "comforting preachers [who] mouth things you've heard all your life." There is a grand and tragic "tone" to the prophet: he would surely denounce "our dropping of the atom bomb on Japan," . . . "the slaughter of Jews by Nazi Christians," . . . "our arrogance in Vietnam." A prophet would demand social justice for the black and economic justice for the poor of the world.

Despite the message of doom, there is, nevertheless, a voiced desire to "hear one of these for a change" and the feeling that "we don't have any prophets today, just men with ideas."

Some subjects spoke of looking at the preacher's teeth while he was preaching; but *mouth* symbolism seems to have little strength. Cosmetics may have created a far stronger secular symbol. One schizophrenic patient, looking at a picture of a speaking prophet, announced, "This is God. He is pretty worn out now."

From the highly charged reactions associated with a papal blessing among Roman Catholics to the less ritualized greeting by hand by the Protestant pastor at the church door, there is an awareness of the *blessing hands* and of hand symbolism in the Christian tradition. The memory of a clergyman "pressing his hand hard at the back of my head" was readily recalled as the primary tactile impression of confirmation. The raised hand at benediction brings a "feeling of finality" to a worship service, though, for many, the act may be loaded with a touch of magic.

The "up and out reaching" hands of the clergy may be losing considerable symbol strength as a consequence of frequent association with hand signals for "stop" in moral prohibition or with "hands out" for something. Such associations act to destroy the warmth of the contact of "blessing hands" in the experience of some.

Despite a heritage which has made it difficult for Christians to identify with their total corporality, *breast* symbols may return from Victorian oblivion. A factor in this may be the increased interest in nursing one's own child—by older women who expressed regret that their milk was not rich enough and by younger women who just "like the idea" of nursing a baby. "If I ever have kids," declared one respondent, "I would certainly breast-feed them."

As a symbol, Mary's nursing of the infant Jesus is seen by some as the "miracle" means by which "she purified the world and made us innocent again." Among Protestant subjects, the focus shifts to the Christ child. In both groups, dependency needs and spiritual nourishment are associated with milk. As the "perfect food" in advertisers' parlance, it is "life-giving," with cosmic associations—the Milky Way or the imagery of stars created by the act of Venus mythically squeezing her breasts.

A backlog of breast symbol embarrassment, coupled with a relutance to admit to the more human aspects of Mary or Jesus, poses an obstacle to a serious revival of breast symbolism. "There's nothing wrong with nursing," said one, "but it is not right for the Madonna to do it." A body-starved religion, however, needs symbols which somehow suggest feeding on vital substance.

It is not clear whether *sacred blood* symbolism is dying or just "seriously ill" in the responses of the subjects. The reaction to human blood from a cut finger appears to be far more immediate than the reaction to the bleeding hands of a dying Christ on the cross. Such phrases as "washed in the blood" and "blood sacrifice" are used, but less frequently. The quantity of blood spilled by men in modern wars and in concentration camps led one person to suggest that "Jesus can be envied; He didn't have to undergo the indignities of these people."

The "Sacred Heart of Jesus" beats with powerful ritual-moral force for Roman Catholics; but one gains the general impression that as blood symbolism becomes more and more sacralized, it appears less and less real. In any case, very strong individualistic blood associations have not mixed with any comparable social response. If this means that the life-blood of Christianity has been drained out of the corporate body, existing only in "isolated individual cells," so to speak, the life expectancy of the symbol cannot be long. On the other hand, the presence of blood associations in a long continuum of symposium involving appeasement, atonement, and purification may provide a much-needed social blood transfusion for the church as the symbolic "body of Christ."

Human blood symbolism receives stronger, more "corporally centered" responses than its sacred counterpart. Humans react with interest ranging through everything from intense fascination to horror at "the sight of my own blood" or "when I saw a truck run over a cat." They long to be "fraternity bloodbrothers" but flee with obvious affect from the memory of dissecting an animal's heart in a biology lab. The picture of a bleeding human hand reminds one person that "I am no stronger than hamburger" but makes another wish she could "go to a bar and order a glass of hot blood." The immediacy of bodily responses and body scores are unequaled by any other corporal symbol.

Human blood symbolism suffers a problem opposite to that confronting sacred blood. While the blood of Christ may have become too holy or too remote from human contact, human blood points to nothing but its mortal self. Theologians might cause the symbolic sacred blood to dry up in the rarefied veins of lifeless concepts. However, if they turned to human blood symbolism, they might well invest it with a new symbol strength.

There are unmistakably strong individual responses to *female reproductive organs,* as symbolized by the womb. "The church is the womb"; said one, "we're all the children of God. Babies develop in the womb; man develops in the church."

The church interior as the womb, however, is not magnified as the symbol referent. There is "no reason," another subject explained, "why we should not have the comfort [of the womb], but Christianity [did not] mean for us to stay in the womb forever." Beyond the womb lies (for the fetus) unimaginable mysteries—breathing, walking, working, laughing, and much more. So beyond the Mother Church are the wider mysteries of social living and spiritual interaction. In short, that there is more to the religious life than can be contained in a womb is the import of these associations.

The "illness" of female reproductive symbolism follows from the fact that the creative preparations and stirrings of development in the church are perceived to be "for individuals" and not for society. The symbolic womb perpetuates life, but does not enlist individuals necessarily for full corporate living. When the biologist eventually succeeds in creating life in his laboratory, womb symbolism will likely be demoted in the technological process. Even though the birth of physical life is becoming a laboratory miracle, preparation for living will still need "a secure place" in which to develop; and the church may again become that place where necessary growth in the spirit takes place. A female reproductive symbol which merely perpetuates life, however, can provide neither protection nor new life.

Male reproductive organs symbolized by the phallus clearly point, in the responses of some subjects, to a superhuman power, though the association is often ambiguous. In current symbolic association the church steeple, for example, is not seen as unambiguously potent. As a landmark it has been surpassed by skyscrapers; but rockets, as man-made structures of power, tend to be identified with nuclear clouds of destruction, issuing more often with murderous showers of fire than with all new seeds of life. A schizophrenic respondent saw the steeple "as phallic. But I don't think I'm applying anything but psychology to it," he added.

Associations reported in connection with pictures of *skin* suggest that body skin symbolism is "thin." Adam's sin is depicted as a "white sin," presumably far less damning than Cain's murderous "black sin." The thought of touching dark skins gave one respondent "creepy feelings." Rather than symbolizing Christian brotherhood or the beautiful colors of created man, pigmentations of the skin are more often smeared into ugly streaks over the image of man and even, it seems, upon the image of God.

Symbols depicting *body sickness* or disease elicited some of the most "promising" responses of any corporal symbol. What are pictured as disease are met by respondents with courage, sometimes head-on with disarming humor, sometimes by escape, often with surprising measures of kindness. The "sickness" of the symbol of body sicknesses consists in dissociation of the latter, under contemporary condition, from the

Christian image of the "healing touch of the Master Physician." The healing miracles of Jesus are apparently outshone for many by the miracles of modern-day hospitals.

In America, *body aging* is taken to be a corporal tragedy. For most respondents, the symbol of a dead Christ seem to take away neither the "sting" of growing old nor the victory of the grave. "There's always an end for everybody," one observed, "even for Jesus Christ. There was an end."

The *death* of one's own body is a thought most men tend to push out of their minds. As one respondent verbalized this: "Few people want to die. Few people want to talk about it.

The scope of associations with body death symbolism appears to be broad. Beyond association with personal death, the symbol evokes ideas concerning the deadly waste of life in war, and much more. Here again, the "sickness" of the symbol seems to lie in its lack of explicit Christian association. In the associations reported in the study, there is a longing to learn how to die with dignity, but no psychological or sociological framework in sight to make it possible.

4. Symbols in a State of "Indeterminate Health." Corporal symbols discussed here seem to reveal extensive potentialities for maintaining vitality. All five of the following symbols appear to hold promise of evoking strong social reference responses or of overcoming "I" responses. If the power of each of these symbols stems from deeply rooted cultural strength, the present liturgical uses to which they are put often appear ineffectual or ill advised.

In its own way, each of these symbols may foreshadow the coming of a new "season" in Christian symbolism. Uncertainty about man's capacity to appropriate their emerging power or potential power constitutes the primary reason for their being categorized here as of "indeterminate health."

With the *nose* or with nose symbolism are associated ideas of the "lifegiving breath of God." The picture of a nose suggested something of this order to about a third of the subjects, the "breath of life" being equated with the Holy Spirit. Another third recollected churchly smells of incense, lilies, candles, freshly polished wood, musty carpets, and the like. Although the Holy Spirit as "breath" or "air" may be receding, one finds the frequent appearance of Light if not of smell in the pattern of associations. Unlike air, Light cannot be captured or "breathed in." By the same token it cannot be "put in a box [and] like God [suffocated] in systematic theology."

In this connection some respondents suggested that "candle light should symbolize the Holy Spirit. . . . You can never point to it and say, 'I've got it.' We know it only when it is gone."

Hands (as distinguished from praying hands discussed previously) appear to have dual association—with terror on one hand and creative power on the other. Hands reaching out toward the unknown or "touching reality" in "new acts of creation" are seen respectively in the pictures presented. Many have left behind the idea of "God shaping the universe by His Hand" and associate hands rather with operations such as handling piles of data in connection with IBM machines and the like. The stylized Hand of God symbol with its self-consciously artistic association has neither life or light enough to touch reality today. Instead there are the hands of the traffic cop and other images that come as frequently (or more so) to mind.

Water as a symbolic purifier for the body has been all but reduced to a trickle over the baby's head at the baptismal font. Except for a few sects, more at home in an agrarian than in an urban society, baptism by immersion in streams of flowing water has been abandoned altogether. Rebirth by water has been demoted from among major practices or "dammed up" in ritual-moral categories. Concerning the font, one respondent said that it was "the last place to look for life-giving water." The idea of living water or the power of water to "make all things new" is not extinct, however.

With respect to *fire* (which like water, is not strictly speaking a *body* symbol but is seen as capable of purifying the body), the situation is somewhat different. Cremation in purifying fire assured kings in some ancient cultures of immediate deification following a dramatic earthly exit. Today the consuming fury of fire symbolism, as far as it touches most lives, has been tamed to the tiny altar candles or hung in "enternal light" containers. The more frightening fire symbols have been pushed away into a remote past or a distant future. While "hell fires" rage with fierce intensity for some Roman Catholics and for some Protestants as well, the picture of a Black Friday cross against a red sky more often looks like lightning or a Camp Fire Girls' campfire than it connotes hell or, in another connection, the seven-tongued flame of the Holy Spirit which descended on the apostles at Pentecost. Fire, then, no longer refines or purifies; at most it is a matter of punishment. Nevertheless there exists a "'social reference" dimension, documented by frequent references to fire storms and atomic bomb holocausts which would destroy "all of us."

It comes as no surprise to learn that the symbolism of a *literal resurrected body* (as distinguished from that of the *abstract resurrected body*, discussed above) is "just not convincing to modern man." The added evidence of a strong skepticism regarding the resurrected Christ, indicated by the statistic that 45 of the 100 Christians interviewed doubted or rejected the prospect of any corporal life after death (either for Jesus or for themselves), would seem to give the coup de grace to this symbol. The majority of the interviewees *wanted* a recognizable body after death. Corporal life in heaven, some anticipated, would be "like summer," "full of warm colors," and even stocked with simple pleasures such as "having a boat of my own up there." But 45% had grave doubts. For those to whom the symbolism of the resurrected body was meaningful, the resurrected Christ was seen as having a very human face and his body was definitely not ethereal—definitely not like a "spook," since "He walked out of the crypt like a normal man:" He didn't float.

5. *"Moderately Healthy Symbols.* A symbol in "moderate health" demonstrates a capacity to activate broadly distributed responses. In this study such a symbol also would necessarily demonstrate strong "social reference" association and show "vitality" in all scoring categories. The term "health" is qualified as "moderate" either because serious statistical gaps in the descriptive dimensions of categories emerged or because analysis of the associations led to questions about the capacity of the symbol to retain its *present "strength."* Only one Christian corporal symbol appears to meet the criteria of "moderate health"—namely, *ritual foods.*

To eat the Eucharistic bread and wine, as the symbolic body and blood of Christ, is to take into one's own body a very vital corporal symbol. These ritual foods evoke social reference scores as strong as those of any other symbol and elicit a distribution among social reference categories exceeded by none. There is a special "we" experience in the common meal which units individuals. Eating the sacred is, of course, universally a dangerous holy act. As a mild example of such dangers, some recall the communion wafer getting "stuck in my throat." Once within the body, such foods are felt to move to the "core of me—very near my heart," and so on.

In our city civilization of supermarkets and frozen foods, bread and wine are essential to but few meals. Bread has moved to the periphery of dinner and may not ever appear on the table of many diet-conscious persons. Wine tends to be a menu luxury item, served when family resources permit. There is little one can point to as visibly essential in the modern fare. Milk for children, perhaps; hamburgers for teenagers, frozen meats for adults—but nothing with the historical continuity required for symbol vitality.

The impressive "we" responses which we have noted, however, often omit concern for the society in which the communicants live. Reference is to a "contained we"—belonging to a closed community. The idea of the community becomes more important than the communal sharing of a gift in the wider society.

Despite these losses of symbol vitality, ritual body foods still nourish man with considerable symbol health. Many live potentialities exist in the sacrament of communion. From the fulfilling of dependency needs to the releasing of hostility through "biting and breaking" food as well as from other associations reported, the Eucharist symbolizes a joyous shared feast in which "for a moment, you imagine you're in a different world. It's very sacred."

6. *"Vibrant" Symbols.* No Christian corporal symbol is today fully "vibrant." Christianity once supplied both the "strength" and appropriate form for each of the thirty body symbols used in this study. Today the forms are time-weakened, both supernaturally and socially detached.

While many of these symbols appear to be capable of attaining restored "health," the needed therapy rarely appears within the body symbols themselves. Active stimulation or injection from outside seems required.

Given the unanticipated association in twenty-three of the thirty body symbols with the noncorporal phenomenon Light, one might conclude that this latter could become properly appropriated as the "tonic" needed for overall body symbol recovery.

Beyond the statistical summaries of the frequencies of the symbols' social references four research inferences may be said to emerge as by-products of the study.

First, the rather astounding agreement between schizophrenic and mentally healthy respondents in the distribution of scores among the ten categories raises a question about the relation of religious experience to psychological states: How is it that a man in psychosis expresses the same or very similar religious characteristics in the scoring categories as a man in mental health? The associational content may vary, but the symbols elicit degrees of social reference, consistently similar for both schizophrenic and mentally healthy subjects.

In the early stages of the study this finding raised more than a few eyebrows among people with whom it was discussed. The idea that a schizophrenic person, although withdrawn from normal society, should omit social references of religious symbols in the same proportion as a healthy person seemed to some absurd, to others disturbing, even insulting.

The underlying premise in these attitudes is that religious experience is dependent upon a psychological condition. A person with schizophenia, psychologically cut off from the social world, is expected to locate social references in symbols less frequently than his emotionally healthy counterpart.

That this did not occur leads the author to challenge psychological reductionism. Religious expression is, by implication, not reducible to psychological states. However, it is still theoretically possible for some to argue, that *all* Christians are collectively psychotic, or may be considered so, or—an entirely different argument—that the scoring categories are invalid instruments of measurement. It would be difficult to establish any convincing empirical evidence either way.

While few would willingly acknowledge themselves as reductionist, there is more than a little evidence that the breed is far from extinct. Theology has developed quite a number of full-blown reductionists, a fact which very early became apparent in this study.

Although the study did not set out to examine differences between Catholic and Protestant associations regarding body symbols, many colleagues thought it should. Religious identity was considered a significant variable; questions about what the differences may be—or those between "believers" and "agnostics"—were raised on every hand. It was assumed (and asserted) that significant differences would emerge statistically.

That such differences did not emerge as shown in Table 2, which exhibits the distributions of scores as between Roman Catholic and Protestant Christians. Only in one category is there any noticeable percentage variance at all: Protestants gave more "we" responses in the subcategory relating to culture among the social reference categories. This may result from the slightly higher educational level reported in the Protestant sample. The eight avowedly agnostic Protestants also responded more frequently in the same subcategory of social references than did Roman Catholics. Apart from this one line, the percentages are frequently identical.

The similarity in the response patterns of subjects in the two major religious traditions also fails to prove the proposition that theological formulations are *not* fundamental to understanding the whole man. It is theoretically possible that the way a man, in response to a symbol, refers himself socially is irrelevant to religious experience, upon which theology occasionally claims to build.

One of the author's own hopes in undertaking this research was that symbolism related to corporality might emerge as a promising (and rewarding) direction for investigation in the field of the sociology of religion. There seemed to be a need for more dynamic descriptions of the actual meanings which people invest in symbols—both people who are mentally ill and those who are not. The vigor of the interviewees' responses, the willing involvement of interviewers for over 260 hours, and

TABLE 2. PERCENTAGE SCORE DISTRIBUTIONS BY
RELIGIOUS GROUPS

Categories	Roman Catholic	Protestant	Total
Individual ("I") references			
Body	2%	3%	5%
Self	16%	17%	33%
Interpersonal	2½%	1½%	4%
Plurality of individuals	12½%	10½%	23%
	33%	32%	65%
Social ("we") references			
Social group	1½%	1½%	3%
Society	—	1%	1%
Culture	5½%	9½%	15%
Supernatural world	1%	1%	2%
	8%	13%	21%
Nonsocial references			
Physical	6½%	5½%	12%
No response	½%	1½%	2%
	7%	7%	14%
Total scores			
(N = 5,700)	48%	52%	100%

the surprising richness of the associations to be scored, highly commend
body symbolism as a topic of inquiry.

The present research by no means exhausts the potential use of the
data already elicited. Much more could be done to analyze them.

While symbols cannot be consciously manufactured by man (nor the
responses to them entirely manipulated), much can be done to reestablish
contact with the strength that still exists in them. What is required is an
artistic sensitivity capable of revising the forms and liturgical and other
uses of symbols without doing injustice or violence to their ideological
references. Man's sensitivity to "see," his will to revise, and his courage
to appropriate could immensely extend the references of corporal symbolism within a particular cultural tradition.

NOTES

1. A symbol is here understood to be a cultural object of empirical reference
which points to something non-empirical.

2. Many other dimensions in symbol responses are, of course, open for study—spatial references, time dimensions, affective expressions, to mention three possibilities—but they are not included here.

3. The criteria of selection of the pictures were that they be "salable"—presumably capable of provoking some response—and that they exhibit artistic clarity. All were found either (1) in religious sections of popular magazines, or (2) in popular religious journals, or (3) in books for sale in religious bookstores in the U.S.

Johannes Fabian

NATIONAL UNIVERSITY OF ZAIRE

Genres in an Emerging Tradition:
An Anthropological Approach
to Religious Communication*

In this paper I propose an anthropological approach to the differentiation of genres. We report on one phase of an ongoing attempt to confront a a system of religious thought and action [1]. Both as ethnographic description and as theoretical discussion the paper has its place in a chain of interconnected arguments, and it will be the task of the first part of the paper to retrace the process of investigation in the briefest possible way.

* To be incorporated in a larger work (in preparation). The study, of which this is a part, was supported by a grant from the Wenner-Gren Foundation for Anthropological Research, New York.

249

The second part will present four major genres: instructions in the doctrine, counseling, testimony, and dream accounts of an "emerging tradition." I shall conclude with a summmary of the implications of a theory of genres for our understanding of religious communication.

I

The Case: The Jamaa Movement. The emerging religious tradition to which our considerations will be applied in the teaching of the Jamaa, a charismatic movement which we studied among Swahili-speaking Africans in the urban industrial centers of Shaba (formerly Katanga) [2]. The founder of the movement was Placide Tempels, a Belgian Franciscan missionary who first became known as the author of *Bantu Philosophy* (1945, 1969). Although the exact date of the movement's origin cannot be determined, all available evidence indicates that by 1953 it had fully developed its present orientations and organization. From the beginning it was characteristically composed of married couples all of them practicing or former Catholic mission Christians. The local groups which formed and rapidly spread from the area of Kolwezi are intertribal, with industrial workers making up the bulk of the male membership. The core of the prophetic message was the same crucial discovery that the founder had expounded in his earlier book: in order to live with dignity as human beings and as Christians, people have to break down the barriers that divide them and, through deep personal encounter, find *umuntu,* the essence of being man. Three fundamental aspirations will then be discovered: life-force, fecundity, and love. A ritual of initiation in three stages, each preceded by a prolonged period of instruction (*mafundisho*), leads the candidates to the progressive realization of these thoughts (*mawazo*) [3], to a new birth by virtue of which relationships of filiation are established between the initiating couple and the candidates. In its earlier stages the Jamaa was hailed as a breakthrough in the translation of Christianity into the African context. But as soon as the first signs of the inevitable routinization of charisma became visible (in patterns of doctrine and organization), the ecclesiastical authorities became increasingly concerned with the control of the movement, and latest reports indicate that earlier sympathetic attitudes gave way to rejection and outright prohibition. At present a break with the mission church seems inevitable, although there is still little evidence for deliberate moves toward separatist organization among the members of the Jamaa.

From Ethnography to Epistemology [4]. Fieldwork in Shaba and the first stages of analysis were carried out in the conceptual framework which seemed the obvious choice given the general ethnographic context and the prevalent sociological orientation at that time: a Weberian-Parsonian view of charismatic phenomena as sources of sociocultural change. Although we experienced some serious difficulties (e.g. with the gathering of hard, statistical data on the membership in this elusive and seemingly amorphous movement), there was sufficient information on which to base a presentation of the history of the movement, the intra- and intergroup organization, and a formal description of the main outlines of the doctrine and its ritual enactment.

For two reasons, however, it was felt that the work on the Jamaa could not be concluded with the customary monograph. One was the disturbing fact that the bulk of the "field data"—consisting of instructions, hymns, interviews, and other sundry language materials, all recorded on tape—was hardly touched upon in the course of our monographic analysis. In our formal semantic analysis of Jamaa doctrinal terminology we had drawn on many of these documents, but its main basis has been a written catechism of teaching, which turned out to contain more than sufficient materials for our analytical purposes.

A second reason for our considerable uneasiness after the task seemed to have been accomplished was the unsolved problem of the "objectivity" of our observations, given the fact that it had proved impossible to procure sufficient survey and other "hard" data to back up our findings and assertions. It looked as if we would have to be content with a largely humanistic and impressionistic rather than scientific outcome. However, a solution to that disconcerting problem had appeared already during fieldwork. Our work took a turn typical for a great deal of current anthropological investigation into systems of belief and phenomena of change: the turn toward language. Language data, recorded on the spot and in situations left by the researcher as undisturbed as possible, were felt to provide objective, empirical grounds. The subsequent application of techniques derived from linguistics was expected to result in objective analysis.

Once we were in a position to look back on our work from a distance, however, to scrutinize our conscious assumptions, and to uncover some of the unconscious ones, it was realized that the turn toward language would not solve the problem of objectivity unless we proceeded from methodological borrowing to epistemological considerations. The point is this: an approach to a religious system through language data does not carry its own justifications by the mere token of employing linguistic methods. One must first establish, through critical reflection on the constitution of ethnographic knowledge [5], in which way language not only signifies and communicates, but articulates and constitutes a social reality. We reexamined our work and the learning processes in which we had acquired command over Jamaa language and formulated the following two theses:

1. In anthropological investigations, objectivity lies neither in the logical consistency of a theory, nor in the givenness of data, but in the foundation (*Begründung*) of human *intersubjectivity*.

2. *Objectivity* in anthropological investigations is attained by entering a context of communicative interaction through the one medium which represents *and* constitutes such a context: *language* (Fabian 1971b: 25 and 27) [6].

From Semantic Analysis to Text Interpretation. Having found the position just characterized, we were then compelled to submit the concept of linguistic "data" to some radical revision. We joined an ongoing debate [7] concerning the limitations of positivist and scientistic orientations in the social sciences and argued that the "givenness" implied in the notion of data seen as discrete items of observation (by analogy to observations in the classical natural sciences) is largely illusory in the social sciences. It is more appropriate to think of these items as *products of processes of communication* with all the consequences this entails. An understanding of products is impossible if it cannot be situated in a context of a community of producers and of socially constituted processes of production. Thus the problem of ethnographic objectivity acquires a second dimension. It is concerned not only with the objective access to data, but also with the nature of data, as intrinsically context-bound and historically constituted. The contextual and historical dimensions of understanding are not merely desirable additions to semantic analysis (a notion which probably everyone in the field of cognitive anthropological studies holds); they are more than that. They are essential to description. Indeed, unless formal semantic analysis of religious thought and language is integrated into those larger frames, such analysis is not only limited but, at least potentially, misguided.

Given these epistemological considerations, there remains the methodological problem of what kind of linguistic material may be submitted to contextual and historical innterpretation. It appears that a study of religious thought and action must be carried out on the *level of texts,* rather than on that of discrete terms or even propositions. More concretely, we may say that the transformation of a prophetic vision into a tradition of knowledge and communal action (which we regard as the crucial process leading to the emergence of movements such as the Jamaa) is dependent on the emergence of a textual dimension of communication. Conversely, an understanding of the Jamaa movement will depend on our ability to translate features of text production into historical process. Such translation we regard as the essence of an interpretative approach.

II

To think of a language, or of any system of symbols, as a depository of meaning has a certain graphic persuasiveness. Yet it is one of those metaphors which must be denied as soon as they are stated. Applying W. von Humboldt's axiom to our specific case, we may say: strictly speaking, Jamaa language only exists in the act of its articulation (cf. Humboldt, 1963: 418. Within certain well-defined limits and for certain analytical purposes it is permissible to treat Jamaa ideology as a system embodied in language. But any attempt to understand the dynamics of such a system must begin with the insight that ideology "acts" only in the *event* of its articulation. A theoretical view of the working of ideology will have to recognize the characteristic features of the process which mediates between *mawazo* (the thought system) and event (the act of articulation). We propose that the results of that mediative process appear in the differentiation of genres of articulated ideology, which we may now call a *doctrine*.

Before we can go about identifying these genres we must explain what we hope to gain by introducing the concept of event. In looking at Jamaa language as an event, we seem to imply the kind of transformation which linguists have seen to occur in utterances that realize *langue* in *parole*. However, in linguistic analysis the temporal aspect of such transformations has received very little attention. It is not being denied, because, obviously, utterances occur in space and time. But linguists, insofar as they envisage the temporal character of speech, at all, tend to think of it as a vector inherent in the act of speaking or in the action of the speaking subject [8]. That may (or may not) be an adequate way of describing the behavior of physical objects It does not make comprehensible the event character of speech. The reason is that speech—except for the unthinkable extreme assumption of a complete monolog [9]—is dependent on shared, intersubjective temporality. In our attempt to understand the articulation of Jamaa ideology through Jamaa language as an event, therefore, we cannot but think of it as a *communicative event* [10]. That general notion will help us to confront Jamaa thought only to the extent that we can differentiate between kinds of communicative events.

Some such criteria of distinction seem obvious. Articulations of Jamaa ideology may vary according to the number and kind of persons who communicate; or according to the character of the occasion (formal, informal, private, public); or according to purpose and goals, and so forth. But our general aim is not to construct a number of criteria according to which communicative events may be *classified;* we propose to *identify* these events through products of communicative processes. Therefore, we cannot simply begin by observing external properties of, let us say, gatherings of Jamaa people in which the members presumably came together in order to exchange their ideas. An interpretative analysis of the results of such exchange must retrace their production. Our understanding of articulated doctrine begins with insights into the ways in which Jamaa people themselves understand communicative events.

Placide Tempels, the founder, has consistently maintained that the Jamaa owes its origin to, and is in fact nothing but, *encounter.* The book of collected essays in which, for the first time after *Bantu Philosophy,* he describes his experiences with African Christians is called *Notre rencontre* (Our Encounter, 1962).

Years after the Jamaa had developed into a movement of massive numerical importance, founder and followers continued to stress deeply personal, unpredictable, and nonmanipulative rapport which suddenly is established between two persons who open themselves up to each other and exchange their innermost experiences. The researcher must accept their claims as a central idea of Jamaa thought. On the other hand, communication has event character; its spatial-temporal extension remains inescapable. Upon closer examination it turns out that the Jamaa constituted itself as a social movement by elaborating ideas and corresponding patterns of action which made it possible to speak of the ineffable, slowly to prepare for the unpredictable, to share the uniquely personal, and to preserve the sudden event.

The question whether or not Tempels consciously devised ritual complements to his prophetic message is of minor importance. Part of the answer is known, and must be affirmative [11]; part of it will remain unknown, probably even to himself. The point is that, given his radical intention to exchange and discuss *mawazo* with his followers, encounter as communication had to result in articulations of thought whose function was to mediate between idea and event, throught and action. From the very beginnings of the movement, therefore, Jamaa language reflectd the continuity and action-oriented character of articulation of *mawazo* by consistently calling it *mafundisho*—teaching, instruction.

If we regard teaching as a communicative event in general, then we may assume that different forms of teaching correspond to different kinds of communicative events. Of course, the predicate "correspond" must be clarified. It cannot imply just any sort of simple genetic relationship such that every unique event would result in a unique form of articulation of *mawazo*. Rather we must start with the assumption that these events are recursive; their occurrence is defined by accepted rules. We face here the kind of circularity which an interpretive approach must take up as a challenge. This is the problem: in order to recognize the shape of communicative events we need to have an understanding of their meaning. In order to understand the meaning of the products of communication we need to have an understanding of the shape of the events that produced them.

In the following discussion of some genres of Jamaa teaching [12] we will follow, whenever possible, the lead of terminological distinctions made in Jamaa language. This procedure will facilitate our task. In no way does it obliterate the problem of hermeneutic circularity, as some students of "native classifications" seem to think.

Mafundisho (Public Instruction). Articulations of *mawazo* in the presence of the entire group (or of a section which can claim to represent a group) invariably are referred to as *mafundisho*, instruction. The teaching situation is characterized not only by its public and formal character, but also by a specific doctrinal content. In its typical form, a *mafundisho* is an uninterrupted speech of varying length, sometimes as brief as five minutes, seldom exceeding half an hour. In theory it may be given by any member of the group; in practice it turns out that only few leading persons give public instructions. A speaker has the freedom to choose the topic and certain stylistic-rhetorical means of expression, but for the genre *mafundisho* it remains characteristic that the speaker must choose the topic from a preexistent corpus of doctrine and adhere in his presentation to certain standardized formulae and organizational schemes.

The main features that characterize *mafundisho,* and which derive from the nature of the communicative event, can be envisaged as products of restrictive rules operating on a communicative situation (see Table 1). Of course, the distinctions we suggest in this schema are tentative and subject to improvement. A more thorough analysis would have to draw on a given text. Nevertheless, we may attempt to make visible the ethnographic reality corresponding to the restrictions upon the communicative situation we described.

TABLE 1.   THE GENRE *MAFUNDISHO*

Restrictions on Communicative Situation	Communicative Event	Features of Text
Group presence		Public address
Speaker vs. audience	Instruction	Authoritative delivery
Purpose: instruction		Standardized content

First of all, the rule which demands that instructions in standardized doctrine be public, that is, carried out as enactment of the community structure of Jamaa, proved quite strong in the field. On several occasions I asked my informants to let me tape one of their *mafundisho* outside the context of the group meeting. The reactions varied: some refused to talk unless at least one other Jamaa member were present; others overcame their embarrassment and tried to please me, but the result was a hurried, abbreviated, and spiritless delivery of doctrinal formulae. In almost all of these cases the speakers tried to maintain the semblance of a public speech by using plural forms to address me, customary interjected greetings, and the rhetoric device of antiphonal word- or sentence- completion. All of these presupposed the presence of a large audience.

Second, it turned out that the de facto selection of speakers, which in many ways contradicts the absolute egalitarianism preached by Tempels and the Jamaa, became one of the most important ethnographic clues for our understanding of the organizational structure of charismatic authority in the movement. Prominent speakers are, in fact, also carriers of authority, although it must be understood that the *legitimation* of their power is based on rhetorical influence and a position as interpreters and manipulators of ideology, and this is only one aspect of authority. More important are criteria derived from the high positions of these leaders in lineages of spiritual filiation that are established through initiation. In any case, a link between teaching and initiation is definitely at the basis of the third restrictive rule operating on *mafundisho*: teaching is never thought of as serving the sole purpose of transmitting knowledge; it always is directed toward the practical and concrete purpose of preparing or, at least, invoking gradual "birth" to the Jamaa [13].

Mashaurio (Counseling). Articulation of *mawazo* is not restricted to formal *mafundisho*. Apart from meetings which may be scheduled on a weekly basis or are called on special occasions (holidays, visits from other groups, celebrations, or crisis events), Jamaa doctrine will be taught, discussed, and recited on many other occasions. It would be hopeless to seek a common denominator for these quite diverse events if it were not for the fact that we find such an effort in Jamaa usage. In the Kolwezi area a distinction was made between *mafundisho*, teachings, and *mashaurio*, counseling. We shall adopt that label for this second genre and may once more give a schematic presentation of the relations between communicative situation and textural genre.

Typically, counseling is done in the presence of only a few members or candidates of the movement. Occasionally only two persons may be involved. Outsiders recognize such sessions as typically Jamaa and often

TABLE 2. THE GENRE *MASHAURIO*

Restrictions on Communicative Situation	Communicative Event	Features of Text
Two couples or few persons Adviser vs. advisee Purpose: practical advice	Counseling	Informal address Admonitory delivery Content contingent on situation/problem

maliciously point out that the two persons may be of the opposite sex. In some places Jamaa members were quite apprehensive about this and made it a point to have at least two or more married couples present. On these occasions, the speaker, that is, the adviser, has a certain position of authority, which, however, will be defined by reference to his (or her) seniority in the movement or the function of initiating those to whom he gives advice. It is not necessarily based on his leading position in the local group.

This lack of formal distinctions between an authoritative speaker and an audience corresponds to the purpose of *mashaurio* sessions. They are aimed at impressing the candidates with the practical consequences of Jamaa ideology in concrete situations of everyday life. Consequently, the formal features visible in *mashaurio* texts are, above all, a more direct form of addressing the audience, aimed at persuading them, proving points to them, and convincing them to take actions. Formulae of standardized doctrine are frequently used, but mostly in a disconnected and repetitive way. The speaker may argue with authority, but his primary interest remains persuasion, not the display of teaching authority.

The form of delivery we recognize in *mashaurio* is appropriate to the content articulated. Counseling is addressed to concrete situations to which Jamaa teaching is seen to apply. It should be noted though that the interrelation between rhetoric form and intentional content acts both ways. What makes a situation that needs advice is largely determined by Jamaa ideas about the nature of counseling. Although we would need to gather more information, we may briefly suggest the main areas in which the Jamaa feels it has to offer advice. These are, above all, marital problems (defined by the concrete demands on people living in a transitory situation between village culture and urban-industrial culture). Others, most often connected with the former, concern attitudes toward magic protection, ancestor worship, and other forms of involvement with traditional religion, all of which are declared incompatible with membership in the Jamaa.

"Testimony." In our texts we can discern a third major genre, for which Jamaa terminology offers no distinct label. Going on similarities with a recognized form of religious expression in enthusiastic movements, we shall call these articulations of *mawazo* "testimony" [14]. Jamaa people would simply call them *mawazo.*

The communicative situation which produces testimony as an event is marked by an emphasis on privacy and personal discretion (see Table 3). In this respect Jamaa testimony is very different from forms of inspired witnessing and public confessions we know from many other religious movements. Interestingly enough, there are reports that during the initial phase of expansion, Jamaa people occasionally tried to introduce public testimony and perhaps even glossolalia into the *mafundisho* meetings. But apparently Tempels himself and, later, his successors in the leadership rejected these tendencies. The reason may have been partly to keep the movement "clean" and free from suspicions of separatism in the eyes of the hierarchy. The privacy and secrecy surrounding the Catholic sacrament of penitence may have also played a role. But probably most important was the logic inherent in Jamaa definitions of communicative situations.

Personal testimony belongs to the event of encounter. Such encounter may have to follow certain ritual rules; yet it is clearly distinguished from both the *mafundisho* and the *mashaurio* situations in that the participating individuals or married couples exchange their experiences strictly qua persons, not as members of the group. Consequently there is in the situation of encounter no single person who would assume the role of a speaker (in the social, not in the linguistic, sense of the word). Ideas of submission and self-humiliation may enter into the event, but always on a mutual basis, not in terms of a leadership hierarchy or a role differentiation between adviser and advisees.

Testimony texts express these definitions of the event in varying degrees. As might be suspected, testimonial exchanges in a pure form will not lend themselves to recording (other than by concealed devices, which I never employed). A few instances of testimony approximating

TABLE 3. THE GENRE "TESTIMONY"

Restrictions on Communicative Situation	Communicative Event	Features of Text
Two couples or two persons		Personal account or dialogue
No role distinction	Encounter-testimony	Emotional delivery
Purpose: "encounter"		Content: personal experience

the pure form were made available to me by leaders who had recorded them for their own purposes. Those, however, cannot be included in public documentation. Still, we are able to draw upon a number of accounts which are less personal. Many of them were given by informants after a long period of mutual acquaintance and cooperation in situations which would customarily be defined as "interviews."

"Dream Account." Finally we must turn to a group of texts which pose considerable difficulties of interpretation. Accounts of dreams, consistently referred to as *mawazo*, signal a kind of communicative event which is of great importance for the Jamaa. Since these accounts, however, are most often surrounded by personal discretion or outright secrecy, our sample of recorded dream accounts is too small to serve as a basis for definitive statements. A further complication derives from the fact that we have here at least two major speakers, the one who tells the dream and the one who gives the interpretation. The recording of these events is therefore much more difficult than in the case of *mafundisho* and *mashaurio* or even testimony talks. Nevertheless, in the course of our work we assembled enough information to project at least a tentative picture (see Table 4).

There remains little doubt that in Jamaa thought a dream experience will always be placed in a social context. Consequently a neat distinction between dream experience (as a primarily visual and private impression on the dreamer) and dream account (as a primarily verbal and communicative activity of the dreamer) is of little interest to Jamaa people. What matters is the articulation and communication of *mawazo* which occurs in dream telling. Jamaa language expresses this definition of dream terminologically in that the current Swahili word *ku-lota,* to dream, is replaced by *ku-pata mawazo,* to receive *mawazo.*

The communicative situation which produces dream accounts as communicative events is of crucial importance and at the same time rather complex. In many ways it is similar to the testimony situation we de-

TABLE 4.   THE GENRE "DREAM-ACCOUNT"

Restrictions on Communicative Situation	Communicative Event	Features of Text
Two persons or (?) two couples		Personal account
Dreamer vs. interpreter	Prophecy	Narrative delivery
Purpose: communication/proof		Content: contingent on situation and standardized images

scribed in the preceding section. Typically dreams will be told only in the presence of one person or one other couple. In fact, since dreams may count as the kind of experience to be communicated in encounter, a distinction between testimony-*mawazo* and dream-*mawazo* is not always possible. On the other hand, striking differences appear as soon as one considers the definition of roles in dream exchange. In contrast to encounter and testimony, which call for mutual accounts and ideal equality and symmetry among the participants, dream telling will most often involve a distinction between "client" and "counselor" similar to the *mashaurio* situation.

Exactly what that asymmetrical relationship entails will depend on the Jamaa's different definitions of the purpose of dream telling. At least one of them is quite explicit: a dream account is part of the ritual of initiation into each of the "three ways." A dream whose content and timing is determined in advance serves as a clue to the initiating couple and to the initiating priest who represent the entire group, that the candidates have in fact reached the degree to which they aspire. Thus the female candidate for the "first way" is expected to have, during one of the nights following the ritual, a dream in which she is united with *Bwana Yesu Kristo,* the Lord Jesus Christ. The idea behind this is that the first degree conveys on the candidates the thought of *uzima,* life-force, to be experienced as a result of unity (see Fabian, 1971a: 168–170).

Apart from these dramatic but relatively rare situations in which the dream account serves as a ritual proof, Jamaa people will frequently consult their spiritual parents (those who gave birth to them through initiation) about dreams in which initiatory experiences and everyday situations of exceptional character may be combined. These may reflect personal crises (marital problems, illness, conflicts with traditional religious beliefs) or situations of stress originating in a group (leadership struggles, schism, relations with the local missionary). The recorded accounts at my disposal and many discussions about their significance indicate that the purpose of dream telling may then become "prophecy," a pronouncement which often implies challenge and innovative claims. The tendency is to express discontent, claims to leadership, and often attempts at reformulating doctrine and changing ritual procedures in the form of expressive *mawazo* rather than through instrumental discussion, litigation, or doctrinal discourse.

Elsewhere I have shown that these dream interpretations may become one of the few explicit prerogatives of Jamaa leaders (see Fabian, 1966 and 1971a: 186–189). In the present context, however, we want to understand the nature of the communicative event which mediates between articulation of Jamaa ideology and the formation of a specific genre.

Why does the Jamaa insist on calling *mawazo* what in another cultural context would cover such a wide range of exchanges as dream accounts, insinuations, expressions of discontent, and so forth?

The most satisfying solution to this problem seems to be that besides instruction, counsel, and encounter-testimony, Jamaa recognizes a fourth definition of communicative event: prophecy. This would cover the two major purposes of dream telling we recognized earlier. Prophecy may announce fulfillment, such as in the account of the initiatory dream; or it may be an announcement of a claim, a vision, a program. In both cases it is absolutely essential that the source of the knowledge to be announced transcend that which can be known from ordinary, everyday experience. The fact that these exchanges are consistently called *mawazo* signifies a concern to dramatize the unifying, common ground of the movement—which is *mawazo*. It seems logical that this should occur in those moments when the individual, claiming the authority of a dream experience, acts as an articulator of Jamaa doctrine.

Given the complexity of the social structures defining the communicative situation and event of dream prophecy, it is not easy to determine the textual features of the genre dream-*mawazo*. Some are quite explicit, though, such as fairly standardized formulae marking the beginning and end of the dream account. Others can be recognized in certain elements of content: imagery and situations, personages, and color symbolism. All of these are in more or less explicit connection with initiatory experiences and tend to express a ritual repetitiveness even though we are not able to assess the degree to which there has occurred a standardization of manifest dream content. Another source of standardization must be sought in the repetitiveness of situations of stress and conflict which find their expression in dream accounts. With more information than we have, it should be possible to compile an inventory of basic situations in which Jamaa thought and everyday life in the mining camps articulate and produce the kind of problems for which the movement provides solutions. Otherwise our limited sample shows that the aspect of strangeness, of distorted and threatening visual experiences often believed to be a universal characteristic of dream experiences, is of little importance in Jamaa dream accounts. What dominates are moral dilemmas arising out of interpersonal relations. Often these are told in a matter-of-fact way with such an aura of concreteness and everyday reality that it becomes indeed impossible to recognize a given narrative as a dream account unless the speaker tells us so.

Summary: Genres of Jamaa Doctrine. In these brief sketches of genres of Jamaa teaching we placed our considerations in the three-part frame of communicative situation, communicative event, and product of communication. We distinguish four major processes in which the differentiation of genres of teaching might occur. We defined the event of articulation of *mawazo* as a mediation between a socially constituted situation and a "literary" product. "Mediation" is the term we use to mark our epistemological position. Approaching a thought system through its expressions in language must include the historical dimension of actual articulation in time and space; linear regressions from the linguistic product either to the habit structure of individual behaving organisms, or to a universal mind, seem to deny that dimension (at least as a necessary element of analysis).

Having established four classes of communicative events (teaching, counseling, testimony, and dream telling), we must now consider the relations between them. After all, our main intention is to present *mawazo* as process; categorization and classes are stated only for that purpose.

One possible translation of classes into scale can be made if the size of the participating personnel and the degree of explicitness of doctrinal content are taken as dimensions of comparison. Within the former we found variations between the presence of an entire group (or several groups, or a significant segment acting as a group) in the teaching situation, the presence of a small number of participants in a counseling situation, and the restriction to initiating and candidate couples in the encounter situation.

With regard to the explicitness of doctrinal content, differences can be recognized in the degree to which the communicative product utilizes predefined, standardized doctrinal formulae. These are used most extensively in the teaching situation. They give way to more and more spontaneous, personalized testimony in counseling and encounter.

Thus there seems to obtain a straightforward correlation between participating personnel and the doctrinal content. The question now is how to interpret that correlation. Does it simply express the trivial fact that formal indoctrination calls for a congregation, whereas personal testimony demands the intimacy of a dialogue? We think not, for several reasons.

First of all, even a superficial comparison with similar religious phenomena can tell us that the relation may be an inverse one. In some movements, such as the Kitawala, explicit doctrinal instructions may be restricted to the secrecy between initiating and candidates; in others, such as the Bapostolo, personal testimony, often in the form of confessions, may ask for the presence of the entire group. We also know of cases in which both formal instruction and personal testimony take place in the presence of the group [15]. We may conclude, then, that the obvious correlation we observe is significant but spurious.

One might point out that the dimension of "size of personnel" really expresses structural rather than quantitative variation. What distinguishes the four situations is not so much the number of participants, but rather the degree to which there occurs a formal differential of roles. Thus in the *mafundisho* situation we observe a marked and rather consistent distinction between speakers, endowed with leadership and authority, and audience. The distinction is somewhat less rigid, but still pronounced, in the counseling situation, and it is supposed to be totally absent in encounter. That would still not constitute an adequate interpretation because it does not take care of the important event of dream telling, in which, as we have seen, we find a combination of little standardized doctrine, reduced personnel, but strong differentiation between dreamer and dream interpreter. A simple translation of variability into process or at least into processual determinants thus proves impossible.

A closer examination of the observed characteristics reveals that explicitness of doctrine and size of participating personnel vary in relation to the process of initiation. In a *mafundisho* meeting, not only candidates for the first degree, but even interested outsiders such as the anthropologist or members of other organizations or movements may be present. In counseling situations one expects only serious candidates. In situations of testimony and dream account, participation is restricted to those who are already involved in the process of initiation.

As a corollary, the decreasing use of standardized formulae of doctrine is often accompanied by increased explicitness in references to the initiatory experience. In *mafundisho*, references to practical application of Jamaa doctrine are expressed in general, stylized terms. The *mashaurio* calls for a confrontation of Jamaa principles with everyday experience. This aspect comes out even more strongly, and often with a pronounced emotional involvement, in testimony. The content of dream accounts often reflects the esoteric images of ritualized encounter, that is, of an achieved translation of Jamaa doctrine into experience.

It seems clear, therefore, that communicative events differ according to the degree to which they are related to the initiatory experience of encounter. The formation of *mawazo* and the products of articulation— those formal features of texts we identify as constituting genres—are crucially linked to the formation of experience. Such formation occurs in an extended ritual in which individual members are called to show proofs of their conversion.

If that is a correct view, then the most appropriate graphic illustration of the relations and processes involved in the articulation of Jamaa

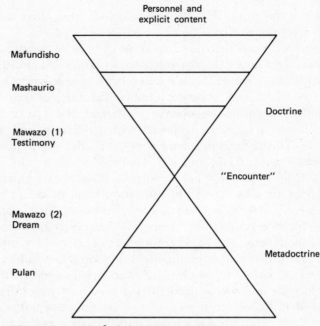

Figure 5.   Articulation of Jamaa ideology.

ideology could be given in the form of an hourglass (Figure 1). Notice that in this presentation the actual event of encounter appears as an unextended point. This reflects the ideas of Tempels and his followers, who view that moment of truth as a "clicking" between two persons, ineffable, a perfect union of undetermined duration and content.

We may now place the genre of dreams on the other side of the nodal point of encounter. This not only takes care of increasing structural differentiation, which would correspond logically to the one observed in teaching and counseling, but it places dream interpretation into the same perspective with another important communicative event we have yet to mention: the *pulan* meeting. Although during my own fieldwork such a meeting was only held at Musonoi, there is no reason to believe that it may not have parallels, especially in the Kasai region. Very briefly, it consists of regular meetings attended by the fully initiated members of several groups. Originally it was organized as a sort of constitutional convention with the aim of formulating a binding text of Jamaa instruction. The result of these discussions was the *Kitabu* (Book) of Musonoi (see Fabian, 1971a: 126–129 and Appendix IV). Once the *Kitabu* was completed, the meetings continued. At the time they were being observed in the field, they seemed to serve a double function. The members attending the *pulan* were the congregation to which new candidates were presented for approval. Second, the *pulan* served as a forum for discussion of doctrinal and disciplinary problems which are kept out of the public *mafundisho* meetings.

As far as I can see, this meeting has several characteristics in common with dream interpretation. There is a pronounced concern with finding acceptable frames for the interpretation of articulated *mawazo*. The *pulan* is the only official event in which doctrine is not only recited but also discussed. Elsewhere I indicated that we may have here an emerging level of meta-doctrine, that is, consistent theories for the meaning and proper application of doctrinal tenets (see Fabian, 1966: 555). Furthermore, the *pulan* meeting shows a pronounced concern with authority and leadership. Challenges to, or by, leaders are tested in these meetings as well as in dream interpretation (see Fabian, 1971a: 179–181). In both instances the direction of communicative exchanges is toward praxis, the implementation of *mawazo* in an individual's or a group's daily life.

If this interpretation is correct, it would mean that religious meta-doctrines, which often are esoteric or at least inconspicuous, may be a more important key to a pragramtic understanding than explicit doctrines and manifest ideology. Obviously this opens an important line of investigation. In the present context, however, we are occupied with the theory of textual interpretation. That restriction to textual material is the reason why we made no attempt to include the *pulan* meeting in our schema of communicative events. *Pulan* meetings often are "enriched" by formal instructions or pieces of *mafundisho,* but as such they are not subject to the kind of social restrictions and formal principles which are involved in production of *mafundisho.* Although they involve participation of a large number of members, they share with encounter-testimony an emphasis on discretion and even secrecy which make them inaccessible to recording or other forms of textual documentation.

A reader of an earlier version of this paper thought that introducing the *pulan* meeting at the end of the discussion of generic differentiation might "wreck the convincingness" of our scheme. It does indeed, if convincingness is equated with analytical neatness. Our model is an open one and attempts to do justice to generic differentiation as an ongoing process, rather than as an established set of rules. The *pulan* clearly can be traced to a contingent event (the preparation of the *kitabu*). It can be shown to postdate the genres of instruction and counseling. And it can be surmised that, as the Jamaa moves from a phase of growth to one of consolidation and stagnation, talk *about mawazo* will become more important than articulation of *mawazo*. If future research shows this to be true, the *pulan* will have "wrecked" not only the convincingness of our scheme but also the Jamaa as it was conceived by its founder and the first followers. The history of religions certainly has enough precedents for such a development.

III

Let us look at the implications of our argument. Our thesis is that generic distinctions in a corpus of oral (or literary) tradition are not adequately understood if the task is defined only as the classification of observable features, organized around certain postulated taxonomic principles, logical rules, or behavioral variables. We envisage a model of text production, the backbone of which is a view of concrete processes of production. These processes are taken to be communicative processes. Hence we are compelled to take account of the intersubjective dimension of social reality, which includes not only the participants who presumably share a given system of belief but also the researcher and the community to which he addresses his findings. Such a position raises a number of questions of general importance.

The first question pertains to the theoretical import of the model. Anthropologists at various stages in the history of our discipline have concerned themselves with the interpretation of texts. Franz Boaz, a founder, has left us with a monumental fragment of carefully recorded, transcribed, and translated "native" texts. Only recently have we come to appreciate once more the theoretical impetus that had led in that direction [16]. Claude Lévi-Strauss, the protagonist of the most influential trend to appear in the last two decades, has sought to construct and elaborate his structuralist theory in confrontation with mythological accounts. Aside from these and other less prominent developments not mentioned here, anthropologists have kept fairly close contact with the problems discussed in folklore studies [17]. In ways which are difficult to ascertain and impossible to summarize in a paper of limited scope, all these efforts have been related to developments in modern linguistics [18].

But the possibility of a fruitful theoretical start, one which the social scientist can make in his own right and not just as a scavenger among neighboring fields, was opened up only recently. We are inclined to locate it at a point where two at first seemingly unrelated developments converge.

One has been labeled sociolinguistics or anthropological linguistics [19]. Although conceived with somewhat different aims and retraceable to different prehistories, the various subdisciplines that make up the category all go beyond taxonomic linguistics by emphasing the contextual, communicative, and social-historical determinants of speech.

The other line of development we see in the renewed philosophical debate concerning the positivist and scientistic paradigm, which has had a dominant position in the rise of *anglo-saxon* social science to its present prominence [20].

Where the two meet, questions arise of a kind we tried to confront in our textual approach to social reality: What exactly constitutes a "datum" of communication? What constitutes a context? What are the conditions of possibility of having access to a context of communication? And so forth.

The methodological turn toward texts (rather than discrete lexical items or elements of grammar) is then based on the epistemological assumption that a system of belief must be approached through the processes of its production, in a community of producers, and through communicative events. Our belated return to the age-old problem of generic distinction among "literary" products reflects the necessity to go beyond taxonomic-classificatory analysis of language materials to a historical-genetic understanding of the emergence of meaning—that is the articulation of thought embodied in language and action governed by thought.

I have pointed out that this interpretative approach follows a circular movement; for instance, an understanding of formal features of genres presupposes some understanding of formal definitions of communicative situations and vice versa. Entrance into that circle is gained only by participation in the mediating communicative events, and by critical reflection on their constitution. The researcher must realize that he will generate scientific knowledge only to the extent to which he participates in the production of ethnographic knowledge. The three-part epistemological frame (situations, events, and products) makes it impossible to conceive of linguistic analysis only as a linear regression from *parole* to *langue*, from surface data to underlying rules or laws. In the tradition which has led to modern hermeneutic philosophy we envisage further progress in textual analysis, seen as an integral part of social science [21]. Many of its implications yet to be worked out.

Perhaps the most urgent problem at this point is the relation of an interpretative approach to the established positions of structuralist-functionalist analysis, statistical work based on survey data, and other variants of behavioral, if not behaviorist, views of social reality. In the immediate context of this paper, such questions arise as: Can there be a "scientific" view of religion which has, so to speak, an in-built objectivity and value neutrality so that it makes possible a gentlemen's agreement between agnostic and believing students of religion? A hermeneutic view which maintains that scientific understanding always has an element of self-understanding and self-critique takes belief in that kind of accommodation to be a limited view at best, and an uncritical and possibly misleading approach at worst.

What we are learning about the processual and constitutive role of language communication in a religious context makes us increasingly uneasy with those neat distinctions between observer and observed, data collection and theory, description and analysis, which still are the stock of the social sciences. Furthermore, since the origins of a hermeneutic social science lie in epistemological rather than in logical considerations, it is to be expected that there will be a debate about fundamentals which ultimately will have consequences on the methodological level. Meanwhile it is to be hoped that further work in sociolinguistics and anthropological linguistics will prepare the field for a confrontation which does not have to degenerate into a mere battle about ultimate concerns.

NOTES

1. I make no attempt to elaborate on the attribute "religious," merely asserting that my ethnographic "case" shows all the characteristics of religious thought and action if measured by commonly accepted criteria. I am aware of the fact that this may "bracket out" an important theoretical problem, and I am not at all certain that such an elimination is so easily justified as it may appear to be in most social-scientific studies of religious behavior. However, the limitations of space do not allow me to take up a problem here for which linguistic considerations might otherwise be of great importance.

2. The present account is reduced to a minimal statement. The author's observations are based on field work in 1966–67 in Shaba (formerly Katanga) and on repeated visits with the founder in Belgium between 1965 and 1970. Those interested in the Jamaa movement will find information on its historical, sociological, anthropological, and semantic aspects in Theuws (1961); De Craemer (1965 and 1968); and Fabian (1969a, 1969b and especially in 1971a). It is examined from the point of view of comparative history of religion in Fabian (1969b), and from that of Catholic theology and mission theory in Janssen (1967) (see also Tanner, 1968). The list, however, is by no means complete.

3. In this paper I employ two words as technical terms: *mawzo*, thought, and *mafundisho*, instruction. The former expresses the totality of Jamaa thought as a domain, the latter its specific articulations.

4. The thesis summarized in this section is more fully developed in Fabian (1971b), and will be developed further in a later publication.

5. The idea of "critical reflection" should not be taken as a vague cover-all concept. It is related to a definite issue in the philosophy of the social sciences. (See below, note 7)

6. Our strong emphasis on language is intended to connote its central, not its exclusive, role in communication. Communication theory explores many other dimensions (e.g., aesthetic, proxemic, kinesic) which we recognize as important although never completely separable from language.

7. Some bibliographic references to that debate are given in Fabian (1971b) and in a forthcoming book by Radnitzky. An informative introduction to the main issues of the debate is contained in Radnitzky (1968).

8. It should be emphasized that we are not dealing with what is usually referred to as the "diachronic" study of language, the main concern of which is to investigate *change* in elements that were determined synchronically. Thus even Greenberg, a linguist who is most sensitive to diachronic temporality, would hold that the problem we raise can be described as applying to the "adequate description of particular forms of speech ('languages') during a *specified chronological period*" (1968: 101, our italics).
In another example, chosen at random, we find the spacio-temporal context of utterances treated in connection with the problem of "meaningfulness," but only as one "ingredient" of context, not as a constitutive element (Lyons, 1968: 413).

9. The "thesis of monologism" in semantic theory is rejected by Habermas (1970).

10. Among other things this implies that the "function" of communication is inseparable from the realization of speech, not because language is a symbol system which evolved and is used as a tool of communication and a vehicle for informative messages, but rather because it is *constituted* as an intersubjective event (see Fabian, 1971b: 28 f). Our notion of communicative events is closely related to the one to which Dell Hymes gives a central place in his ethnography of speaking (1964); see also Fabian (1971b: 32).

11. In the monograph we showed some instances in which he consciously adopted ritual forms from the Luba tradition as models for his movement (Fabian, 1971a: 172–174).

12. For the sake of accuracy, we should note that two kinds of textual material have been excluded. For practical reasons, we are unable to deal with Jamaa hymns representing a corpus which is simply too extensive to be handled at the present stage. Secondly, we prefer, on theoretical grounds, to deal with narrative accounts modeled on traditional African storytelling in the context of stylistic choice rather than generic differentiation. The reason is that we are unable to identify a communicative situation specific to the narration of these exemplary stories.

13. For an account of a concrete situation in which this became visible, see Fabian (1969a: 169).

14. In doing this, we are following a usage adopted by many of the non-

African members and observers of the movement who refer to these accounts as *tèmoignage*.

15. Concerning the isolation and secretiveness of Kitawala, see Greschat (1967, esp. 88f). I observed public witness talks in groups of the Bapostolo during fieldwork in Shaba. The third possibility is suggested by the work of Marcene Marcoux on the cursillo (a Catholic revival) in the Boston area.

16. See G. Stocking's essay on Boas's turn from "Physics to Ethology" (1968: 133–160).

17. A recent synthesis, covering an amazing number of topics and problems, is Munro S. Edmonson's *Lore* (1971). An excellent example of the convergence of views, derived from the point of view of a student of folklore, is a paper by Dan Ben-Amos (1971).

18. The best and most comprehensive account of the role of linguistic method in ethnography was given by Dell Hymes (1970).

19. Readers should consult the brief descriptive and bibliographic background provided by W. J. Samarin in his paper introducing the session on language and religion at the 1971 meeting of the Society for the Scientific Study of Religion at Chicago (1971: 7–9, note 1).

20. See note 7 on page 269.

21. In this paper I have made no attempt to confront recent literature on the differentiation of genres. I should like at least to point to an article by E. Schwartz (1971) with whom I share a view of the epistemological signifi-cance of the problem. Dan Ben-Amos has published an excellent review of past approaches. His theory of genre is quite similar to mine (Ben-Amos, 1969).

REFERENCE

BEN-AMOS, DAN

1969	"Analytical Categories and Ethnic Genres." *Genre* **2:** 275–301.
1971	"Toward a Definition of Folklore in Context." *Journal of American Folklore* **84:** 3–15.

DE CRAEMER, W.

1965	*Analyse sociologique de la Jamaa.* Leopoldville: Centre de Recherches Sociologiques.
1968	"The Jamaa Movement in the Katanga and Kasai Regions of the Congo." *Review of Religious Research* **10:** 11–23.

EDMONDSON, MUNRO S.

1971	*Lore: An Introduction to the Science of Folklore and Literature.* New York: Holt, Rinehart and Winston.

FABIAN, JOHANNES

1966   "Dream and Charisma: 'Theories of Dreams' in The Jamaa Movement (Congo)." *Anthropos* **61**: 544–560.

1969a   "Charisma and Cultural Change: The Case of the Jamma Movement in Katanga (Congo Republic)." *Comparative Studies in Society and History* **11**: 155–173.

1969b   "An African Gnosis: For a Reconsideration of an Authoritative Definition." *History of Religions* **9**: 42–58.

1971a   *Jamaa: A Charismatic Movement in Katanga.* Evanston, Ill.: Northwestern University Press.

1971b   "Language, History and Anthropology." *Philosophy of the Social Sciences* **1**: 19–47.

1973   "Kazi: Conceptualizations of Labor in a Charismatic Movement among Swahili-Speaking Workers." *Cahiess d'etueles africaines* **3**: 293–325.

GREENBERG, J. H.

1968   *Anthropological Linguistics.* New York: Random House.

GRESCHAT, H. J.

1967   *Kitawala—Ursprung, Ausbrietung und Religion der Watch-Tower—Bewegung in Zental-afrika.* Marburg: Elwert.

HABERMAS, J.

1970   "Towards a Theory of Communicative Competence," *Inquiry* **13**: 360–375.

HUMBOLDT, W. VON

1963   *Schriften zur Sprachphilosophie.* Ed. by A. Flitner and K. Giel. *Werke* III Stuttgart: Cotta.

HYMES, DEL

1964   "Toward Ethnographies of Communiction." Pp. 1–34 in J. J. Gumperz and D. Hymes, (eds.), *The Ethnography of Communication.* Menasha, Wis.: American Anthropological Association.

1970   "Linguistic Method in Ethnography: Its Development in the United States." Pp. 249–325 in Paul Garvin (ed.), *Method and Theory in Linguistics.* The Hague: Mouton.

JANSSEN, TH. M.

1967   "Religious Encounter and the Jamaa." *Heythrop Journal* **8**: 129–151.

LYONS, JOHN

1968   *Introduction to Theoretical Linguistics.* Cambridge: Cambridge University Press.

RADNITZKY, G.

1968   *Continental Schools of Metascience.* Vol. 2. Goteborg: Akademiforlaget.

SAMARIN, WILLIAM J.

1971   "The Language of Religion." Paper presented at the annual meeting of the Society for the Scientific Study of Religion, Chicago, 1971.

SCHWARTZ, ELIAS

1971   "The Problem of Literary Genres." *Criticism* 13: 113–130.

STOCKING, G. W.

1968   *Race, Culture and Evolution: Essays in the History of Anthropology.* New York: Free Press.

TANNER, R. E. W.

1968   "The Jamaa Movement in the Congo." *Heythrop Journal* 9: 164–178.

TEMPELS, PLACIDE

1945   *La philosophie bantoue.* Elisabethville: Lovania.

1962   *Notre rencontre.* Léopoldville: Centre d'Etudes Pastorales.

1969   *Bantu Philosophy.* Paris: Présence Africaine.

THEUWS, TH.

1961   *The Jamaa Movement in Katanga.* London: Mission Press.

Part Six

"Soundings" in the Study
of Religious Commitment
and Religious Behavior

Donald R. Ploch

NATIONAL SCIENCE FOUNDATION, WASHINGTON, D.C.

Religion as an Independent Variable: a Critique of Some Major Research

The use of religion as an independent variable has centered on differences between religious groups or the influence of religiosity (usually religious orthodoxy). Major studies include Lenski, *The Religious Factor* (1961); and Glock and Stark's work, especially *Christian Beliefs and Anti-Semitism* (1966) and *American Piety* (Stark and Glock, 1968). Because these studies are widely read and cited, and because they represent some of the best work in the field, it is important to review their findings to see whether different analyses of their data will lead to different conclusions. Using these studies as major foci I show that differences between religious groups are exaggerated, especially when one takes account of within-group variation. Also, the effect of religious orthodoxy is more clearly stated if analyses use specific causal models and techniques associated with them, for example, path analysis rather than the accumulation of indices. Greater attention to the findings may cause us to shift the focus of both research and theory.

Reading survey studies of religion is like traveling through Wonderland: it gets curiouser and curiouser. Evidence concerning a religious upswing or downturn is contradictory. Longitudinal evidence—in the form of survey results—is largely nonexistent. Guesstimates of the past situation vary from one survey to the other. Methods of analysis vary from percentage distributions to factor analyses touching all stops in between but concentrating at the extremes. Predictions of the future of organized religion in America vary from estimates of a continuance of activity and influence to those of a massive falling away of members and influence. Through it all, imperialistic Americans tend to equate religion with Western Christendom. Normally there is some attempt to handle the Jews, because they are here, but they are not handled well—there are too few of them for a sophisticated analysis. In addition, despite the relative lack of centrality to social science as currently practiced, there are enormous numbers of research monographs of survey studies of religion. Theological seminaries—especially Protestant ones—have been cranking out survey data as if both data and technique were going out of style. We are inundated with facts, each of which seems enmeshed in its own peculiar theory. What, then, shall we do?

In this paper I shall address two specific problems: differences between religious groups and the use of causal models in sociology of religion. In the first instance I shall center on Lenski's *Religious Factor,* and in the second on Glock and Stark's *Christian Beliefs and Anti-Semitism.* These issues are picked because they are critical ones which the scientific study of religion needs to face. The works are chosen because they are widely recognized as the best of their type. I have not chosen them to be contentious or to bury them. I would like to begin to step beyond them. As good as they are, they are milestones on the journey, not signs that we have arrived.

DIFFERENCES BETWEEN SOCIORELIGIOUS GROUPS

The first issue has to do with unity and diversity between and within denominations. Since accidents of history decreed that America was to take shape as a white, Anglo-Saxon, Protestant nation, we have wondered about the ability of our society to absorb others outside the WASP stream, and we have wondered about the reliability of those minorities who stubbornly resist absorption. Because blacks are basically Protestant, they are not a major focus of this research area. The cultural emergence of blacks will change this. The predominant strands of this research are Protestant-Catholic difference and denominational differences within Protestantism.

The research and analysis in Lenski's *Religious Factor* were carefully done. If the scientific study of religion is to improve, then we must improve on the methods used in that book—not because they are bad but because newer ones are better. Much progress in methods has occurred since Lenski wrote. My analysis uses summary statistics instead of tables of frequencies and percentages.

That my conclusions differ from Lenski's ought not be surprising. We use different approaches. He concluded that religious differences were as important as social class for explaining differences on a wide variety of dependent variables. I will suggest that, in his data, neither variable accounts for much variation.

In most of Lenski's tables socioreligious groups, membership [1] and social class [2] have independent and additive effects. His major table for religion and class (Table 7, p. 80) yields the following summary statistics:

$$T_{class, \ religion} = .04$$
$$T_{religion, \ class} = .07$$

where T is Goodman and Kruskal's Tau and the first variable the dependent. If one abstracts the 2×2 table for white Protestant and white Catholic, with class collapsed to middle and working, $T = .00$. These values are all small enough for us to declare no relation between religion and class. Therefore in tables which have both religion and class as variables, they are independent of each other. Inspection shows their effects to be additive as well. Neither alters the other's relation to the dependent variable.

This being the case, the major summary table (Table 50, pp. 324f.) can be treated as a summary of 2×2 tables: the effect of religion being the same whether or not controlled for class, and the effect of class being the same whether or not controlled for religion. We can get a rough idea of the magnitude of the explained variation by converting the percentages to proportions and squaring them. This gives us a figure which approximates Tau (Goodman and Kruskal) [3].

T (Tau) is chosen for several reasons. First it has direct meaning in terms of variance explained. If $T = .05$, then 5% of the variance in the dependent variable is explained. Second, the meaning of the statistic is the same regardless of table size. A difference of proportions can be considered a special case of slope in a 2×2 table. In a $2 \times K$ table this analogy is harder to draw. In a 2×2 table, difference of proportions across the rows times difference of proportions across the columns equals r^2 (square of a point biserial correlation). This is analogous to the coefficient of determination from regression analysis. In a $2 \times K$ or $I \times K$ table this analogy breaks down. Thus use of T provides a focus on variance explained that is readily generalized to other tables. For example it is possible to compare T for class and religion with T for any other pair of variables.

Finally T is asymmetric. It assumes causal flow or at least predictive flow. Lenski wants to predict from religion or class to specific dependent variables. T measures the predictive power of independent variables in units of variance explained. Thus if $T_{republican, class} = .14$ and $T_{republican, religion} = .05$, then we can conclude that class is about three times as strong as religion in predicting party preference.

Table 1 gives the results of the conversion of percentages to T. For all

TABLE 1. COMPARISON OF THE RELATIVE DISCRIMINATING POWER OF CLASS AND SOCIORELIGIOUS GROUP MEMBERSHIP FOR A SAMPLE OF DEPENDENT VARIABLES (WHITE PROTESTANT AND CATHOLICS ONLY). STATISTIC REPORTED IS TAU[b] (GOODMAN AND KRUSKAL).

	Estimates of Tau[b]	
Dependent Variable	Between Classes[1]	Between Religion[2]
1. Happy working (males only)	.00	.01
2. Installment buying wrong or unwise	.00	.00
3. Multiple reasons for saving	.00	.01
4. Chances for upward mobility good (1952)	.01	.01
5. Ability more important than family (1952)	.00	.02
6. Republican preference (1957 and 1958)	.14	.05
7. Nonvoter in 1956 elections	.02	.00
8. Constitution allows attacks on religion	.03	.00
9. Constitution allows Communist speeches	.01	.00
10. Much thought given world problems	.00	.00
11. Spend abroad only for national defense	.01	.00
12. Prefer segregated schools	.02	.00
13. Disturbed if Negro moved into block	.01	.00
14. Public officials not interested in average man	.01	.01
15. Government should do more	.02	.02
16. Government should run big industries	.01	.01
17. Favors national health insurance (1952)	.02	.02
18. Favors stronger price controls (1952)	.03	.02

19. Expects CIO members to agree with him re controversial issues (1952)	.14	.03
20. Expects businessmen to agree with him re controversial issues (1952)	.03	.01
21. Relatives in Detroit (1952)	.00	.01
22. Visits relatives once a week (1952)	.00	.00
23. Native Detroiter	.01	.03
24. Future-oriented in child rearing (1953)	.01	.00
25. Uses physical punishment on 10-year-old (1953)	.03	.04
26. Indulgence-oriented re leisure time (1953)	.06	.05
27. Values autonomous thought over obedience	.04	.02
28. Four or more children	.00	.03
29. Gambling wrong	.02	.06
30. Birth control wrong	.00	.20
31. Moderate drinking wrong	.00	.01
32. Sunday business wrong	.00	.01
33. Divorce wrong	.00	.09
34. Jews less fair in business dealings	.00	.00
35. Jews trying to get too much power	.00	.00
Mean value	.02	.02
Median value	.01	.01

[1] With religious group held constant.
[2] With class held constant.
Source: Table format and headings taken from Lenski, Table 50, pp. 324f. For computation of Tau which is based on percentages reported by Lenski, see the text, especially note 3.

practical purposes, relations between religion (with or without class controlled) and a broad spectrum of dependent variables is moderate to non-existent. If one takes values of .05 or more as indicators of socially important differences [4], these can be accounted for by chance since they are no more in number than we would expect given a 5% significance level and correlated dependent variables. More important, they present a pattern of meaning. Strong religious differences and weak class ones cluster about behavioral issues which are focused on by the churches (gambling, birth control, and divorce). Of the other three issues, the one on leisure times shows little class-religion difference, one is a statement that class is more relevant to party preference than religion, and the last is clearly an economic policy issue more relevant to class than to religion. On the whole, I conclude that if the binary dependent variables are value-loaded such that one side represents progress while the other represents a problem (e.g., preference for democratic religious organization is progress, while preference for authoritarian organization is a problem), then if the percentage differences between groups vanished overnight, the magnitude of the problem would not be altered in any important sense.

At the risk of belaboring the obvious, I am taking a different approach from Lenski. He says that a shift from Catholic to Protestant (with class controlled) will result in a shift of a certain percentage of responses (12% on the average). While this is true, and while the larger differences are statistically significant given the sample size, I am saying that the distribution of responses within religious groups is such that even if a shift were to occur, the population distribution would not be changed in a socially significant manner.

All of this is reinforced by the finding of Glock and Stark and Hadden. The series of studies directed by Glock (1959; Glock and Stark, 1965, 1966; Stark and Glock, 1968) clearly shows more internal variance between Protestant denominations than between Protestants and Catholics. The studies show a clear progression from Congregational to sectarian on several variables. Examples: Congregationalists are least orthodox in doctrine and belief, poorest attenders of religious services, poorest givers (despite being second only to Episcopalians in median income), and most socially-ethically concerned. For the most part, means move in a steady progression from Congregational through Episcopalian, Methodist, Presbyterian, American Baptist, Lutheran (American, then Missouri Synod), Southern Baptist, to sectarian. Roman Catholics are in general a little more orthodox, better attenders, better givers, and less socially-concerned than the average Protestant. However, the Protestant-Catholic difference is never as large as the Congregational–Southern Baptist one. Hadden (1970) corroborates the variance within Protestant denominations and points out that it occurs in individual churches also.

The fact that the Catholic Church has not divided into denominations means that the laity have no convenient way to find religious soulmates. There appears to be as much internal variance on most religious matters within Catholicism as within Protestantism. Without a denominational structure there is no way for this variance to differentiate since there are no obvious means for clustering points of view. Ethnic churches are one way, but the differences between ethnic Catholics is not so large as that between Protestant denominations (Greeley and Rossi, 1966). Perhaps we should look at Holy Name Societies, Sodalities, and other voluntary groups within local congregations to get at effects similar to Protestant denominations. Perhaps this effect is missing among Roman Catholics. We are still waiting for as thorough a study of Catholics as the Glock and Stark studies of Protestantism.

Whether or not Catholics are self-sorted into differentiated groups as

Protestants are, the fact that internal variance among Protestants overshadows Protestant-Catholic differences ought to give us pause when we interpret these differences. To talk about them as socially important when the nature of variation within religious groups is unknown (or known to be large) is to give way to flights of fancy or to ideological mongering, which is a social science equivalent of demagoguery. We need to pay careful attention to the gathering, accumulating, analyzing, and displaying of data so that intragroup variation can be shown.

At this point the choice of accumulating, analyzing, and displaying data works against the analysis. One assumes that most of the variables analyzed (doctrinal orthodoxy is a good and widely used example) are continuous where every shade of opinion is to be found in the population. Choosing to accumulate data item by item and summing them into an index with a few well-defined values serves to restrict the range of variation. Collapsing the index into a dichotomy for analysis and presentation alters the distribution still further. What is gained in clarity and force of presentation does not make up for loss of information and misrepresentation of the population. Dichotomizing a display tends to overemphasize between group differences and minimize within group differences [5]. We would all be helped by the development of scales that could display within denomination variance as well as between. The progression of means across denominations (e.g., with Congregationalists more liberal and Southern Baptists more orthodox) would remain. What we would gain is a better picture of within-denomination dispersions.

This issue is crucial for two reasons. First, it will help us avoid overinterpreting new data. For we tend to make too much of interdenominational differences. Second, there is much talk that a formal merger of churches (e.g., consummation of talks now listed as the Consultation on Church Union, COCU) will be followed by a liberal-orthodox split. We need some grip on intradenominational distributions of responses if we are to predict such a split accurately.

Viable conclusions at this point are as follows. (1) Protestant-Catholic differences are overrated and center on a few behavioral items. (2) Protestantism, with its denominations serving as means of focusing opinions and behaviors of many people, appears more highly differentiated than Catholicism. (3) If COCU were to succeed, then on the basis of Glock and Stark's work we could predict that American Catholicism would wind up between COCU and the "orthodox" denominations on most issues. (4) If Protestant-Catholic differences are overrated, what accounts for the animus between these bodies? The answer is stated explicitly by Herberg (1961) and implicitly by Lenski (1967). There is a struggle for social honor [6]. Historically, most Catholics were working-class immigrants with a mother tongue other than English. Their numbers are large enough and their integration into American society thorough enough that they challenge the WASP image of America. Thus the animus about social honor tends to focus on and magnify differences. It is important to recognize that the differences persist because of the animus and not vice versa. As the animosity lessens, so will the differences. (5) The Protestant-Catholic differences in survey research may be small partly because they center on self-reported data and ignore equally important information which is not gathered in questionnaire surveys. Examples of data not ordinarily gathered are: Underwood's mapping of Protestantism and Catholicism in Paper City (1957: 406), urban-rural and regional distributions (Soper, 1967), patterns of dominance and submission between clergy and laity, and structural-organizational differences between church organizations would be other possibilities. (6) The data seem to confirm Herberg's conclusion that large segments of American religious life are more American than confessionally religious (1955). Continuing to center on matters of verbalized doctrine and belief is to focus on matters of public rhetoric which may bear a different relation to social reality than nonverbalized beliefs. The former concentrate on that part of the advertising-packaging complex of religion which serves to promote customer loyalty by differentiating an essentially similar product (see Berger, 1963). This complex has received so much attention because it is the overt focus of much covert hostility. (7) Another intriguing point for sociologists is the amount of between-group difference necessary to support hostile stereotypes. Research on intergroup differences documents the real basis for stereotypes—mean tendencies are different. But the differences are slight, and the dispersion about them is great. What magnitude of difference is essential to support a stereotype, and does this differ under different conditions?

CAUSAL MODELS

Anyone who has wrestled with a four- or five-dimensioned table recognizes the difficulty of seeing relationships—especially partial associations which call for holding the effect of one or more variables constant. In addition, most variables are conceptualized as continuous. Categories for tabular presentation are the limits of measurement ability (or lack thereof) rather than the result of theory. Thus it seems best if we can convert tabular arrays to summary statistics so that we can evaluate causal models.

Glock and Stark's (1966) study of anti-Semitism is a most ambitious attempt at causal modeling. It deserves extended comment. First, the general theoretical outline that orthodoxy leads to stereotyping of Jews, which leads to anti-Semitism is plausible. Second, the attempt to spell out an operational paradigm is commendable. The research attempts to verify the following causal model (p. 132, Figure 2),

$$O \longrightarrow P \longrightarrow J \longrightarrow RH \longrightarrow AS \tag{1}$$

$$RL$$

where O = orthodoxy, P = particularism (God's chosen people), J = implication of historic Jew in crucifixion, RL = religious libertarianism, RH = religious hostility toward the modern Jew, AS = secular anti-Semitic beliefs. Glock and Stark state that RL is a crucial intervening variable. They also label the complex $O + P + J + RL$ as religious dogmatism (RD). This yields a simpler model:

$$RD \rightarrow RH \rightarrow AS \tag{2}$$

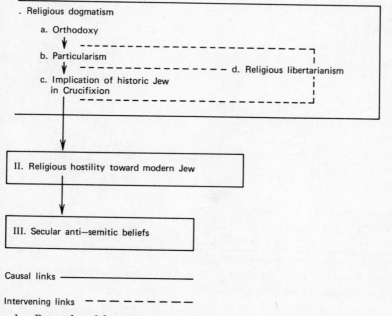

Figure 1.   Reproduced from Glock and Stark (1966, p. 132, their Figure 2).

TABLE 2. DOGMATISM, RELIGIOUS HOSTILITY, AND ANTI-SEMITISM

(Percentage of respondents who ranked High or Medium High on Index of Anti-Semitic Beliefs)

Rank on Index of Religious Hostility Toward Modern Jews	Religious Dogmatism Index		
	High	Middle	Low
Protestants			
High (4)			
Percent	77	62	a
Number	(97)	(50)	(7)
Score of 3			
Percent	53	54	56
Number	(75)	(73)	(32)
Score of 2			
Percent	35	34	38
Number	(79)	(93)	(92)
Score of 1			
Percent	19	21	15
Number	(21)	(96)	(151)
Low (zero)			
Percent	5	16	10
Number	(19)	(82)	(217)
Catholics			
High (4)			
Percent	a	a	a
Number	(6)	(1)	(1)
Score of 3			
Percent	55	a	a
Number	(20)	(5)	(3)
Score of 2			
Percent	37	39	33
Number	(27)	(28)	(15)
Score of 1			
Percent	32	19	23
Number	(28)	(37)	(22)
Low (zero)			
Percent	12	12	6
Number	(26)	(32)	(31)

a: Too few cases to compute stable percentages.
Source: Data and table reproduced from Glock and Stark (1966, p. 134, their Table 50). Summary statistics computed from table.

Group	Kendall's Tau	Goodman and Kruskal's Tau	
		$RH \rightarrow RD$	$RD \rightarrow RH$
Protestant	.44	.17	.07
Catholic	.20	.05	.02
Total	.38	.11	.05

The first model is more interesting and important; but it is not treated adequately by Glock and Stark.

In the following discussion I shall try to present a formal analysis of the data analysis and hypothesis testing. To this end I shall refer to variables by a code, defined in conjunction with model (1) and modified as new variables are entered. This is done to strip the analysis of overtones and value loadings from the variable names. It also helps us to see that the summary names have no substance apart from the operations used to construct the indices. This should make us wary, for too often the research is reported in terms of catchy variable titles rather than reasonable summaries of operations [7].

The authors declare that absence of RL strengthens these relationships: $O \rightarrow P, P \rightarrow J, J \rightarrow RH$. Though RL is the subject of a chapter, its function as intervening variable is never explored. Links between O and P, P and J, J and RH are never "interpreted," not even in the limited sense expounded by Hyman (1955). The reader is given tables of bivariate relations between RL and O, and RL and J. Would RL "wipe out" the $O \rightarrow J$ relations as P had done earlier? Unless Glock and Stark tell us, we shall never know.

At some points logical analysis serves to undercut the authors' argument. When RD is cross-classified with forgiveness for contemporary Jews (JG) and punishment of contemporary Jews (JP) Glock and Stark (1966: 96) point out that the analysis of JG leads to the conclusion that RD is a necessary condition for JG for Catholics and a sufficient condition for Protestants. Though they don't point it out, RD is a necessary but not sufficient condition for JP. Furthermore, their Table 50 (p. 134), which is reproduced as Table 2 here, shows dramatically that RD is not correlated to RH [8] for Roman Catholics. Inspection of parenthesized numbers in the bottom of the table shows this. There is a correlation for Protestants. My conclusion is that for Catholics it is clear that RD does not cause RH. Among Protestants, while it is possible that RD is a sufficient condition for RH, this is not always the case. Thus at a crucial point the causal model fails.

Further, though it is clear that controlling for RH wipes out the RD effect on AS, it is not clear whether model (2) above or model (3) applies.

$$RD \leftarrow RH \rightarrow AS \qquad (3)$$

Glock and Stark must assume that (2) is correct since (3) is equally well supported by the data. Without longitudinal data which show changes of individuals on these variables, one cannot choose between (2) and

(3). An alternative would be to go to a more sophisticated type of analysis which would allow the evaluation of a larger system as well as exogenous effects. One way would be to decompose RD into its constituent elements to produce a model such as:

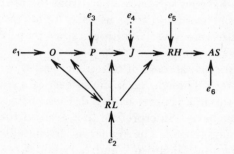

$$(4)$$

which is similar to (1) with exogenous variables added. This model can be tested with path coefficients or, if we treat RL as a categorized variable, with covariance. It demands working with frequency distributions and summary statistics rather than percentages. The analysis closest to the theory would treat the scales as continuous variables with equal intervals. This would be a routine path analysis. If one does not wish to make metric assumptions of this sort, one can collapse to dichotomies and compute phi coefficients, which can be treated as product moment coefficients for purposes of path analysis (Boudon, 1968). On the other hand, if effects are different for high versus low RL, then covariance analysis is a logical procedure.

Such analyses would have been helpful since the authors combine RD and RH to form a scale of Religious Bigotry (RB), which Table 3 (their Table 51) shows is strongly related to AS. The entries in Table 3 are determined by collapsing Table 2 about the main diagonal. Thus, for example, 59 Catholic respondents with $RB = 3$ are found by summing entries from Table 2 for Catholic $RH = 1$, $RD = $ Hi (28); $RH = 2$; $RD = M$ (28) $RH = 3$, $RD = $ Lo (3). This cross checking allows us to establish all but two missing percentages in Table 2. Solutions for the cells Catholic, $RH = 3$, $RD = M$, and Catholic, $RH = 4$, $RD = $ Lo are dependent on one another. With these percentages established we can present the relation between HR and AS as in Table 4. The second line for Catholics is due to the non-unique solutions noted above.

TABLE 3.   RELIGIOUS BIGOTRY AND ANTI-SEMITIC BELIEFS

Rank on Index of Anti-Semitic Beliefs	Index of Religious Bigotry						
	0	1	2	3	4	5	6
Protestants							
High	2%	3%	9%	20%	16%	28%	54%
Medium high	8	12	19	17	30	29	24
High and medium high	(10)	(15)	(28)	(37)	(46)	(57)	(78)
Medium	57	54	52	49	45	40	22
None	33	31	20	14	9	3	0
Total	100%	100%	100%	100%	100%	100%	100%
Number[1]	(216)	(233)	(206)	(146)	(159)	(124)	(97)
Catholics							
High	6%	4%	6%	7%	18%	29%	50%
Medium high	0	13	13	32	22	29	33
High and medium high	(6)	(17)	(19)	(39)	(40)	(58)	(83)
Medium	42	48	50	46	51	42	17
None	52	35	31	15	9	0	0
Total	100%	100%	100%	100%	100%	100%	100%
Number	(31)	(54)	(78)	(59)	(33)	(21)	(6)[2]

[1] There are minor discrepancies in the numbers of Protestants coded Religious Bigotry 0, 2, 5. These are all 1 less than computations based on Table 2.
[2] The stability of a percentage based on so few cases is questionable, and this finding is presented only for its descriptive interest.
Source: Reproduced from Glock and Stark (1966, p. 136, their Table 51).

What Tables 3 and 4 clearly show is that *RH* predicts *AS* as well as *RB* does. They show that the addition of *RD* to *RH* to form *RB* adds little or no information. That this would be the case ought to be obvious from Table 2. The relation between *RD* (and its constituent elements) and *RH* needs to be specified. Combining variables into indices is not the way to specify conditional relationships implied by Figure 1 or model (4). These conditional relationships need specification if the theory proposed is to be taken as true.

In a later publication, *Wayward Shepherds* (1971), Stark and his co-workers use path analysis to attempt a more sophisticated test and explication of their theory. They use the data from the anti-Semitism study and additional data from a sample of clergymen. The analysis omits *RL* and all interaction effects. In addition it fails to come to grips with the

TABLE 4. RELIGIOUS HOSTILITY AND ANTI-SEMITIC BELIEFS

Rank on Index of Anti-Semitic Beliefs	Index of Religious Hostility				
	0 (Low)	1	2	3	4 High
Protestants					
High and medium high	36	47	95	97	112
Other	282	121	169	83	42
% High and medium high	(11)	(28)	(35)	(54)	(73)
Catholics					
High and medium high	9	21	26	17[1]	6[1]
Other	80	66	44	11	2
% High and medium high	(10)	(24)	(37)	(61)	(75)
Alternative[2]					
High and medium high				16[1]	7[1]
Other				12	1
% High and medium high				(57)	(87)

Source: These data are computed from Tables 50 and 51 Glock and Stark (1966). Those tables are reproduced in this article as Tables 2 and 3.

[1] These numbers are interdependent. There are too many unknowns for a unique solution.

[2] This row is to show the alternate solution. These two solutions are mutually exclusive and exhaustive.

model suggested in Figure 1 or models (1) or (4). Their model (Stark at al., 1971: 81,83), is:

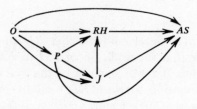

$$(5)$$

This is a fully recursive model in which one variable is dependent on all previous variables. If error paths are added, the equation set is:

$$P \leftarrow p_{PO}O + p_{PA}A$$
$$J \leftarrow p_{JO}O + p_{JP}P + p_{JB}B$$
$$RH \leftarrow p_{RH,O}O + p_{RH,P}P + p_{RH,J}J + p_{RH,C}C$$
$$AS \leftarrow p_{AS,O}O + p_{AS,P} + p_{AS,J}J + p_{AS,RH}RH + p_{AS,D}D$$

$$(1)$$

where A, B, C, D are combined effects of all variables exogenous to the model and their coefficients are indicators of the size of the effects of these variables. These effects are error or unexplained variance because the model does not take them into account.

On the other hand, if RL is dropped from models (1) and (4), one gets:

$$
\begin{array}{cccc}
A & Z & Y & X \\
\downarrow & \downarrow & \downarrow & \downarrow \\
O \to P & \to J & \to RH & \to AS
\end{array}
\tag{6}
$$

The equation set is:

$$
\begin{aligned}
P &\leftarrow p_{PO}O + p_{PA}A \\
J &\leftarrow \qquad\quad p_{PJ}P + p_{PZ}Z \\
RH &\leftarrow \qquad\qquad\qquad p_{RH,J}J + p_{RH,Y}Y \\
AS &\leftarrow \qquad\qquad\qquad\qquad\quad p_{AS,RH}RH + p_{AS,X}X
\end{aligned}
\tag{2}
$$

Coefficients present in equations (1) but missing from (2)—i.e. p_{JO}, $p_{RH,O}$, $p_{RH,P}$, $p_{AS,O}$, $p_{AS,P}$, $p_{AS,J}$—are assumed equal to zero by model (6). If they are non-zero, then the theory of *Christian Beliefs and Anti-Semitism* is subject to modification.

It turns out that $p_{RH,O}$ and $p_{RH,P}$ are both positive and moderately strong. This suggests that model (6) (drawn from Figure 1) is not accurate and ought to be modified.

The size of the error terms also indicates a need to modify the theory. The smallest error path coefficient is more than twice the size of the largest path coefficient. If one were to display error paths with widths proportional to size of effects, one could construct a black background to border the model. The relationships reported are very weak. Less variance is explained by the model than by variables outside and independent of it.

The above, though important in detail, is peripheral to the central methodological issue. Model (6) is expected to hold only in the absence of RL. This suggests two separate path analyses within separate subsamples. The sample is divided into two groups: one with RL and one without. Model (6) is tested in each group with these predictions:

1.   It will hold for the absence of RL group.
2.   It will not hold for the presence of RL group.
3.   Therefore, the coefficients for the two groups will be different from each other.

Since predictions 1 and 2 imply 3, it will suffice to examine the data to see if these predictions hold. If so, the case is made as argued. If not, modification is called for. They have not yet put the theory to the test in this fashion. The path analysis in *Wayward Shepherds*, while suggestive, is not relevant to the hypotheses being tested.

Returning from our formal analysis to the language of everyday discourse, the data presented by Glock and Stark do *not* demonstrate a causal connection between Christian beliefs and anti-Semitism. Further, any correlation between them may be spurious rather than developmental.

Christian Beliefs and Anti-Semitism has signal importance for its attempt to validate a causal model. This will be a pattern for future research. Causal models of this type can be evaluated by one of the many varieties of path analysis (Duncan, 1966; Blalock, 1968; Boudon, 1968) using interval level statistics or phi coefficients for dichotomies (Boudon, 1968) or by covariance analysis (Schuessler, 1969). It requires working with dummy variable regression, ordinal measures of association, or multiple classification analysis. These procedures are now available. Many were not available to Glock and Stark when the data were analyzed; so they cannot be faulted for not using them. Despite any shortcomings, their anti-Semitism study is a step forward. It is necessary to specify hypotheses before we can test them. It is only by attempting such work as this that we can assess where we are in development of theory, method, and the testing of hypotheses. This assessment is fundamental to any forward thrust of the discipline.

CONCLUSIONS

I have chosen to examine a few works rather than catalog an extensive survey of studies of religion. These detailed examinations lead to suggestions for the future:

1. Differences between religious groups in American society are magnified out of proportion by the survey literature. In the first place, intergroup differences are so small that we can call them trivial. In a fourfold (2 × 2) table, if differences between groups do not equal or exceed 40 percentage points, they are probably not large enough to worry about. Such a difference accounts for about 16% of the variance in the dependent variable. Manipulation of this amount of variance may be socially useful. To move to manipulate less than this may be to expend more energy than is worthwhile. If we are looking for solutions to problems, variables which account for less than 16% of the variance appear to be poor solutions. My bet is that there are better ones. Moreover, intragroup differences seem so large that intergroup differences are small by comparison. We need to develop reliable and standard scales to report the range of variation within groups. Once this is done, it will be seen that differences in means are insignificant compared to the overlapping of ranges.

2. Failure to find major differences between groups ought to lead us

n new research directions. I suggest that intergroup tension in society is more closely related to the struggle over the distribution of social honor, goods, and services than to religious differences between groups. In effect, society is, in a limited sense, a zero-sum game (more so if the economy is stationary) in which genuine religious or theological differences between groups are not as important as the distribution of power, prestige, and products. Religious differences which are relatively small and trivial become the centers of public debate, but the real struggle concerns other issues. In this sense trivial differences are socially important because they serve as overt foci for tension and conflict. No Christian group has a theology which bars intercommunion (or even justifies separation) on grounds of economic or social status. Yet these appear to be basic reasons for intra-Protestant schism even though the argument between groups proceeds along lines of doctrine and polity (Niebuhr, 1929).

3. Flaws in the last major study of Christianity and anti-Semitism should not lead us to reject the research thrust. An explicit causal model was proposed. If religion has effects on secular aspects of society, then the testing of explicit causal models is the way to test the form and magnitude of these effects.

In closing, I should emphasize that the studies discussed were chosen for their importance to the future of survey studies of religion. Where I have dealt harshly with them, it was not in an attempt to point the finger at bad work. My contention is that recent methodological advances in the handling of survey data could make them even better.

NOTES

1. White Protestant, white Catholic, Negro Protestant, and Jew. But for many tables only white Protestant and white Catholic are included because of small numbers of others. The major summary table (Table 50, pp. 324f.) has this restriction.

2. Middle and working classes are defined as white collar or nonmanual versus all other (pp. 48f.). The operational definition is given in footnotes to Table 7, p. 80.

3. This conversion procedure is based on the fact that Tau = r^2 for 2 × 2 tables. Unless the margins are quite differently skewed, percentage differences by rows will nearly equal those by columns (Blalock, 1963). r^2 = % diff. rows × % diff. col. Thus the procedure, while "quick and dirty," is essentially reliable.

4. This value is lower than I feel comfortable with. I prefer .20.

5. This is an optical illusion. We are impressed by percentage differences which

are dramatic and easily grasped. We tend to forget that dichotomizing usually attenuates relationships thus reducing the size of summary statistics. Internal variance tends to be large but is obscured by the fact that we have only two values. That each value has a group of observations tends to be ignored. Attenuation due to categorization will affect results negatively when the team attempts a path analysis. In general, individual correlations are low. In two samples coefficients of determination for AS as a linear function of O, P, J and RH are .05 and .13. This means that coefficients of alienation, measures of the effect of variables left out of the model, are .95 and .87. Clearly, much work is left to be done.

6. I use this term in its Weberian sense.

7. See Dittes (1967), for extended comment in connection with this book.

8. Religious Hostility Index is composed of two items: "Jews can never be forgiven for what they did to Jesus until they accept Him as the True Savior" (JG), and "Among themselves, Jews think Christians ignorant for believing Christ was the Son of God" (p. 133). Curiously, the item labeled JP above is not part of this index.

REFERENCES

BERGER, PETER L.
LUCKMANN, THOMAS

1963   "Sociology of Religion and Sociology of Knowledge." *Sociology and Social Research* 47: 417–427.

BLALOCK, HUBERT M., JR.

1963   *Causal Inference in Non-experimental Research.* Chapel Hill: University of North Carolina Press.

1968   "Theory Building and Causal Inferences." Pp. 155–198 in H. M. Blalock and A. B. Blalock (eds.), *Methodology in Social Research.* New York: McGraw-Hill.

BOUDON, RAYMOND

1968   "A New Look at Correlation Analysis." Pp. 199–235 in H. M. Blalock and A. B. Blalock (eds.), *Methodology in Social Research.* New York: McGraw-Hill.

DITTES, JAMES

1967   "Review of Glock and Stark *Christian Beliefs and Anti-Semitism." Review of Religious Research* 8: 183–187.

DUNCAN, O. DUDLEY

1966   "Path Analysis: Sociological Examples." *American Journal of Sociology* 72: 1–6.

GLOCK, CHARLES Y.

1959   "The Religious Revival in America." Pp. 25–42 in Jane Zahn (ed.), *Religion and the Face of America.* Berkeley: University of California Press.

GLOCK, C. Y.
STARK, RODNEY

1965   *Religion and Society in Tension.* Chicago: Rand McNally.

1966   *Christian Beliefs and Anti-Semitism.* New York: Harper and Row.

GREELEY, ANDREW M.
ROSSI, PETER

1966   *Education of Catholic Americans.* Chicago: Aldine.

HADDEN, JEFFREY K.

1969   *The Gathering Storm in the Churches.* Garden City, N.Y.: Doubleday.

HADDEN, J. K.
HEENAN, EDWARD F.

1970   "Empirical Studies in the Sociology of Religion: An Assessment of the Past Ten Years." *Sociological Analysis* **31**: 153–171.

HERBERG, WILL

(1955)   *Protestant-Catholic-Jew: An Essay in American Religious*
1960   *Sociology.* Garden City, N.Y.: Doubleday Anchor.

1961   "Religion and Education in America." In J. W. Smith and A. L. Jamison (eds.), *Religious Perspectives in American Culture.* Princeton: Princeton University Press.

HYMAN, HERBERT H.

1955   *Survey Design and Analysis.* Glencoe, Ill.: Free Press.

LENSKI, GERHARD

(1961)   *The Religious Factor.* Garden City, N.Y.: Doubleday
1963   Anchor.

1967   "Religion's Impact on Secular Institutions." Pp. 217–236 in J. Brothers (ed.), *Reading in the Sociology of Religion.* Oxford: Pergamon Press.

NIEBUHR, H. RICHARD

(1929)   *The Social Sources of Denominationalism.* New York:
1957   Meridian.

SCHUESSLER, KARL

1969   "Covariance Analysis in Sociological Research." Chapter 7 in E. F. Borgatta (ed.), *Sociological Methodology*. San Francisco: Jossey-Bass.

SOPER, DAVID E.

1967   *Geography of Religions*. Englewood Cliffs, N.J.: Prentice-Hall.

STARK, RODNEY
GLOCK, CHARLES Y.

1968   *American Piety: The Nature of Religious Commitment*. Berkeley: Universiy tof California Press.

STARK, RODNEY
FOSTER, BRUCE
GLOCK, C.
QUINLEY, HAROLD

1971   *Wayward Shepherds*. New York: Harper and Row.

UNDERWOOD, KENNETH

1957   *Protestant and Catholic*. Boston: Beacon Press.

W. Clark Roof

UNIVERSITY OF MASSACHUSETTS, AMHERST

Explaining Traditional Religion in Contemporary Society

Among advances of the past decade in the sociology of religion, one of the most significant has been the conceptualization of religious commitment as multidimensional. Beginning with Glock's (1959) essay, a host of research studies, including those by Fukuyama (1961), Lenski (1961), Faulkner and DeJong (1966), King (1967), Clayton (1968), and Stark and Glock (1968), have shown empirically that the dimensions of religiosity vary independently, and that the use of any single indicator may be a poor predictor of the others. These studies have helped us to understand the conceptual and measurement aspects of a complex phenomenon. Instead of viewing religiosity as a unitary construct, social scientists have now begun to define the term more fully.

At the present time, however, it is probably fair to say that what we need in studying religious commitment is not the unfolding of more dimensions, important as that may be; rather, we need better *theories* of religious commitment. We need theories which explain religiosity in its multidimensional structure and link the latter to other sociological variables both as causes and consequences. For if by "theory" we mean explanation, and ultimately the knowledge necessary for predicting empirical regularities, then it is apparent that at present our interpretive skills in the sociology of religion lag behind our descriptive insights.

Some progress in developing more systematic theories is already underway, largely as a result of the multidimensional studies. Previously postulated theories, often based upon an unidimensional conception of religiosity, are being reexamined. We shall review some of these studies, but the primary task of this paper will be to explore some uses of the local-cosmopolitan orientation concept for explaining traditional religiosity. Elsewhere I have discussed the broad outline of such a theory (Roof, 1972); here I intend to explore further how this orientation concept may contribute to more systematic theories of religiosity in contemporary society.

In particular, I shall briefly outline and assess theories of religiosity that involve at least two independent variables and that build upon the conventional notions of specification and statistical interaction in social science literature. Although the proposals for more systematic theoretical models are more suggestive than substantive at the present time, I shall argue that such approaches in theory building are more promising, and conceptually neater, than single-variable explanations.

EXPLAINING TRADITIONAL RELIGIOSITY

If we want theories which explain religious phenomena but yet are empirically testable, at some point we must confront seriously underlying conceptual and methodological problems in the sociology of religion. That researchers continue to use the term "correlate" to describe the social realities associated with religiosity is perhaps an indication of how little sociological theory we actually have regarding the matter. Two considerations seem particularly pertinent in obtaining more satisfactory theories: (1) multivariable explanations, and (2) new explanatory concepts. Each of these deserves detailed comment.

Multivariable Explanation. Of all the "social correlates" of religiosity studied, social class has received the most attention. Several researchers have offered theories of social class and religious commitment which utilize multidimensional measures (Demerath, 1965; Davidson, 1966; Goode, 1966, 1968). Formal religious participation, such as church attendance, is generally found to be positively linked to social class, whereas devotionalism and orthodoxy measures are negatively associated. Other, less embracing explanations using multidimensional conceptions focus on sex (Glock, Ringer, and Babbie, 1967), age (*ibid.*; Lazerwitz, 1964; Orbach, 1961), and local-cosmpolitan orientations (Roof, 1972).

Most studies of this kind, as is true for much social science research, concentrate upon a single independent variable for formulating a "theory" of religiosity. Often little or no consideration is given to the fact that the explanatory factors themselves may be interrelated and perhaps causally dependent upon one another. If the problem of spuriousness is dealt with at all, it is frequently done by looking at control variables one at a time without much attention to the question of how the variables are causally ordered. Such neglect of the interrelations among independent variables, as Blalock observes (1969: 35), is a major source of fruitless debates in sociology over the relative importance of one set of explanatory variables as compared with another. If one can correctly assume no relations among the religiosity predictors, then relative importance can be assessed easily in terms of variance explained in the dependent variable. But if there are causal influences of one independent variable upon another, the reasoning for using such straightforward procedures breaks down. Unless replaced by simultaneous-equation methods, it is easy to make biased or incorrect inferences about the importance of a a single explanatory factor.

In order to arrive at more reliable estimates of the effects of independent variables, it is necessary to examine the interrelationships among social correlates. Multivariate models specifying linkages among all variables also help establish which variables should be controlled, and make more explicit the entire verification process. Path analysis procedures, in the case of recursive models [1], provide a means of obtaining measures of the relative importance of factors, including direct and indirect influences. Where the dependent variable can be taken as a joint function of two or more independent variables multiplicative models can be constructed which specify more precisely the relations among a set of variables. As we shall see later, this approach promises to shed light upon several substantive problems in the sociology of religion.

New Concepts. Multicausal explanations alone are not sufficient. Also needed are new analytical concepts, that is, alternative variables that are sensitive predictors of traditional religious beliefs and practices in a secular society.

Generally, theories of religious commitment employ structural variables as major causal factors. By structural we refer to those correlates which describe a status or role position within the social order, such as social class, education, sex, or age. Structural concepts are not problematic in themselves, but they are often couched in explanatory schemes loaded with assumptions about the manner in which religious values function to integrate society. In functional theories of religion, for example, it is often assumed that a single, overarching belief system exists in society, characterzed by congruence among the cultural, structural, and personality levels of the social system. When a religiously based moral order is taken for granted, a person's role is likely to be viewed as embodying opportunities for expressing religious commitments—in varying forms, perhaps, but to the same underlying tradition. In this way, role and status are often understood as affecting the "style" of commitment, but such interpretations do not tell us much about the plausibility of the institutionalized belief system itself.

What if it can no longer be assumed that traditional religious symbols and rituals provide the basis for the cultural integration of modern society? Various writers, including Eister (1957), Fenn (1970, 1972), and Luckmann (1967), suggest the need for a sociology of religion based upon alternative presuppositions. Instead of assuming that the "official" religious system is internalized by individuals, no matter what their role or position, we need theoretical approaches that rest upon the premise that modern society offers plural meaning systems, among which individuals may choose. Thus, in a secular society the plausibility of a religious tradition should be viewed as problematic, not simply accepted for granted. Commenting on how secularization affects motivation, Fenn observes that the "determination of goals by actors, whether these actors be individuals or collectivities, is increasingly related to contextual considerations such as individual proclivities and situational exigencies. In the process of internalizing systems of ultimate meaning, furthermore, the same situational and subjective considerations acquire greater salience than officially sanctioned and institutionalized normative systems" (1970: 135.)

Rather than reify institutional religion as a societal universal, it would seem more promising to view traditional religiosity today as essentially symbolic expressions of a broader set of traditional values, which are operative in certain social contexts more than in society as a whole. One's commitment to a particular value orientation may be regarded as containing the meaning of the religious, and in a society characterized by pluralistic meaning systems, the values and beliefs institutionalized in traditional religion are only one set among many alternatives. Estus and Overington (1970), in fact, call for abandoning the "institutional" model of religion and suggest instead an approach focusing upon meanings and values acted out in religious behavior.

In a secular society, we shall increasingly need analytical concepts for studying religiosity that are sensitive predictors of such underlying value commitments. We can look upon traditional religion not as an end in itself, but as an opportunity for studying a distinctive set of values, attitudes, and life styles, many of which may be at odds with the prevailing moral sentiments of the society at large. One approach to the question of why people are involved in traditional religion is to examine the "social location" of the values affirmed by religious expressions of this kind, and to link the social realities involved to their symbolic meanings. More attention to the social context in which traditional world views persist, therefore, is a necessary step toward developing sociological theories in keeping with the functional realities of traditional religion in contemporary society.

THE LOCAL-COSMOPOLITAN ORIENTATION AND THE PLAUSIBILITY OF TRADITIONAL RELIGION

To the extent that traditional religious symbols continue to provide a basis for cultural integration, they do so within specific social sectors rather than for society as a whole. One sector that has retained greater plausibility than most is the local sphere. By local sphere is meant the immediate community that an individual is involved in and affiliated with, as compared to the larger social world of which he is a participant. Like the family, the local community is, as Benita Luckmann (1970) puts it, a major "small life-world"—a micro-universe around which experiences may be structured and interpreted in the modern world.

Empirical studies have utilized the local-cosmopolitan distinction for tapping orientational proclivities toward one's immediate sphere of social experiences. Merton (1957) was the first to put forth a local-cosmopolitan theory, in which localism and cosmopolitanism are viewed as alternative modes of reference group orientation. Following his usage and that of others, the measure has come to be construed as one of community reference, ranging from one's immediate social environment to the broader national society. Essentially, it gauges the varying degree to which a local community reference is instrumental in affecting a person's perceptual, cognitive, and behavioral patterns, either through pressures to conform to local norms or by providing an interpretative frame of reference.

In recent years, the distinction has become quite useful for delineating behavioral and ideological patterns in modern society. Community ideologies based on old symbolic associations continue to persist, reinforced by community newspapers (Janowitz, 1952) and the romanticizations of small-town life by the mass media (Vidich and Bensman, 1958). Not only does local community attachment offer a persisting basis of identification; it also provides a sense of contact with supporting groups having similar backgrounds, values, and attitudes. Family relations, neighborhood ties, and communal rituals may all be invested with locality-specific meaning, in a manner permitting an individual to achieve a degree of closure of social experience. Furthermore, such orientations may contribute to what Berger and Luckmann (1966) describe as a "reified" view of social reality, that is, a conception of reality as a fixed, superordinate phenomenon infused with transcendental authority.

My previous study of local-cosmopolitan correlates of religiosity suggests, at least for a sample of Southern Baptists, that localism is a strong predictor (Roof, 1972). Treating localism as a single variable, I examined five separate measures of religiosity to see if this orientational factor would explain as much variance as more frequently used structural variables such as occupational prestige, education, age, and sex. Not only were the correlations generally higher, but the regression analysis showed this measure to be a better predictor than any of the other independent variables. For devotionalism, age was a stronger predictor than was local orientation, but on all four of the remaining religious dimensions the latter clearly surpassed. A multiple regression analysis revealed, moreover, that on three of the five dimensions localism explained as much or more of the total variation in religiosity scores as did the combined set of occupational prestige, education, sex, and age variables.

THE CONCEPT OF STATISTICAL INTERACTION,
WITH THE LOCALISM MEASURE USED FOR DEVELOPING
MULTICATIVE EXPLANATIONS

Rather than view localism as simply an orientational correlate of traditional religiosity, we may usefully employ it to "specify" conditions under which other relationships are expected to hold. After a brief discussion of specification and its relevance for theory building, generally, I shall suggest two ways in which this measure may lend itself to such possibility.

In simplest terms, specification involves a situation where the relations between an independent variable and a dependent variable differ according to some third factor (Hyman, 1955). If an investigator finds, for example, that the relations between x and y vary within categories of z, he should, to be precise, offer a statement describing that relation which includes the specification, rather than speak of a single bivariate relation between the independent and dependent variables. From a statistical point of view, the presence of z as a specification suggests "interaction"—that is the *nonadditive* effects of x and z on y. Statistical interaction suggests, among other things, multiplicative relations where a dependent variable is a joint function of two or more independent variables. Whereas the notion of specification implies an asymmetric approach involving one variable as a conditioning influence, statistical interaction suggests a symmetric formulation of the same events in terms of jointly produced effects.

It would appear that social scientists have yet to explore the range of possibilities using either notion for theory construction. The asymmetric specification approach is straightforward, and in a field of study such as sociology of religion, where the underlying causal structure among variables is often poorly understood, the search for theoretically important control variables may be a necessary first step. But increasingly, as Blalock points out (1968: 180–85), it is preferable to think in terms of interaction, in order to advance hypotheses in the form of multiplicative relations among three or more variables. Such an approach should be useful particularly when one wants to argue that *two* conditions are simultaneously necessary in order for an event to occur. As our understanding of religiosity increases, we can expect to find researchers giving more attention to formulations of this kind..

Plausibility of Traditional Religiosity. One interesting problem that deserves further attention is how the dimensions of traditional religiosity are related to each other and, in particular, how the structures of religious commitment may be changing currently. For if by secularization is meant the decline of traditional forms of religiosity, sociologists should specify in more detail how the dimensions of religiosity may be expected to change. Aside from Weigert and Thomas's work (1970), almost no research has attacked this problem.

If we view secularization as "declining plausibility," as does Berger (1967), it is possible to develop a rationale for using the local orientation concept for predicting changing patterns of religious commitment. By distinguishing between the objective social structures which support a given world view and the subjective realities of consciousness, Berger makes it possible to examine plausibility in terms of the degree of congruence between reality-as-experienced and the institutionalized values and beliefs (see also Berger and Lockmann, 1966: 163–173). A plausible world view is one in which there is symmetry between the objective experiences and the internalized meanings. Religious beliefs and values, in this instance, are "real" because the social experiences confirm those realities. Similarly, to the extent that there is asymmetry between the two, the chances are the symbolic meanings will begin to totter and to lose their motivational power. Psychic gaps emerge between everyday experiences and traditional interpretations of life events.

In accounting for disparities of this kind, Berger makes explicit the primacy of structural factors. Subjective realities are socially created and maintained, and if there are changes in the "plausibility structures" on which they rest, then alterations in subjectivity are likely to follow. If in modern society, as we have suggested, it can no longer be assumed that the society as a whole encompasses the fundamental "plausibility structure" for traditional religiosity, then the local sphere persists as one context in which traditional values retain their plausibility. At the very least, such values should be *more* plausible and have *more* legitimating power in this sphere than they would in many other sectors of modern experience.

Such reasoning would lead us to expect that localistic orientation "specifies" the relation between socioreligious group involvement on the one hand, and subjective religiosity on the other. This latter distinction refers essentially to the difference between an individual's interaction within a religious community and his orientational commitments [2]. Associational and communal activities are not direct measures of religiosity; rather, such measures of involvement are better viewed as aspects of the "plausibility structure"—the infrastructure supportive of religious commitment. We would expect, in fact, *that among locals there should be stronger relations between socioreligious group involvement and subjective religious commitment.* This hypothesis rests on the assumption that a person's social interaction in the religious institution will buttress his individual religiosty if he is sensitive of, and conforms to, the norms and values of those with whom he interacts. If a person is not locally oriented, then we would not expect the intercorrelations among religiosity measures to be as great.

Figure 1 diagrams the causal relations implied in this argument and shows the indicators which are taken as measures of socioreligious group involvement and subjective religiosity. The vertical arrow is intended to suggest that localistic community reference specifies the substantive relation between the two religious factors, thereby establishing a condition for the plausibility of traditional religiosity; empirically, the strength of the horizontal relationship is expected to vary depending on the level of localistic orientation.

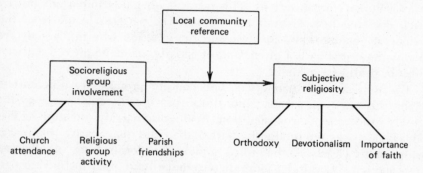

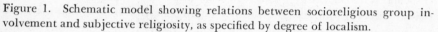

Figure 1. Schematic model showing relations between socioreligious group involvement and subjective religiosity, as specified by degree of localism.

Associational Involvement. Another unresolved issue in the sociology of religion concerns the relations between social class and religious participation. Studies usually show that participation such as church attendance and involvement in organized religious activities is positively associated with social class. But how do we explain it?

Greater middle-class participation is regarded by some as an indication of a greater degree of religiosity and of religious concern. Rodney Stark (1964), for example, argues that middle-class individuals display a higher level of religiousness, and that their higher level of church activity measures this involvement. Others hold that the relation is explained by factors extrinsic to religiosity, arguing that the greater level of religious group participation on the part of middle-class individuals is an artifact of other sources. Lenski (1962), for one, maintains that members of the middle class generally have a higher level of associational activity in formal organizations. Church participation is one expression of middle-class associational activity and thus need not be explained in terms of religious motivation.

Empirical studies have uncovered some support for the Lenski argument, although the explanations given are not totally satisfactory. Goode (1966) finds that when "general associational activity" is controlled, the relation between social class and church activity attenuates but does not disappear. Lazerwitz comes to a similar conclusion. Noting that the relations between the number of organizational memberships and social class indicators are stronger than those between education or occupational prestige and church attendance, he concludes that the latter "cannot be conceived of as merely another manifestation of over-all activity in voluntary associations" (1964: 436).

It is not enough, then, simply to look at middle-class propensities toward voluntary organizations. This factor is obviously important but by itself does not fully account for the observed patterns. Aside from the extent of organizational involvement, the question why individuals are highly associated with a given *kind* of activity, namely religious activity, must be dealt with as well.

The local-cosmopolitan orientation concept promises to differentiate along this latter dimension, and hence, provides a complement to the purely socioeconomic consideration. In the original Merton study (1957: 389–399), it was the qualitative rather than the quantitative differences which most clearly distinguished middle-class locals from middle-class cosmopolitans. Locals, far more than cosmopolitans, were inclined to participate in voluntary organizations having locally based memberships, where personal relations were valued more highly than professional skills. As religious commitments come to be more and more "privatized" in contemporary society, we would likewise expect those who are involved in traditional religious institutions to be disproportionately inclined toward local interests and organizational affiliations.

A multiplicative model is thus proposed as a means of explaining church participation. Figure 2 shows such a causal model, where socioeconomic status and local community reference are taken as having joint effects upon religious participation. That there are linear additive relations among the variables is of course also possible, but the argument here is that religious participation may be conceptualized as a multiplicative function of (1) high socioeconomic status and, by implication, formal organizational activity; *and* (2) local community reference and participation in local organizations. Put differently, one would expect these two variables to produce effects in interaction with one another that would not occur if the two independent variables were operating separately. Conceptually, it makes sense to explain this outcome in terms of middle-class

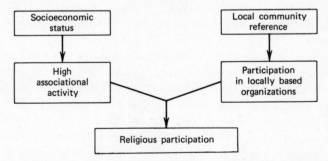

Figure 2.   Schematic model showing religious participation a multiplicative function of local reference and socioeconomic status (linear additive relations omitted).

associational involvement plus a propensity to carry out religious activity in the local sphere. But since we do not have measures for these intervening variables, we shall look for interaction effects among the causally prior influences. Such reasoning, extended to continuous variables, suggests the following hypothesis: *As local community reference increases, the relations between socioeconomic status and religious participation will increase.*

DATA AND METHODS

Data collected in 1968 as part of an Episcopal Church survey in the North Carolina Diocese permit us to examine these hypotheses. Questionnaires were sent to a sample of 890 adult Episcopalians from the diocese membership list. Usable questionnaires were returned by 518 respondents. Discounting twenty-eight errors in listing, a response rate of 70% was obtained. Although the response rate was low, subsequent questionnaires mailed to ninety-one nonrespondents revealed only negligible differences with respect to background characteristics.

As would be expected with a systematic sample of this kind, the population is characterized by relatively high status, professional occupations, and college-plus education. The general sample characteristics are as follows: 59% female, 55% less than fifty years of age, 58% in either a professional or managerial occupation, 53% college graduates, and 70% Southerners by birth. Sample representativeness of a larger population is not easy to determine, but the results with respect to one item suggest comparability with Episcopalians nationally. Concerning the number of Episcopal church members previously affiliated with other denominations, the results are almost identical to those of a 1965 National Opinion Research Center study. Whereas 45% of the NORC national sample were previously members of other churches (Stark and Glock, 1968: 195), 44% had been so affiliated in the North Carolina sample.

The major exploratory variable—local community reference—was measured by a multiple-item scale. The scale items were:

1.   Despite all the newspaper and TV coverage, national and international happenings rarely seem as interesting as events that occur in the local community in which one lives.

2.   Big cities may have their place but the local community is the backbone of America.

3.   When it comes to choosing someone for a responsible public office in my community, I prefer a person whose family is known and well-established.

4. The most rewarding organizations a person can belong to are local clubs and associations rather than large nation-wide organizations.

These items, previously used by Dye (1963) and in my earlier exploratory research, were randomly distributed in the questionnaire. Respondents were asked whether they strongly agreed, agreed, disagreed, or strongly disagreed with each item. An average product-moment intercorrelation of .37 was obtained for the set of items as a whole. These responses were summated according to Likert procedures, following an item analysis indicating reasonable internal consistency (Cromback's alpha = .81). For present purposes, scale scores range from 4 to 16 and are classified into four categories, ranging from low localism to high localism.

Six measures of religiosity were used. (1) *Church attendance* was measured by asking respondents to indicate frequency of attendance. (2) *Religious group activity* was measured by the number of religious organizations and church groups individuals frequently participated in. (3) *Devotionalism* was measured by combining responses to two questions concerning the frequency of reading religious literature and of Bible reading (Tau = .38). (4) *Parish friendships* refer to the number of the respondent's four closest friends who were members of the same parish. (5) *Orthodoxy* was measured by combining traditional responses to four statements of personal belief (average inter-item phi = .51). Items refer to traditional beliefs regarding God, eternal life, the soul, and heaven and hell. (6) *Importance of faith* was measured by asking the respondents to indicate if their religious faith was extremely important for their life, fairly important, not very important, or not at all important.

Interval measurement is assumed in the analysis in order to utilize product-moment correlation and analysis of covariance procedures. Errors resulting from the treatment of ordinal measures as interval are usually negligible (Labovitz, 1967), and the gains in terms of higher-powered methodological procedures are considerable. Product-moment correlation coefficients are used as measures of association in examining Hypothesis 1, looking at these measures as they vary from one category of localism to another. With the second hypothesis, analysis of covariance is used in testing for interaction effects. Category slopes (regression coefficients) reveal changes in the predictive power of one independent variable upon the dependent variable, from one category of the control variable to another.

FINDINGS

Religious Dimensions. In order to assess the hypothesis regarding the relations among associational-communal involvement and subjective reli-

TABLE 1. INTERCORRELATIONS BETWEEN
ASSOCIATIONAL-COMMUNAL INVOLVEMENT AND SUBJECTIVE
MEASURES OF RELIGIOSITY.

	Classification Variable			
Measures of Religiosity	Low Localism	Moderately Low Localism	Moderately High Localism	High Localism
Church attendance with				
Orthodoxy	.14	.15	.22	.31
Devotionalism	.17	.19	.27	.17
Importance of faith	.56	.55	.60	.71
Religious group activity with				
Orthodoxy	−.07	−.05	.06	.12
Devotionalism	.21	.21	.14	.14
Importance of faith	.20	.39	.39	.42
Parish friendships with				
Orthodoxy	.01	.00	.16	.29
Devotionalism	.27	−.05	.05	.00
Importance of faith	.28	.27	.34	.38

giosity, it is necessary to examine the measures of association for these two sets of indicators. Table 1 reports the correlation coefficients. The data generally show the relations to be stronger among the locally oriented respondents. Both the orthodoxy and the importance of faith measures are interrelated with socioreligious group involvement, and, as expected, these relations are stronger for locals. Moreover, their magnitude increases across categories of the classification variable in predictable fashion. The stronger the respondent's local community reference, the greater the association between socioreligious group involvement and personal religious commitment. The findings, therefore, support the view that subjective plausibility rests upon a strong interactional base.

In the case of devotionalism, the expected patterns do not hold. It is clear that the devotionalism measure is less interrelated with religious group activities and parish friendships among locals than among nonlocals. With respect to church attendance and devotionalism the pattern is erratic. One interpretation might be that devotionalism taps a dimension of religiosity that is less bound to other forms of institutional religiosity generally and hence may be less dependent upon a strong plausibility structure.

Tables 2 and 3 report the interrelations among religious dimensions for the two separate sets of indicators, controlling for degree of localism.

TABLE 2. INTERCORRELATIONS AMONG ASSOCIATIONAL-COMMUNAL INVOLVEMENT MEASURES WITHIN CATEGORIES OF LOCALISM

Classification Variable	Church Attendance–Religious Group Activity	Church Attendance–Parish Friends	Religious Group Activity–Parish Friends
Low localism	.19	.12	.08
Moderately low localism	.29	.10	.25
Moderately high localism	.41	.37	.47
High localism	.55	.45	.41

TABLE 3. INTERCORRELATIONS AMONG SUBJECTIVE RELIGIOSITY MEASURES WITHIN CATEGORIES OF LOCALISM

Classification Variable	Orthodoxy–Devotionalism	Orthodoxy–Importance of Faith	Devotionalism–Importance of Faith
Low localism	.01	.14	.41
Moderately low localism	.07	.16	.21
Moderately high localism	.21	.16	.17
High localism	.25	.38	−.01

Except for minor inversions, the correlations among the associational-communal indicators increase as the categories of localism increase (see Table 2). Locals exhibit a pattern of commitment involving strong ties to the socioreligious group as well as numerous associational activities in the religious participation. Among nonlocals we observe that the measures of associations are substantially reduced, suggesting that for the latter there is less interrelation between associational activity and communal involvement. Thus, differences in "style" of institutional commitment distinguish locals from nonlocals. Whereas for locals there are broad-based involvements within the religious institution, the patterns of socioreligious group involvement are much more fragmented for nonlocals.

With the subjective measures, once again we see that devotionalism is interrelated differently than are the other similar measures. Table 3 shows that, among locals, devotionalism is a correlate of orthodoxy but bears little or no relation to importance of faith. Importance of faith and devotionalism hang together among the nonlocals, but here the association between devotionalism and orthodoxy reduces to near zero. In effect, the data suggest that subjective religiosity is probably *less* of a unitary phenomenon for locals than for nonlocals. Individuals who are devotionalistic may or may not be "religious" on other subjective dimensions. This is not surprising, since devotional religiosity has become very much "privatized" in modern society. It is likely true, as Luckmann suggests (1967: 105), that the proliferation of inspirational religious literature in recent years signifies an emergent form of invisible religion, directly accessible to individuals, and one which will likely be less and less linked to other modes of institutional religiosity.

Associational Involvement. The interaction hypothesis explaining formal church participation is examined using analysis of covariance procedures. Table 4 reports the results of this analysis.

As is evident by the regression coefficients, the socioeconomic status measures are better predictors of church participation under conditions of strong local community orientation. We observe, in using church attendance as the participation measure, a pattern of increasing slopes across categories of localism. Using occupational prestige and education as predictors, the *F* ratios suggest that the interaction effects of the two independent variables are statistically significant. With income as a predictor, the differences in slopes are in the expected direction but are less strong.

Where religious group activity is used as the measure of associational involvement, the support for the hypothesis is less conclusive. The differences among slopes are not statistically significant, although they do fall into the expected pattern; moreover, in two instances, we observe negative slopes under conditions of low localism, which become positive as the classification variable changes.

We find, then, limited support for the interaction hypothesis. The evidence is stronger when church attendance is used as a measure of participation. But it is also likely that the latter is a more valid indicator of associational activity in the religious institution. Church attendance as a measure probably does not confuse associational activity and personal religious commitment to the extent that religious group activity does. People may "attend" church just as they occasionally participate in other voluntary organizations, but involvement in religious organizations likely presupposes a greater degree of religious commitment in the form of leadership roles and program responsibilities.

The findings, on the whole, are suggestive. Sufficient evidence is mustered to indicate that the joint conditions of high socioeconomic status and local community reference do, in fact, produce empirical results not likely to be detected if either of the independent variables were studied

TABLE 4. REGRESSION OF FORMAL RELIGIOUS PARTICIPATION
MEASURES ON SOCIOECONOMIC STATUS INDICATORS WITHIN
CATEGORIES OF LOCALISM AND F TESTS FOR
INTERACTION EFFECTS

Independent Variable Classification Variable	Dependent Variables			
	Church Attendance	F	Religious Group Participation	F
Occupational prestige				
Low localism	.043		−.054	
Moderately low localism	.150	8.63[1]	.042	< 1.0
Moderately high localism	1.641		.228	
High localism	1.775		.100	
Income				
Low localism	.095		−.217	
Moderately low localism	.090	1.09	.191	1.27
Moderately high localism	.109		.141	
High localism	.329		.146	
Education				
Low localism	.026		.024	
Moderately low localism	.095		.022	
Moderately high localism	.231	2.47[1]	.053	< 1.0
High localism	.405		.189	

[1] Statistically significant at the .01 level.

alone. With more direct measures of organizational activity, the results
may be more conclusive.

CONCLUSIONS

This study attempts to go beyond the conventional approaches to the
study of religious commitment. In so doing, we have proposed (a) that a
local community reference concept offers insight into the social location of
traditional religion in contemporary society, and (b) that an orientational
measure of this kind provides a means of empirically specifying relations
among selected variables, which in themselves are of theoretical interest.

The findings, though far from conclusive, generally support the specification and/or interaction hypotheses. Under conditions of localism, the
relations between socioreligious group involvement and subjective re-

ligiosity were stronger, except in the instance where the devotionalism measure was used. Likewise, support was obtained for the interaction hypothesis predicting formal religious participation as a joint function of socioeconomic status and local community reference.

In each instance, the findings are consistent with the theoretically derived expectations. The concept of local community reference serves to "fill out," or specify more exactly, a set of empirical results, and at the same time extends or complements the theoretical approaches. If, as our results suggest, the localism measure taps traditional value orientations, further work is needed to determine the "styles" of religiosity associated with locals and nonlocals. Moreover, as the secularization of traditional religion continues, many of our conventional explanations may need reexamining from the perspective of religious plausibility. Structural explanations of religiosity are likely to be less and less satisfactory, except when applied primarily to people whose religious commitments are highly plausible or salient. For this reason, in developing explanations of traditional religiosity it will be necessary to utilize concepts such as localism for purposes of specification.

Multiplicative formulations of the kind proposed here should also be more useful in the future. Interaction models, examining three or more variables simultaneously, promise to increase the specificity of our theories and to generate predictions that would not be readily suggested by common sense or alternative theories. At the very least, such endeavors in model building should serve to sensitize researchers to the complexities of the religious phenomenon in its social settings, while at the same time cautioning against simplistic explanations.

NOTES

1. By a recursive model is meant essentially one-way causation. Ruling out feedback effects and reciprocal causation, linear regression procedures can be used, provided that the additional assumptions of additive relations, negligible measurement error, and uncorrelated error terms can be met. See Blalock (1968).

2. The distinction between socioreligious group involvement and personal forms of commitment is conventional in the sociology of religion. It was first made by Gerhard Lenski in *The Religious Factor*. Subsequently others have classified religious dimensions along this line, noting differences between group involvement and personal orientation commitments. For further discussion and review of literature, see Robertson (1970: 51–58).

REFERENCES

BERGER, PETER

1967   *The Sacred Canopy*. Garden City, N.Y.: Doubleday.

BERGER, PETER
LUCKMANN, THOMAS

1966   *The Social Construction of Reality*. Garden City, N.Y.:
                       Doubleday.

BLALOCK, HUBERT M., JR.

1968   "Theory Building and Causal Inferences." Pp. 115–198
                       in H. M. Blalock and Ann B. Blalock (eds.), *Methodology
                       in Social Research*. New York: McGraw-Hill.

1969   *Theory Construction*. Englewood Cliffs, N.J.: Prentice-
                       Hall.

CLAYTON, RICHARD R.

1968   "Religiosity in 5-D: A Southern Test." *Social Forces* **47**:
                       80–83.

DAVIDSON, JAMES D.

1966   "The Relationship between Social Class and Five Dimen-
                       sions of Religious Affiliations." Unpublished Ph.D. dis-
                       sertation, University of Notre Dame.

DEMERATH, N. J. III

1965   *Social Class in American Protestantism*. Chicago: Rand
                       McNally.

DYE, THOMAS R.

1963   "The Local-Cosmopolitan Dimension and the Study of
                       Urban Politics." *Social Forces* **42**: 239–246.

EISTER, ALLAN W.

1957   "Religious Institutions in Complex Societies: Difficulties
                       in the Theoretic Specification of Functions." *American
                       Sociological Review* **28**: 387–391.

ESTUS, CHARLES W.
OVERINGTON, MICHAEL A.

1970   "The Meaning and End of Religiosity." *American Jour-
                       nal of Sociology* **75**: 760–778.

FAULKNER, J. E.
DE JONG, G. F.

1966   "Religiosity in 5-D: An Empirical Analysis." *Social
                       Forces* **45**: 246–254.

FENN, RICHARD K.

1970   "The Process of Secularization: A Post-Parsonian view."
               Journal for the Scientific Study of Religion 9: 117–136.

1972   "Toward a New Sociology of Religion." *Journal for the
               Scientific Study of Religion* 11: 16–32.

FUKUYAMA, YOSHIO

1961   "The Major Dimension of Church Membership." *Review
               of Religion Research* 2: 154–161.

GLOCK, CHARLES Y.

1959   "The Religious Revival in America?" Pp. 25–42 in Jane
               Zahn (ed.), *Religion and the Face of America*. Berkeley:
               University of California Press.

GLOCK, CHARLES Y.
RINGER, B. R.
BABBIE, E. R.

1967   *To Comfort and to Challenge*. Berkeley: University of
               California Press.

GOODE, ERICH

1966   "Social Class and Church Participation." *American Jour-
               nal of Sociology* 72: 102–111.

1968   "Class Styles of Religious Sociation." *British Journal of
               Sociology* 19: 1–16.

HYMAN, HERBERT H.

1955   *Survey Design and Analysis*. Glencoe, Ill.: Free Press.

JANOWITZ, MORRIS

1952   *The Community Press in an Urban Setting*. Glencoe; Ill.:
               Free Press.

KING, MORTON

1967   "Measurement of the Religious Variable: Nine Proposed
               Dimensions." *Journal for the Scientific Study of Religion*
               6: 173–190.

LABOVITZ, SANFORD

1967   "Some Observations on Measurement and Statistics."
               Social Forces 46: 151–160.

LAZERWITZ, BERNARD

1964   "Religion and Social Structure in the United States."
               Pp. 426–439 in Louis Schneider (ed.), *Religion, Culture,
               and Society*. New York: Wiley.

LENSKI, GERHARD E.

1961   *The Religious Factor*. Garden City, N.Y.: Doubleday.

1962   "The Sociology of Religion in the United States." *Social Compass* 9: 313–324.

LUCKMANN, BENITA

1970   "The Small Worlds of Modern Man." *Social Research* 37: 580–596.

LUCKMANN, THOMAS

1967   *The Invisible Religion*. New York: Macmillan.

MERTON, THOMAS

1957   *Social Theory and Social Research*. Glencoe, Ill.: Free Press.

ORBACH, HAROLD

1961   "Aging and Religion." *Geriatrics* 16: 530–540.

ROBERTSON, ROLAND

1970   *The Sociological Interpretation of Religion*. New York: Schocken.

ROOF, W. CLARK

1972   "The Local-Cosmopolitan Orientation and Traditional Religious Commitment." *Sociological Analysis* 33: 1–15.

STARK, RODNEY

1964   "Class Radicalism, and Religious Involvement in Great Britain." *American Sociological Review* 29: 698–706.

STARK, RODNEY
GLOCK, CHARLES Y.

1968   *American Piety: The Nature of Religious Commitment*. Berkeley: University of California Press.

VIDICH, ARTHUR J.
BENSMAN, JOSEPH

1958   *Small Town in Mass Society*. Garden City, N.Y.: Doubleday.

WEIGERT, ANDREW J.
THOMAS, DARWIN L.

           "Secularization: A Cross-National Study of Catholic Male Adolescents." *Social Forces* 49: 28–36.

Clarence H. Snelling
and Oliver R. Whitley

Problem-Solving Behavior
in Religious and
Para-Religious Groups:
An Initial Report

This paper reports some preliminary findings of a study of what is happening in the religious behavior of Americans outside of the traditional institutional settings.

As we sought to decide among groups we might most profitably study, we found a major motif in each group we considered. Each emphasized some kind of problem-solving—with consequences, as it seemed to us, reminiscent of the so-called Protestant ethic. Although it varied consider-

315

ably, the concern for solving problems was present in some form, either explicitly or implicitly.

Two related but distinct foci developed in our study. One was the emergence of para-religious phenomena in groups where the emphasis was clearly upon problem-solving; the other, the appearance of problem-solving behavior in manifestly religious groups. Up to the time of writing, we have been engaged in the study of behavior as problem-solving in four groups: (1) a small, neighborhood-centered Alcoholics Anonymous group; (2) Cenikor House, a Denver live-in center for drug addicts and persons convicted of various crimes; (3) a group associated with the Denver Temple of Krishna Consciousness; and (4) a Denver astrology group. The present paper presents some observations on Cenikor House and the Temple of Krishna Consciousness group—each representing one of the two categories identified above.

At the outset we determined that participant observation would be our best approach, taking a position similar to that described by George C. Homans in *The Human Group* (1950). We found that Homans' question was our kind of question: Just what in human behavior do we see?

We approached each group we were interested in investigating through its leaders, identifying ourselves as professors in a theological seminary and requesting permission to attend meetings of the group in order to observe its on-going activities. Having revealed our intentions and objectives, we accepted participation on the terms on which it was offered. In general, we attended meetings of a given group as many times as seemed necessary to arrive at an initial sense of what was *happening* in that group. As the work proceeds, we expect to return for additional visits with a clearer idea of the things we need to look for and ask about. Whenever possible, we both attended meetings, assuming that what one of us missed, the other might notice.

Our overt participation was kept to a minimum, and in our judgment our presence in the groups had no perceptible effect upon what was going on. We did, however, engage in what was happening on a few occasions. When we attended the Krishna Consciousness meeting, we were each invited to participate—as were all others present—in the reading of the portion of the sacred literature being considered at the time. Here it would have been conspicuous *not* to participate.

The participant observer role, as Bruyn suggests, involves sharing life activities and sentiments of people in face-to-face relationships. Though sharing experiences, the participant observer is not entirely *of* them. We have, we think, managed to achieve sympathetic identification with the people whose activities we have been sharing but have avoided projective distortion that might result from overidentification (Bruyn, 1963: 224–

225; 1966). At no time has either of us felt any need to make judgments or moralizations about what we were observing.

THE BROTHERS AND SISTERS AT CENIKOR HOUSE: SELF-STYLED "ASSHOLES IN THE FAITH"

A few yards off the major thoroughfare in a residential suburb of Denver is a two-story modern brick building with a contemporary glass-walled entry and reception area. Our impression, upon arrival, was that of entering an office building. A well-dressed young man ushered us down a hall to a large room which turned out to be a dining room, with one end furnished as a living room–television lounge and, along one side, a cafeteria-style serving area adjacent to a well-equipped kitchen. The floor was carpeted and the atmosphere was one of a college dormitory or fraternity house. Small groups of neatly groomed people of a variety of ages and both sexes were seated around the tables. Except for one rather nervous young man, and another man with a scar or two showing through his close-cropped hair, there were no indications that those present had all been narcotic addicts or alcoholics and that they had collectively spent almost two hundred years in prison.

The Cenikor Foundation, Inc., is a self-help program founded by Luke Austin, a "graduate" of the Synanon program [1]. It combines a residential setting, group therapy, vocational training, and family-type relationships into a rehabilitation program, the goal of which is arresting addiction and rehabilitating ex-convicts.

The group was called together by one of the leaders, who asked if there were any items to be brought up for "the good of the house." One young man asked about keeping the dog out of the halls when the floors were being mopped. The director asked who had been letting the dog in; three people raised their hands. He said, "Well, let's have some respect around here. Cut that out. You wouldn't want the dog to mess up a floor you had just mopped" [2]. Someone else mentioned that the coffee had not been kept brewing. "You're assigned to that chore, aren't you?" the director asked one of the girls. "Yes, but . . ." "Don't bother about the 'buts.' Just get the coffee made. Why did the rest of you wait for the meeting to get this out? Give her a pull-up if she messes around with the coffee."

After several, similar items, names were read in three groups, and these dispersed to separate rooms for "the Game." Having been introduced as guests earlier, we were virtually ignored during the session that followed. About eight residents sat in armchairs in a circle; the assigned leader asked if anyone wanted the Game on him tonight. The man with the close-cropped hair said he needed the Game. The director responded, "Well, our fuckin' prizefighter has begun to learn something from his fuckin' haircut. You've finally decided to use the tools instead of bullying your way through life; is that what's finally gotten into that shithead of yours?" The prizefighter responded, "You just make me so fuckin' mad that I keep wanting to bust your balls. What's going on with you and that other bastard? You got a contract going?" "Listen, man, I don't have no contract with nobody in the house. You want to know why I'm always shitting around with him? You asshole, it's because that asshole is my brother. And you'll be a lot better off when you stop fuckin' around and bullying people and start treating all these assholes like brothers" [3].

The Game then moved to a young man who had been in the house for just four months. "Where's your head at, man? You're tripping on the street; you're just doing time; you remember down at Canon City [Colorado State Penitentiary] how it was? Just doing time, drinking lots of water and walking slow. Man, that's the story of your fuckin' life. You're still taking a trip outside the Foundation; you're putting something else ahead of saving your life. We have to hold your head and show you everything." Another added, "Shit, man, you're just playing with the tools. How do you think Luke feels when you just fuck around with these tools that have been put together for us [4]?"

The Game then turned to a young woman. "How do you feel about being the Virgin Mary of Cenikor? The only woman in the world who has never used the word 'fuck'? The philosophy says that you have to express your convictions to the utmost. What have you got? A Florence Nightingale complex? Are you some kind of a social worker? Other people's problems are *theirs,* not *yours.* That's a mind game, making other people's problems yours. And while we're at it, what's this Jesus Christ shit? That kind of talk indicates you think you're better than we are. 'Go in peace, O fucked-up one!' That's the line you're giving everyone. You don't have to accept what everybody says as true, but look at it, examine it. This is not on your *personally,* it's your behavior that needs to be pulled up" [5].

The Game continued around the circle with such admonitions as: "We're not here for selling Bibles, we're all fucked up; that's why we're here." "Stop trying to give reasons for not doing what we all need to do. Games are not punishment, not a Kangaroo Court." "The real revolution is inside ourselves. Playing mind games or tripping on insanities from the street isn't going to get our heads together. You're here, man, you've got a chance. If you don't change you'll die. Remember the dinosaurs." The Game moves quickly, but the name of it is the same. "How do you feel about all that shit that's being unloaded on you? Why can't you remember to leave the keys? Don't trip—you'll fall off your cloud. Man, you don't even have balls enough to ask Luke for another set of keys." "You're not very aware. Are you carrying attitudes away from the Game?" [6]. The Game had gone almost around the room. The newest resident had been told that it would not be "on him" that night. The director suddenly said, "Let's all go get a cup of coffee." The Game was over. The residents that had been shouting obscenities at one another a moment before headed upstairs in a quiet and friendly mood. There were groups of people playing cards, others were drinking coffee, some were just sitting around talking. The conversation was totally free of even everyday and mild forms of cursing. It was clear that the Game was over. Now everyone was "on the floor."

On our other visits to Cenikor when we were allowed to attend sessions of the Game, the content and dynamic were the same [7]. After we had been present several times and had spent a good deal of time "on the floor" listening to the residents' conversations and visiting with them, we began to be accepted as a part of the fellowship, at least to a limited extent. This acceptance was symbolized by one of us being given a "pull-up" for tilting back in a chair. When the "bad behavior" was unthinkingly repeated an hour later, he was threatened with a "verbal hair-cut."

One visit to the Cenikor Foundation was arranged in order to be present for lunch and the seminar which follows every afternoon. On a large chalkboard were the words: "If you can find a path with no obstacles, it probably doesn't lead anywhere." After the tables had been cleared and the dishes washed, all the residents returned to the tables for a discussion of this "concept." The director explained that it describes the way life *is*. "Wherever you're going, the changes you go through are the obstacles. These are necessary. In Cenikor the hassles are a part of getting your head together. . . . Persecution is often essential. Look at the Jews; the Christians wouldn't be anywhere if they hadn't been persecuted. . . . We just think we've been persecuted when we were on the streets. We created our own obstacles. We are banded together because of our insane habits" [8]. All the residents were then invited to make their own observations about the concept. There was no debate. There were no "right" or "wrong" answers or opinions. Each person said what he thought the concept meant, or offered an illustration, for example: "Some things are not good or bad, they just *are*." "Feelings of accomplishment are one of the greatest things we can have." "The concept is dishonest. The nobility of suffering is an illusion. In Cenikor we want to become self-actualized people. Attitudes like this keep people down." "Without obstacles, life would be boring." "Our problem is we haven't all learned to say no to the insanities. When we do, we will be pretty good people." "We always look for paths without obstacles" [9]. The interpretive task of the seminar was in a low key and almost seemed secondary to the first-level need for as many as wished to express themselves.

After several visits to Cenikor we began to sort out the obvious problem-solving behavior and methods that were explicitly offered as the "tools" with which a resident could move toward "self-actualization." The primary tool is the group therapy session known as the Game. As described above, this is conducted by the residents themselves, without the aid of a professional therapist [10]. The Game is held three nights a week. The method has become so popular that outsiders have asked to be a part of the process. Therefore a "Game for Squares" is held every Thursday evening. A Game may be "called" at any point in the day by any resident. Those who are "on the floor" join in for a short session which is only "on" the person who called for it. As residents become better adjusted to the house and start getting themselves "together," they do not need to call a Game so often, and are able to hold out for the regularly scheduled ones [11].

The other problem-solving tools include the "pull-up," whereby one resident calls another into accountability for some infraction or points out some "insanity" in which the other is engaged. Pull-ups are usually between peers, but if the behavior is not corrected, it might bring a "verbal" from one of the directors. The pull-up, like other tools, may be misused. When the pull-up is used to cut another down, it becomes, not a helping device, but a moral weapon. This practice is called, in the group argot, "lugging" (which means carrying excess baggage).

There are only two absolute rules in Cenikor, although the minor rules appear to be endless and all-encompassing. First, there is to be no alcohol and no narcotics. Second, there is to be no expression of physical hostility. Violation of these is likely to bring on a "hair-cut." For males, this is a literal shaving of the head. For females, it consists of covering the head with a stocking cap, removing all cosmetics, wearing baggy men's clothing and floppy boots. This ceremony of degradation is carried out as a final resort in the effort to get the resident to conform to the standards of the Foundation. Like other degradation ceremonies, it "falls within the scope of the sociology of moral indignation. . . . Both event and perpetrator must be removed from the realm of their everyday character and be made to stand as 'out of the ordinary'. . . . Finally, the denounced person must be ritually separated from a place in the legitimate order" (Garfinkel, 1956: 421–423). It was obvious from our conversations with men who had experienced the hair-cut and women who had undergone the female equivalent that they held no feelings of anger at having been so treated, except the anger they reserved for themselves and their own "bad behavior."

Other tools include normative vocational programs such as a small shop which makes saw-horses for sale, a gasoline station next door which is operated by the residents, and the program of "hustling," which provides needed goods and services as contributions from the business community to the Foundation. Responsibilities within the house structure are carefully assigned and just as carefully supervised, not only by the directors but, indeed, by the entire community. There is almost total group accountability on every score. Job assignments are made on the basis of ability or desire to "accept responsibility." Perhaps the most important tool is, after all, the atmosphere of "family" structure that is built within the house. The brothers and sisters are placed in a climate of support and trust, which for the majority is a new life situation. A whole matrix of new learnings is perhaps enabled by this deliberate structure.

The family structure is also the most obvious form of boundary maintenance used by Cenikor as an inclusive form of behavior. A new resident is introduced as "a new brother." Chastisement for failing to "care" for the brothers and sisters is verbalized with some frequency in sessions of the Game. The mere fact of being in residence naturally offers a precise line of division between those on the "inside" and those who are still "on the streets." This symbolism is constantly referred to and made explicit in the therapy process. One young man was called to account during a session of the Game for having failed to notify the authorities when a customer at the service station, whom he had known earlier in criminal contexts, was "casing the station" for a possible later burglary. "Whose station is that? Is it yours to hand to that guy on a platter? Hell no! Hhat station belongs to all of us here at Cenikor. Where is your loyalty at, man? Get with the brothers and sisters or get out [12]!"

Behavior that describes a more implicit form of boundary maintenance is evidenced by the clear distinction made between acceptable and unacceptable thought patterns, conversational content, and attitudes. Anyone caught in a nostalgic mood about the past, talking about "insanities" (former modes of behavior during periods of addiction on "the outside"), or failing to "take responsibility" to a proper degree, is immediately given a pull-up and directed to the proper behavior which would indicate that "you're inside the Foundation, man! Not out on the street [13]!" Such differentiations between "outside" and "inside" modes of thought are instances of the group's methods of handling cognitive dissonance (cf. Festinger et al., 1956). A similar distinction is made quite explicitly between Cenikor's self-actualization program and other types of therapy used with addiction problems in other settings and by agencies operated by professionally trained persons.

Perhaps the most distinctive aspect of the Cenikor program is the particular function of language patterns. As we have noted, severe sanctions are employed in reference to cursing, epithets, and obscenities while residents are "on the floor" or going about their normal routines each day. These sanctions disappear as soon as the Game begins. It is quite clear that the style of language that might be considered normative among convicts has been given special designation at Cenikor. This style of language is treated as though it were a "sacred symbol system" by the residents. Within this system a private argot has been developed which allows for the coding of a variety of relationships and the labeling of proscribed behavior patterns. Even the dynamics of friendship and affection are thus coded. The rehabilitation program of Cenikor operates within such a language circle. Those who have learned the language codes are "inside"; those who have not are "outside." The fact that the same or similar expressions are used "on the street" by other ex-convicts or in other types of therapy programs does not diminish the special nature of the coded language for Cenikor residents.

Such identity and language structures are among the more obvious institutional processes at Cenikor. Another basic process is the social contract which serves as both an entrance and a continuation function. Persons coming to Cenikor, off the street or by court referral, are told that the door is open. Their participation in the program is self-directed and may be terminated by simply walking out. On several occasions within the Game, a resident was reminded that the door was not locked; if he didn't wish to shape up, he could always leave.

The self-direction of the therapy program is structured, however, by an elaboration of accountability structures. No resident is ever unobserved. Every entrance and return is recorded in the "sign-in book," even if the exit is only to the back yard with the garbage. The business sessions (described above) include the reporting of infractions and an opportunity for confessions by wrongdoers. The Game and pull-ups offer the strongest forms of accountability. These may also be described as modes of peer education. Models of approved behavior within the peer group are provided by persons who have been granted more responsibility in the house or given positions of trust in relation to the outside community. As a resident begins to "get his head together" and indicates a desire for responsibility, he may be assigned a position as supervisor of a dorm. Later he is eligible to become a director, which allows him to lead the Game and join the founder in major decision-making. A small group of advanced residents under the leadership of a vice-president has recently been sent to Houston to open a second Cenikor center [14].

This hierarchical arrangement suggests that some residents may choose to remain with the program rather than be "graduated" in the third year. In the normal sequence, the first year consists of intensive therapy and the beginning of assuming responsibility. The second year finds the resident assigned out to a full-time position, but he continues to reside at the house and participates in the Game. His wages are kept for him as savings (with 15% withheld for room and board). In the third year he is given his savings and moves out to private quarters. It is evident that many elect to remain, at that point, with the Foundation. When one young man was asked if he was looking forward to completing the program and being on his own, he answered, "Well, we owe a great deal to Cenikor, and we feel like we want to help others in turn" [15]. Some observers might describe this desire for continued association as a dependency syndrome. However, it could also be called the development of a particular life-style which has highly specialized institutional associations.

The socialization process eventuating in this particular life-style appears to be related to the precise moral code and system of sanctions which is operative at Cenikor. Every detail of daily living is accounted for. Whereas most therapy programs are directed toward the resolution of specific problems or the handling of particular stress situations, the Cenikor program is holistic in its scope. A parallel might be found in the toilet-training program in a middle-class suburban home. One of the major tacit understandings of the Foundation is that there is ultimate value in the normative standards of the American middle class. Values related to industry, thrift, morality, sobriety, and initiative are unquestioned. These form a part of the "taken-for-grantedness" of the Cenikor world view (See Gurwitsch, 1962; Schutz, 1962).

The ritual use of language within Cenikor, as well as the accountability structures and social contract inherent in the program, have parallels in many religious movements. The most notable parareligious function might be seen in the strict code of conduct laid out for the residents of Cenikor House. When observing the content and the dynamic of this code of behavior, we were impressed by the similarity of the "fundamental rules" of the Fetter Lane society as issued by John Wesley in 1738. "That we meet together once a week to confess our faults to one another, and pray for one another, that we may be healed. That the persons so meeting be divided into several *bands*, or little companies, none of them consisting of fewer than five or more than ten persons. That everyone in order speak as freely, plainly, and concisely as he can, the real state of his heart, with his several temptations and deliverances, since the last time of meeting. . . . That no particular member be allowed to act in anything contrary to any order of the society. . . ." [16]. This paradigm of the class meeting seems to have been reproduced by Cenikor in almost exact detail.

The motif of soteriology in Cenikor is quite explicit. The entire program is geared to help the resident "save his life." The salvific function of "these life saving tools," going to court to request referral of a new resident in order to "give him back his life" and "save the life of a new brother" [17], indicates that the members of the Foundation are explicitly aware of both the seriousness of the business in which they are engaged and the semi-religious character of the Cenikor program.

BACK TO GODHEAD: KRISHNA CONSCIOUSNESS AND THE "NICE'" *BHAGAVAD-GITA*

Our introduction to the Krishna Consciousness group took place at one of the regular Sunday afternoon "celebrations" to which the public is especially invited. We entered the temple (a former church, purchased from the Church of the Brethren and undergoing remodeling), and after a quiet and friendly "Hare Krishna" greeting were requested to remove our shoes before proceeding. Once inside, we were ushered to the part of the building where about a dozen devotees (pronounced "devotees" by adherents of the movement) were already engaged in dancing and chanting in the presence of images of Krishna and the photographic likeness of His Divine Grace, A.C. Bhaktivedanta Swami Prabhupada. Some thirty minutes later we were invited to accompany the devotees to a larger room. By this time, seventy to eighty people had arrived.

The young man who acts as leader of the group set the tone for what was to follow, and for much of what we were to learn later about the group. His brief remarks appeared to us to set forth the *charter* of the group. "Our Spiritual Master has directed us," he said, "to seek our true transcendental position. Things like a new car, or a healthy body, do not give us the nectar [18] we seek. One should want nothing on his own account. Krishna has sent us this nice temple. If we did not have this we should be prepared to sleep under a tree, for we are, after all, mendicants. Our chanting of the holy name of God leads to perfection. Hearing from the authorities is the first requirement. Hearing the name leads to inquiring about God's *form*. So our purpose is to perfect our chanting of the name of God. In this way, our consciousness will expand to the fullest. We have nice surroundings and food, but we don't claim them for ourselves."

These remarks were a prelude to the invitation to join the devotees in the ritual processes of chanting and dancing. "I will now chant Hare Krishna. Please practice this here and at home. Chanting is a very nice thing; so is dancing, which we can also do." The chanting and dancing began quietly and slowly, but as they continued the volume and the pace increased. Krishna devotees, we soon learned, "talk" with their bodies. The rhythmic movements are graceful and expressive and, judging from the looks on the devotees' faces, a source of obvious sensual delight. The chant and dance continued for about thirty minutes. Just as the process appeared to be heading toward sheer physical exhaustion of the participants (or looked as though it could become orgiastic), the leader gave the signal for the dancing to stop.

As though he was explaining what had just been concluded, the leader commented that "it was good of the Divine Master to give us such a simple process. Five thousand years ago, there was a wonderful culture. Half of the population was searching for perfection in God-realization. The spiritual masters of today teach exactly what was taught then. They teach us that we have a temporary body, and a soul. Krishna is All-Soul, and we are small parts of his soul. We should act for our eternal soul. Krishna is eternal form, never changing. But we forget who we are and identify with the body and the delights of the body. Krishna invites us to a 'nectaring relationship' with him. When we forget about Krishna, we run after the things of the body. They drag us here and there, and we are anxious about questions such as 'Where am I going to be a year from now?' The fruits we taste are never enough, and we always want more. There are really only two paths: we can accept the temporary self, or Krishna, the search for perfection. We can try for the eternal, or we can mingle around in the temporary. Our goal is spiritual identification and enlightenment. Everything we do has a 'taste.' If we use the chanting of the name of Krishna rightly, we can have eternal happiness. For those who can read philosophy, the *Bhagavad-Gita,* this nice philosophy, is available. It is not, however, essential. You can reach the goal just by chanting" [19].

We returned within a few days, and during the next two weeks spent several evenings at the temple. In this period we were able to learn much about the place, and the importance, of "the nice *Bhagavad-Gita*" in the Krishna Consciousness subculture. Each evening, after a round of ritual dancing and chanting, the devotees gather in the sacred room for exegesis and hermeneutic of the Krishna Consciousness scripture. The passage being considered for the day is read aloud by one of the devotees. The edition of the *Gita* used in the "class" includes, following each section, a body of material called "Purport." This is, of course, the "authorized" hermeneutic for the passage that immediately precedes it. The Purport is read in such a way as to suggest that it, too, is a part of the scripture. The reading of the Purport is used as the point of departure for a process of informal group hermeneutic and, it seemed to us, a kind of group therapy. Boundary maintenance, ideological socialization, and reinforcement functions were much in evidence. Participating in this process, we gained a number of insights into the lives of the devotees, the major themes in the Krishna Consciousness subculture, and the functions being performed in the participation of individual devotees in the group scenario.

The portion of scripture being considered on the evening we first attended the class dealt with the assertion that a yogi is greater, respectively, than an ascetic, an empiricist, and a fruitive worker, and with the question of knowledge of the absolute. The group hermeneutic was, in the context of our total participation in what the group is doing, quite revealing. "One may know awe and reverential aspects (of life in Krishna) but one must go beyond this to truest knowledge," the discussion leader began. "The trouble is that we fall into the material world. Krishna says, 'Surrender unto me.' We are to worship Krishna in loving service, drawing away from sexual desire and other *things*. When you speculate and analyze, you have to control your senses. There are no hashish Yogis, or tobacco Yogis, or sex Yogis. If we do as he says we will actually know God. But we have to qualify by developing an offense-less attitude—by *giving up the idea* of 'I and mine' (false egoism) and understanding that everything belongs to Krishna.

"As for the knowledge of the Absolute, we have, in order to obtain this, to 'hear perfectly from Krishna.' If we are in Krishna consciousness, we understand and participate in all the earlier stages of Yoga. If you know Krishna, you know *everything*. 'Hear from me!' Krishna tells us. You come to see everything in relation to Krishna. But you can't do it with this burden on your back [a reference to sensuous desires]. The knowledge is like turning on a light switch in the darkness. Taking the trash out is keeping the temple clean for Krishna. It's so nice! Why am I doing this? For Krishna! Why am I tired? Because I identify with my body! If you have this knowledge but smoke, go to movies, and play golf, then what good is the knowledge? Don't hover on the mental plane" [20] (a reference to employing Krishna knowledge as if it were "head stuff," when it really deals with man's whole selfhood).

The path to Krishna Consciousness is only opened by his grace, and only a very few (the illuminati?) ever really try to understand the truth. "Most people," said one of the devotees, "are just going here and there after cars, family, vacations, and not really seeking knowledge. They are caught up in the illusion that there is pleasure in the world. The camel thinks what he is eating tastes good, but it is really only the thorns pricking his tongue. The path is difficult for many to follow, but for us it is easy, since we are not seeking material things. We don't want to go downtown or sleep on a big thick mattress! It is so nice to have all our desires fixed on Krishna. The 'nectar of devotion' tells us what pure devotion is" [21].

Krishna Consciousness, it was pointed out at a subsequent meeting, is a *hearing* process. But then, we don't hear very well. So that is why we have been given the *Bhagavad-Gita*, which, if we hear it, enables us to become perfect, for *it* is perfect. The major concern here was a discussion of the kinds of people whose knowledge is "stolen by illusion," and who are "of the atheistic nature of demons." (Bhagavad-Gita, Book VII: 14–15, in Bhakivedanta, 1972). The leader began the hermeneutic by suggesting that "atheists are not using their intelligence; they try to find happiness without Krishna. At an earlier time, great leaders surrendered to Krishna, but not today. People are full of misery. They work hard to get things to minister to the senses and the body. We're always trying to avoid Krishna. We don't want to go home. We miss what is really human, because we are spoiling our time by not spending it seeking Krishna Consciousness."

In the Purport for this passage, there is a discussion of four types of miscreants (Duskritina) who are capable of performing meritorious work but live on a low plane or use their abilities for wrong purposes. Of the four types, the one most important to understand is the person whose erudite knowledge has been nullified by "illusory material energy." According to the group hermeneutic, these are the speculative philosophers who "hover on the mental plane." Said one devotee, "Intellectuals direct their brains in the wrong way. Their knowledge is not worthwhile because it is not directed toward Krishna. They win Nobel prizes but their learning is null and void. Wilhelm Reich, a psychoanalyst some think is more important than Freud, used his intellect in the wrong way when he announced the ridiculous conclusion that there can be no true human happiness without a satisfying sex life." At this point, a young woman devotee blurted out: "Wow, what an illusion!" to which the response was generally a nodding of heads in assent and a murmur of agreement.

The devotee who was leading the discussion was not content to let matters rest here. He was constrained to point out that even *we* are not really pure devotees. "We even came *here* [to the temple] to find something—happiness, food, a place to stay," he said. Before we can become devotees in the purest sense, it was indicated, we must become free of desires and willing to know Krishna only. We should not try to figure out (in a calculating way) what will advance Krishna Consciousness, but we should surrender to Krishna, and take what comes as a result [22].

In a subsequent session of the class, attention was given to the questions of how one can know Krishna as the Supreme Lord and how one works in the material world on his behalf. Passages were cited from the *Bhavagad-Gita* (Book VII: 29–30, and Book VIII: 1–2), and we were afforded some insights into how Krishna Consciousness devotees understand their relations to the world and to each other. "When you want to know how a computer works," it was said, "you ask the engineer. When you want to know how to work in the material world, you go to Krishna. To be sure, we all have doubts at times. But if one is fixed in Krishna knowledge, he will know what to do (he will not be caught up in desires or lamentations). We are getting ready *now* to be able to accept our death. Even now, when the police come and take away some of the devotees, there is nothing to do but depend upon Krishna [23]. Krishna gives us the facility to do what we need to do. We must proceed on the assumption that 'if Krishna throws a thought into your mind, then do it. That's sensible.' Of course, everything *is* confusing until we surrender to Krishna. We can feel Krishna's directions coming through. They are *different*. A subtle thing (not like someone saying 'move aside'). When someone says something foolish, we may respond by saying, 'I don't know what little voice you're listening to, but that wasn't Krishna.' The expert devotee knows. Krishna directs us very sanely, so if you can't hear out here, how can you hear in there?''

This had been the leader of the group speaking. At this point he seemed to become aware of what *surrender* meant for him, and for the devotees who live together at the temple. "We get ample opportunities every day to surrender," he commented. "I've been told by a higher authority to do something, so I should do it. We have to learn to take instructions. It really comes out nice. We learn to surrender by taking directions. Through this, Krishna controls the whole show. If my parents tell me not to come to Krishna Consciousness, I will say no to them—Krishna is higher" [24]. Mixed in with these comments were some remarks clearly indicating that the leader was using the opportunity to "make points" about devotees "surrendering to Krishna" when they were asked to clean floors or do other temple household chores.

In trying to understand what we participated in and observed, we have found that its meaning tends to cluster in four main categories: boundary maintenance (as this would be identified in sociological terms); playing, as we would say, the group's "language game"; processes of institutionalization in group life; and efforts at socialization within the group. In the Krishna Consciousness movement, boundary maintenance mechanisms appear at once to include and to exclude outsiders. They also operate both explicitly and implicitly. Efforts are made to include all who are willing to come: Krishna Consciousness is definitely to be shared. Visitors are allowed to observe and to participate in the ritual processes—receiving consecrated flowers which are in turn offered to the gods, the purification ceremony of fire which involves touching a flame and then placing the hand on the forehead, the reading and discussing of sacred literature, sharing the Prasadam (the sacred meal), chanting and dancing. Visitors are, in a sense, explicitly excluded in terms of social visibility since they do not wear saffron robes or gowns and cannot chant (or can do so only with difficulty), since the chants are in a strange language not easily accessible. (An English translation is provided, but we appeared to be the only visitors making use of it.) Visitors learn as they participate, when they are violating in-group norms. One of us accidentally dropped a consecrated flower on the floor; a young woman devotee "rescued" it immediately and handed it back. The same thing occurred when one of us allowed his copy of the *Bhagavad-Gita* to slip onto the floor; it was quickly snatched up and handed back to him. In neither instance was a word spoken, but a gesture and a look of reproach made the message clear. A word was spoken, however, when one of us, feeling his legs cramped from sitting in the "lotus position" too long, stretched his legs out in front of him while the scripture was being read The devotee who was reading stopped and said, "Please cross your legs again." Perhaps the most serious instance of this violation of norms took place when one of us touched some of the food set aside for the sacred meal without waiting to be served. "You may have contaminated that food. Do not take it from the common dish!" said the devotee who was responsible for the ritual serving.

An additional insight into the mechanisms for boundary maintenance was gained in connection with responses we encountered to questions that had pointed toward the possibility of "cognitive dissonance" (inconsistency, etc.). To certain kinds of questions, group members with whom we talked responded evasively; it was clear to us that the questions were threatening. For example, when we asked how the group was supported, we were told, after some hesitation, that Krishna had provided the devotees with a nice temple and with this nice spiritual food. Krishna devotees were, we discovered, not without awareness of the physical necessities of life in the world, for they are pragmatically concerned with the support of the temple. But even on this level the language used indicates that "all material things belong to Krishna." In answer to a specific question from a young woman "inquirer," a devotee quoted the rule: "A householder [one who maintains a home outside the temple] should contribute 50% of his annual income to the temple because 100% belongs to Krishna." The devotee added, "We will help you make a nice budget" [25]. We had the impression, however, that whenever the discussion appeared to be leading to a consideration of the world outside, the conversation was quickly changed and brought back to the firm ground of Krishna Consciousness language.

That language, we are convinced, is of crucial importance if one wants to understand this culture—or subculture. As noted earlier, a central belief in the group is that the recurrent chanting of the name of God

(Krishna), practiced several times each day, will bring devotees ever closer to the achievement of Krishna Consciousness. The ritual functions of language are very much in evidence. Each day, devotees participate in the chanting process and in the study of the *Bhagavad-Gita*, together with a highly ritualized reading (no exegesis or hermeneutic as known in theological school accompanies this) of what they refer to as "the nice Krishna book." Devotees, incidentally, are surrounded by pictures showing various aspects of Krishna's life, and these pictures are constant reminders of the devotees' involvement with in-group language. The word "nice" appeared to be almost a code word, being repeatedly attached to any thing or experience that is positively valued in the group. The scriptural passage and its Purport are treated reverentially and in a manner that suggests the importance of constant playing on Krishna Consciousness language—or, as we came to feel, playing the Krisha consciousness language game—for the sake of reinforcing group norms and collective sentiments.

Institutionalization of group processes is rapidly taking place. We observed, for example, an implicit moral contract that appears to bind the devotees together, as well as "accountability structure" and emerging patterns of leadership and authority. The *explicit* statement of the contract focuses on a commitment to Krishna. A moral contract with other members of the group is implicit, since what is done for Krishna (and this includes everything, ideally) is manifestly done for the group—namely, keeping the temple clean, preparing food, answering mail, walking the streets to invite potential converts or to solicit gifts. Members of the group are clearly accountable to each other for the various tasks that form the division of labor in the temple. Part of the accountability structure has to do with leadership. One of the young male devotees is the president of the group, and the others look to him regularly for leadership and decisions [26]. He, in turn, considers himself under the authority of the top leadership of the national headquarters of the Krishna Consciousness movement.

Socialization of the devotees goes on continuously; it is evident in almost everything done at the temple. Krishna Consciousness moral codes and sanctions are apparently acquired in stages, with more and more items being transmitted as devotees get farther "into" the group. The most committed male members have submitted themselves to a species of degradation ceremony (although it may not be so regarded by them), involving the shaving of the head except for a strand of hair which hangs pigtail fashion down the back, and the donning of a saffron gown. Female members completely dispense with make-up, but do give attention to their hair. Much of the socialization process takes place in the daily round of chanting and dancing as well as in the daily study of the *Bhagavad-Gita* which they do together. Members of the group socialize each other as the interpretations of the scripture take place. Reinforcement of values and commitments already shared is very much in evidence during this process.

Our participation in several facets of the life of this group has made it abundantly clear that most of the devotees understand themselves to be in the process of overcoming various kinds and degrees of alienation, anomie, and apathy which they experienced prior to their entry into the Krishna Consciousness subculture. We believe it may be necessary to see them as participating in a contraculture (Yinger, 1960: 625–635) rather than a subculture. Judging from our conversations with several of them, Krishna devotees are experiencing a new sense of personal identity—an identity that becomes firmer as they begin to understand themselves (in these terms), daily moving toward "real" Krishna consciousness and away from the enticements of the world they have left behind.

CONCLUSION

Our study is not yet complete, and we have at this point only the data derived from our initial participant observation. We do, however, have two reasonably well-substantiated observations to offer which seem to us important. First, in all four of the groups we have observed, there is a noticeable strain or predisposition toward reductionism in the sense of cutting down or narrowing the "size" of the world in order to make it more "manageable." In Cenikor, life in the house is made into a kind of microcosm of the way things will be "when we get it all together." In the Hare Krishna group, life is reduced to dealing with sensuality and how to "get rid" of it. For the Alcoholics Anonymous group, getting rid of the compulsion to drink is the key to everything else. And the sojourner in the realm of astrology has made things simpler by hitching everything from interpersonal relations to the destiny of nations to the stars. In each case, the reductionism has helped group members to scale down the booming, buzzing confusion of life as they had experienced it before becoming involved in the group.

Second, we are impressed with the continuing viability, in some contexts, of the Protestant ethic. Our study has convinced us that the funeral rite for this culture pattern that has been so solemnly (or joyously, as the case may be) conducted by various students of American society, as well as by ideologists for one or the other brand of the "counterculture," may have been premature. In all four groups, the Protestant ethic is far from dead. Our observation has made this so clear that we are increasingly disposed to accept Anthony Wallace's remark that "old religions do not die; they live on in the new religions which follow them" (Wallace, 1966: 4). Cenikor might be described as a group acting out a secularized version of the Protestant ethic. Alcoholics Anonymous picks up aspects of this ethic—especially, of course, the emphasis upon sobriety. The astrology group is much concerned with system and order, along with a disciplined and calm acceptance of the world that the stars and planets have made. The Krishna Consciousness group, while it is, in some ways, better understood as a "contraculture" than as a "subculture" group, is nevertheless also acting out parts of the Protestant ethic, especially the heavily moralistic emphasis on "doing everything for the glory of Krishna" [27].

As our study proceeds, we will continue to test these impressions. We are planning to return to each of these groups for the purpose of conducting depth interviews with leaders we have been able to identify, and holding follow-up conversations with as many members of each group as possible. We hope to make successful contact with at least two more groups. We want, among other things, to see whether the connection we have found between problem-solving behavior and religious and parareligious subcultures holds for other, and different, kinds of groups.

NOTES

1. When we asked about a possible model for the Cenikor House approach, we were promptly referred to Lewis Yablonski (1967).
2. Field notes (Snelling, hereafter "S"), Cenikor, January 14, 1972.
3. *Ibid.*
4. Field notes (Whitley, hereafter "W"), Cenikor, January 15, 1972.
5. Field notes (S, W), Cenikor, January 14, 1972.
6. *Ibid.*
7. Up to this time the authors are the only outsiders who have been permitted to observe the Game. The Foundation founder appears to be sensitive about outsiders getting "too close to the secrets of the tribe."
8. Field notes (S and W), Cenikor, January 21, 1972.
9. *Ibid.*
10. Negative feelings toward professionals are evident in the use of "social worker" as a term of reproach.
11. Conversation with Director of Cenikor House, January 21, 1972.
12. Field notes (S), Cenikor, January 17, 1972.
13. *Ibid.*

14. The authors were asked to write a letter of introduction for these Cenikor "missionaries." This we take to be an indication of the kind of rapport we were able to establish, although it may have other meanings as well.

15. Conversation "on the floor" at Cenikor House, January 21, 1972.

16. Entry for May 1, 1738, *Journal of John Wesley*, Vol. I, pp. 458–459.

17. Conversation, Cenikor House, January 21, 1972.

18. The use of the term "nectar" seems to be important; we were to hear it used frequently, and we found its use revealing in this cultural context.

19. The foregoing account of the Krishna celebration is based on detailed notes taken by the authors during their first evening at the temple. (We continued to use the tape recorder, but decided that it was not really useful.)

20. Field notes (W), Krishna Temple, February 11, 1972.

21. *Ibid.*

22. Field notes (W) , Krishna Temple, February 15, 1972.

23. In recent weeks the Denver police have apparently been "hassling" the Krishna devotees. The American Civil Liberties Union has filed a court case requesting an injunction against police activities in this regard.

24. Field notes (W), Krishna Temple meeting, February 17, 1972.

25. Field notes (S), Krishna Temple meeting, February 21, 1972.

26. The president is a young man approximately twenty-three years old; he appears to be the oldest in a group where the age range is from about eighteen to twenty-three.

27. This point has already been made concerning another non-Judaic-Christian group, the Black Muslims (see Laue, 1964: 315–323).

REFERENCES

BHAKTIVEDANTA SWAMI PRABHUPADA, TRANS.

1972   *The Bhagavad-Gita: As It Is.* New York: Collier Books.

BRUYN, SEVERYN T.

1963   "The Methodology of Participant Observation." *Human Organization* 22: 224–225.

1966   *The Human Perspective in Sociology.* Englewood Cliffs, N.J.: Prentice-Hall.

FESTINGER, LEON
RIECKEN, H. W.
SCHACHTER, S.

(1956)   *When Prophecy Fails.* New York: Harper Torchbooks.
1964

GARFINKEL, HAROLD

1956   "Conditions of Successful Degradation Ceremonies." *American Journal of Sociology* **61**: 420–424.

GURWITSCH, ARON

1962   "The Common Sense World as Social Reality." *Social Research* **29**: 50–72.

HOMANS, GEORGE C.

1950   *The Human Group*. New York: Harcourt, Brace.

LAUE, JAMES H.

1964   "A Contemporary Revitalization Movement in American Race Relations: The Black Muslims." *Social Forces* **42**: 315–323.

MALINOWSKI, BRONISLAW

1945   *The Dynamics of Culture Change*. New Haven: Yale University Press.

SCHUTZ, ALFRED

1962   "Common Sense and Scientific Interpretation of Human Action." Pp. 3–47 in *Collected Papers*, Vol. 1. The Hague: Nijhoff.

WALLACE, ANTHONY F. C.

1966   *Religion, an Anthropological View*. New York: Random House.

WESLEY, JOHN

n.d.   *The Journal of the Reverend John Wesley*. Ed. by Nehemiah Curnock. London: Robert Culley.

YABLONSKI, LEWIS

1967   *Synanon: The Tunnel Back*. Baltimore: Penguin Books.

YINGER, J. MILTON

1960   "Contraculture and Subculture." *American Sociological Review* **25**: 625–635.

David O. Moberg

MARQUETTE UNIVERSITY, MILWAUKEE

Evaluation Research
on Religion

Systematic and scientific approaches to the determination of the success or failure of social institutions and their programs are gaining attention. One result of the increasing demand for *evaluative* research by social and behavioral scientists is a growing volume of literature.

A group of distinguished social scientists was invited to advise the U.S. Department of Health, Education, and Welfare on the measurement of social change and the charting of social progress in the nation. The work of this panel led to a highly significant document, *Toward a Social Report* (1969), calling attention to the need to develop a regular system of social reporting. Just as the nation has an Economic Report, required by statute, in which the President and his Council of Economic Advisors report the economic health of the nation, together with a comprehensive set of fairly sensitive and reliable indicators, the panel report proposed governmental procedures for periodic stock taking of national social health. It urged that a set of social indicators be developed for this purpose. It discussed health and illness, social mobility, the physical environment, income and poverty, public order and safety, learning, science, art, and participation and alienation; but it included nothing on religion except one casual reference to memberships in voluntary associations "including religious groups."

Is religion indeed irrelevant to the social health of the nation? Or is its apparent irrelevance a false impression resulting from interpretations of the separation of church and state which compel governmental agencies to omit the subject from their direct concerns? If religion is important to national well-being, can it be evaluated through associations and programs in the private sphere, or must it be incorporated into a national set of social indicators in order to receive due attention?

An innovative approach to the subject is the evaluation of research itself. The greater reliance professional and lay church leaders place upon social science research as a guide to action, the greater will be their need for an understanding of how, under what conditions, and with what degree of confidence they should proceed. The increasing significance of evaluation research is evident in nearly all areas of institutional behavior. Professional literature in almost all fields includes items on the subject [1]. Although primarily interested in health fields. Schulberg and others (1969), for example, have produced a valuable collection of studies on program evaluation which includes contributions on general issues as well as precise techniques of design and measurement, applications of findings, examples of evaluative studies, and experiences and problems in implementing research findings.

Evaluation is implicit in a great deal of sociological analysis. Efforts to identify "causes" and "effects" often lead to implicit if not explicit evaluation of what factors lead to benevolent, benign, or malign results. The determining and the investigation of (eu)functions and dysfunctions is not purely objective, but rests in the final analysis upon value judgments and a process of evaluation; the history of sociology shows this. Today, however, as evaluation research and other applied aspects of the social sciences are seen as bundles of knowledge and services that are "for sale" (see Horowitz, 1970), value-laden decisions are becoming more complicated. Indeed the more "relevant" these disciplines become, the more it is apparent that "value-free" research is impossible (Sjoberg, 1967; Shostak, 1966; Denzin, 1970).

EVALUATION PROJECTS

In some ways applied religious research stands in a position similar to that of government-supported research on social problems; proposals for the latter are usually required to include an evaluation component. But requests for evaluation have tended to be ritualistic, with vague statements of intent and procedure for assessing the impact of the proposed project, rather than demanding a systematic study based upon scientific procedures with clearly specified objectives and indicators of relative degrees of success and/or failure. Suchman's *Evaluative Research* (1967) was an effort to correct these and other shortcomings.

In the area of religious organizations and programs, the activity most closely related to evaluation research is church planning. Planning specialists have been concerned with evaluating priorities among goals for action, the feasibility of achieving policy changes necessary for the attainment of the preferred goal or goals, identifying resistance to proposed changes, the organization's power to overcome resistance, changes of goals necessary to achieve maximum results from effort expended, and so forth.

One of the earliest guides to evaluation research in churches suggested several survey instruments for the study of churches and their community contexts. It included criteria for evaluation and many suggestions for the "conservation of survey results." H. Paul Douglass, in *From Survey to Service* (1921), also offered criteria for evaluating success in achieving goals and pleaded for objective tests of the adequacy of service to people by the church as a service agency. Even today his analysis is generally consistent with current social science knowledge, but the hortatory tone is more in keeping with a descriptive treatise on home missions than with a textbook on evaluation research.

Evaluation was a major component in the studies of the Institute of Social and Religious Research during its fourteen-year history from 1921 to 1934. It conducted or sponsored forty-eight research projects published in seventy-eight volumes—the most famous of which, at least among social scientists, was the study of *Middletown* (1929) by Robert S. and Helen Merrill Lynd and their students. The most significant findings from all of these studies were masterfully summarized by Douglass and Brunner (1935).

In 1922, the Institute (under its initial name, the Committee on Social and Religious Surveys) undertook a first-hand investigation of the "forty most successful town and country churches which could be found anywhere in the United States" (Brunner, 1923a, 1923b). Cooperative ministries were favored by the Institute and received evaluative attention in most of the projects. Brunner's study (1934) of the larger parish focused directly upon such programs, as did another by Hallenbeck (1934).

The Institute's study of 1,044 churches in cities of 100,000 or more population was oriented primarily to the goal of classifying churches into major types.. The provisional use of averaged statistical characteristics of a given type was considered as an alternative to the construction of an idealized scale from which to measure deviations in fact (see Douglass, 1926: 299–316).

Another project of the Institute involved analysis of 1,950 churches from eight denominations in sixteen large cities. The progress of these churches over the preceding decade was measured by "the best available evidence of institutional validity and progress . . . proven by experience to be valid, and . . . uniformly available" (Sanderson, 1932: 73).

Evaluation of the effects (or effectiveness) of religious education, especially among youth, has been attempted rather frequently.

An interdisciplinary project on Christian education, conducted for the Board of Christian Education of the United Presbyterian Church in the United States, compiled a vast amount of survey data on the attitudes, backgrounds, and characteristics of ministers, teachers, communicant members, and youth. Among Lutherans (in the American Lutheran Church) the problem of post-confirmation dropouts was the focus of a follow-up study of a sample of youth of that denomination two years after their high school confirmation classes (Brekke, 1966). A preceding study had sought to evaluate the curriculum and educational materials with specific hypotheses about levels of interest, understanding of the purposes of particular lessons, comprehension of the connections sought between activities and purposes, and so on (Johnson, 1961).

Using both cross-sectional and longitudinal analyses, the University of Santa Clara studied its own impact as a theologically value-oriented institution on student attitudes. The study suggested that while attendance at such a university may reduce deviation from ethical and theological doctrines, the initial self-selection of the institution by the students may have greater impact than the instructional program. Other attitudes and beliefs also were modified, but all the changes were small (California Province of the Society of Jesus, 1969). This study calls to mind other studies by Fichter (1958), Greeley and Rossi (1966), Greeley and Gockel (1971), and Johnstone (1966).

Much evaluative survey research has been done by the Research and Statistics Department of the Sunday School Board of the Southern Baptist Convention (SBC). These studies cover a very broad range of topics from opinions and attitudes of Southern Baptists toward the SBC's broadcast ministry through reader evaluations of SBC magazines, appraisals of the annual conference program, and the extent of use of SBC curricular materials [2].

A project now in progress is designed to test the relative degrees of effectiveness of the three approaches to training youth in the synagogue and church; it is described by M. P. Strommen in his *Profiles of Church Youth* (1963).

Another area of interest, which might be loosely designated as "clergy evaluation studies," is represented in part by the Danforth Foundation Commission's Study of Campus Ministries (1969) directed initially by Kenneth Underwood. In the context of a strong conviction of the strategic importance of the campus ministry and a desire to serve ministry, university and church, the study combined ethical commitment and reflection on one hand with technically competent empirical research on the other. A policy of continuous reformation of campus ministries was urged. Evaluative activities by the ministers studied made the "subjects" of research themselves become researchers, involving them in reflection that changed their ways of thinking and acting during the course of the study. The process, described as one of "prophetic inquiry," sought to involve all individuals and groups engaged in religious ministries on college and university campuses and resulted in a number of suggestions for the university, the church, and theological seminaries.

In a different direction, a Pilot Project for Clinical Training of Clergymen in the Field of Alcoholism instituted in Georgia tried to evaluate its performance. It encountered difficulties since it was not possible to obtain comparable groups of clergymen and seminary students with (and without) training in this specialty. Moreover, it was difficult to isolate and measure the training variable; self-reports had to be taken at face value, and follow-up testing was suspected of being contaminated by the influence of earlier tests. Several standardized psychological instruments were used but found unsuitable for the needs of the project. Since the new attitudes and conceptual orientations may have been developed through training, a time lag or "sleeper effect" was thought to be at work (Fox et al,. 1967).

The Ministry Studies Board (of the National Council of Churches) undertook a pilot evaluation study of three continuing educational programs for ministers. Both this and another project, Research on Training for Metropolitan Ministry, have been reported on. The latter involved study of three major action-training programs—the Urban Training Center in Chicago, the Clergy Internship Program in Cleveland, and the Metropolitan Urban Service Training facility in New York (McCune and Mills, 1968; Mills, ca. 1966; Winter et al., 1971).

Numerous studies of role-perceptions of clergymen in relation to their own professional or personal satisfaction have been described. A nation-wide survey of Episcopal parish clergymen, their wives and vestries, found the absence of any system of job-performance evaluation (with accompanying criteria) among sources of discontent. This was thought to be related to the apparent inability of seminaries and continuing education programs to prepare individuals for clergy roles [3].

Important components of evaluation are included in surveys of church "strength" and related concerns in several denominations, although typically they are implicit rather than explicit. Many studies (too many to review here) have been made specifically for the purpose of diagnosing and proposing solutions for difficulties into which churches have run. The American Baptist Extension Corporation, among other bodies, has conducted many such studies. Descriptive studies of religious orders like the Brothers of the Christian Schools have included evaluation (see, for example, Ammentorp and Fitch, 1968). Also worth mentioning are Fr. Benjamin Tonna's evaluation report on the Servizio di Documentazione e Studi in Rome (1966), Frank Pagden (1968), Ralph D. Mitchell (1970) [4].

The Effective City Church Study of the National Council of Churches should be noted, although it has been criticized for the vagueness of the criteria used as a basis for evaluation. Data assembled in connection with this study from over 1,700 members of eight Lutheran churches in various parts of the nation provided a basis for comparison of personnel, programs, and problems (Kloetzli, 1961). One of the best illustrations of efforts to enhance effectiveness in achieving goals through the use of cumulative studies is exemplified by the Institute of Church Growth at Fuller Theological Seminary in Pasadena, California.

Denominational appraisals, sometimes apologetic in tone, are usually more descriptive than genuinely evaluative. An exception is Schaller's recent study of the Cumberland Presbyterian Church (1971). Moberg's sociological interpretation of the growth of the Baptist General Conference cross-checks trends by reference to other internal developments of the denomination as well as to conditions in the society and in the ecclesiastical world which he thought might have contributed to rapid expansion (Moberg, 1959; 1960).

Three major studies of an evaluative sort are currently in progress in Reform Judaism's efforts to keep up with the rapid changes in contemporary society. One of these involves the "testing" of five "experimental" Shabat services throughout the country. A second is an in-depth study of the rabbinate, and the third is a pilot project for synagogue change under the aegis of the Union of American Hebrew Congregation's Long Range Planning Committee (cited in Schoen, 1971).

EVALUATION CRITERIA

One of the greatest problems posed by evaluation of church-related programs is that such programs are usually conducted for the purpose of attaining only general, broadly stated goals. How does one determine whether or not an activity—or even a bundle of activities and programs— is "glorifying God," "advancing the Kingdom," or fulfilling other grandly formulated objectives? Unless these concepts are operationalized in terms of specific objectives, they remain "in the heavens," and it is impossible to determine whether or not they have been attained.

In the past, "evaluations" of religious programs and projects have often been based upon casual, impressionistic, subjective, and intuitive responses of nonrepresentative "authorities" to selected bits of evidence, ignoring latent and indirect consequences, paying little or no heed to "target populations" which fail to respond to evangelistic or other efforts, and ignoring voices of dissent which are, by virtue of their criticisms, regarded as "disloyal to the leadership of our significant ministry."

Value-conflicts often arise when an attempt is made to translate broad goals into specific objectives. Inevitably all of the theological and methodological debates of a religious body are brought to a head when any effort is made to specify precise indicators of the success or failure of religious programs.

Since there is disagreement about what constitutes a successful or a "vital" church, disagreements about evaluation outcomes and indicators are not surprising (see Bigman, 1961; Moberg, 1962). "A good program" frequently means something different to its administrator from what it means to its sponsor, to nonmember observers, or to regular participants. Different indices may have different degrees of importance in different situations. An index of evangelism, for instance, should be used with recognition of the opportunity or the need for such work in a given community. Any overall index of church effectiveness must inevitably be a composite of many factors, yet any criteria used will be valid only for the groups that accept them. Such are the problems when theological factors become involved in goal-setting decisions and in evaluation.

EVALUATION METHODOLOGY

Most major religious bodies have developed methods, techniques, and tools for evaluative studies of local churches or parishes of other areas either by staff members or on a self-study basis. Numerous instruments have been developed for use in self-studies of churches (the most comprehensive, possibly, being *Exploration of Mission* developed by the Board of National Missions of the United Presbyterian Church in the U.S.A. Institute of Strategic Studies (1965)) [5]. An important study, currently in progress, is the international project of the Society of the Divine Word (Rashke, 1970). Elsewhere the Jesuit self-study of the California/Oregon Provinces (1969), using a research instrument developed by Sr. Marie Augusta Neal (1970), provided rich data for comparison as well as for self-examination. In an afterword to the report, John L. Thomas concluded that:

> the basic problems we are currently experiencing in the Society stem from lack of agreement regarding the fundamental beliefs and rationales underlying our . . . values, attitudes and practices relating to religious life. Research studies can reveal some of the dimensions of this lack of agreement, but only a profound, concerned and continued rethinking of these beliefs and rationales can provide the basis for the unity and consensus required for survival. (Thomas, 1969)

Scientific technology of evaluation, Thomas felt, can never replace theological and philosophical reflection and the careful scrutiny of value-commitments; but it may help to sharpen such study—make it more precise.

EVALUATION OF EVALUATION RESEARCH

Although a large number of studies have been undertaken, few show a high level of performance. Indeed, those investigators that do maintain high standards may claim that no evaluative research is being done at all. The comments cited in this concluding section are selected from personal letters sent to the author by some of the nation's leading researchers in religion—all presented anonymously here. Wrote one,

> We have done little evaluation research that we care to admit that we did . . .

Much of the so-called research has been superficial in the opinion of another:

> So far as my knowledge goes, real evaluative research has been very scarce within the church. Many programs have been evaluated

by intuition, budget or politics. Occasionally leaders have sat together to ask, "How did we do, boys?" But seldom has there been any real measurement or even an attempt to gather objective data or to control personal judgment.

As if echoing his words, a social scientist wrote:

> In response to your letter concerning evaluative research in religion, I must confess I can report nothing . . . of a contemporary nature which would fit that description. We have one venture in religious experimentation . . . which has been written up, but on which no evaluation has been done. I regard this as an unfortunate condition because far too much expensive and unchecked appraising has gone on in many of these ventures.

The director of a program of professional education for the clergy suggested:

> . . . we don't really know how effectiveness is identified, indicated or measured. In fact, part of our problem is that we have not been able to move beyond that statement of objective [in the program description]. We have not been able to state in behavioral and measurable terms what we mean by enhancement of effectiveness. And until we can so state it, we cannot measure it.

A socioreligious research investigator expressed a similar idea:

> A problem . . . is the haziness with which goals are defined in the first place. Since evaluation cannot occur except against a backdrop of fairly clearly specified goals, evaluation becomes next to impossible in many cases. Overriding it all, I suppose, are the twin problems of reluctance adequately to fund evaluation research and a reticence to be fully open to the outcomes and conclusions of such research.
>
> . . . The basic problem with evaluation research in the church is that the idea of evaluation does not appear soon enough if it appears at all. Nearly always a project such as an experimental ministry is already underway or even completed before someone gets the idea that it would be good to have some kind of evaluation that is more than personal reflection and anecdote . . .

When evaluation is conducted by staff members of the agency or program that is being evaluated, or when it is done for the purpose of preparing reports to the board or the constituency, strengths are likely to be accentuated while failures or weaknesses are correspondingly ignored or glossed over. Annual reports at conventions, news releases prepared by the organization itself, speeches by officials or other promotional representatives, and summaries of progress in fundraising are relatively poor sources of evaluative data, tinged as they often are with self-interest or with other biases.

Clinical evaluations of clients by psychologists or social workers sometimes betray the "Barnum effect," presenting selected diagnostic statements that are universally valid or nearly so and therefore tend to be accepted as perceptively correct. They may also be "Aunt Fanny descriptions," diagnostically valid for the client but equally true of his or anybody else's Aunt Fanny (Kadushin, 1963). In similar fashion, "evaluative reports" of religious programs and projects are sometimes phrased in cliché-ridden generalities that may be technically accurate but of such broad applicability that they carry little more than an outward appearance of pertinence.

Much evaluation, moreover, has been "means-oriented," focusing upon organizational and operative instrumentalities and processes rather than upon goals. In ecclesiastical as well as in educational institutions, means-oriented planning predominates (Palola et al., 1968). It emphasizes quantitative criteria (numbers of persons involved, size of facilities, and so on) in a context of crisis-oriented efforts and using only piecemeal research data. By contrast, end-oriented planning places more stress upon the qualitative aspects of institutional functions and activities and emphasizes continuous planning, the establishment of priorities among goals, and research on key issues that extend beyond routine services of the institutional personnel. Measures of input are not measures of output, nor is efficiency of operation equivalent to effectivenesss of implementation.

The impact of religious factors upon aspects of personal and social well-being has been demonstrated on numerous occasions through empirical research findings in the sociology and psychology of religion (Strommen, 1971). In the face of such findings, the stark neglect of religion in efforts to evaluate social institutions and national welfare may reflect a major gap which will be overcome only if academicians, social and behavioral scientists, and religious leaders cooperate to evaluate the effects of religious orientations and programs upon individual and group life.

The lack of continuity in evaluation efforts probably operates to the detriment of religious programs and institutions. Longitudinal studies and follow-up research projects having a baseline of data from which to measure change are almost nonexistent. There has been no systematic process of building research upon past findings related to the effectiveness and efficiency of churches. The major strides toward general principles of religious behavior and institutions that were made by the Institute of Social and Religious Research until its demise in 1935 have not been followed by any coordinated evaluative studies.

Part of the problem is the failure of investigators to be informed about the work of others. Much evaluative research relevant to religious institutions is reported only in fugitive documents which may serve their immediate purpose by reaching one or two, a dozen, or perhaps a hundred readers before being buried in institutional or denominational archives. A coordinated effort to disseminate information, the establishment of consolidated indexes of archives, and the development of a consortium of religious information systems might help to overcome that difficulty.

Methodological shortcomings plague evaluative research. Respect for human dignity precludes the arbitrary assignment of people to experimental groups and other forms of manipulation, so that it is difficult to perfect research designs. Outcome measures are weak, not covering the full scope and richness of human experience. Religious life itself is complex; seldom if ever does a simple, single indicator suffice as a measure of the outcome of treatment or experimentation. Major topics for evaluation need to be broken down into manageable components, but when they are, critics claim with some justice that the essence of the phenomenon has been lost.

Systematic summaries of research on the success and failure of various types of religious bodies should be compiled. The criteria of success need clarification. Since ultimately they rest upon theological values that undoubtedly vary from one religious group to another, what is considered success by one may be interpreted as failure by another. It is possible that no universal criteria can be developed. Nevertheless, when objective indicators of church characteristics or of performance are used, the results should be observable to those who are pleased as well as to those who are dismayed by the findings. Cooperative work should be possible, in short, on the level of data-gathering even among groups that disagree.

The generalizations that grew out of the research on Protestant churches by the Institute of Social and Religious Research between 1921 and 1934 could now be followed up with careful tests and more refined methodological tools to determine the extent to which (and the conditions under which) they may still be valid. It may be hypothesized that Protestants and Catholics, though formerly affected by different factors, are now increasingly alike with respect to the influences which affect their success or failure, growth or decline, prosperity or recession.

With its record of shortcomings and deficiencies, evaluation has been plagued by the same problems in all areas of human action. Religious research is part of a vast company, for evaluative research as a whole is an underdeveloped specialty. When scientific rigor and precision are possible, the results are often too narrow to be of much practical use. But evaluations based on sweeping generalizations are undependable as a basis for action.

Nevertheless, a great deal has been accomplished. Discoveries of failures to achieve goals have led to program modifications, and in some instances successes are becoming more apparent than they have been in the past. Attention to the problems of evaluative research has led to more sophisticated research designs and techniques. The "soft" methods which now dominate will provide a base for better studies in the future. The very act of initiating an evaluation study clarifies the objectives an institution or a group seeks. In itself that may be an adequate reward. Many concepts of current concern are linked with evaluation—accountability, quality control, assessment of objectives, social accounting, social indicators, goal performance, goal displacement, management by objectives, functional consequences, policy-formation, and performance funding, to name but a few. When these elements of evaluation enter into the thought patterns of ecclesiastical leaders, their conduct inevitably is modified.

NOTES

1. Among the most significant general works on the subject are Suchman (1967), Caro (1971), and Weiss (1971). All of these present valuable information on the uses of evaluative research, guidelines for conducting it, and examples of its effective and defective applications. Other very useful general works on various aspects of evaluation methodology include Cook (1966), Fellin et al. (1969), Herzog (1959), Hesseling (1966), Hyman et al. (1962), Tripodi et al. (1969), and Wright (1968).

2. A conference on Evaluation in Christian Education was held in 1959 at Drew University under the joint sponsorship of the Bureau of Research and Survey of the National Council of Churches and the latter's Commission on Christian Education. The summary and critique of the conference noted that evaluation was the key to discovering "relevancy," listed some basic assumptions and themes in evaluation, indicated the difficulties of conducting good evaluation, and urged the acceptance of "negative findings" (Sibley, 1970: 78–83).

3. See Wilson (1971), Coville et al. (1968), Fukuyama (1965), Leonardini (1969), and others.
   [Ed. note: In addition to the studies cited here, the readers' attention is called to several papers presented at the 1971 meetings of the Society for the Scientific Study of Religion—by Laile Batlett, Raymond Carey, Jackson Carroll, John Biersdorf, Regina Flesch, William Newman, Ronald Johnstone, and Andrew Sorenson.]

4. In 1969 Roper Research Associates conducted a survey of a sample of the constituent members of the American Baptist Convention to determine the level of effectiveness of its leaders in communicating the accomplishments of the denomination and its related agencies, to discover which issues and interests were foremost among the members, and to investigate the knowledge of (and attitudes toward) the Convention and its leadership. Data were interpreted by a professional sociologist who had formerly been an ABC pastor (Campolo, 1971).

5. See Biever and Gannon (1969), Campolo (1971), Myers (1963), Mitchell (1970), Johnson (1971), National Council of Catholic Men (1969), in addition to studies prepared under the American Baptist Home Mission Societies, Church Strategy Program, by the Columbus (Ohio) Council of Churches, the Presbyteries and Synod of Michigan, Detroit (1971) and the Institute of Strategic Services of the United Presbytertian Church in the U.S.A. (1965).

REFERENCES

AMMENTORP, WILLIAM
FITCH, BRIAN

    1968   *The Committed: A Sociological Study of the Brothers of Christian Schools.* Winona, Minn.: St. Mary's College Press.

BIEVER, BRUCE
GANNON, THOMAS (EDS.)

    1969   *General Survey of the Society of Jesus, North American Assistancy,* 5 vols. Oak Park, Ill. National Office of Pastoral Research.

BIGMAN, STANLEY K.

    1961   "Evaluating the Effectiveness of Religious Research." *Review of Religious Research* **2**: 97–121.

BOUMA, GARY

    1971   "Assessing the Impact of Religion." *Zygon* **6**: 55–64.

BREKKE, MILO

    1966   "A Sample of Findings from Stage I of a Study of Post-Confirmation Drop-out in the American Lutheran Church." Minneapolis: American Lutheran Church (mimeographed).

BRUNNER, EDMUND DE S. (ED.)

    1923a   *Churches of Distinction in Town and Country.* New York: George H. Doran.

1923b   *Tested Methods in Town and Country Churches.* New York: George H. Doran.

1934   *The Larger Parish: A Movement or an Enthusiasm?* New York: Institute of Social and Religious Research.

CALIFORNIA/OREGON SOCIOLOGICAL
SURVEY COMMISSION

1969   *The Santa Clara Study: The Impact of a Value-oriented University on Student Attitudes and Thinking.* Santa Clara: The California Province of The Society of Jesus and The Pioneer Educational Society.

CAMPOLO, ANTHONY, JR.

1971   *A Denomination Looks at Itself.* Valley Forge, Pa.: Judson Press.

CARO, FRANCIS G. (ED.)

1971   *Readings in Evaluation Research.* New York: Russell Sage Foundation.

CARROLL, CHARLES E.

1915   *The Community Survey in Relation to Church Efficiency: A Guide for Workers in the City, Town and Country Church.* New York: Abingdon Press.

COMMISSION ON THE DANFORTH
STUDY OF CAMPUS MINISTRIES

1969   *New Wine.* St. Louis, Mo.: Danforth Foundation.

COOK, DESMOND L.

1966   *Program Evaluation and Review Technique: Applications in Education.* Washington, D.C.: Office of Education, U.S. Department of Health, Education and Welfare.

COVILLE, WALTER J., ET AL.

1968   *Assessment of Candidates for the Religious Life.* Washington, D.C.: Center for Applied Research in the Apostolate.

DENZIN, NORMAN K. (ED.)

1970   *The Values of Social Science.* Chicago: Aldine.

DOUGLASS, H. PAUL

1921   *From Survey to Service.* New York: Council of Women for Home Missions and Missionary Education Movement.

1926   *1900 City Churches.* New York: George H. Doran.

DOUGLASS, H. P.
BRUNNER, E. DE S.

1935   *The Protestant Church as a Social Institution.* New York: Institute of Social and Religious Research.

FELLIN, PHILLIP, ET AL. (EDS.)

1969   *Exemplars of Social Research.* Itasca, Ill.: F. E. Peacock.

FICHTER, JOSEPH H.

1958   *Parochial Schools: A Sociological Study.* Notre Dame, Ind.: University of Notre Dame Press.

FOX, VERNELL, ET AL.

ca. 1967   *Pilot Project for Clinical Training of Clergymen in the Field of Alcoholism.* Atlanta: Georgia Department of Public Health.

FRY, C. LUTHER

1924   *Diagnosing the Rural Church: A Study in Method.* New York: George H. Doran.

FUKUYAMA, YOSHIO

1965   "Some Reflections on the Evaluation of New Forms of Ministry." New York: United Church of Christ Board for Homeland Ministries (mimeographed).

GREELEY, ANDREW M.
ROSSI, PETER

1966   *Education of Catholic Americans.* Chicago: Aldine.

GREELEY, A. M.
GOCKEL, GALEN L.

1971   "The Religious Effects of Parochial Education." Pp. 264–301 in M. P. Strommen (ed.), *Research on Religious Development.* New York: Hawthorn Books.

HALLENBECK, WILBUR C.

1934   *Urban Organizations of Protestantism.* New York: Harper, for the Institute of Social and Religious Research.

HATHORNE, BERKLEY C.

1964   *A Critical Analysis of Protestant Church Counseling Centers.* Washington, D.C.: Board of Christian Social Concerns, The Methodist Church.

HERZOG, ELIZABETH

1959   *Some Guidelines for Evaluation Research.* Washington, D.C.: Social Security Administration.

HESSELING, P.

1966   *Strategy of Evaluation Research.* Assen, Netherlands: Van Gorcum.

HOROWITZ, IRVING L.

1970   "Sociology for Sale." Pp. 279–286 in L. T. and J. M. Reynolds (eds.), *The Sociology of Sociology*. New York: David McKay.

HYMAN, HERBERT H., ET AL.

1962   *Applications of Methods of Evaluation*. Berkeley: University of California Press.

INSTITUTE OF STRATEGIC STUDIES

1965   *Exploration of Mission: Tools for Exploration by the Local Congregation*. New York: Board of National Missions, United Presbyterian Church in the U.S.A.

JOHNSON, DOUGLAS W. (ED.)

1971   *Program Planning and Budgeting for the Churches*. New York: Office of Planning and Programs, National Council of Churches.

JOHNSON, MARVIN A.

1961   *Operation Parish Education Research, Planned Lesson Evaluation*. Minneapolis: American Lutheran Church.

JOHNSTONE, RONALD L.

1966   *The Effectiveness of Lutheran Elementary and Secondary Schools as Agencies of Christian Education*. St. Louis, Mo.: Concordia Seminary.

KADUSHIN, ALFRED

1963   "Diagnosis and Evaluation for (Almost) all Occasions." *Social Work* **8:** 12–19.

KLOETZLI, WALTER

1961   *The City Church—Death or Renewal*. Philadelphia: Muhlenberg Press.

LEONARDINI, RAYMOND J. ED.

1969   "The Jesuit Seminarian." Part 5, pp. 265–291, in B. F. Biever and T. M. Gannon (eds.), *General Survey of the Society of Jesus, North American Assistancy*, Vol. 3, Research Studies. Oak Park, Ill.: National Office of Pastoral Research.

LYND, ROBERT S.
LYND, HELEN M.

1929   *Middletown*. New York: Harcourt, Brace.

MC CUNE, SHIRLEY D.
MILLS, EDGAR W.

1968   *Continuing Education for Ministers: A Pilot Evaluation* of *Three Programs*. Washington, D.C.: Ministry Studies Board.

MILLS, EDGAR W.

ca. 1966   "Relating Objective and Evaluation." Washington, D.C.: Ministry Studies Board (mimeographed).

MITCHELL, RALPH D.

1970   "The Role of the Non-Metropolitan Church in the Midst of Rapid Social Change." M.S.T. thesis, San Francisco Theological Seminary.

MOBERG, DAVID O.

1959   "A Sociologist's Interpretation of the Recent Rapid Growth of the Baptist General Conference." *Bethel Seminary Quarterly* **7** (4): 19–24.

1960   "Evaluation of Reasons for Conference Growth." *Bethel Seminary Quarterly* **8** (3): 58–66.

1962   *The Church as a Social Institution*. Englewood Cliffs, N.J.: Prentice-Hall.

MYERS, RICHARD

1963   *Lincoln Park and Its Churches*. Chicago: Church Federation of Greater Chicago.

NATIONAL COUNCIL OF CATHOLIC MEN

1969   *Iowa South East Evaluation, Diocese of Davenport, Iowa, Interpretive Analysis*. Washington, D.C.: National Council of Catholic Men.

NEAL, SR. MARIE A.

1970   "The Relation between Religious Belief and Structural Change in Religious Orders: Part I, Developing an Effective Measuring Instrument." *Review of Religious Research* **12**: 2–16.

PAGDEN, FRANK

1968   "An Analysis of the Effectiveness of Methodist Churches of Varying Sizes and Types in the Liverpool District." Pp. 124–134 in D. A. Martin (ed.), *A Sociological Yearbook of Religion in Britain*. London: SCM Press.

PALOLA, ERNEST G., ET AL.

1968   "Qualitative Planning: Beyond the Numbers Game." *Research Reporter* (Center for Research and Development in Higher Education, University of California) **3** (2): 1–4.

RASHKE, RICHARD

1970   *Society of the Divine Word Self-Study Reports*. Washington, D.C.: Society of the Divine Word.

SANDERSON, ROSS

1932   *The Strategy of City Church Planning.* New York: Institute of Social and Religious Research.

SCHALLER, LYLE E.

1971   *Report of the In-Depth Study of the Cumberland Presbyterian Church.* Naperville, Ill.: Center for Parish Development.

SCHOEN, MYRON E.

1971   "Change on All Sides Considered by Reform." *The Jewish Post and Opinion* 38 (33): 8.

SCHULBERG, HERBERT C., ET AL. (EDS.)

1969   *Program Evaluation in the Health Fields.* New York: Behavioral Publications.

SHOSTAK, ARTHUR (ED.)

1966   *Sociology in Action.* Homewood, Ill.: Dorsey.

SIBLEY, LEONARD A.

1960   "Summary and Critique." Pp. 78–85 in Helen F. Spaulding (ed.) *Evaluation and Christian Education.* New York: National Council of Churches.

SJOBERG, GIDEON (ED.)

1967   *Ethics, Politics and Social Research.* Cambridge, Mass.: Schenkman.

STROMMEN, MERTON P.

1963   *Profiles of Church Youth.* St. Louis, Mo.: Concordia Publishing House.

1971   *Research on Religious Development.* New York: Hawthorn Books.

SUCHMAN, EDWARD A.

1967   *Evaluative Research.* New York: Russell Sage Foundation.

THOMAS, JOHN L.

1969   "Afterword." Pp. 295–319 in B. F. Biever and T. M. Gannon, *General Survey of the Society of Jesus, North American Assistancy.* Oak Park, Ill.: National Office of Pastoral Research.

TONNA, BENJAMIN

1966   *Evaluation Report on SEDOS.* Rome: Servizio di Documentazione e Studi.

TRANTOW, D. J.

1970   "An Introduction to Evaluation." *Rehabilitation Literature* **31** (1): 2-9, 12.

TRIPODI, TONY, ET AL.

1969   *The Assessment of Social Research: Guidelines for the Use of Research in Social Work and Social Science.* Ann Arbor: University of Michigan Press.

UNDERWOOD, KENNETH

1969   The Church, the University and Social Policy, Middletown, Conn.: Wesleyan University Press, 2 vols.

WEISS, CAROL H.

1971   *Bibliography on Evaluation Research.* Washington, D.C.: National Institute of Mental Health, U.S. Department of Health, Education and Welfare.

WILSON, ROBERT L.

1971   *Drop-Outs and Potential Drop-Outs from the Parish Ministry.* New York: United Methodist Church. (Abstract in Review of Religious Research 12:188.)

WINTER, J. ALAN
MILLS, EDGAR W.
HENDRICK, POLLY S.
YOUNGER, GEORGE D.

1971   *Clergy in Action Training: A Research Report.* New York: IDOC. (Washington, D.C.: Ministry Studies Board.)

WRIGHT, CHARLES R.

1968   "Evaluation Research." Pp. 197–202 in *International Encyclopaedia of the Social Sciences,* Vol. 5. New York: Crowell, Collier and Macmillan.

WRIGHT, C. R.
HYMAN, HERBERT H.

1967   "The Evaluators." Pp. 140–163 in P.E. Hammond (ed.), *Sociologists at Work.* Garden City, N.Y.: Doubleday Anchor.

Index